Cells at Work! CODE BLACK

はたらく細胞

01

WARNING
MATURE CELLS ONL
AGES
18+

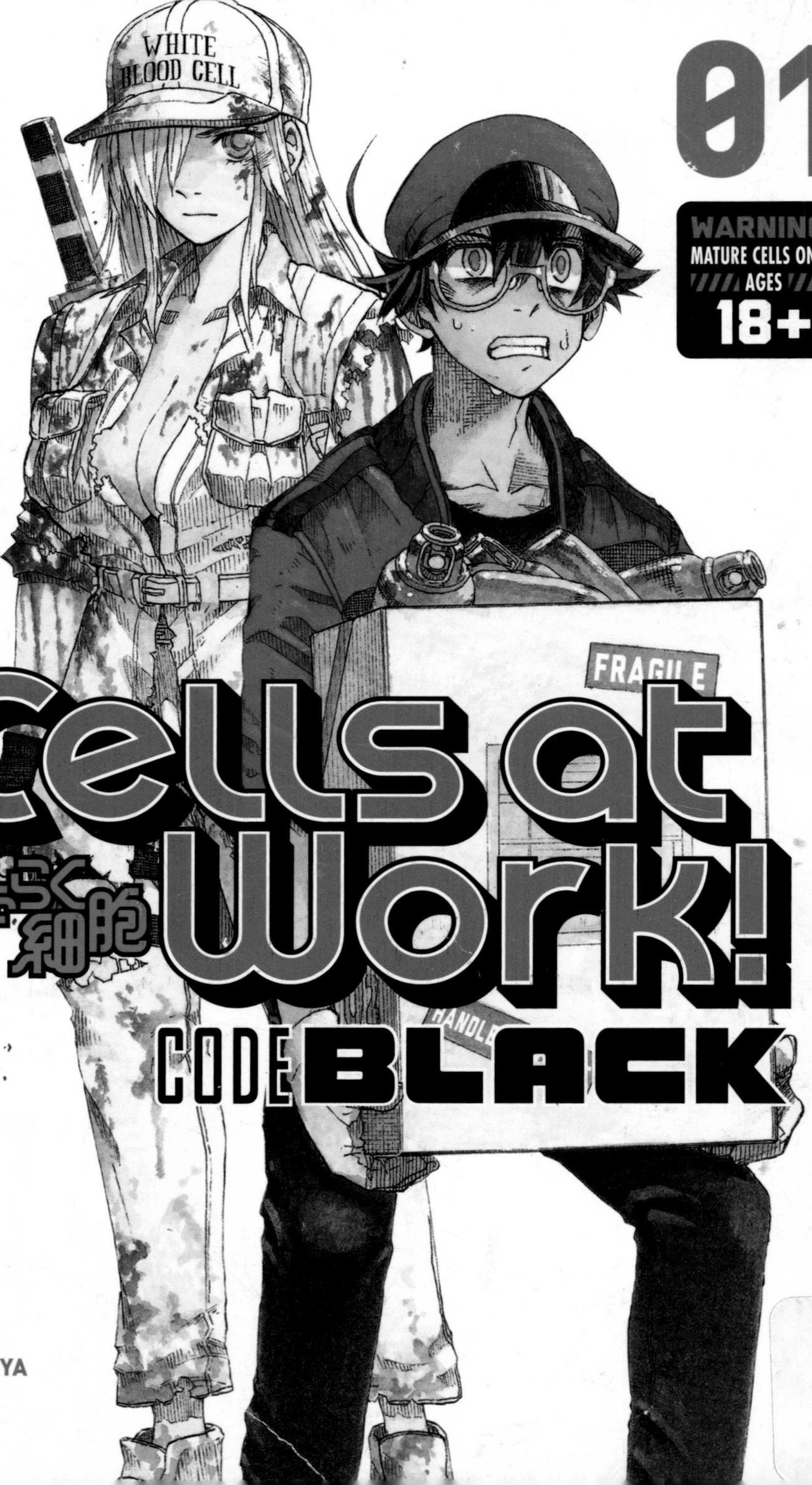
WHITE
BLOOD CELL
FRAGILE
HANDLE

STORY BY
SHIGEMITSU
HARADA
ART BY
ISSEI
HATSUYOSHIYA
CREATED BY
AKANE
SHIMIZU

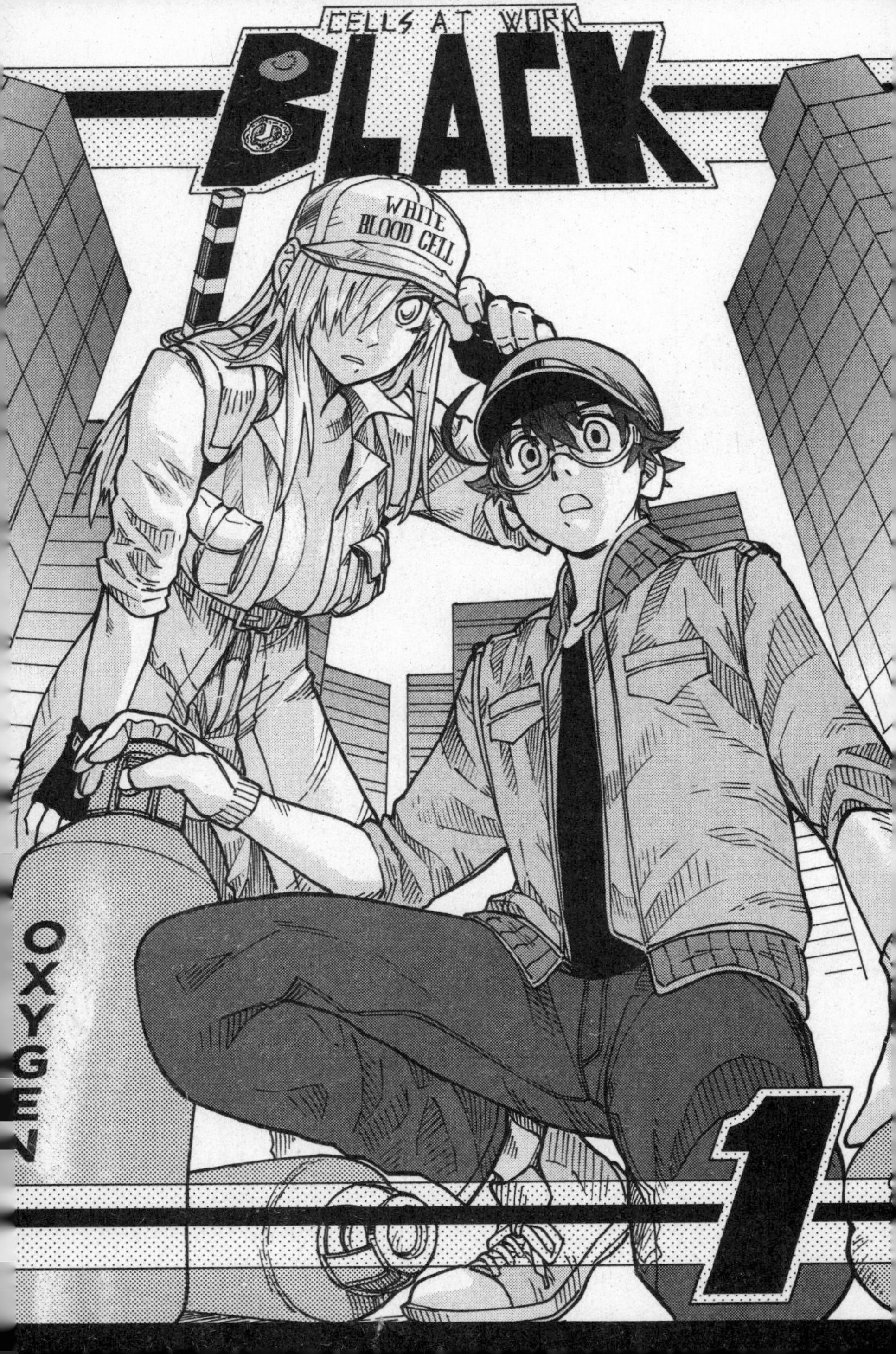
CELLS AT WORK
BLACK
WHITE BLOOD CELL
OXYGEN
1

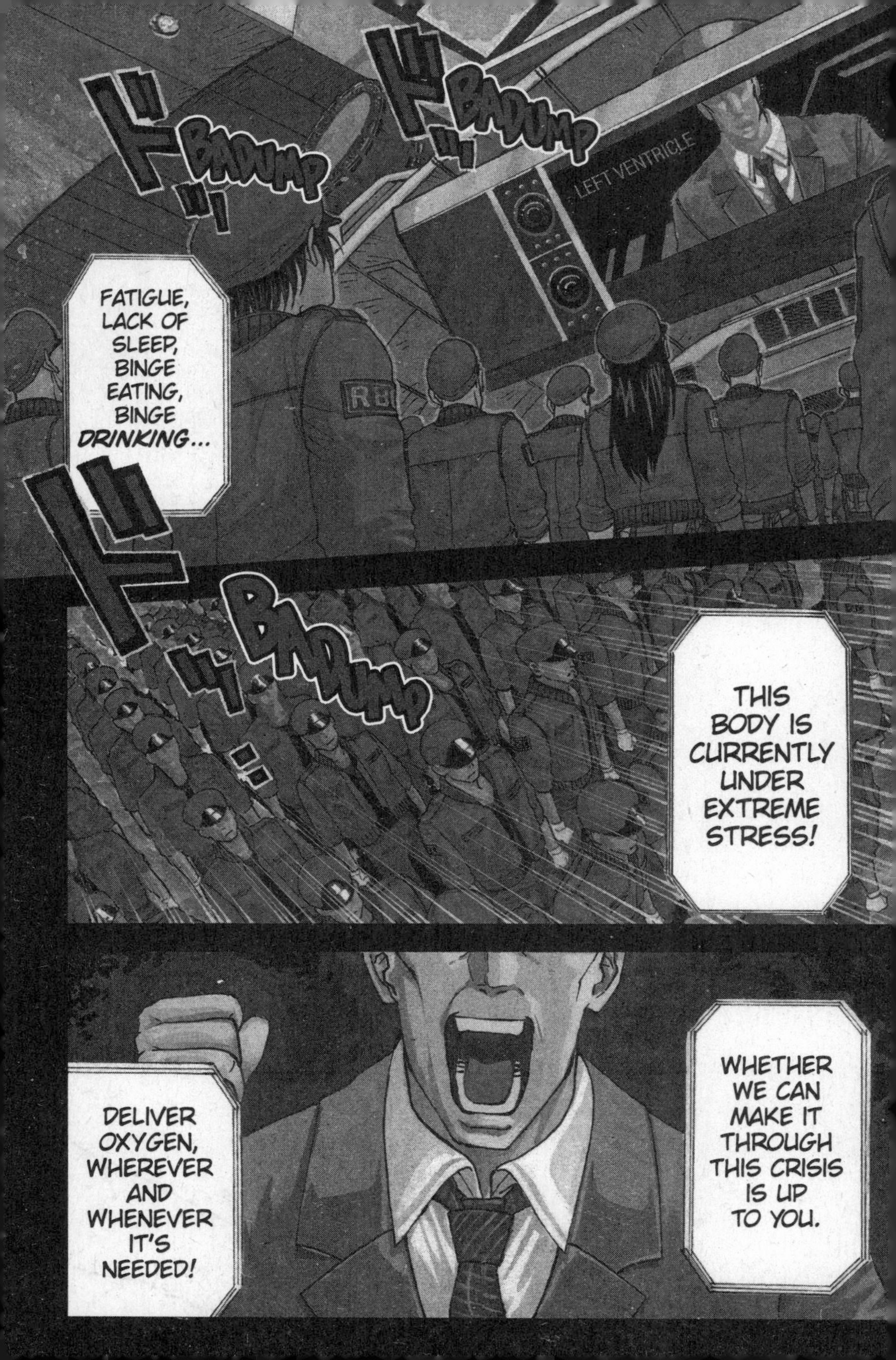
BADUMP
LEFT VENTRICLE
BADUMP
FATIGUE, LACK OF SLEEP, BINGE EATING, BINGE *DRINKING*...
BADUMP
THIS BODY IS CURRENTLY UNDER EXTREME STRESS!
WHETHER WE CAN MAKE IT THROUGH THIS CRISIS IS UP TO YOU.
DELIVER OXYGEN, WHEREVER AND WHENEVER IT'S NEEDED!

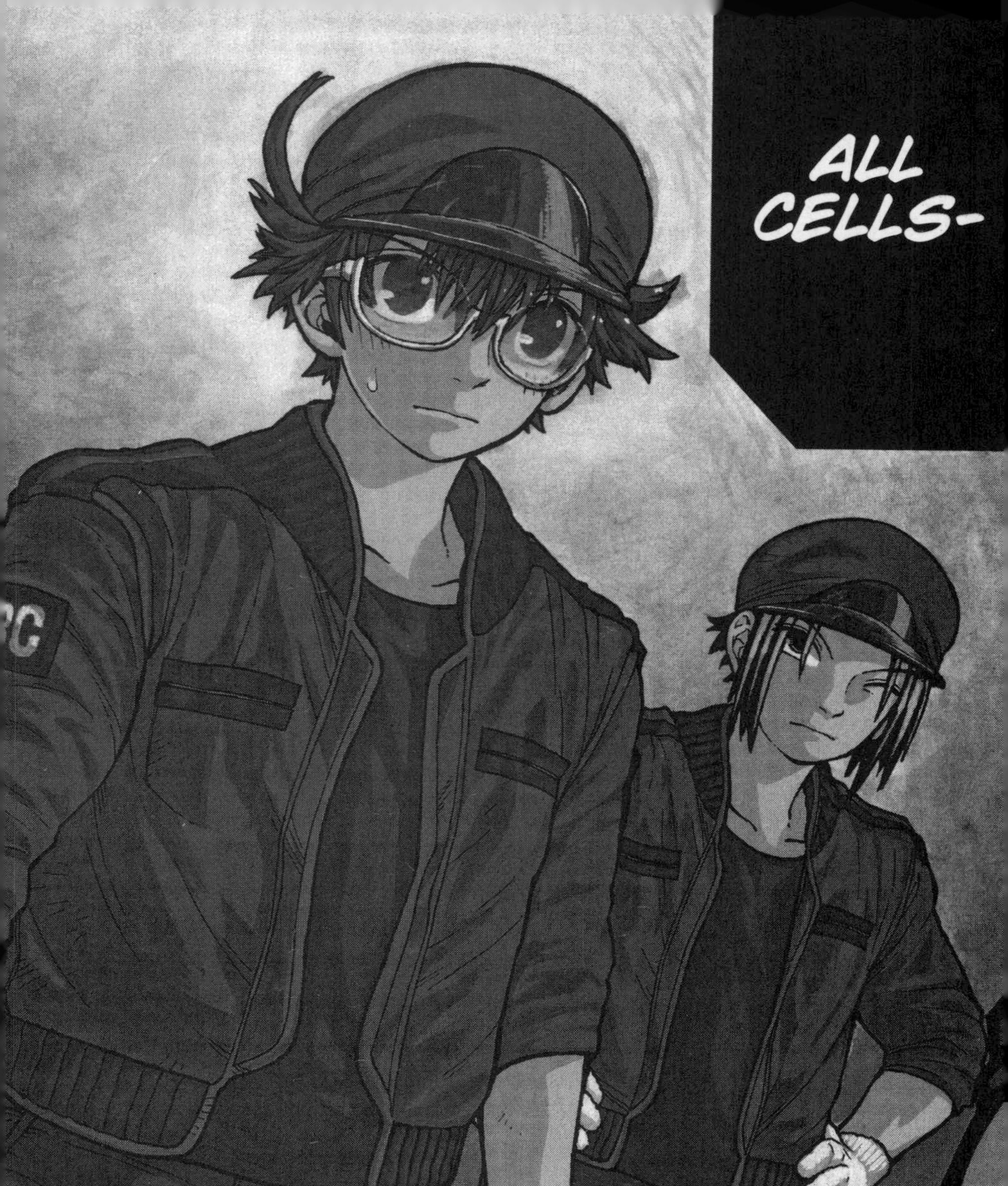
ALL CELLS-

01. SMOKING, BACTERIA, AND THE BEGINNING OF THE END

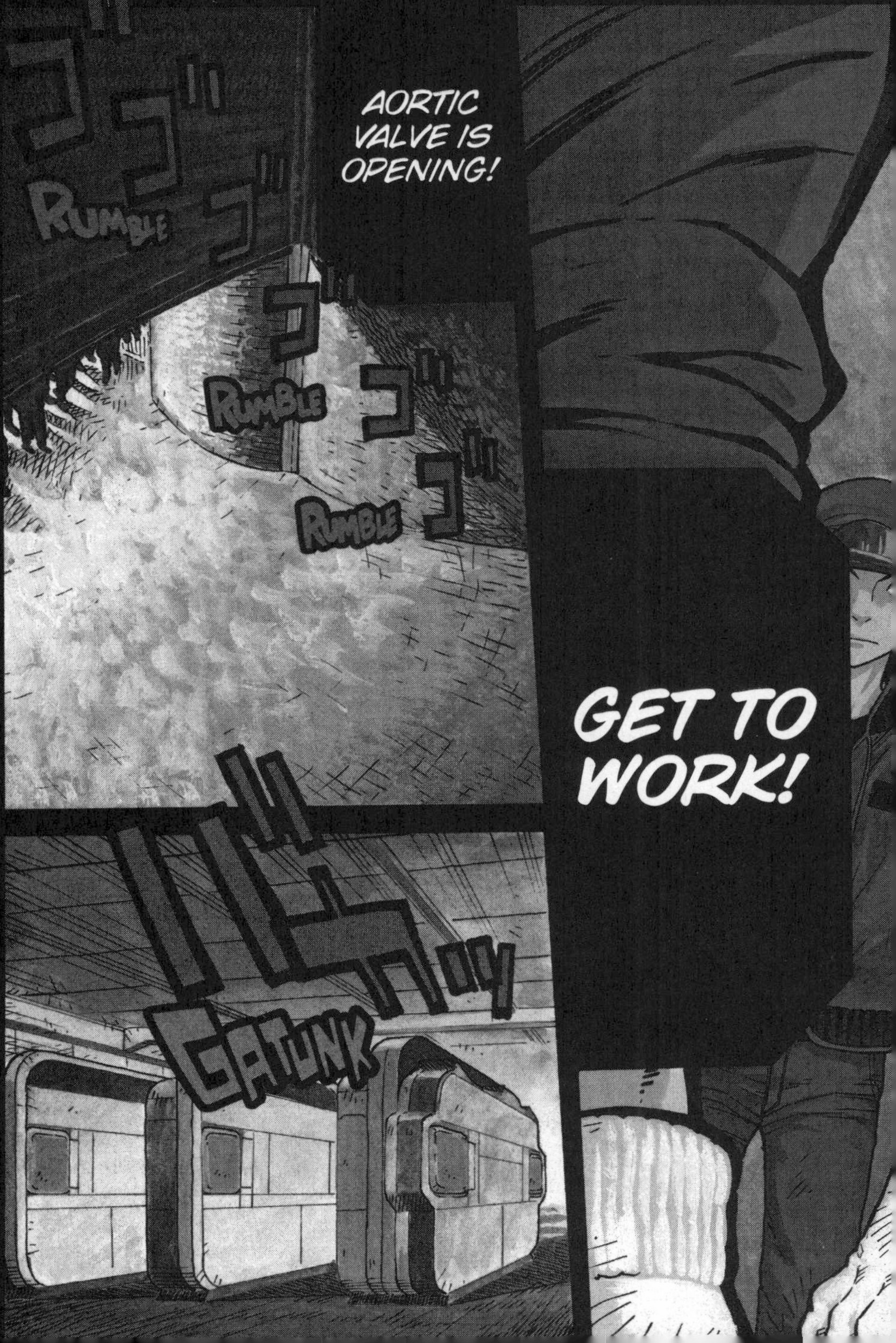
RUMBLE
AORTIC VALVE IS OPENING!
RUMBLE
RUMBLE
GET TO WORK!
CATUNK

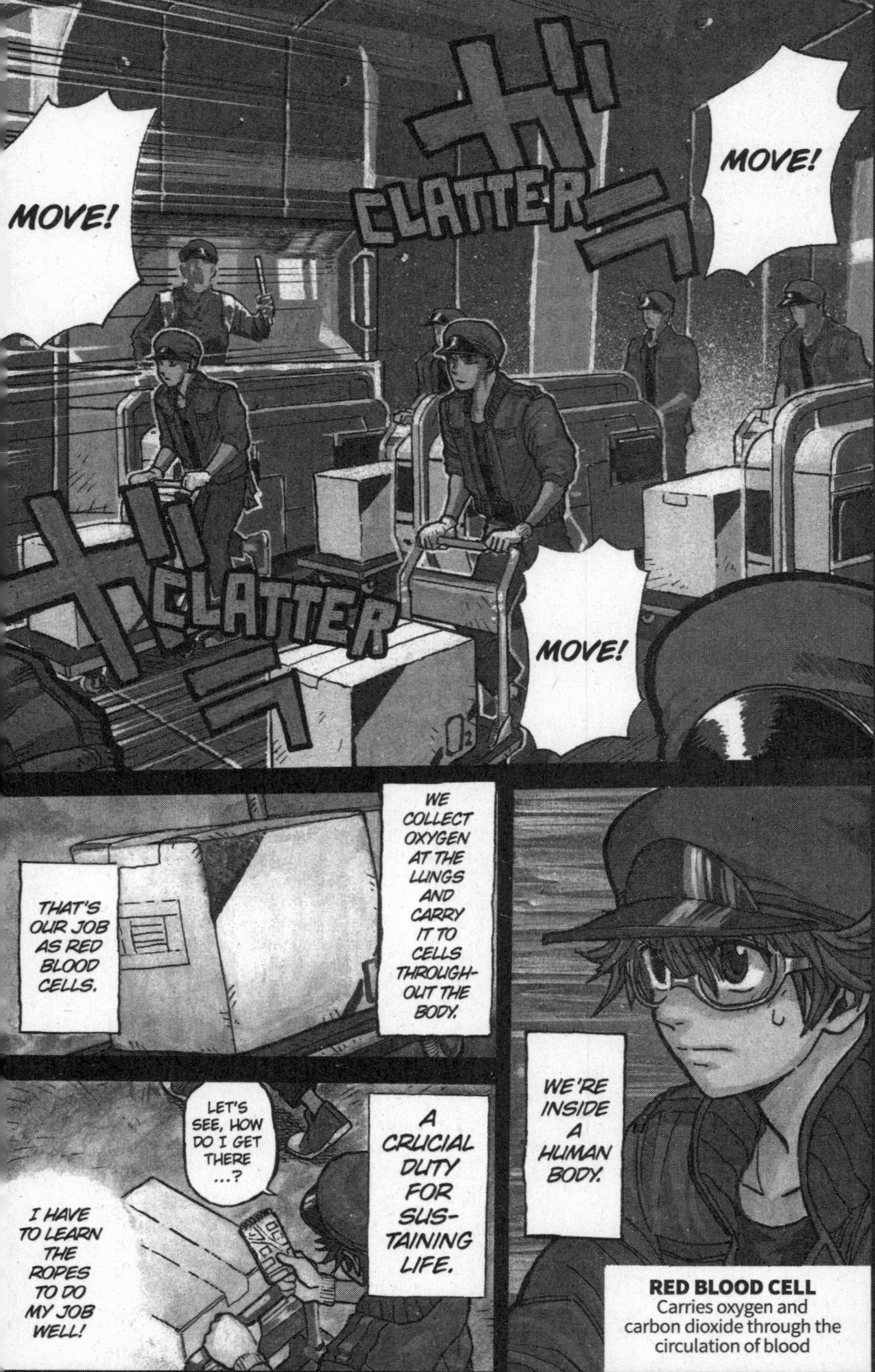
MOVE!
CLATTER
MOVE!
MOVE!
CLATTER
WE'RE INSIDE A HUMAN BODY.
RED BLOOD CELL
Carries oxygen and carbon dioxide through the circulation of blood
WE COLLECT OXYGEN AT THE LUNGS AND CARRY IT TO CELLS THROUGH-OUT THE BODY.
THAT'S OUR JOB AS RED BLOOD CELLS.
A CRUCIAL DUTY FOR SUS-TAINING LIFE.
LET'S SEE, HOW DO I GET THERE ...?
I HAVE TO LEARN THE ROPES TO DO MY JOB WELL!

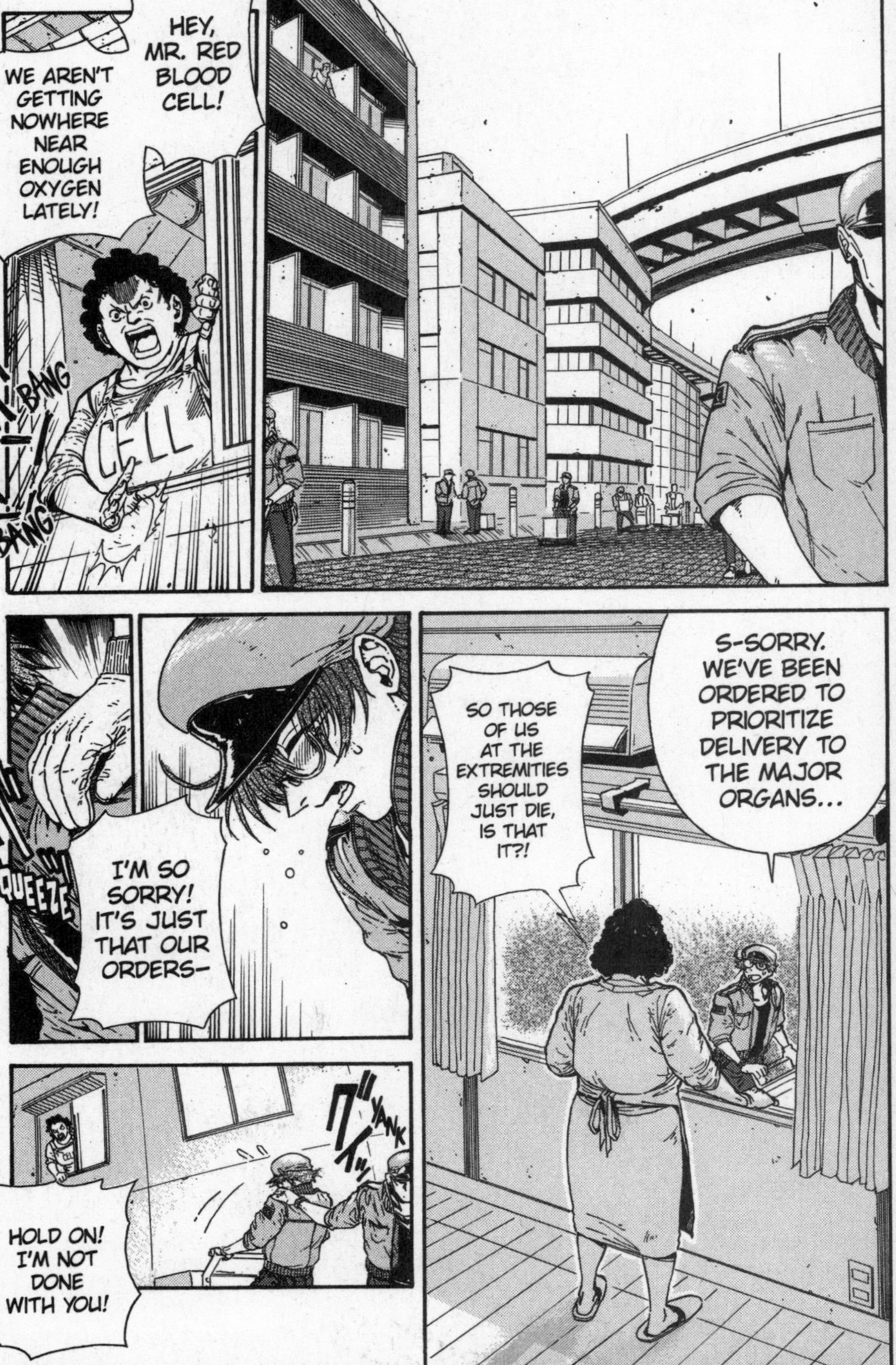
HEY, MR. RED BLOOD CELL!
WE AREN'T GETTING NOWHERE NEAR ENOUGH OXYGEN LATELY!
BANG
BANG
CELL
S-SORRY. WE'VE BEEN ORDERED TO PRIORITIZE DELIVERY TO THE MAJOR ORGANS...
SO THOSE OF US AT THE EXTREMITIES SHOULD JUST DIE, IS THAT IT?!
I'M SO SORRY! IT'S JUST THAT OUR ORDERS-
SQUEEZE
YANK
HOLD ON! I'M NOT DONE WITH YOU!

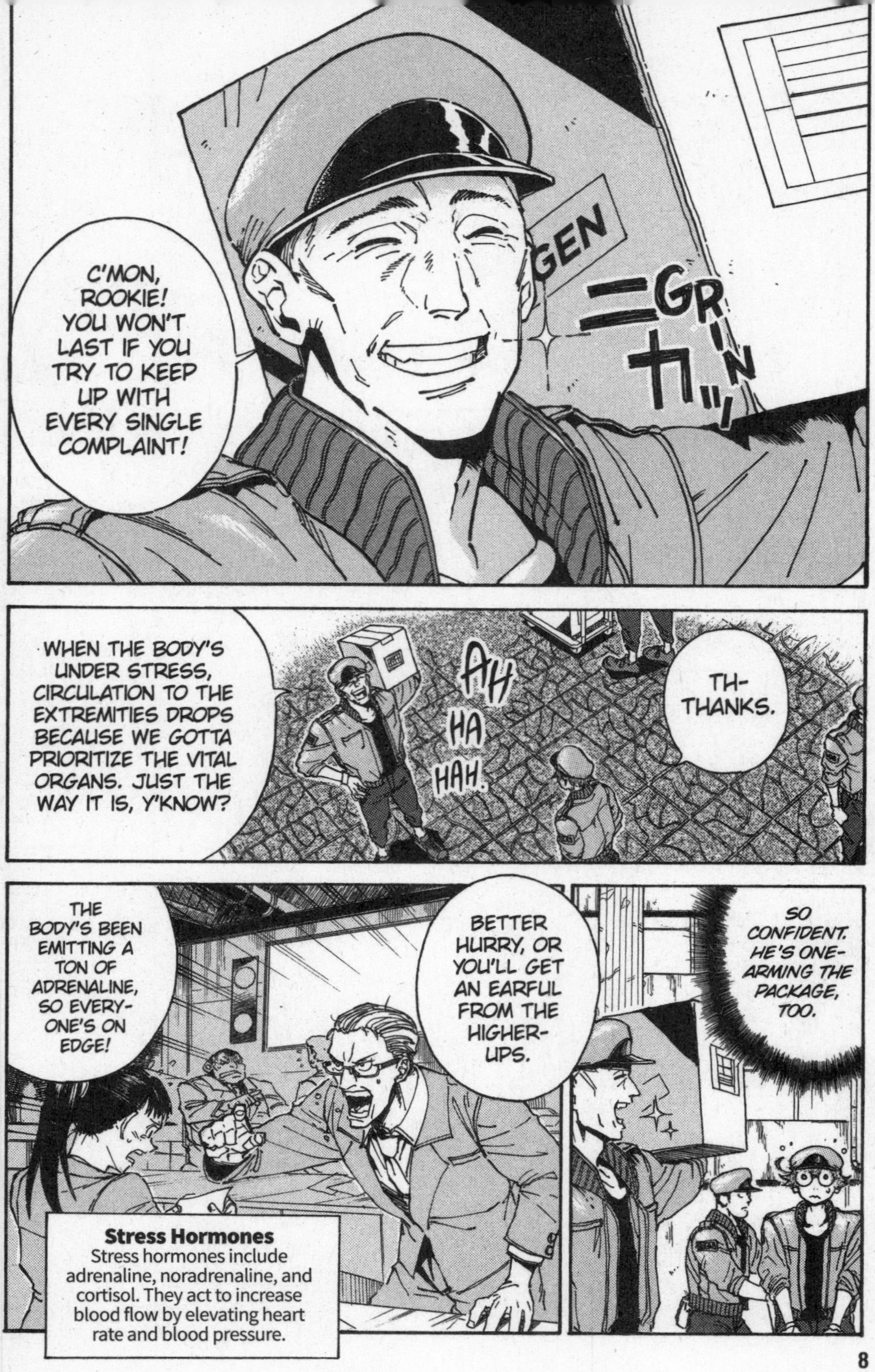
GEN
GRIN
カッ
C'MON, ROOKIE! YOU WON'T LAST IF YOU TRY TO KEEP UP WITH EVERY SINGLE COMPLAINT!
TH- THANKS.
AH HA HAH.
WHEN THE BODY'S UNDER STRESS, CIRCULATION TO THE EXTREMITIES DROPS BECAUSE WE GOTTA PRIORITIZE THE VITAL ORGANS. JUST THE WAY IT IS, Y'KNOW?
SO CONFIDENT. HE'S ONE-ARMING THE PACKAGE, TOO.
BETTER HURRY, OR YOU'LL GET AN EARFUL FROM THE HIGHER-UPS.
THE BODY'S BEEN EMITTING A TON OF ADRENALINE, SO EVERY-ONE'S ON EDGE!

Stress Hormones
Stress hormones include adrenaline, noradrenaline, and cortisol. They act to increase blood flow by elevating heart rate and blood pressure.

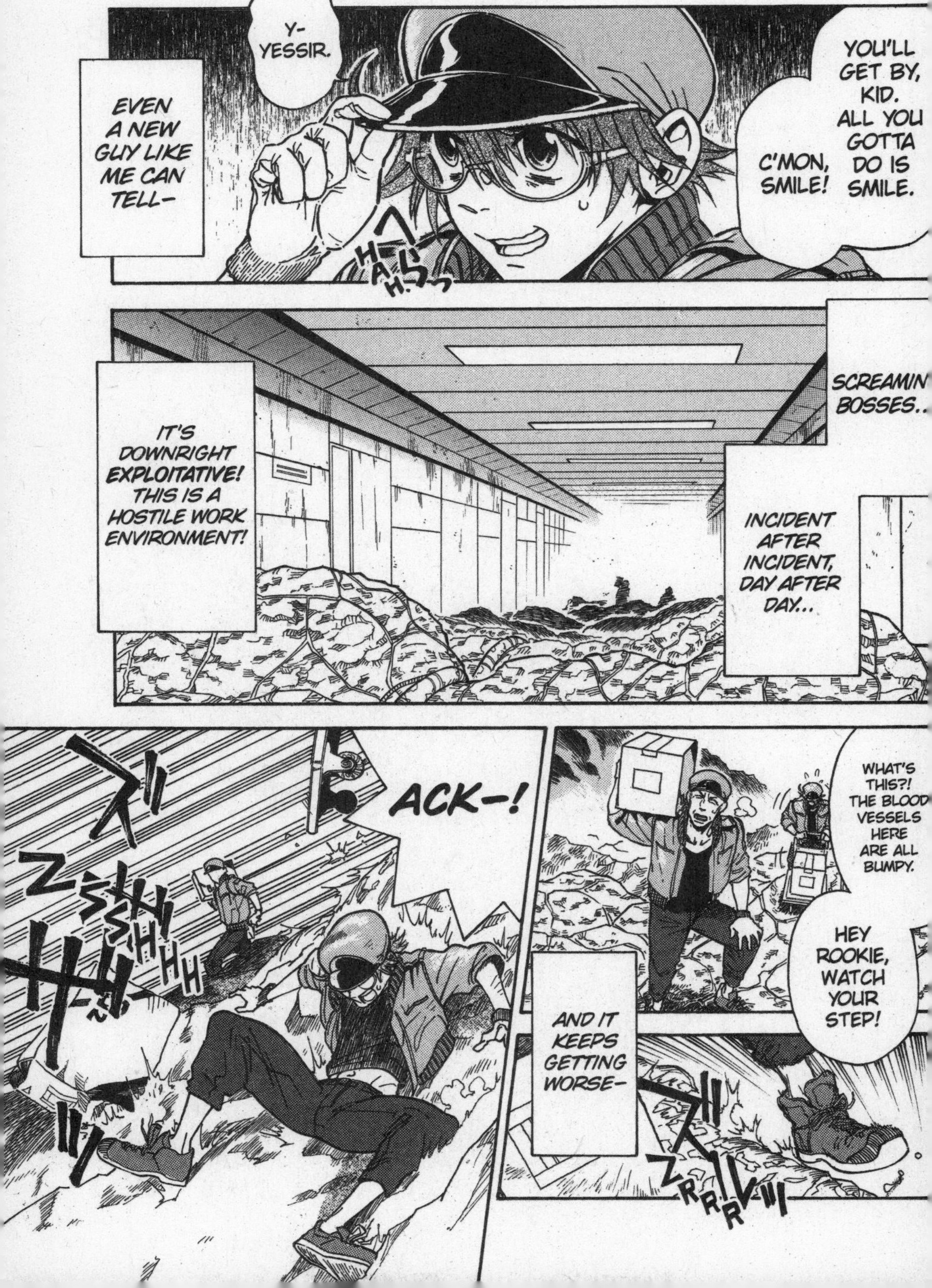
YOU'LL GET BY, KID. ALL YOU GOTTA DO IS SMILE.
C'MON, SMILE!
Y- YESSIR.
EVEN A NEW GUY LIKE ME CAN TELL-
HAH HAH
SCREAMIN BOSSES...
INCIDENT AFTER INCIDENT, DAY AFTER DAY...
IT'S DOWNRIGHT EXPLOITATIVE! THIS IS A HOSTILE WORK ENVIRONMENT!
WHAT'S THIS?! THE BLOOD VESSELS HERE ARE ALL BUMPY.
HEY ROOKIE, WATCH YOUR STEP!
AND IT KEEPS GETTING WORSE-
ACK-!

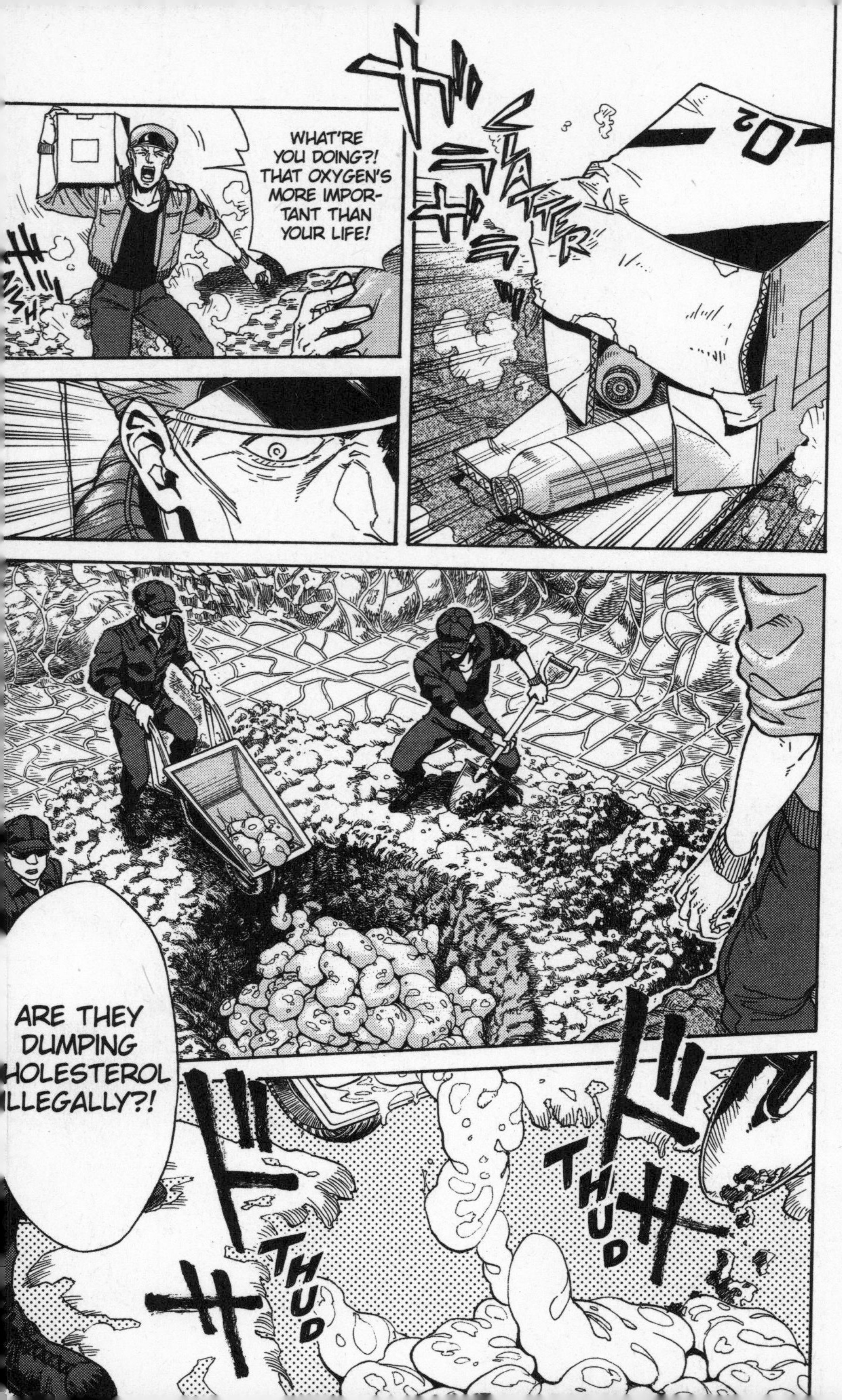
CLATTER
WHAT'RE YOU DOING?! THAT OXYGEN'S MORE IMPOR- TANT THAN YOUR LIFE!
ARE THEY DUMPING HOLESTEROL LLEGALLY?!
THUD
THUD

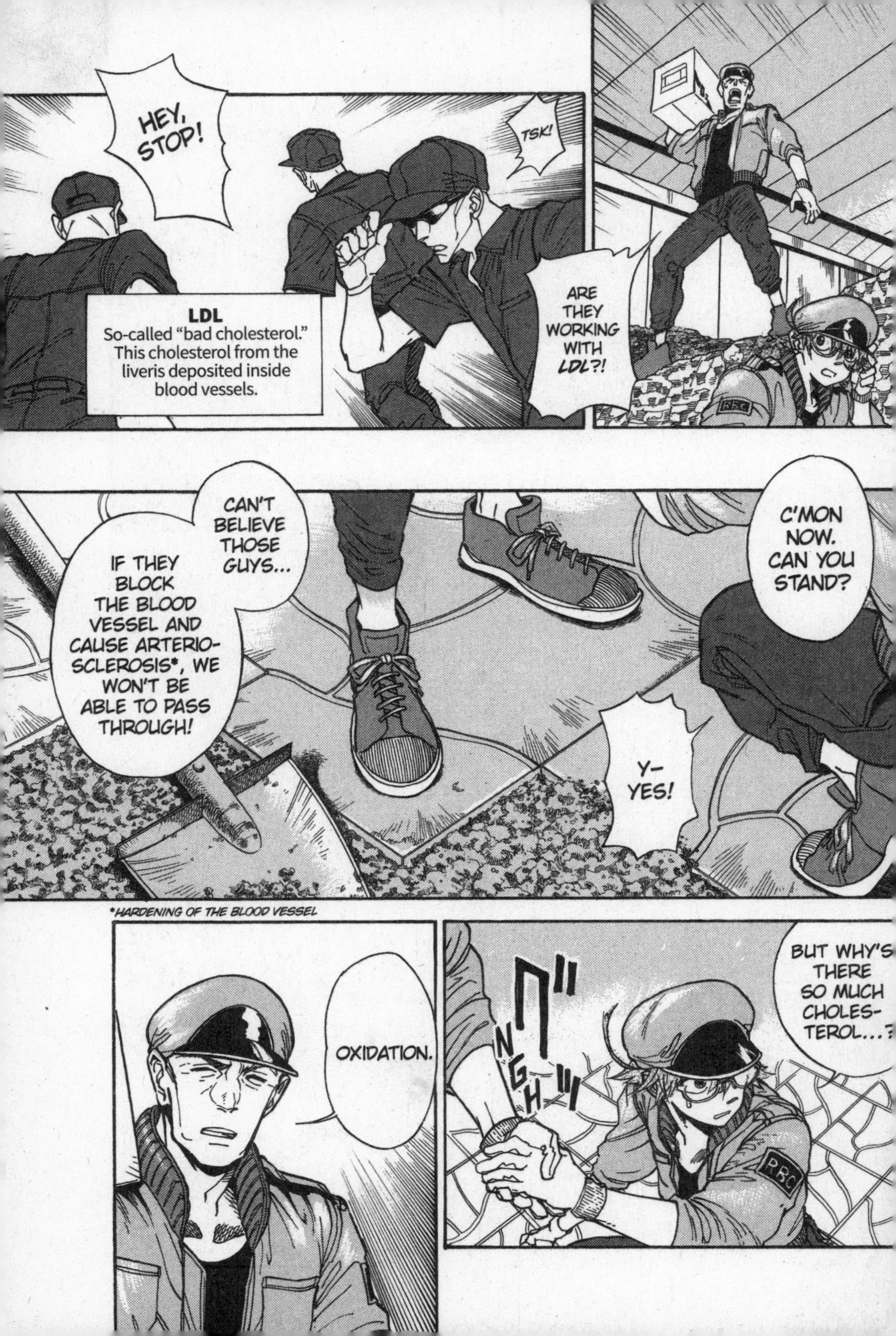

HEY, STOP!
TSK!
ARE THEY WORKING WITH *LDL*?!
LDL
So-called "bad cholesterol." This cholesterol from the liveris deposited inside blood vessels.
C'MON NOW. CAN YOU STAND?
Y-YES!
CAN'T BELIEVE THOSE GUYS...
IF THEY BLOCK THE BLOOD VESSEL AND CAUSE ARTERIO-SCLEROSIS*, WE WON'T BE ABLE TO PASS THROUGH!
*HARDENING OF THE BLOOD VESSEL
BUT WHY'S THERE SO MUCH CHOLES-TEROL...?
NGH
OXIDATION.

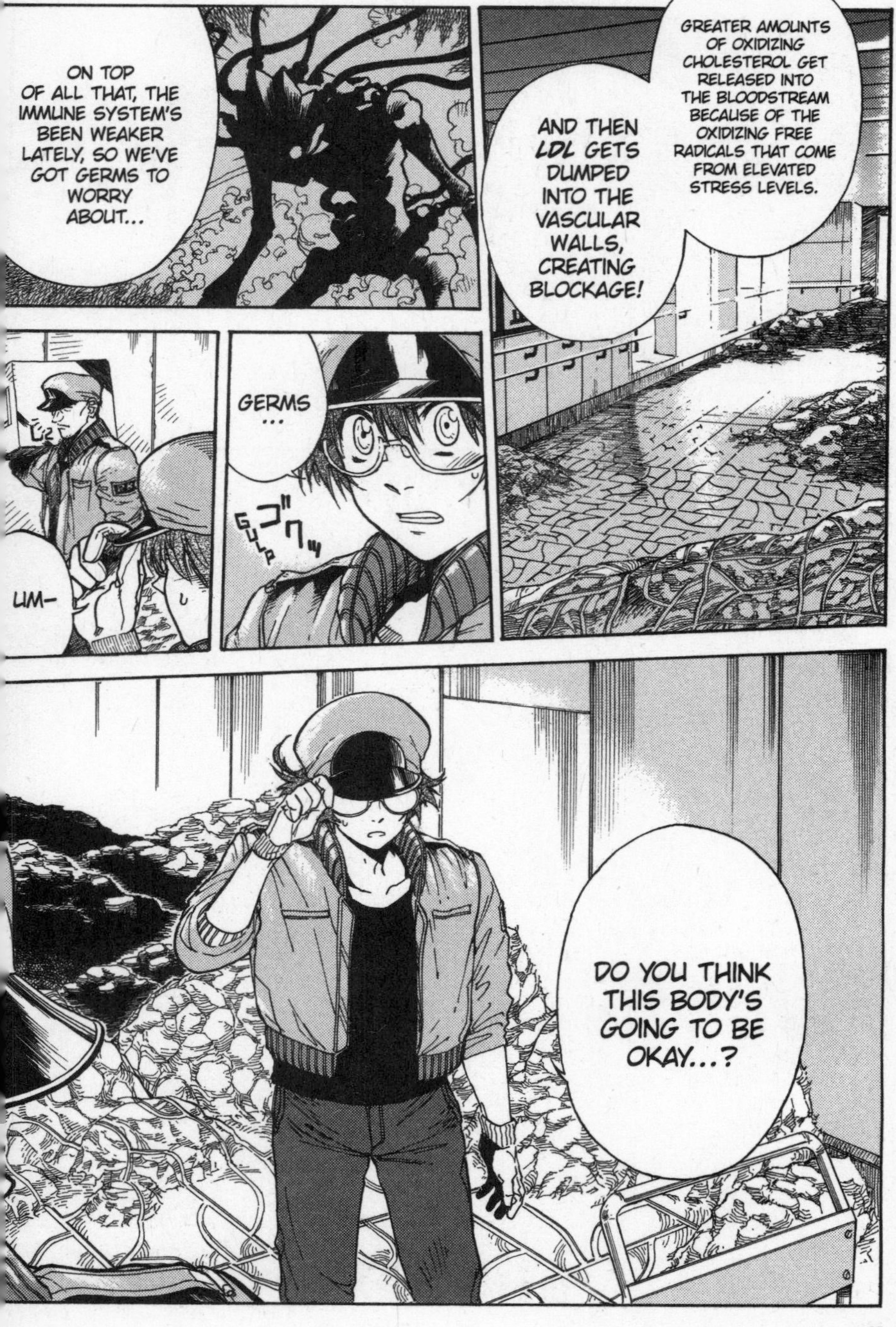
GREATER AMOUNTS OF OXIDIZING CHOLESTEROL GET RELEASED INTO THE BLOODSTREAM BECAUSE OF THE OXIDIZING FREE RADICALS THAT COME FROM ELEVATED STRESS LEVELS.
AND THEN *LDL* GETS DUMPED INTO THE VASCULAR WALLS, CREATING BLOCKAGE!
ON TOP OF ALL THAT, THE IMMUNE SYSTEM'S BEEN WEAKER LATELY, SO WE'VE GOT GERMS TO WORRY ABOUT...
GERMS...
ゴクッ
GULP
UM-
DO YOU THINK THIS BODY'S GOING TO BE OKAY...?

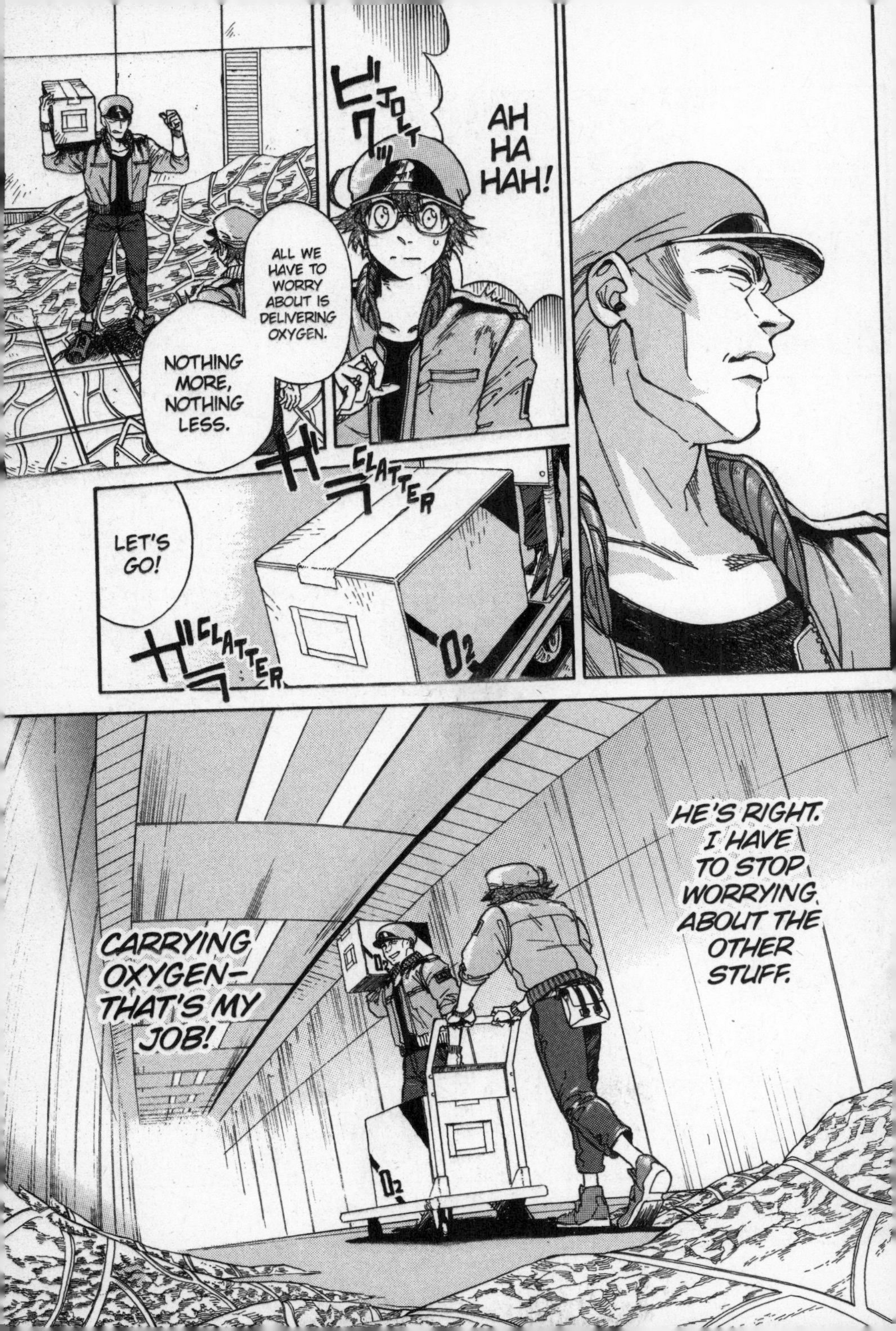

AH HA HAH!
ビクッ
JOLT
ALL WE HAVE TO WORRY ABOUT IS DELIVERING OXYGEN.
NOTHING MORE, NOTHING LESS.
ガラ
CLATTER
LET'S GO!
ガラ
CLATTER
O_2
HE'S RIGHT. I HAVE TO STOP WORRYING ABOUT THE OTHER STUFF.
CARRYING OXYGEN—THAT'S MY JOB!

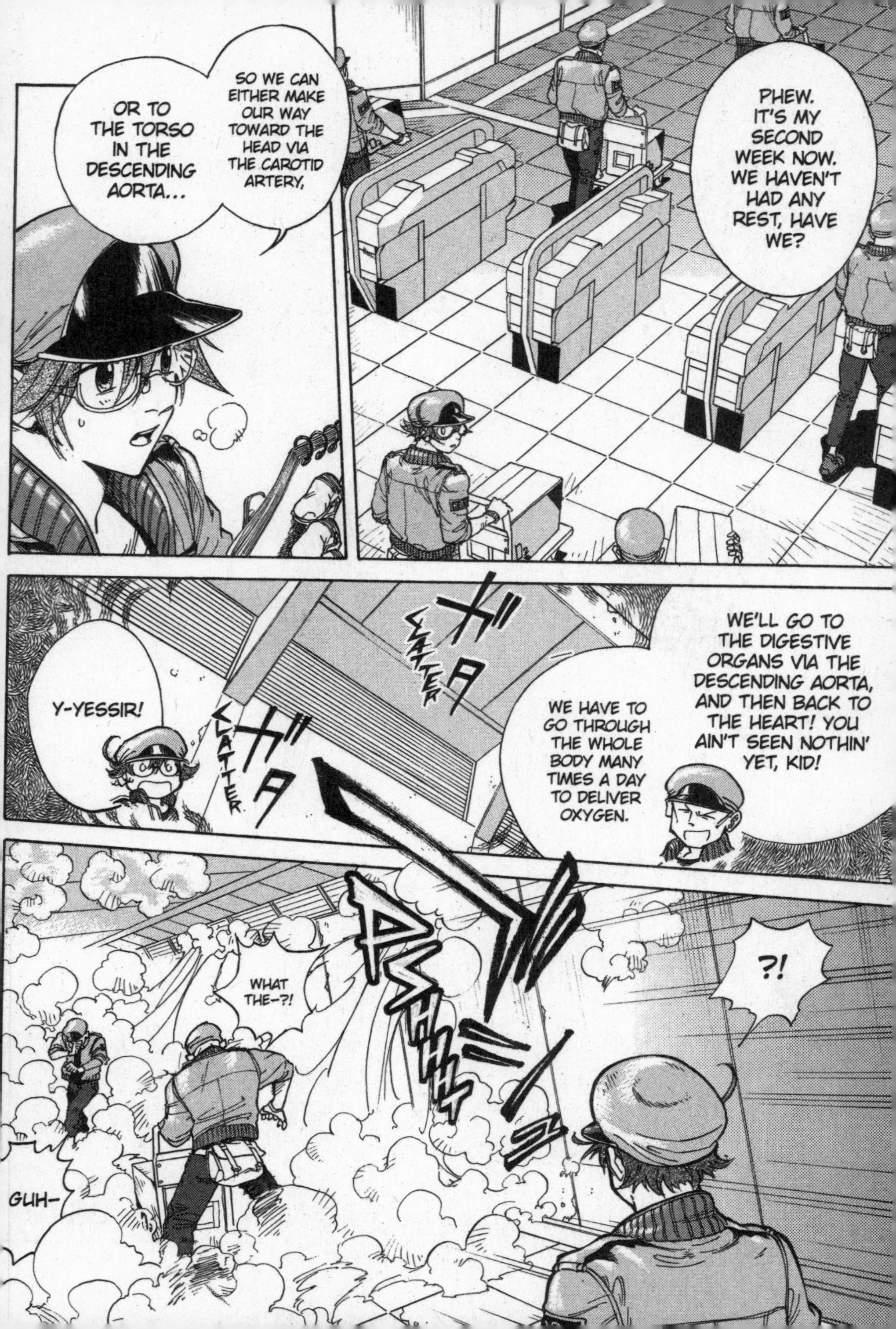
PHEW. IT'S MY SECOND WEEK NOW. WE HAVEN'T HAD ANY REST, HAVE WE?
SO WE CAN EITHER MAKE OUR WAY TOWARD THE HEAD VIA THE CAROTID ARTERY,
OR TO THE TORSO IN THE DESCENDING AORTA...
WE'LL GO TO THE DIGESTIVE ORGANS VIA THE DESCENDING AORTA, AND THEN BACK TO THE HEART! YOU AIN'T SEEN NOTHIN' YET, KID!
WE HAVE TO GO THROUGH THE WHOLE BODY MANY TIMES A DAY TO DELIVER OXYGEN.
CLATTER
CLATTER
Y-YESSIR!
?!
WHAT THE-?!
GUH-

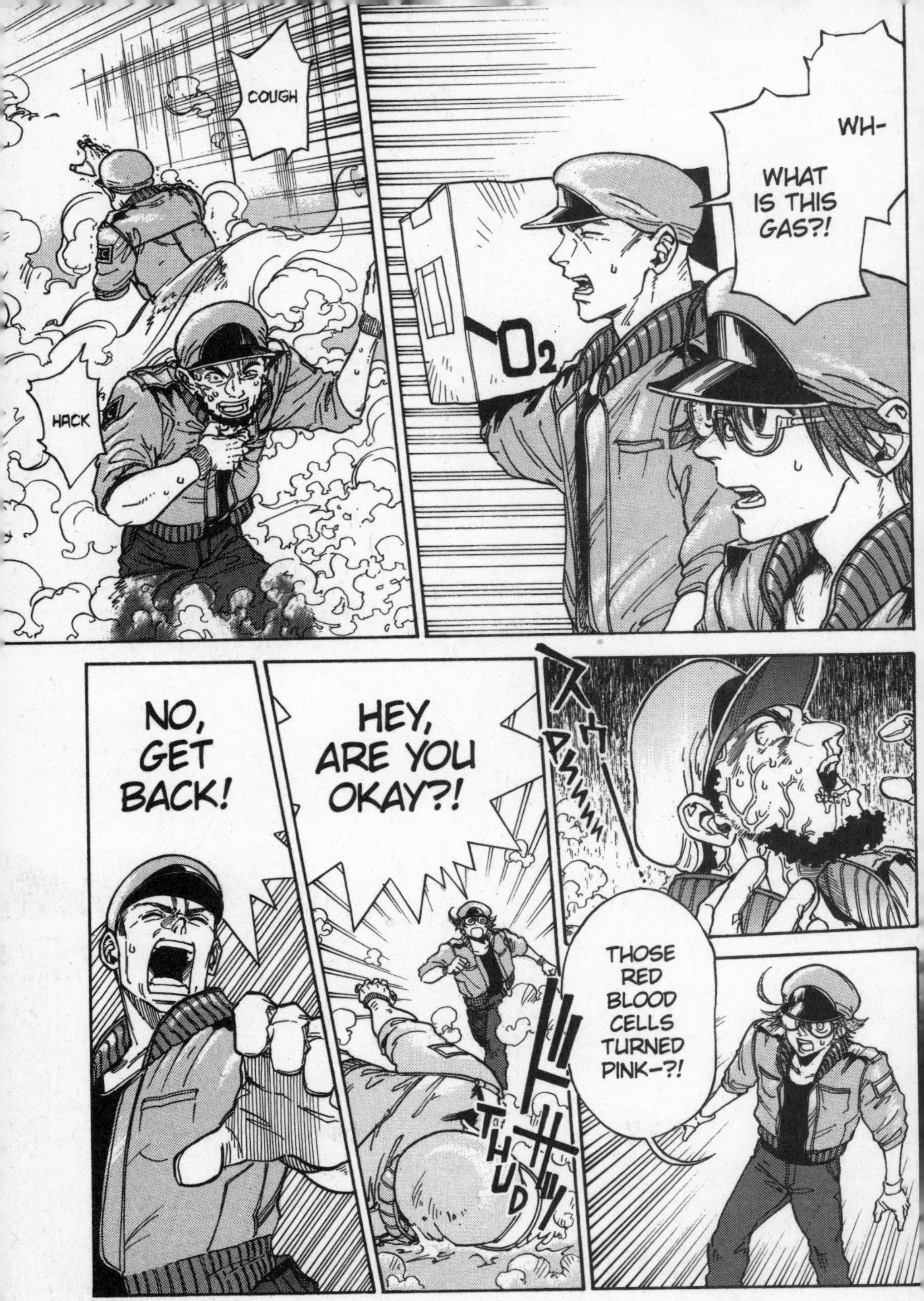
WH-
WHAT IS THIS GAS?!
COUGH
HACK
THOSE RED BLOOD CELLS TURNED PINK-?!
THUD
HEY, ARE YOU OKAY?!
NO, GET BACK!

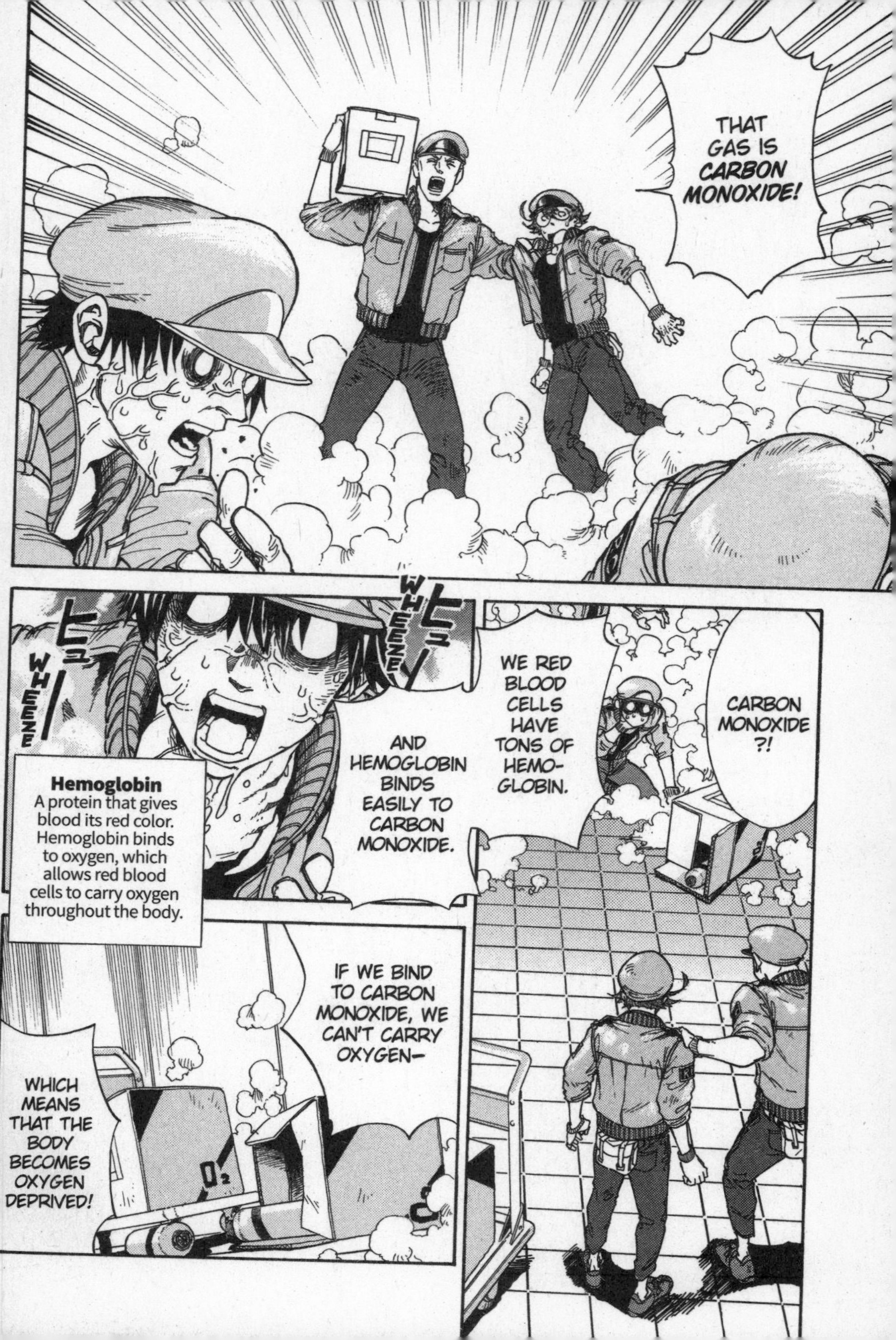
THAT GAS IS CARBON MONOXIDE!
CARBON MONOXIDE ?!
WE RED BLOOD CELLS HAVE TONS OF HEMO-GLOBIN.
ヒュー WHEEZE
ヒュー WHEEZE
AND HEMOGLOBIN BINDS EASILY TO CARBON MONOXIDE.
Hemoglobin
A protein that gives blood its red color. Hemoglobin binds to oxygen, which allows red blood cells to carry oxygen throughout the body.
IF WE BIND TO CARBON MONOXIDE, WE CAN'T CARRY OXYGEN—
WHICH MEANS THAT THE BODY BECOMES OXYGEN DEPRIVED!

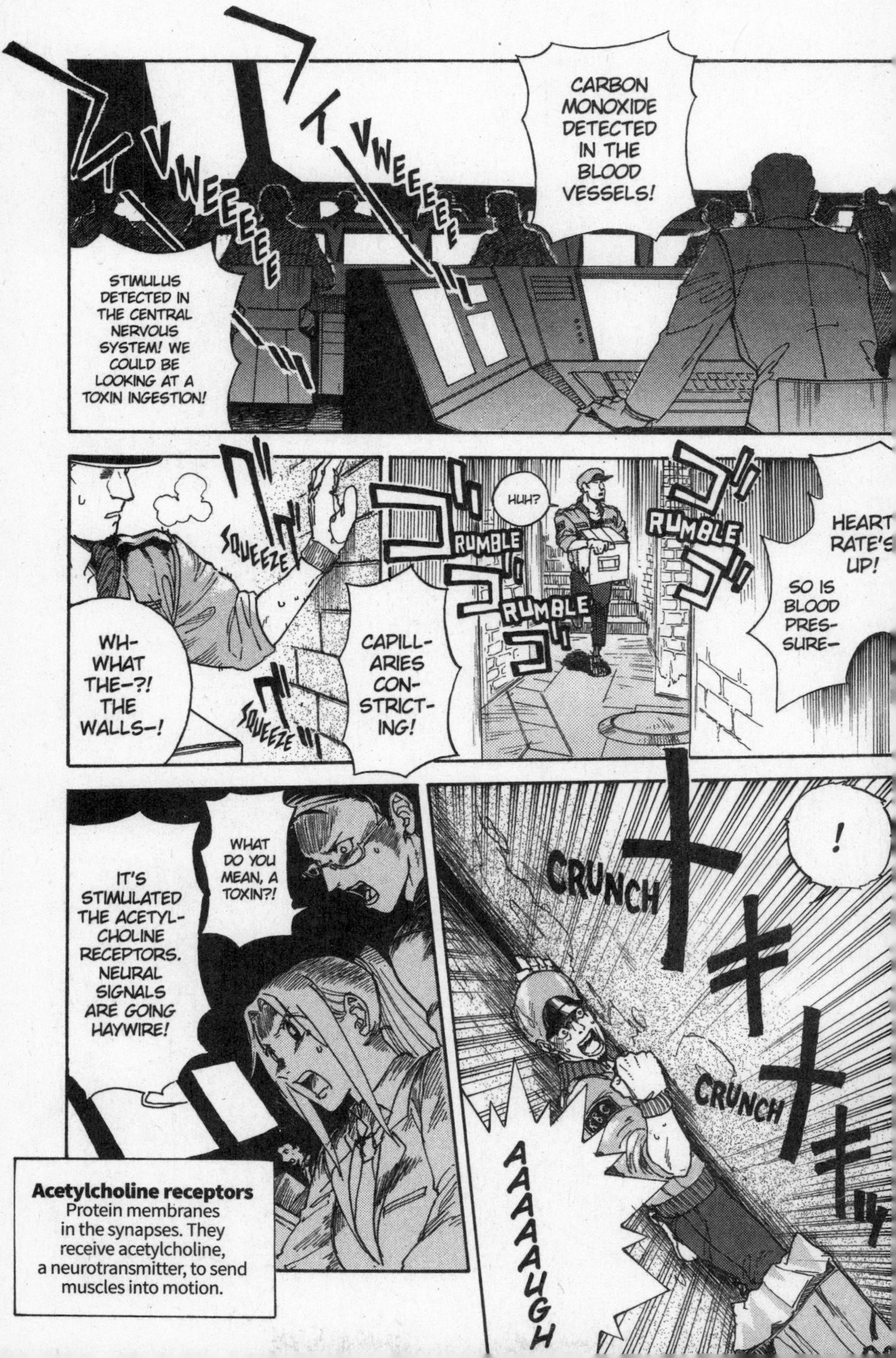

CARBON MONOXIDE DETECTED IN THE BLOOD VESSELS!
VWEEEEEE
VWEEEEEE
STIMULUS DETECTED IN THE CENTRAL NERVOUS SYSTEM! WE COULD BE LOOKING AT A TOXIN INGESTION!
HEART RATE'S UP!
SO IS BLOOD PRES-SURE–
RUMBLE
HUH?
RUMBLE
RUMBLE
CAPILL-ARIES CON-STRICT-ING!
SQUEEZE
SQUEEZE
WH-WHAT THE–?! THE WALLS–!
!
CRUNCH
CRUNCH
AAAAAAUGH
WHAT DO YOU MEAN, A TOXIN?!
IT'S STIMULATED THE ACETYL-CHOLINE RECEPTORS. NEURAL SIGNALS ARE GOING HAYWIRE!

Acetylcholine receptors
Protein membranes in the synapses. They receive acetylcholine, a neurotransmitter, to send muscles into motion.

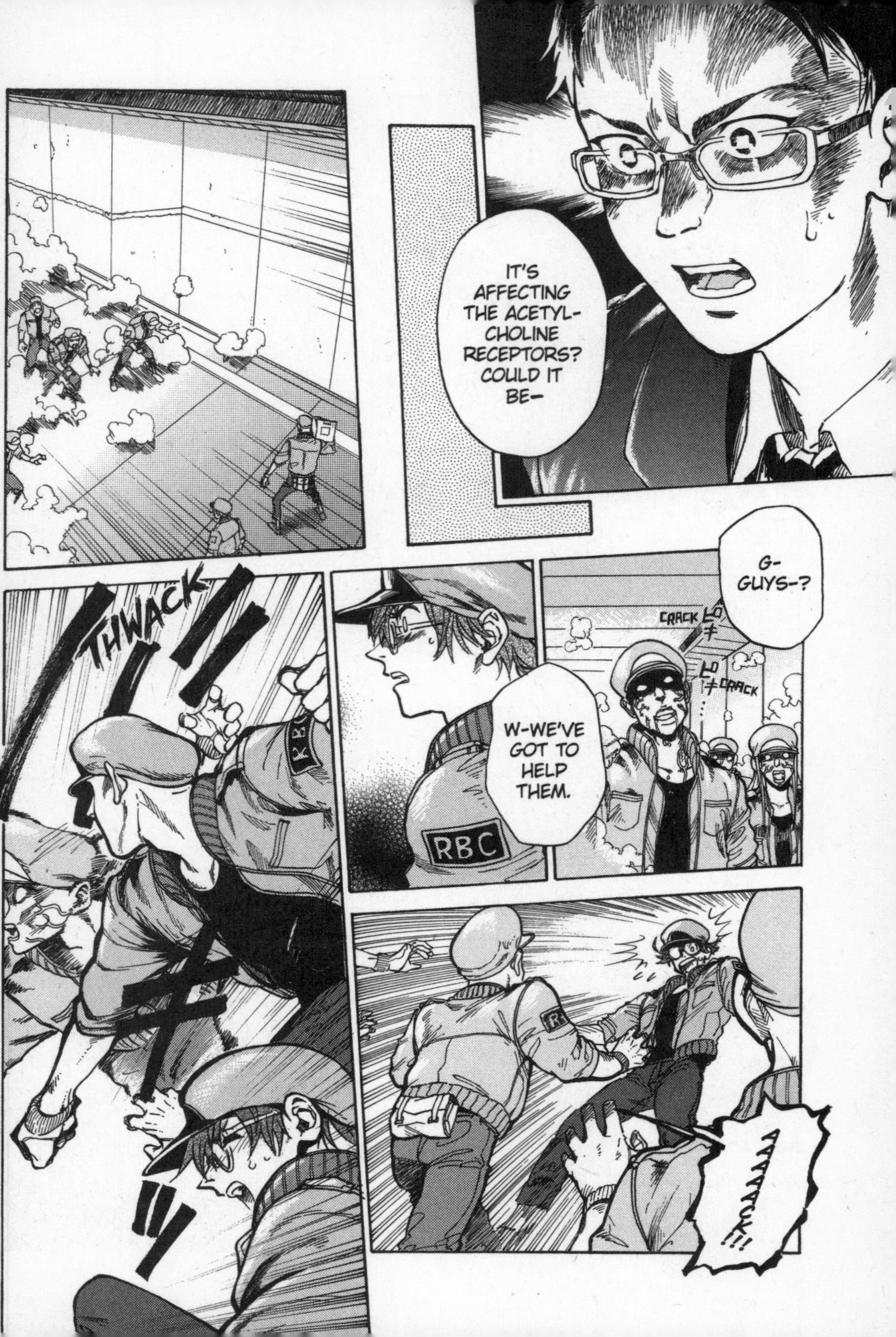
IT'S AFFECTING THE ACETYL-CHOLINE RECEPTORS? COULD IT BE—
G-GUYS-?
CRACK ピキ
ピキ CRACK
W-WE'VE GOT TO HELP THEM.
RBC
THWACK
AAAAAACK!!!

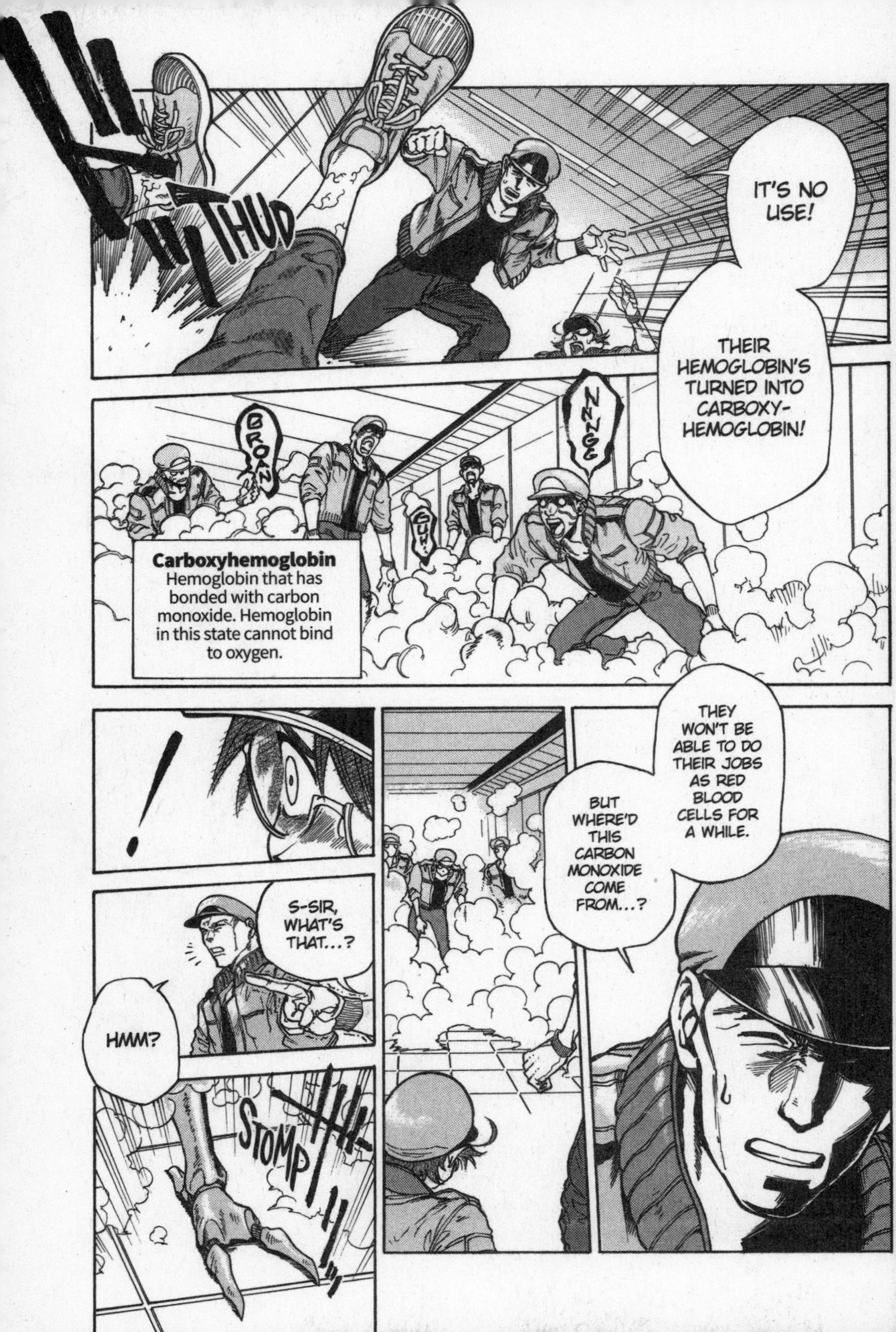
IT'S NO USE!
THEIR HEMOGLOBIN'S TURNED INTO CARBOXY-HEMOGLOBIN!
THUD
NNNGG
GUH...
GROAN
Carboxyhemoglobin
Hemoglobin that has bonded with carbon monoxide. Hemoglobin in this state cannot bind to oxygen.
THEY WON'T BE ABLE TO DO THEIR JOBS AS RED BLOOD CELLS FOR A WHILE.
BUT WHERE'D THIS CARBON MONOXIDE COME FROM...?
!
S-SIR, WHAT'S THAT...?
HMM?
STOMP

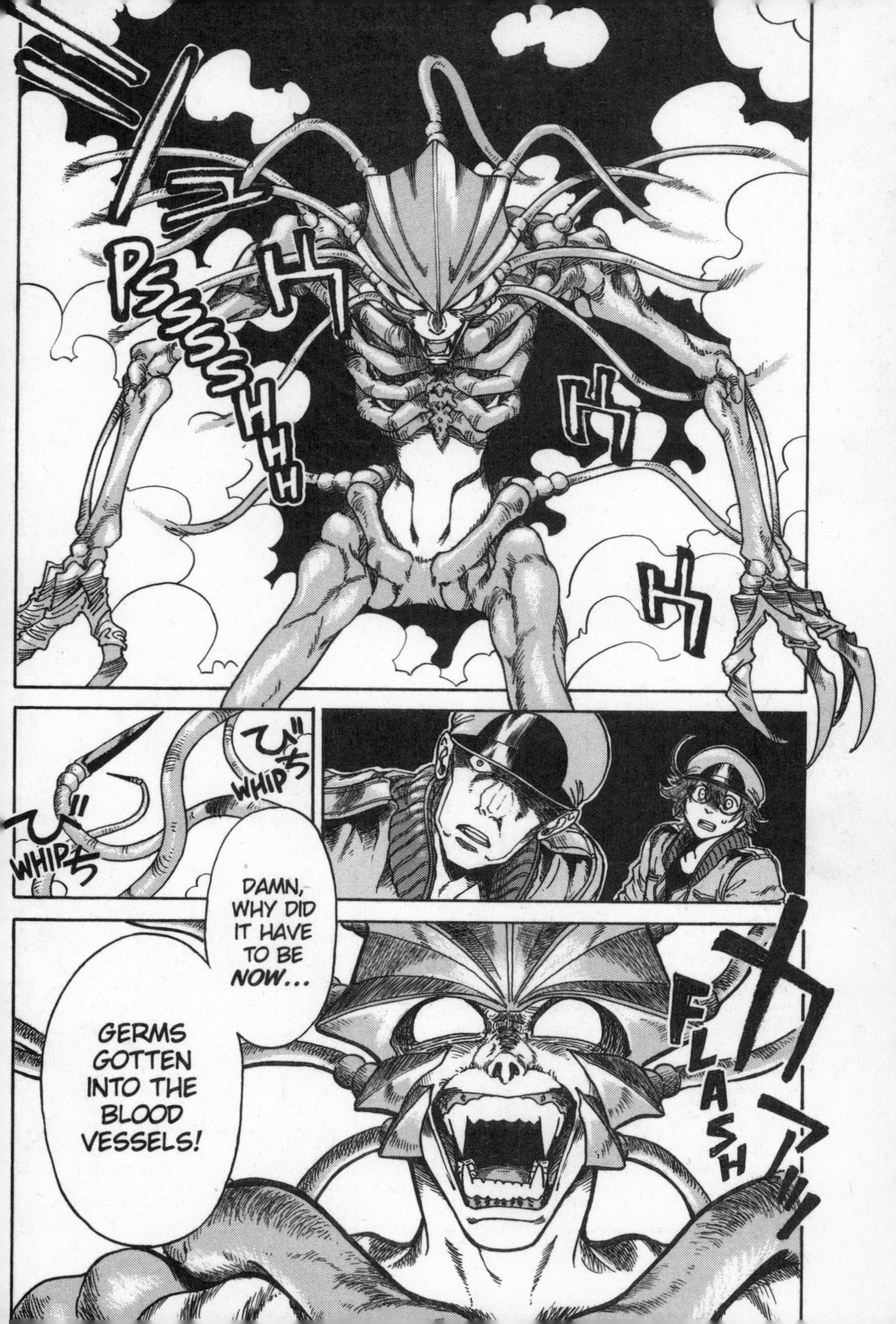
PSSSSHHHH
DAMN, WHY DID IT HAVE TO BE *NOW*...
びち
WHIP
びち
WHIP
FLASH
GERMS GOTTEN INTO THE BLOOD VESSELS!

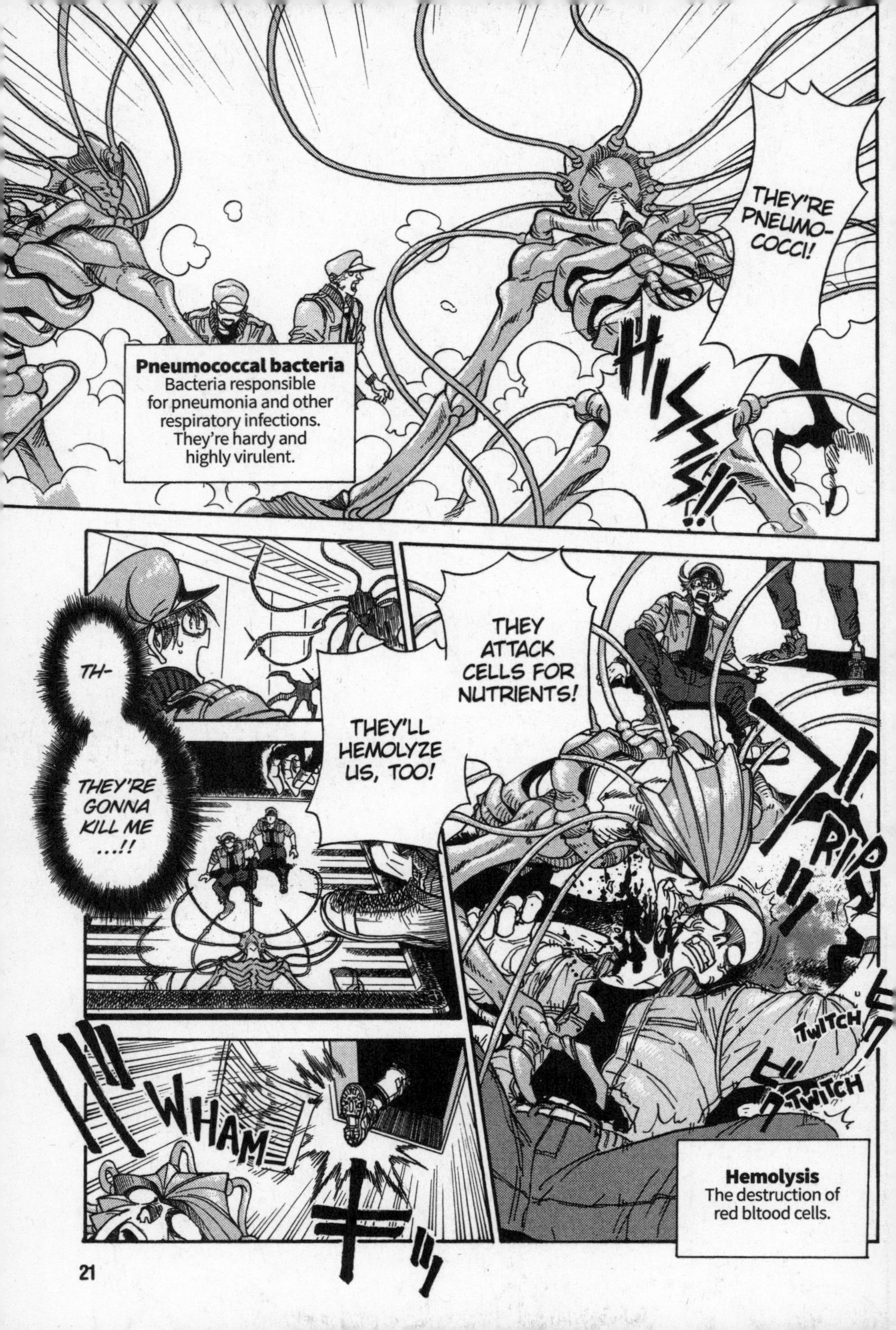
THEY'RE PNEUMO-COCCI!
HISSS!!
Pneumococcal bacteria
Bacteria responsible for pneumonia and other respiratory infections. They're hardy and highly virulent.
THEY ATTACK CELLS FOR NUTRIENTS!
THEY'LL HEMOLYZE US, TOO!
RIP
TWITCH
TWITCH
Hemolysis
The destruction of red bltood cells.
TH-
THEY'RE GONNA KILL ME ...!!
WHAM

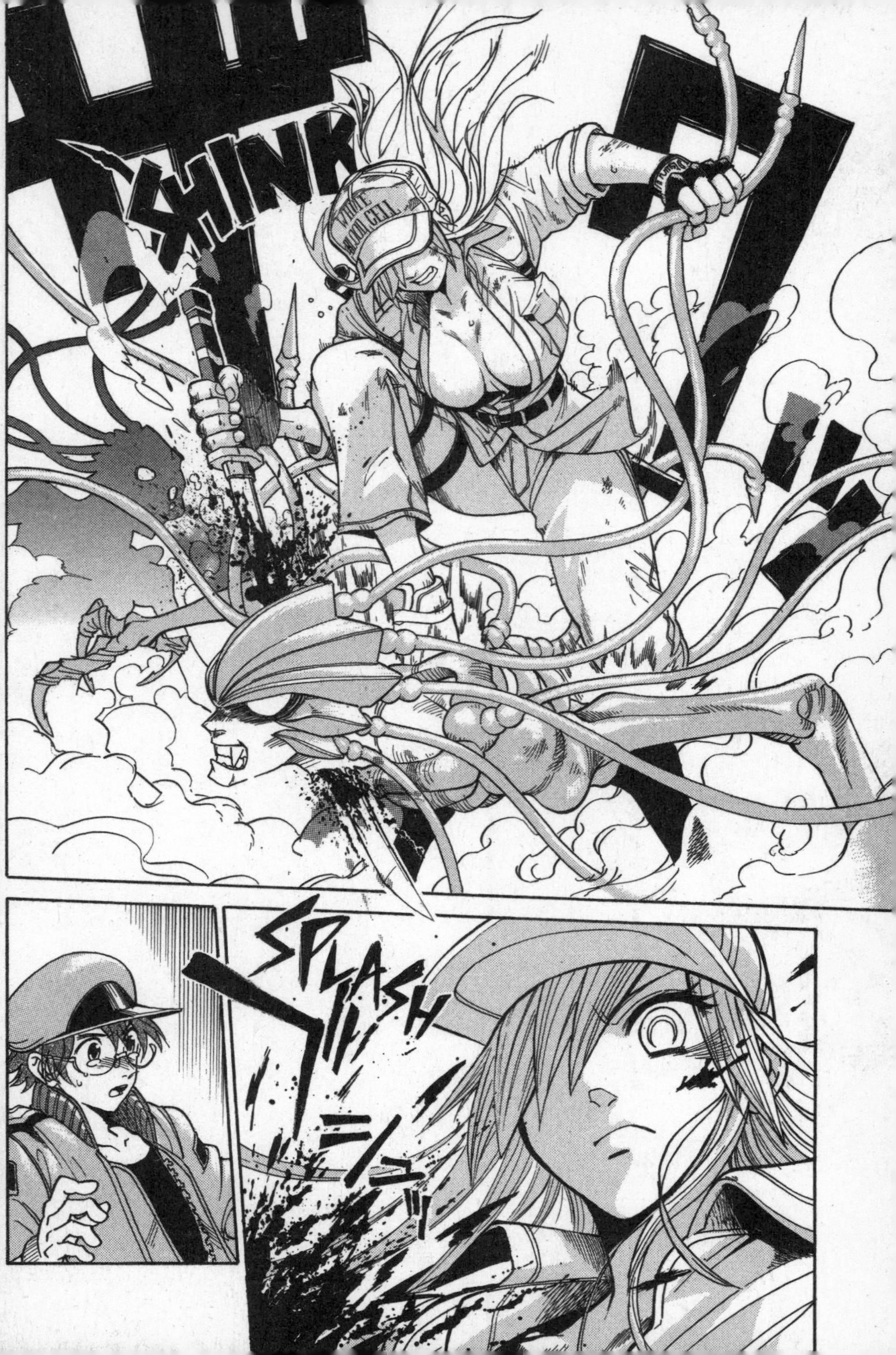
SHINK
SPLASH

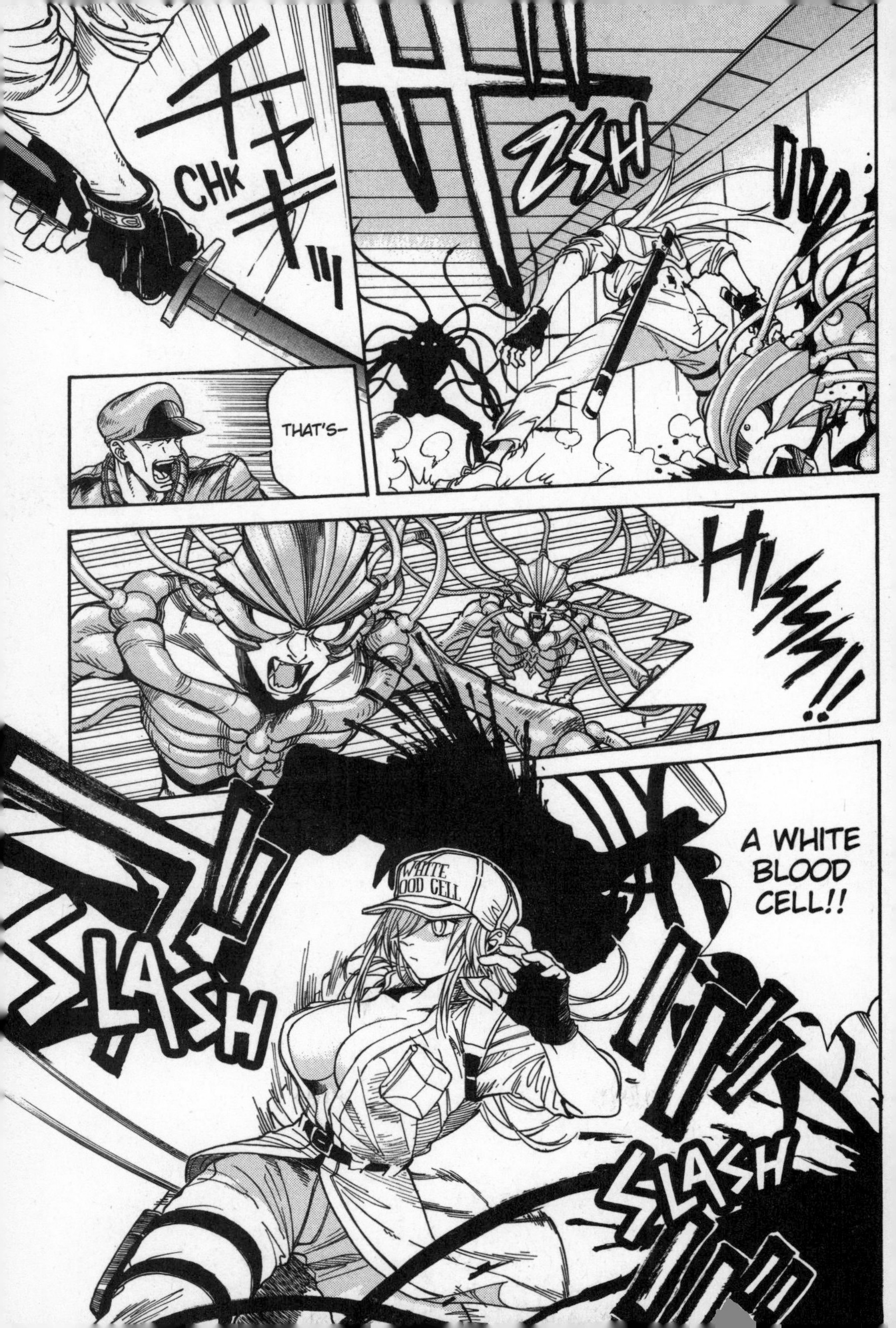
ZSH
CHK
THAT'S-
HISSSS!!
A WHITE BLOOD CELL!!
SLASH
SLASH

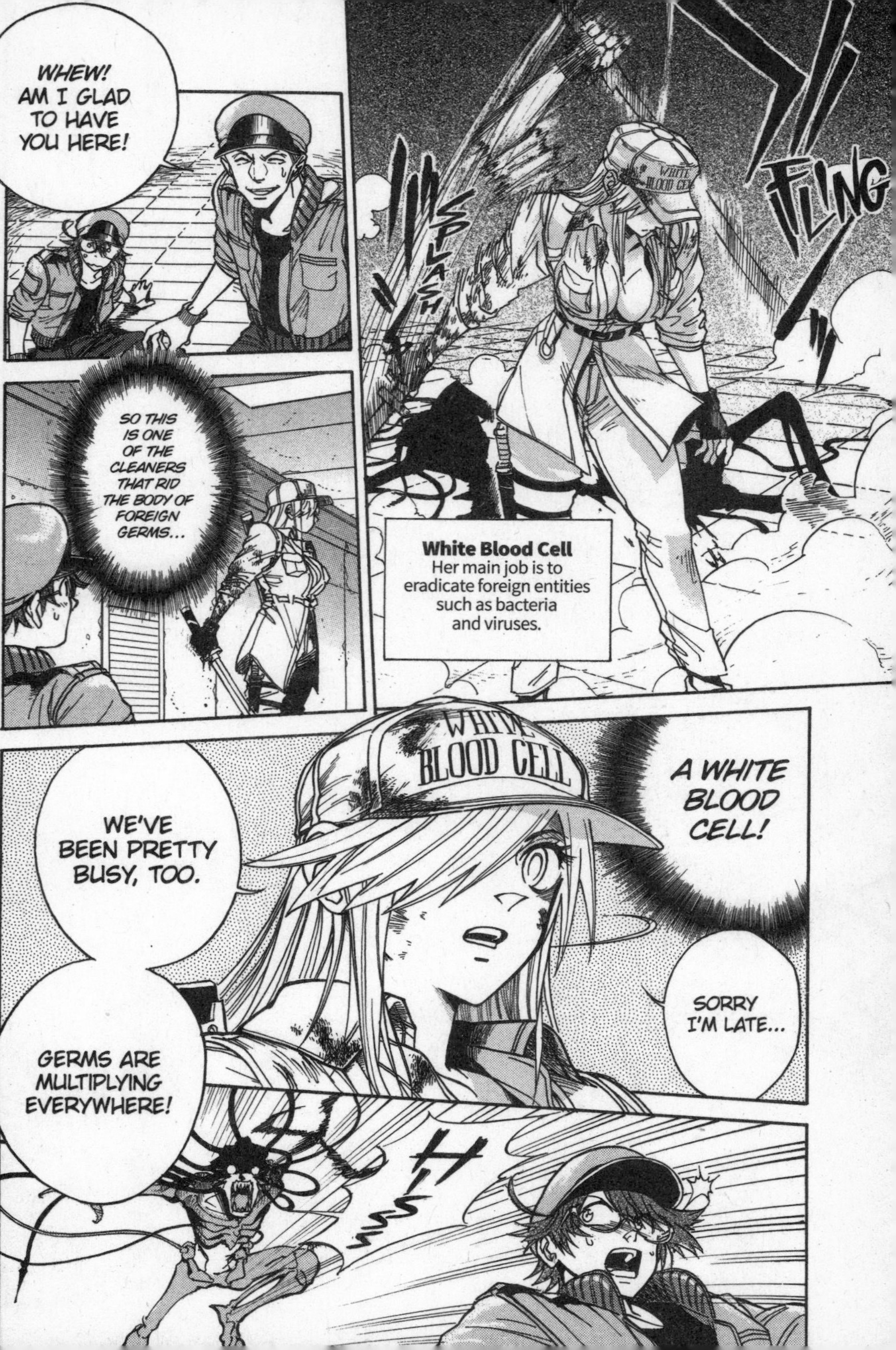
FLING
SPLASH
White Blood Cell
Her main job is to eradicate foreign entities such as bacteria and viruses.
WHEW! AM I GLAD TO HAVE YOU HERE!
SO THIS IS ONE OF THE CLEANERS THAT RID THE BODY OF FOREIGN GERMS...
WHITE BLOOD CELL
A WHITE BLOOD CELL!
SORRY I'M LATE...
WE'VE BEEN PRETTY BUSY, TOO.
GERMS ARE MULTIPLYING EVERYWHERE!
HISS

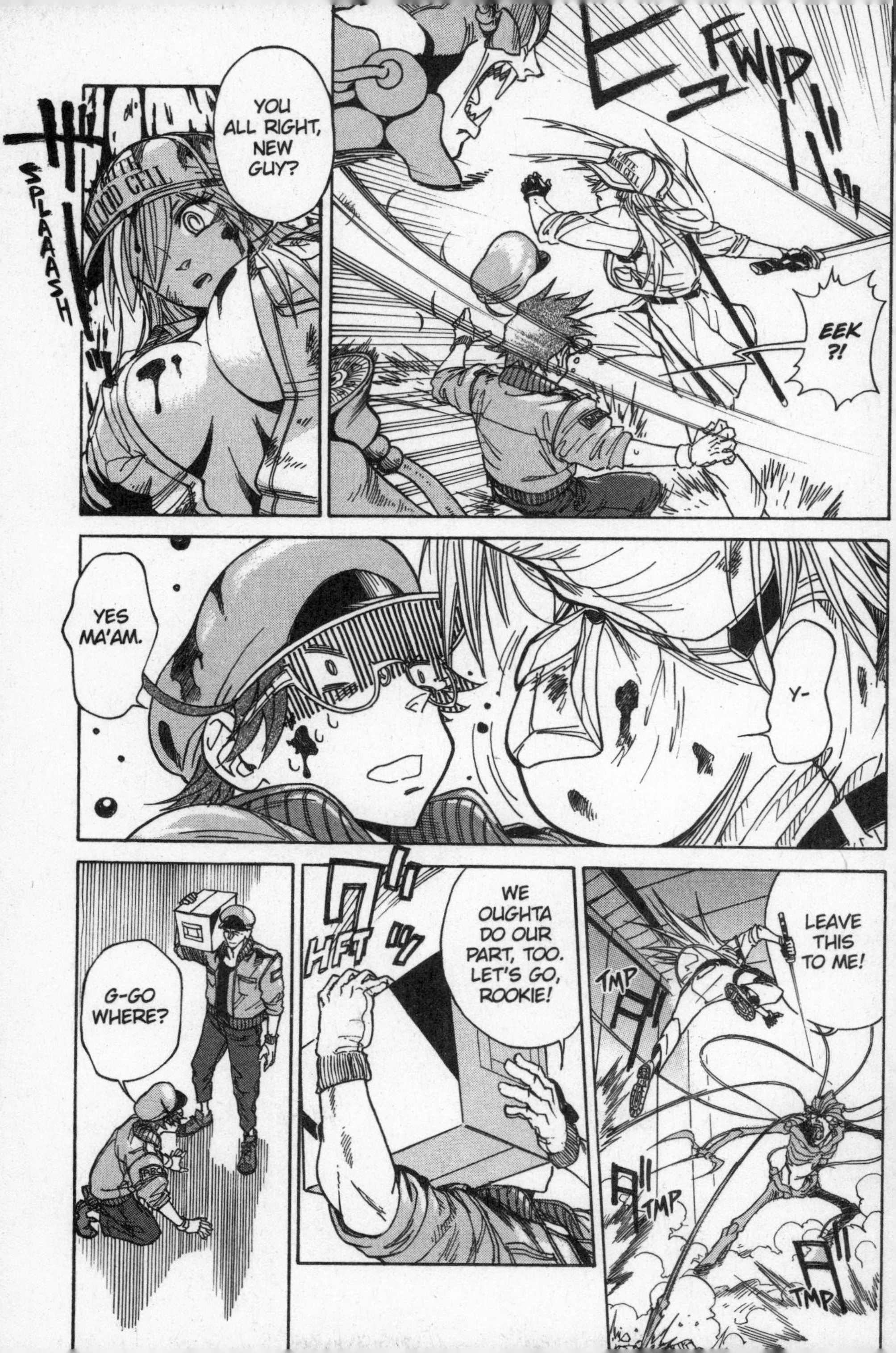
FWIP
EEK?!
YOU ALL RIGHT, NEW GUY?
SPLAAASH
Y-
YES MA'AM.
LEAVE THIS TO ME!
TMP
TMP
TMP
HFT
WE OUGHTA DO OUR PART, TOO. LET'S GO, ROOKIE!
G-GO WHERE?

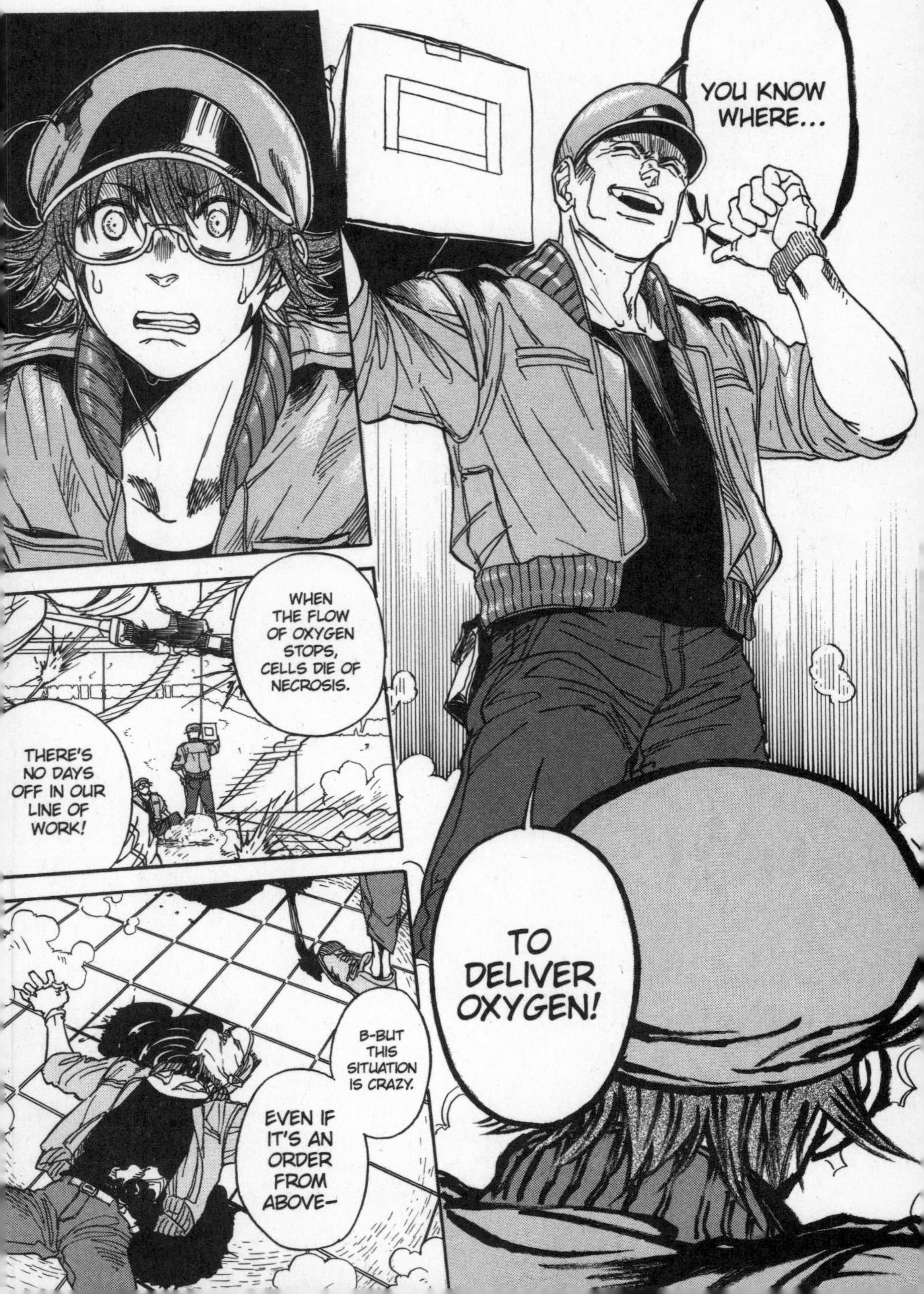
YOU KNOW WHERE...
TO DELIVER OXYGEN!
WHEN THE FLOW OF OXYGEN STOPS, CELLS DIE OF NECROSIS.
THERE'S NO DAYS OFF IN OUR LINE OF WORK!
B-BUT THIS SITUATION IS CRAZY.
EVEN IF IT'S AN ORDER FROM ABOVE-

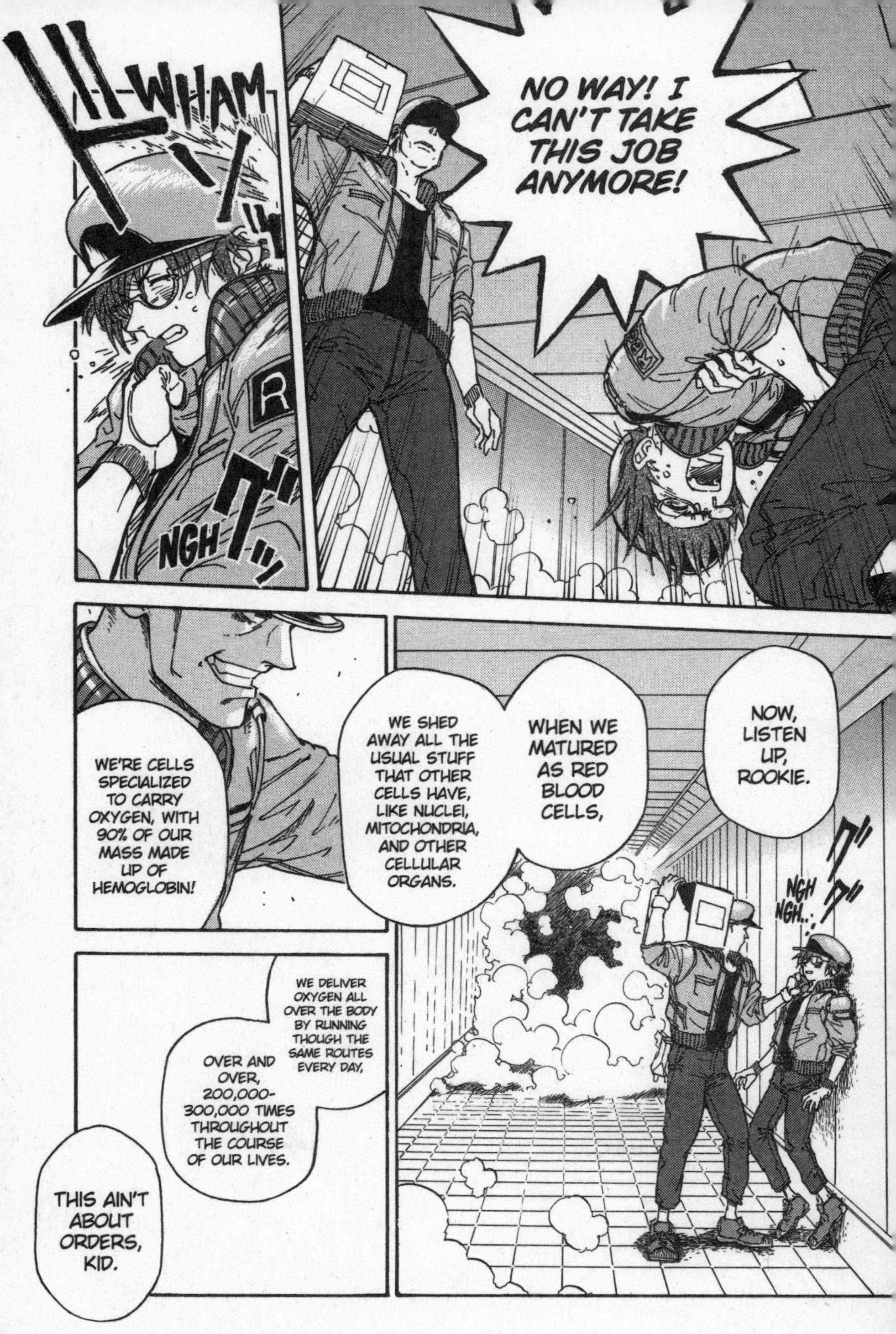
NO WAY! I CAN'T TAKE THIS JOB ANYMORE!
WHAM
NGH
NOW, LISTEN UP, ROOKIE.
WHEN WE MATURED AS RED BLOOD CELLS,
WE SHED AWAY ALL THE USUAL STUFF THAT OTHER CELLS HAVE, LIKE NUCLEI, MITOCHONDRIA, AND OTHER CELLULAR ORGANS.
NGH NGH...
WE'RE CELLS SPECIALIZED TO CARRY OXYGEN, WITH 90% OF OUR MASS MADE UP OF HEMOGLOBIN!
WE DELIVER OXYGEN ALL OVER THE BODY BY RUNNING THOUGH THE SAME ROUTES EVERY DAY,
OVER AND OVER, 200,000-300,000 TIMES THROUGHOUT THE COURSE OF OUR LIVES.
THIS AIN'T ABOUT ORDERS, KID.

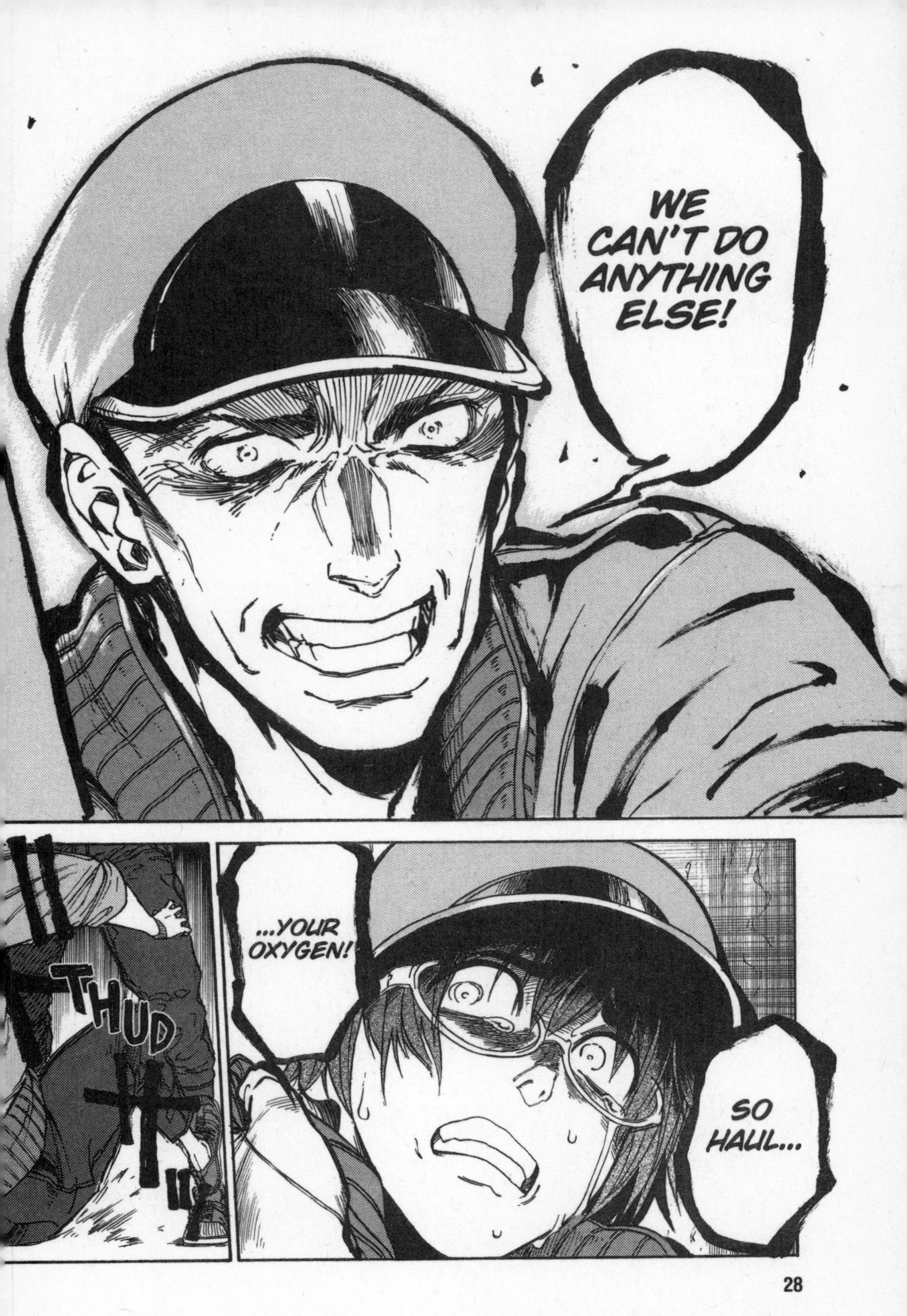
WE CAN'T DO ANYTHING ELSE!
SO HAUL...
...YOUR OXYGEN!
THUD

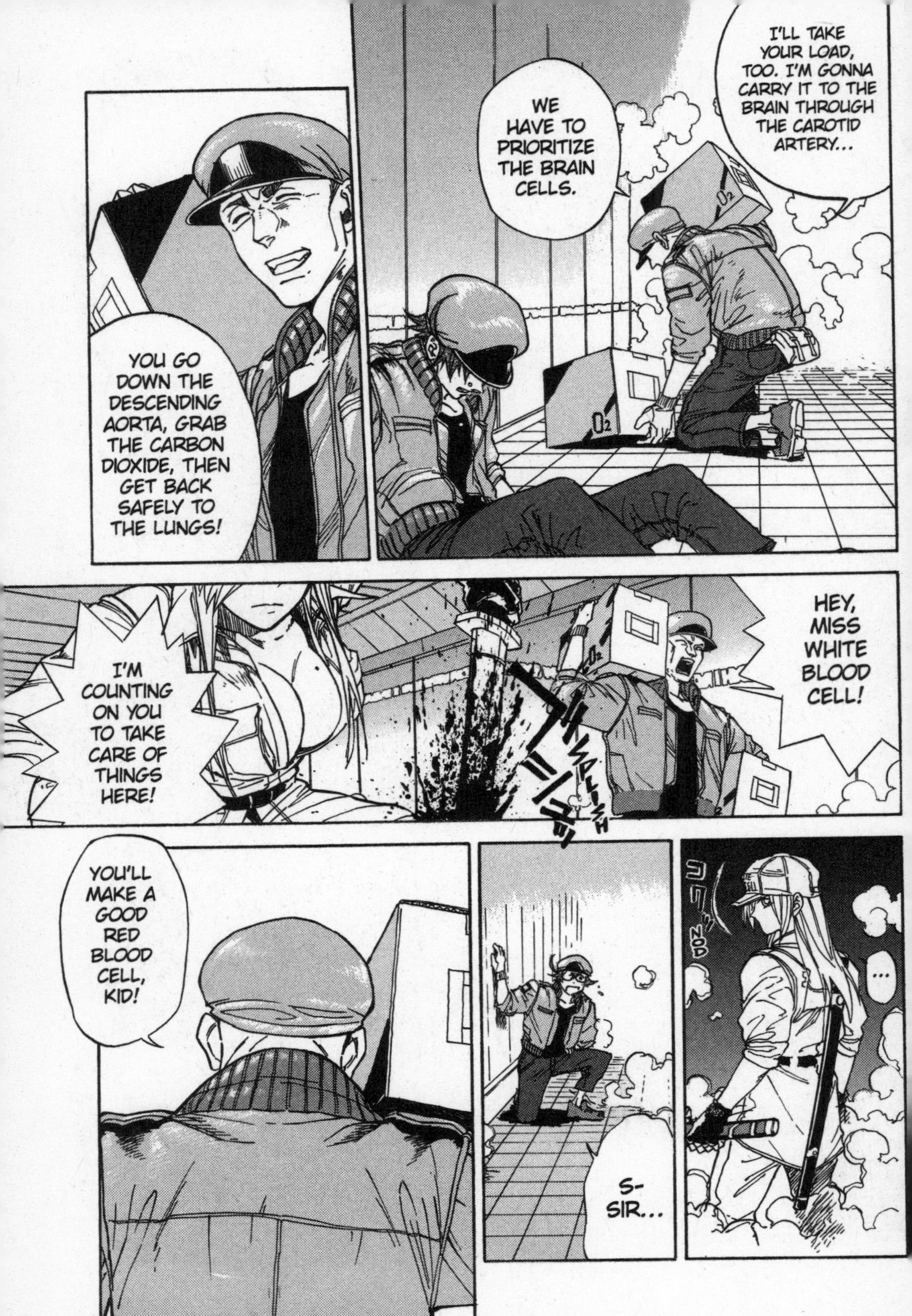
I'LL TAKE YOUR LOAD, TOO. I'M GONNA CARRY IT TO THE BRAIN THROUGH THE CAROTID ARTERY...
WE HAVE TO PRIORITIZE THE BRAIN CELLS.
YOU GO DOWN THE DESCENDING AORTA, GRAB THE CARBON DIOXIDE, THEN GET BACK SAFELY TO THE LUNGS!
HEY, MISS WHITE BLOOD CELL!
SPLISH
I'M COUNTING ON YOU TO TAKE CARE OF THINGS HERE!
NOD
...
S-SIR...
YOU'LL MAKE A GOOD RED BLOOD CELL, KID!

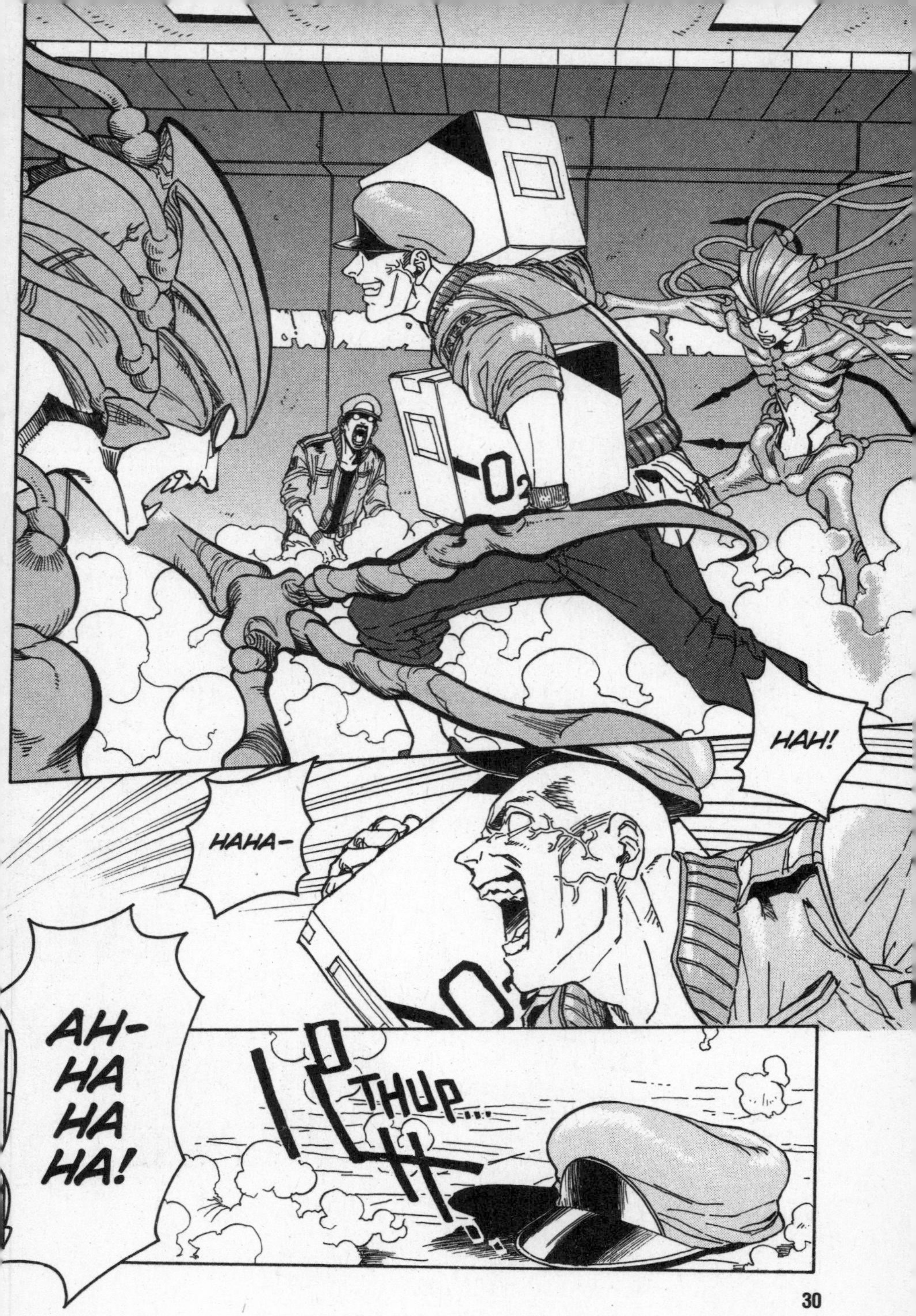
HAH!
HAHA-
AH-HA HA HA HA!
THUP...

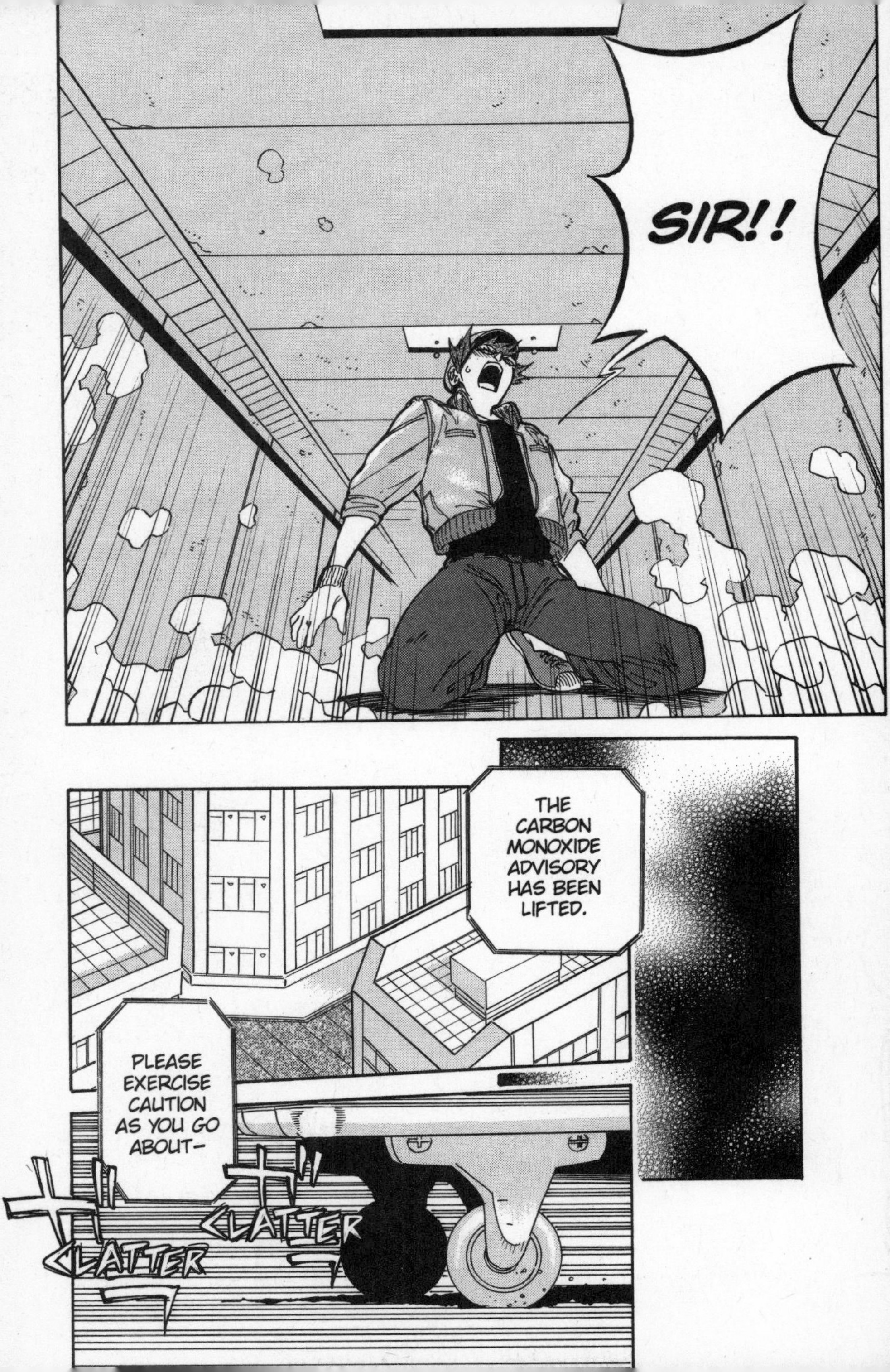
SIR!!
THE CARBON MONOXIDE ADVISORY HAS BEEN LIFTED.
PLEASE EXERCISE CAUTION AS YOU GO ABOUT-
CLATTER
CLATTER

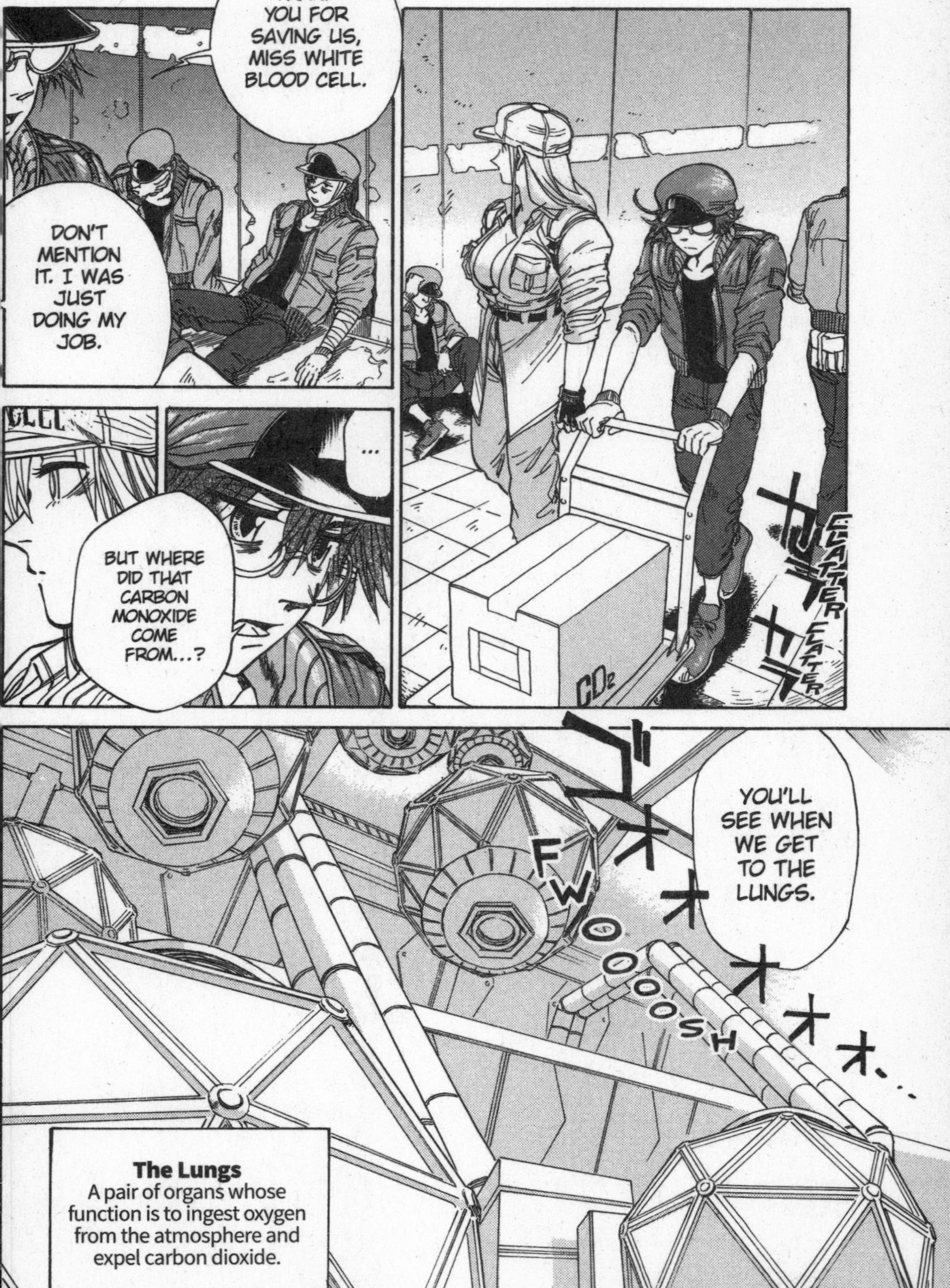
CLATTER
CLATTER
THANK YOU FOR SAVING US, MISS WHITE BLOOD CELL.
DON'T MENTION IT. I WAS JUST DOING MY JOB.
...
BUT WHERE DID THAT CARBON MONOXIDE COME FROM...?
FWOOOOOSH
YOU'LL SEE WHEN WE GET TO THE LUNGS.
The Lungs
A pair of organs whose function is to ingest oxygen from the atmosphere and expel carbon dioxide.

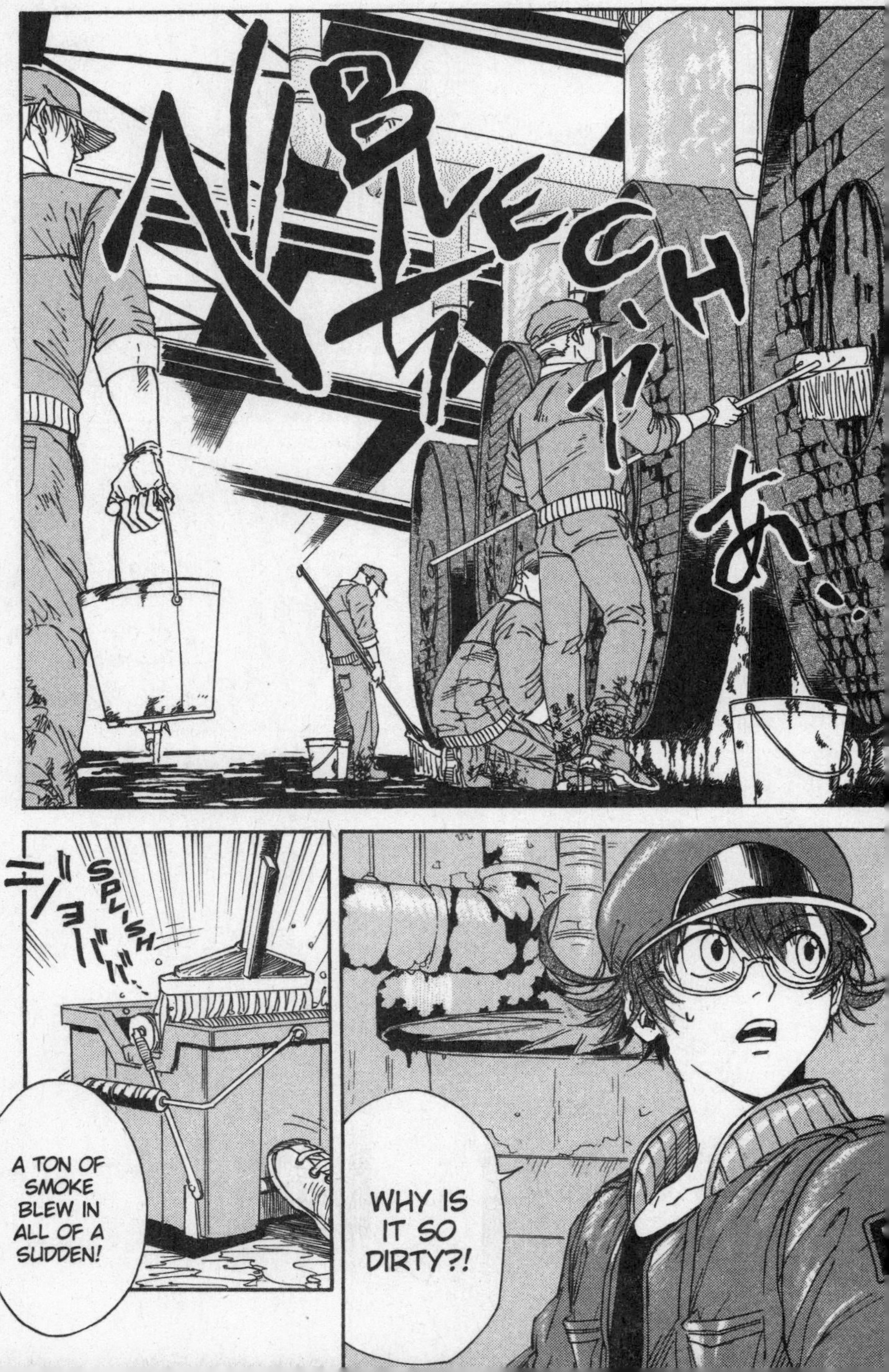
BLECH
SPLISH
WHY IS IT SO DIRTY?!
A TON OF SMOKE BLEW IN ALL OF A SUDDEN!

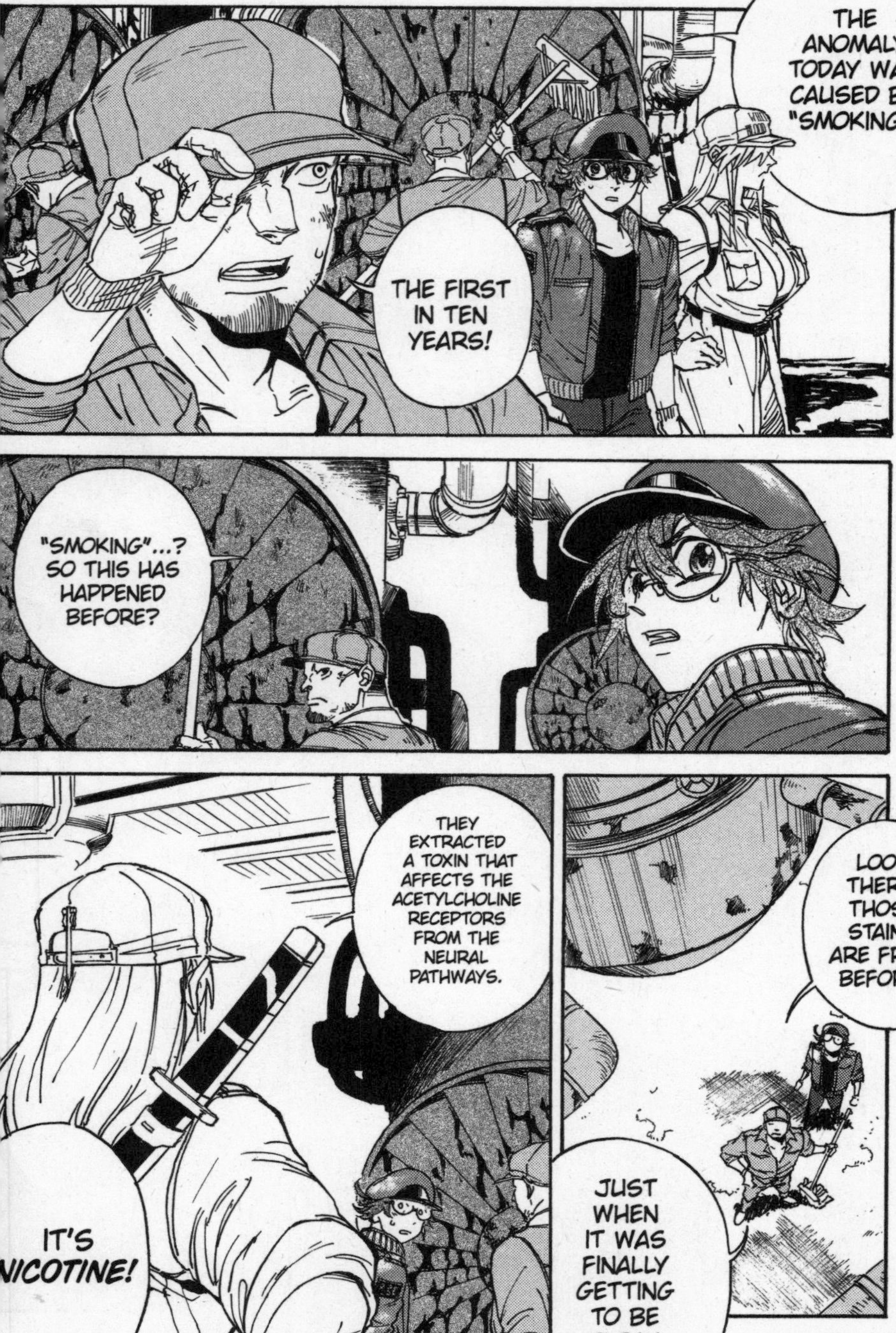
THE ANOMALY TODAY WAS CAUSED BY "SMOKING."
THE FIRST IN TEN YEARS!
"SMOKING"...? SO THIS HAS HAPPENED BEFORE?
LOOK THERE. THOSE STAINS ARE FROM BEFORE.
JUST WHEN IT WAS FINALLY GETTING TO BE CLEAN TOO...
THEY EXTRACTED A TOXIN THAT AFFECTS THE ACETYLCHOLINE RECEPTORS FROM THE NEURAL PATHWAYS.
IT'S NICOTINE!

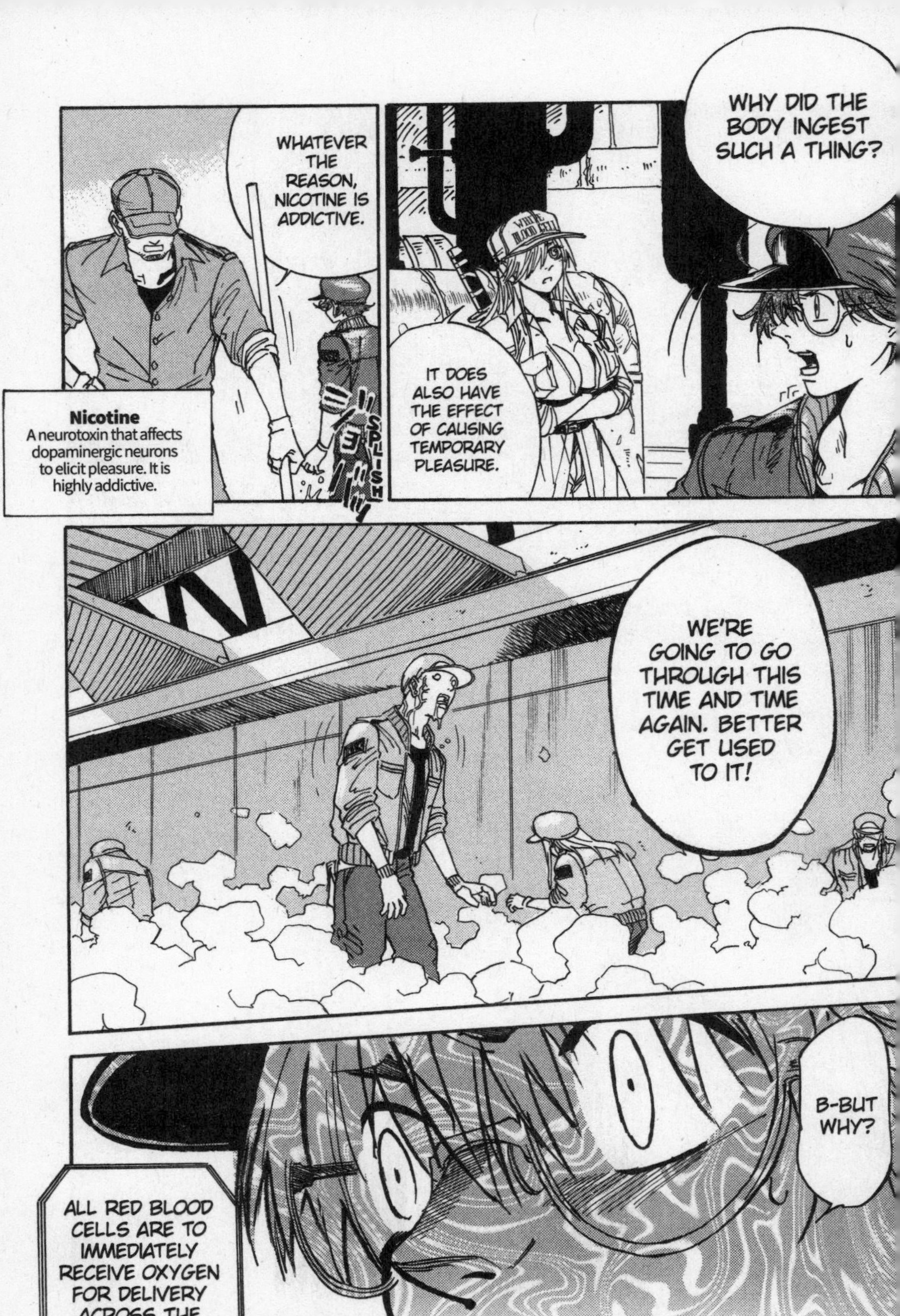
WHY DID THE BODY INGEST SUCH A THING?
IT DOES ALSO HAVE THE EFFECT OF CAUSING TEMPORARY PLEASURE.
WHATEVER THE REASON, NICOTINE IS ADDICTIVE.
SPLISH
Nicotine
A neurotoxin that affects dopaminergic neurons to elicit pleasure. It is highly addictive.
WE'RE GOING TO GO THROUGH THIS TIME AND TIME AGAIN. BETTER GET USED TO IT!
B-BUT WHY?
ALL RED BLOOD CELLS ARE TO IMMEDIATELY RECEIVE OXYGEN FOR DELIVERY ACROSS THE BODY!

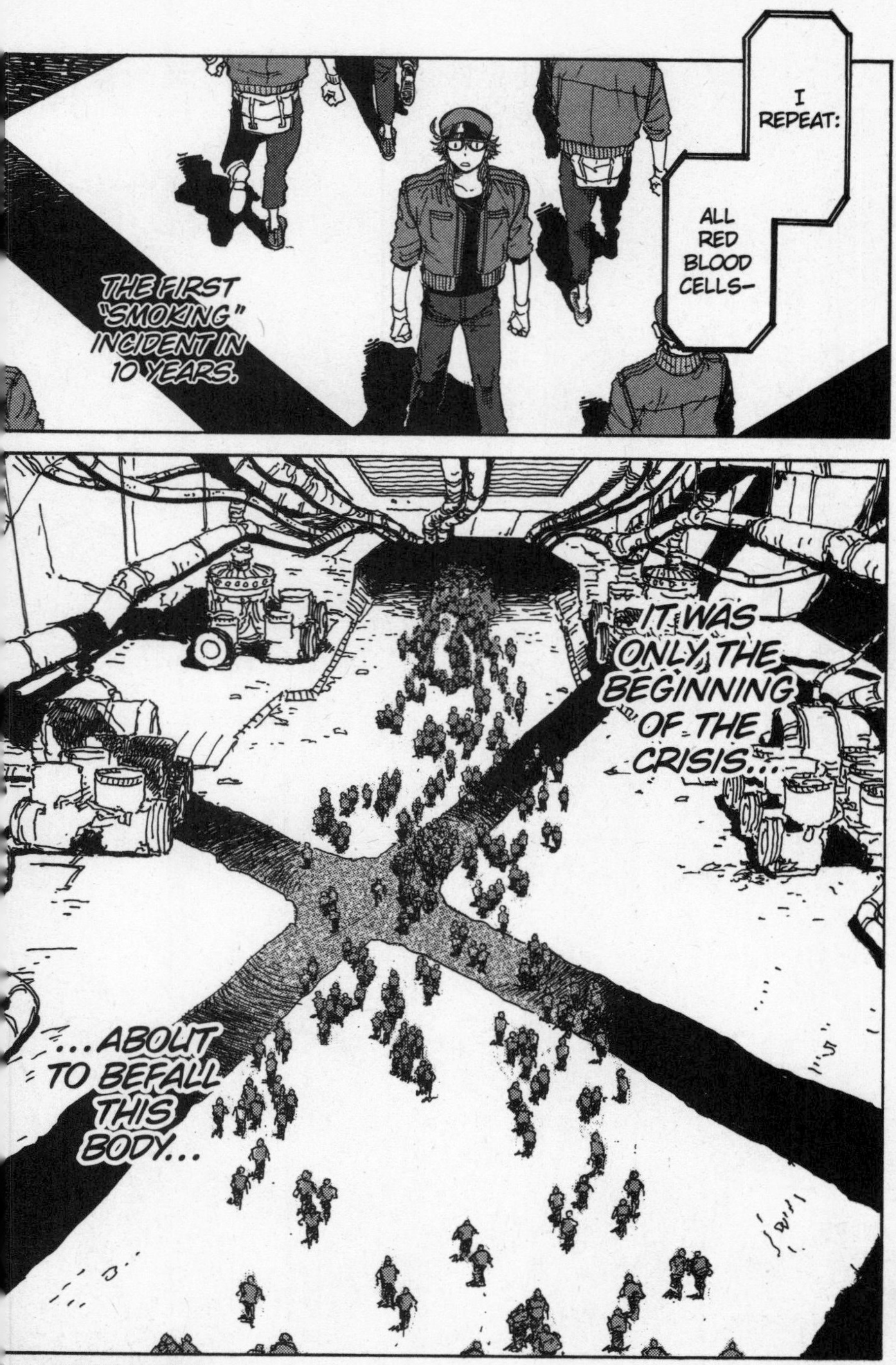
I REPEAT:
ALL RED BLOOD CELLS—
THE FIRST "SMOKING" INCIDENT IN 10 YEARS.
IT WAS ONLY THE BEGINNING OF THE CRISIS...
...ABOUT TO BEFALL THIS BODY...

CHAPTER 1: END

CHAPTER 2: THE LIVER, ALCOHOL, AND PRIDE

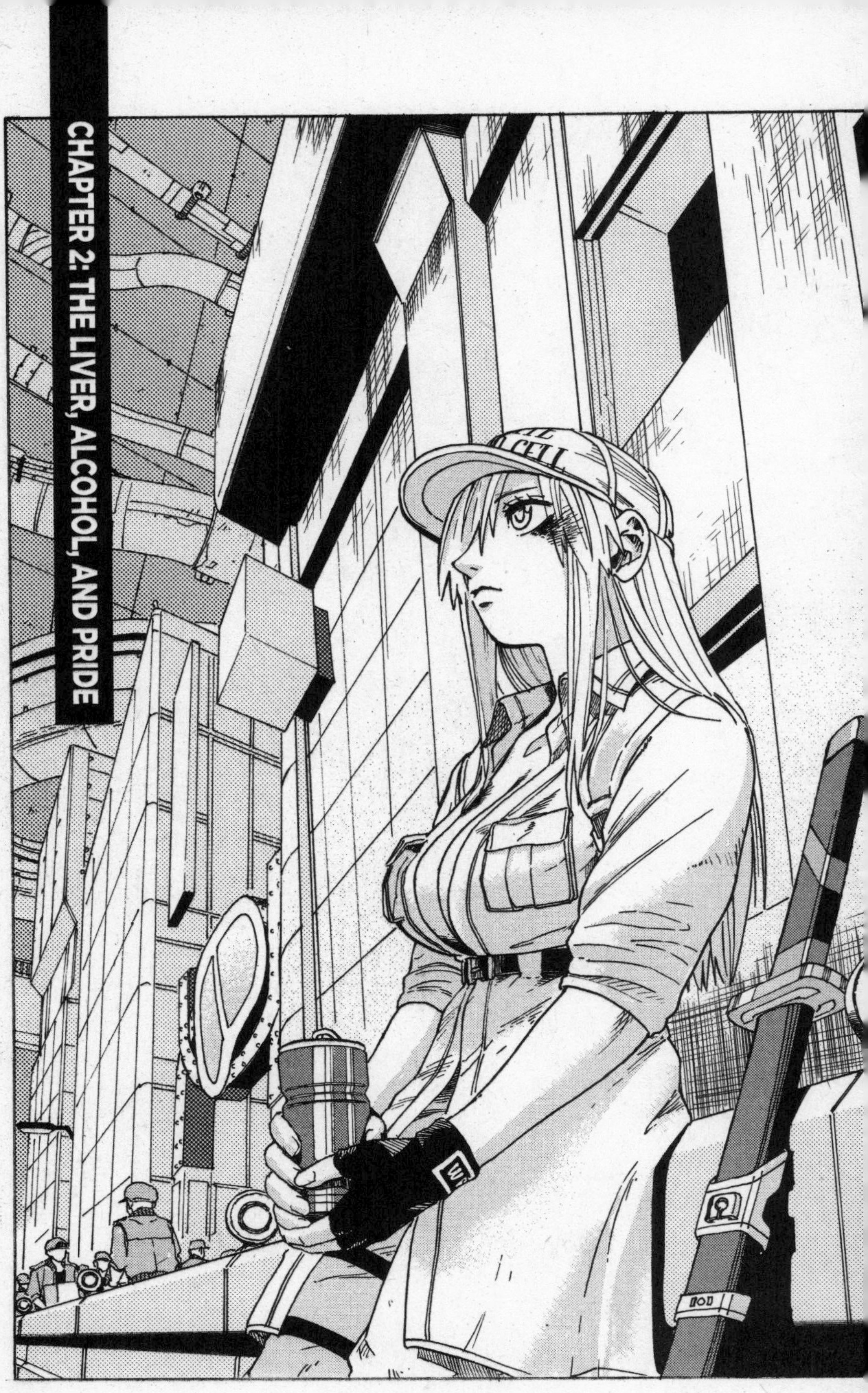

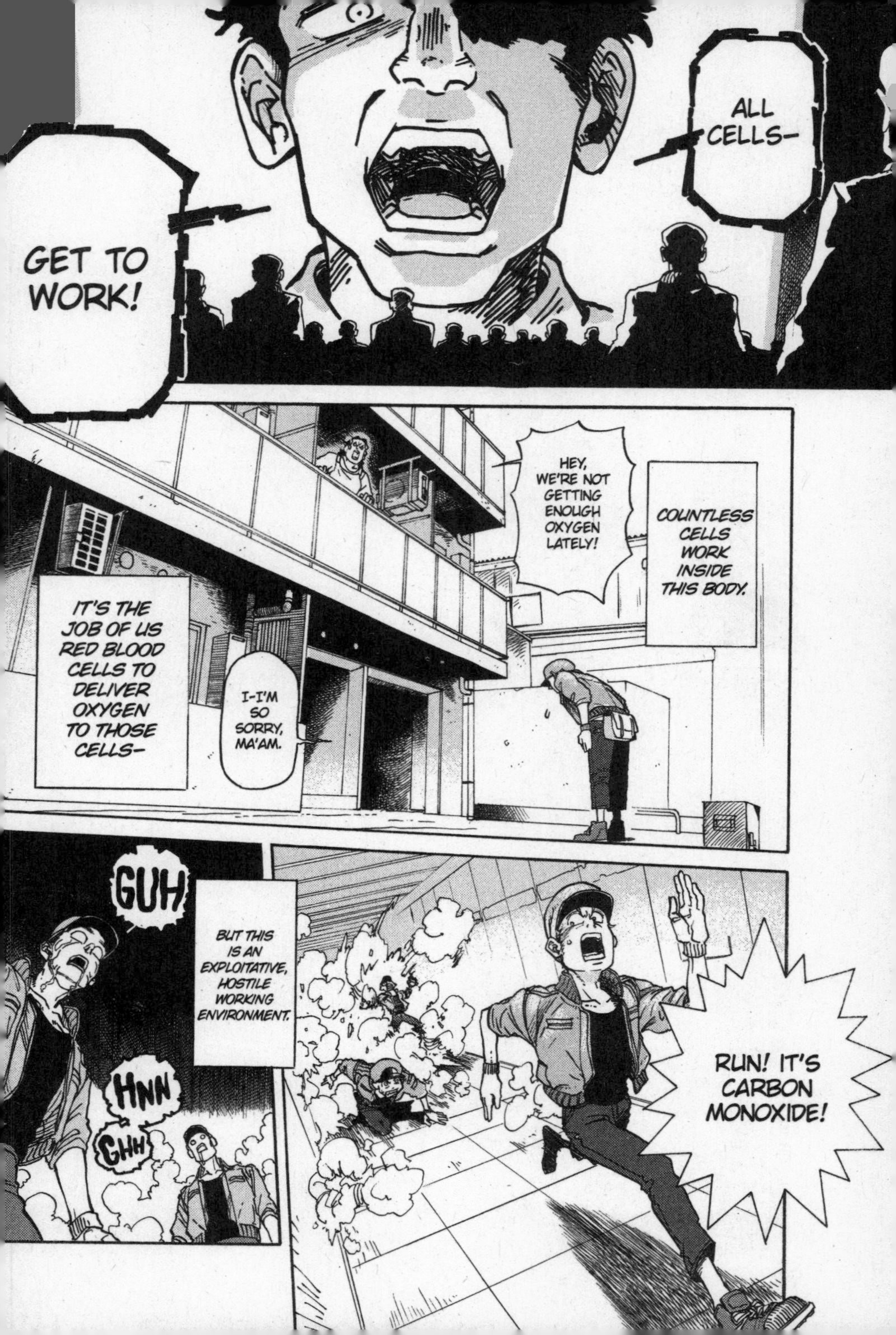
ALL CELLS—
GET TO WORK!
COUNTLESS CELLS WORK INSIDE THIS BODY.
HEY, WE'RE NOT GETTING ENOUGH OXYGEN LATELY!
I-I'M SO SORRY, MA'AM.
IT'S THE JOB OF US RED BLOOD CELLS TO DELIVER OXYGEN TO THOSE CELLS—
RUN! IT'S CARBON MONOXIDE!
BUT THIS IS AN EXPLOITATIVE, HOSTILE WORKING ENVIRONMENT.
GUH
HNN
GHH

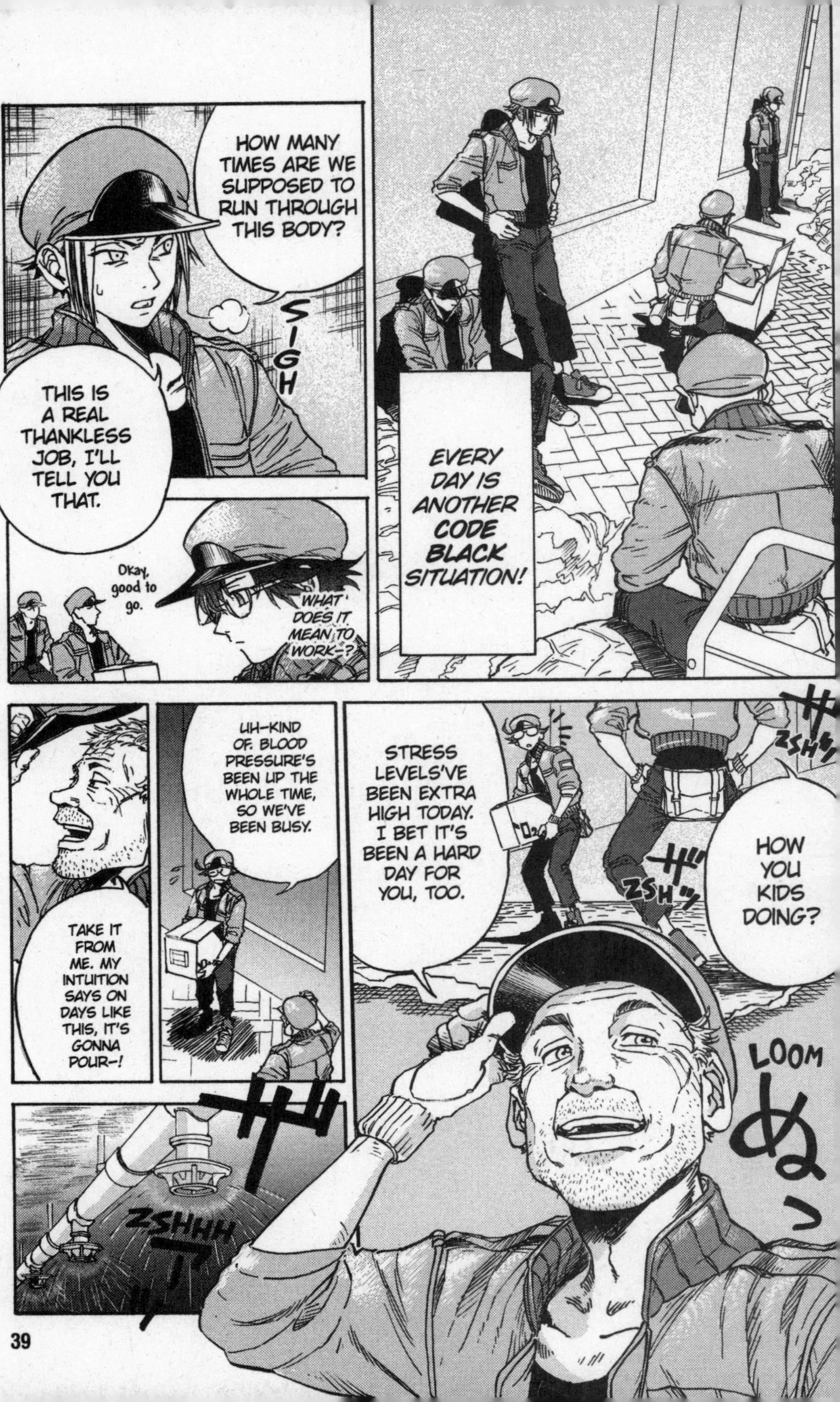
EVERY DAY IS ANOTHER CODE BLACK SITUATION!
HOW MANY TIMES ARE WE SUPPOSED TO RUN THROUGH THIS BODY?
SIGH
THIS IS A REAL THANKLESS JOB, I'LL TELL YOU THAT.
WHAT DOES IT MEAN TO WORK-?
Okay, good to go.
ZSH
HOW YOU KIDS DOING?
STRESS LEVELS'VE BEEN EXTRA HIGH TODAY. I BET IT'S BEEN A HARD DAY FOR YOU, TOO.
ZSH
LOOM
ぬっ
UH-KIND OF. BLOOD PRESSURE'S BEEN UP THE WHOLE TIME, SO WE'VE BEEN BUSY.
TAKE IT FROM ME. MY INTUITION SAYS ON DAYS LIKE THIS, IT'S GONNA POUR-!
ZSHHH

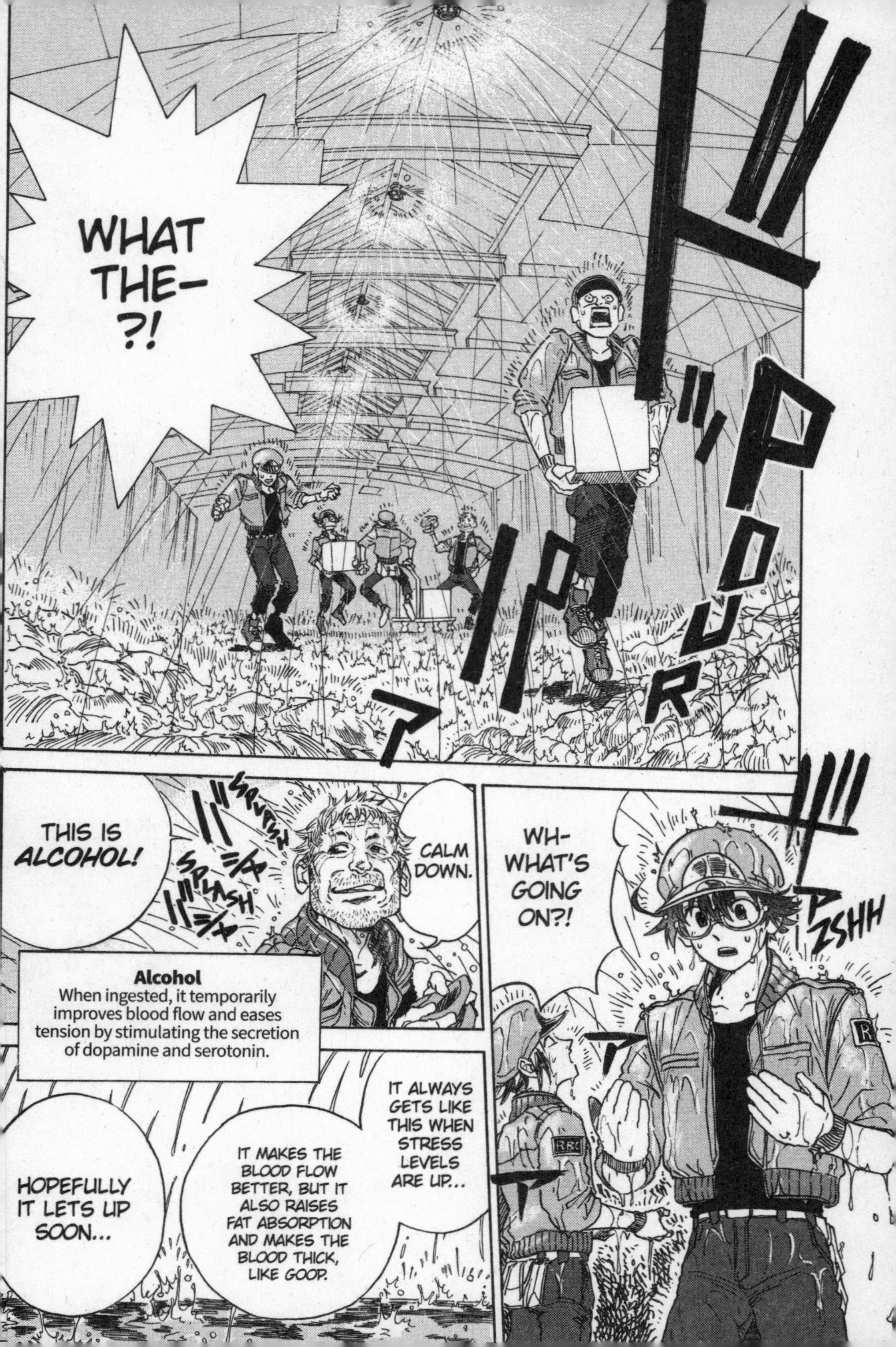
WHAT THE-?!
POUR
WH- WHAT'S GOING ON?!
ZSHH
SPLASH
SPLASH
CALM DOWN.
THIS IS ALCOHOL!
Alcohol
When ingested, it temporarily improves blood flow and eases tension by stimulating the secretion of dopamine and serotonin.
IT ALWAYS GETS LIKE THIS WHEN STRESS LEVELS ARE UP...
IT MAKES THE BLOOD FLOW BETTER, BUT IT ALSO RAISES FAT ABSORPTION AND MAKES THE BLOOD THICK, LIKE GOOP.
HOPEFULLY IT LETS UP SOON...

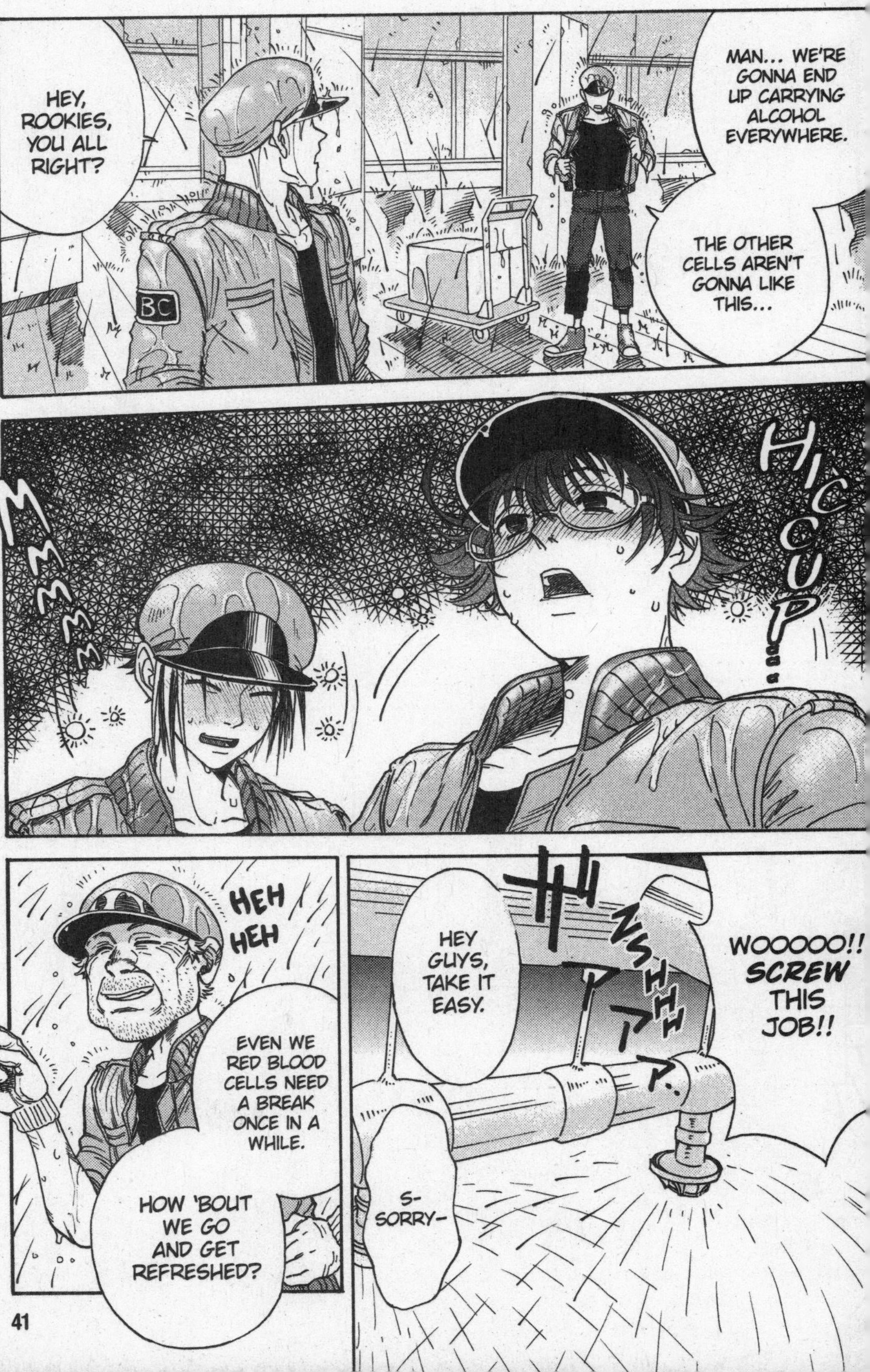
MAN... WE'RE GONNA END UP CARRYING ALCOHOL EVERYWHERE.
THE OTHER CELLS AREN'T GONNA LIKE THIS...
HEY, ROOKIES, YOU ALL RIGHT?
HICCUP...
MMMMMM
WOOOOO!! SCREW THIS JOB!!
HEY GUYS, TAKE IT EASY.
S-SORRY-
HEH HEH
EVEN WE RED BLOOD CELLS NEED A BREAK ONCE IN A WHILE.
HOW 'BOUT WE GO AND GET REFRESHED?

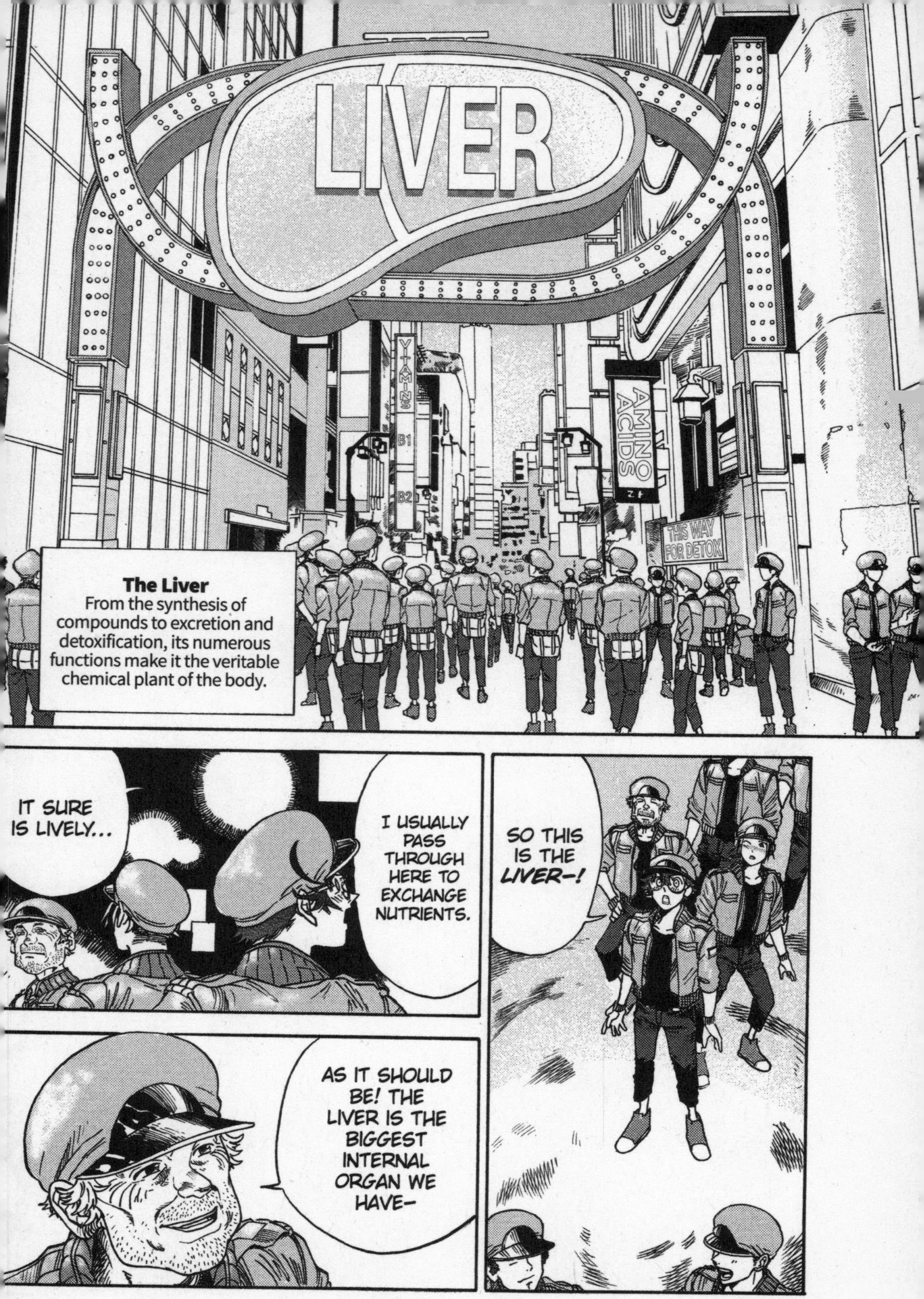
LIVER
VITAMINS
B1
B2
AMINO ACIDS
THIS WAY FOR DETOX
The Liver
From the synthesis of compounds to excretion and detoxification, its numerous functions make it the veritable chemical plant of the body.
SO THIS IS THE *LIVER*—!
I USUALLY PASS THROUGH HERE TO EXCHANGE NUTRIENTS.
IT SURE IS LIVELY...
AS IT SHOULD BE! THE LIVER IS THE BIGGEST INTERNAL ORGAN WE HAVE—

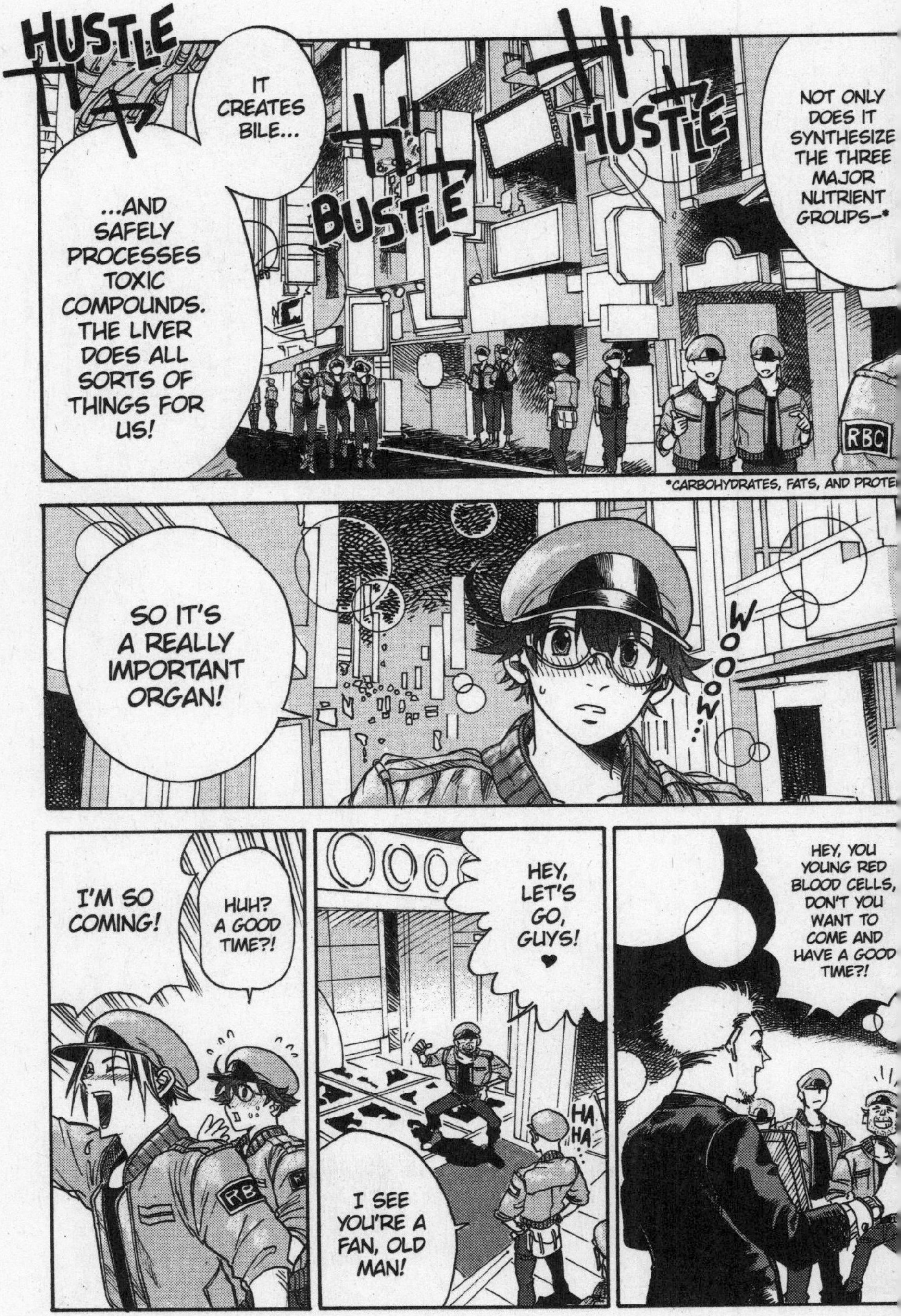
NOT ONLY DOES IT SYNTHESIZE THE THREE MAJOR NUTRIENT GROUPS—*
HUSTLE
BUSTLE
HUSTLE
IT CREATES BILE...
...AND SAFELY PROCESSES TOXIC COMPOUNDS. THE LIVER DOES ALL SORTS OF THINGS FOR US!
RBC
*CARBOHYDRATES, FATS, AND PROTE
WOOOOW...
SO IT'S A REALLY IMPORTANT ORGAN!
HEY, YOU YOUNG RED BLOOD CELLS, DON'T YOU WANT TO COME AND HAVE A GOOD TIME?!
HEY, LET'S GO, GUYS! ♥
HA HA
I SEE YOU'RE A FAN, OLD MAN!
HUH? A GOOD TIME?!
I'M SO COMING!
RB

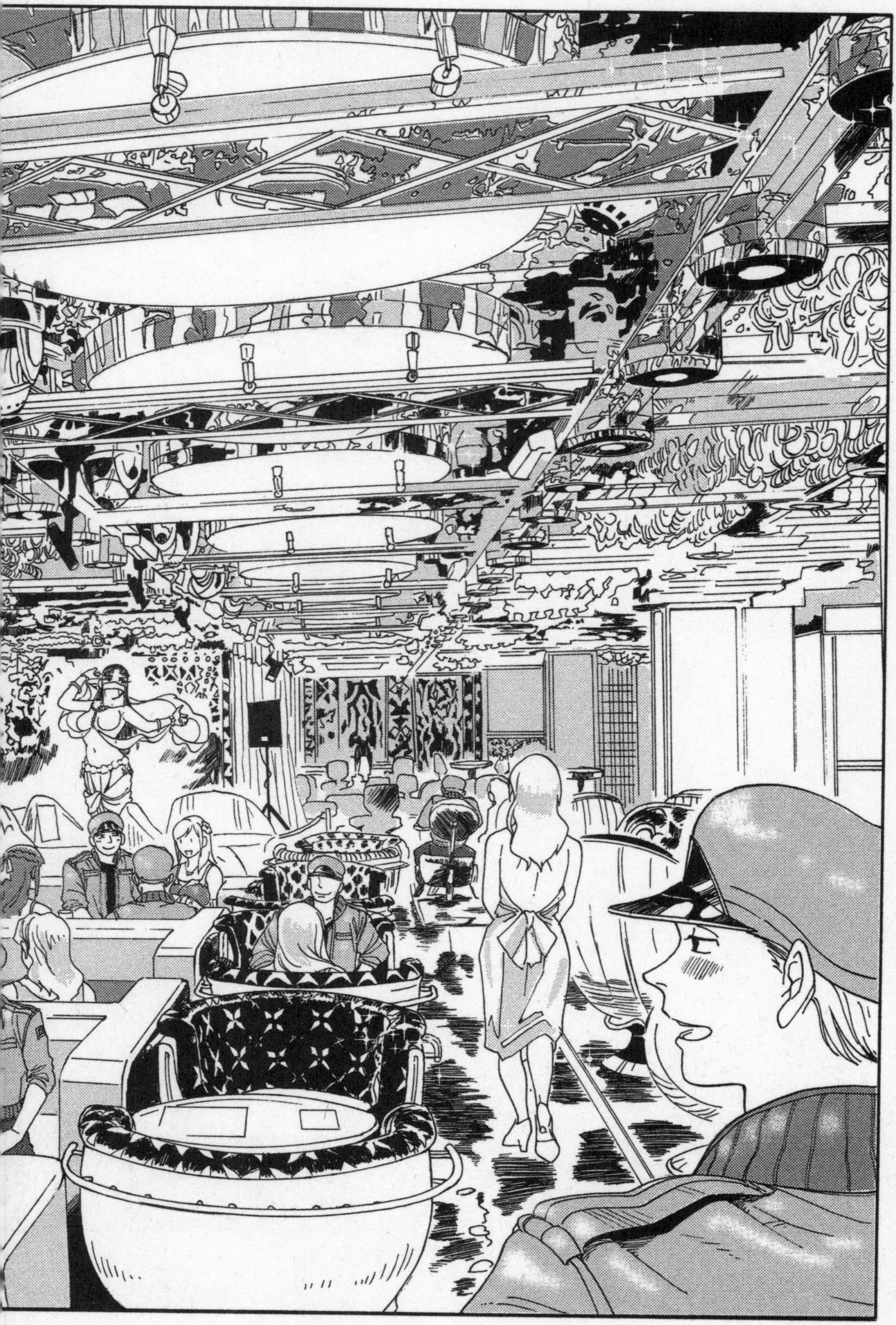

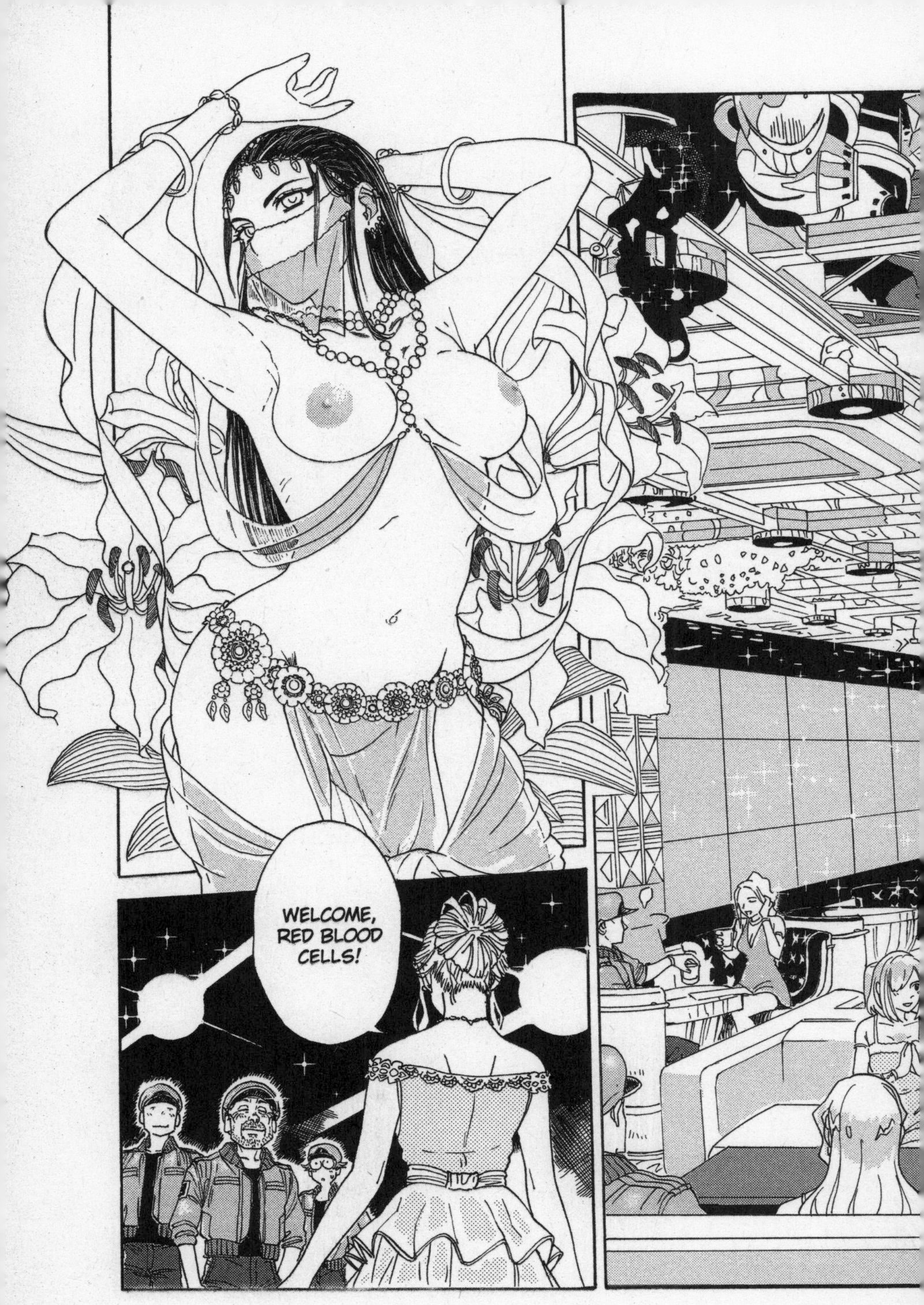
WELCOME, RED BLOOD CELLS!

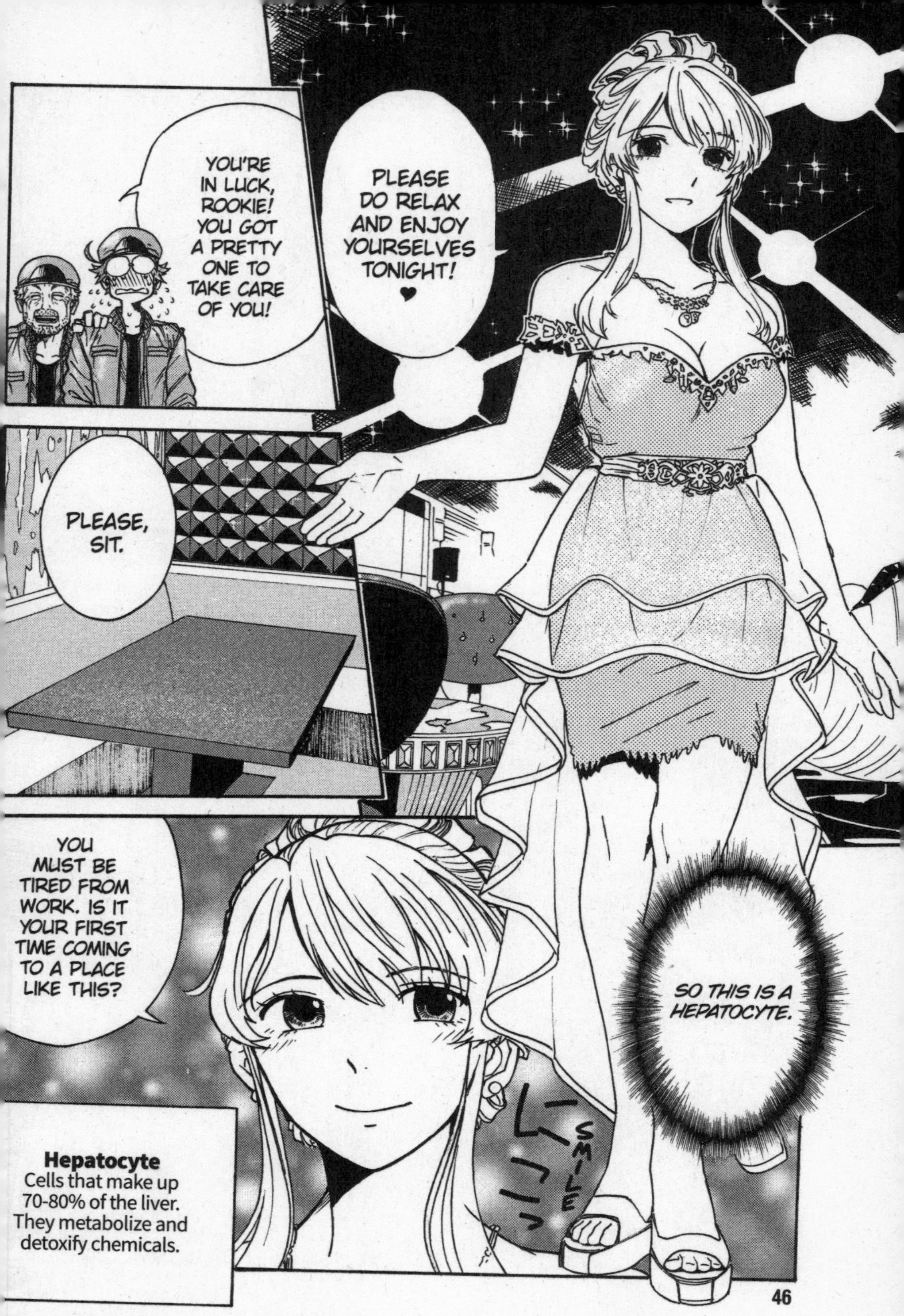
PLEASE DO RELAX AND ENJOY YOURSELVES TONIGHT! ♥
YOU'RE IN LUCK, ROOKIE! YOU GOT A PRETTY ONE TO TAKE CARE OF YOU!
PLEASE, SIT.
SO THIS IS A HEPATOCYTE.
YOU MUST BE TIRED FROM WORK. IS IT YOUR FIRST TIME COMING TO A PLACE LIKE THIS?
SMILE
Hepatocyte
Cells that make up 70-80% of the liver. They metabolize and detoxify chemicals.

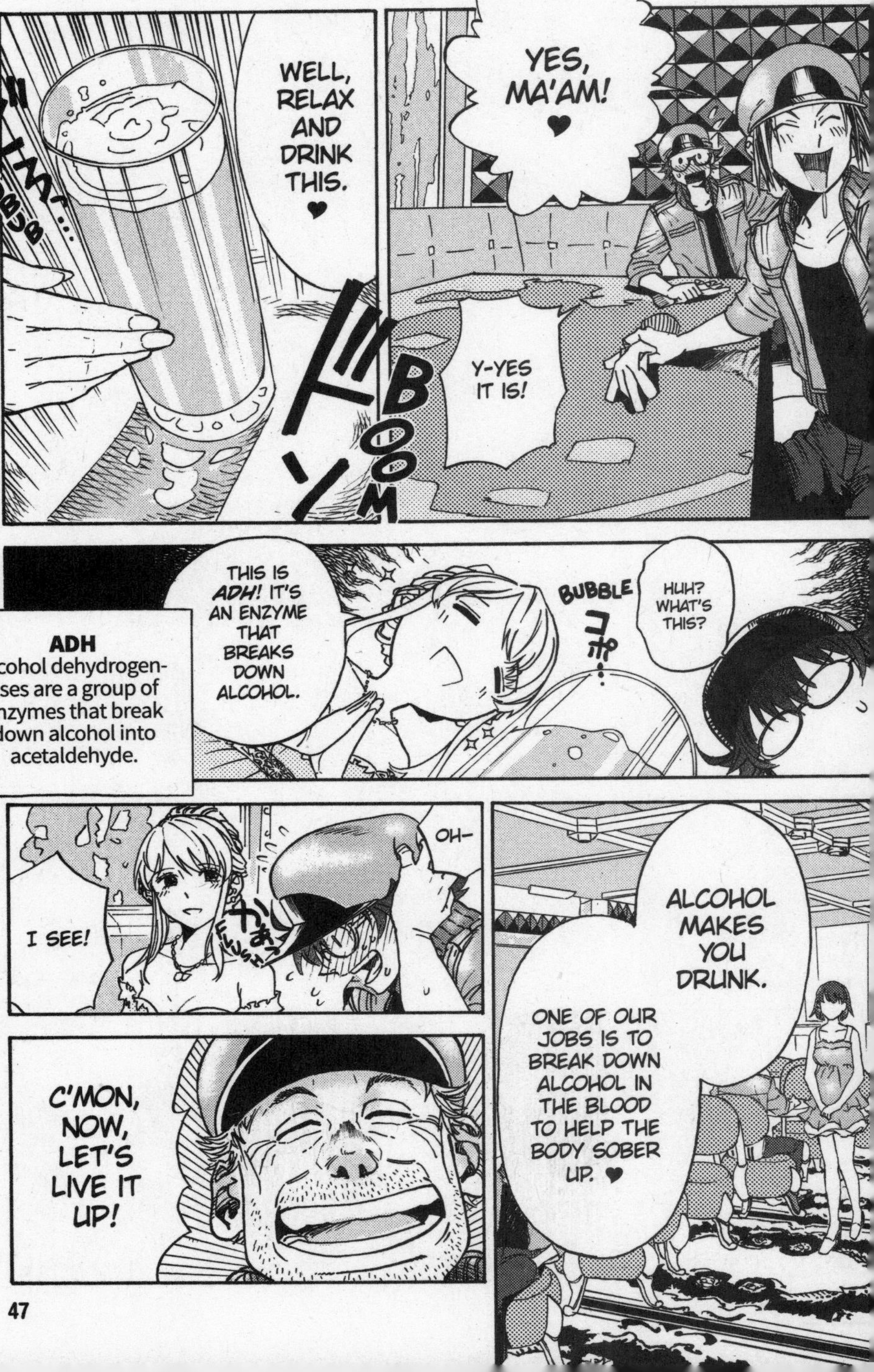
YES, MA'AM! ♥
Y-YES IT IS!
WELL, RELAX AND DRINK THIS. ♥
GLUBGLUB...
BOOM
HUH? WHAT'S THIS?
BUBBLE
THIS IS *ADH*! IT'S AN ENZYME THAT BREAKS DOWN ALCOHOL.
ADH
Alcohol dehydrogenases are a group of enzymes that break down alcohol into acetaldehyde.
ALCOHOL MAKES YOU DRUNK.
ONE OF OUR JOBS IS TO BREAK DOWN ALCOHOL IN THE BLOOD TO HELP THE BODY SOBER UP. ♥
OH-
I SEE!
C'MON, NOW, LET'S LIVE IT UP!

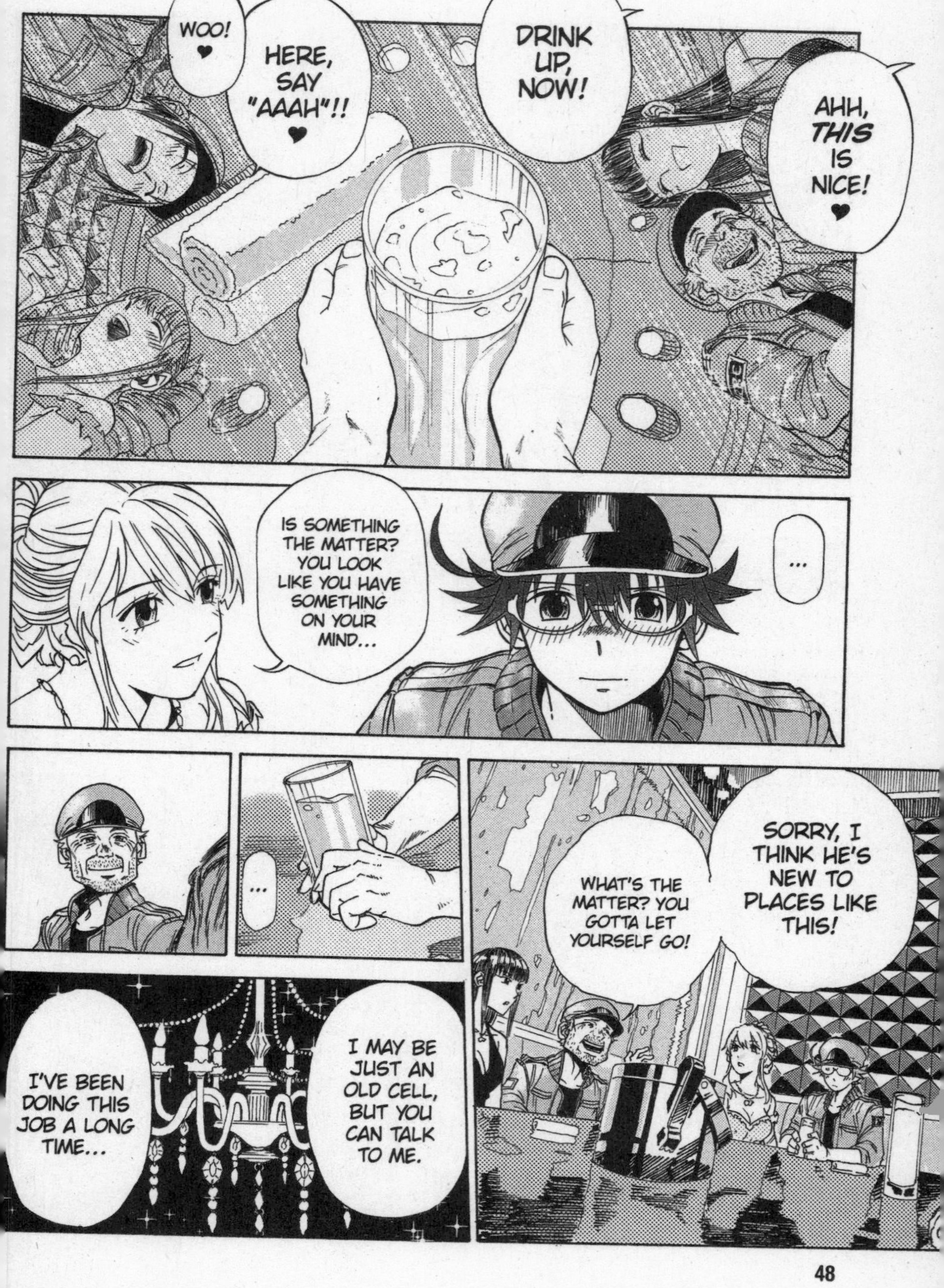
AHH, *THIS* IS NICE! ♥
DRINK UP, NOW!
HERE, SAY "AAAH"!! ♥
WOO! ♥
...
IS SOMETHING THE MATTER? YOU LOOK LIKE YOU HAVE SOMETHING ON YOUR MIND...
SORRY, I THINK HE'S NEW TO PLACES LIKE THIS!
WHAT'S THE MATTER? YOU GOTTA LET YOURSELF GO!
...
I MAY BE JUST AN OLD CELL, BUT YOU CAN TALK TO ME.
I'VE BEEN DOING THIS JOB A LONG TIME...

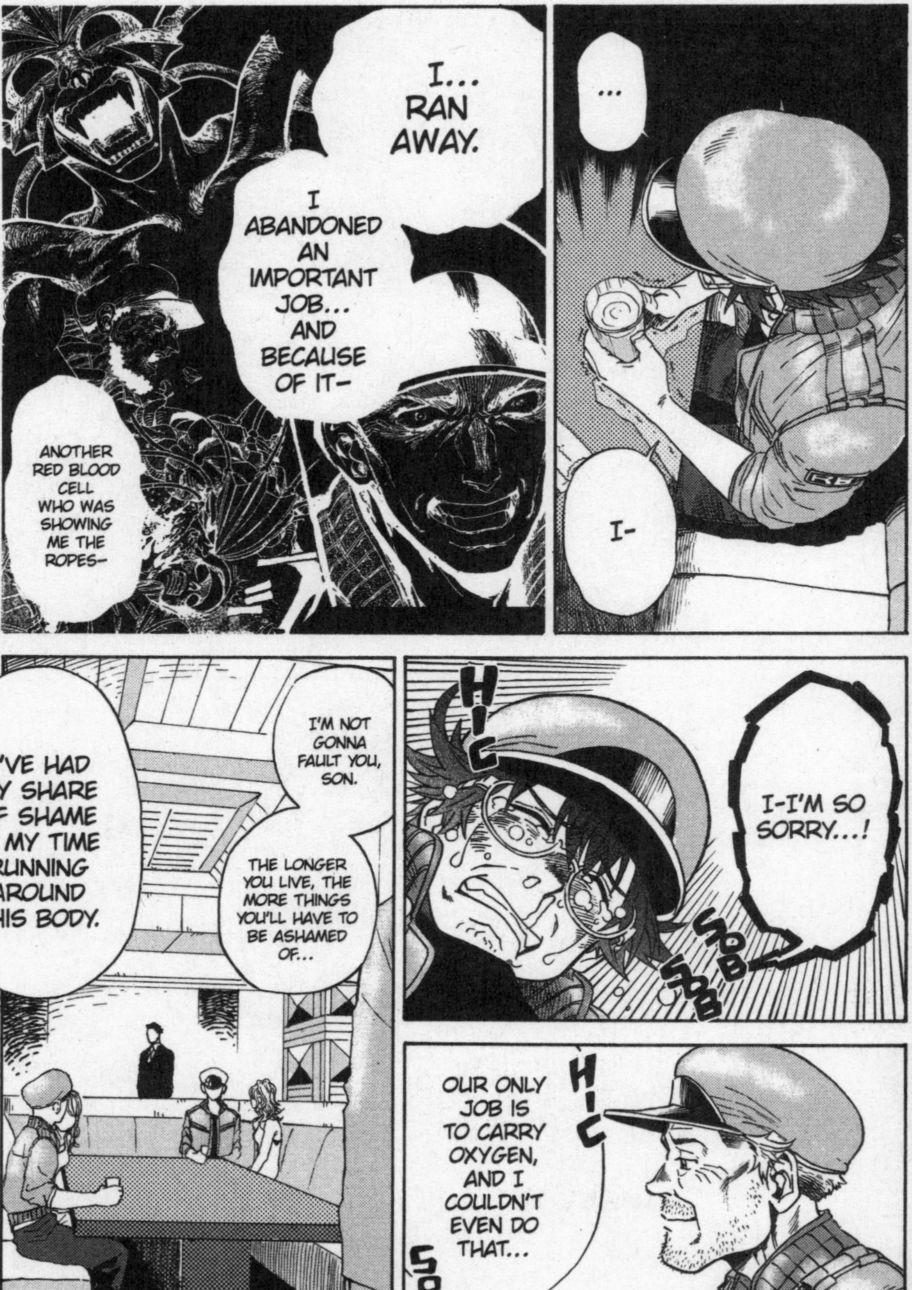
...
I-
I... RAN AWAY.
I ABANDONED AN IMPORTANT JOB... AND BECAUSE OF IT—
ANOTHER RED BLOOD CELL WHO WAS SHOWING ME THE ROPES—
HIC
I-I'M SO SORRY...!
SOB SOB
HIC
OUR ONLY JOB IS TO CARRY OXYGEN, AND I COULDN'T EVEN DO THAT...
SOB
I'M NOT GONNA FAULT YOU, SON.
THE LONGER YOU LIVE, THE MORE THINGS YOU'LL HAVE TO BE ASHAMED OF...
I'VE HAD MY SHARE OF SHAME IN MY TIME RUNNING AROUND THIS BODY.

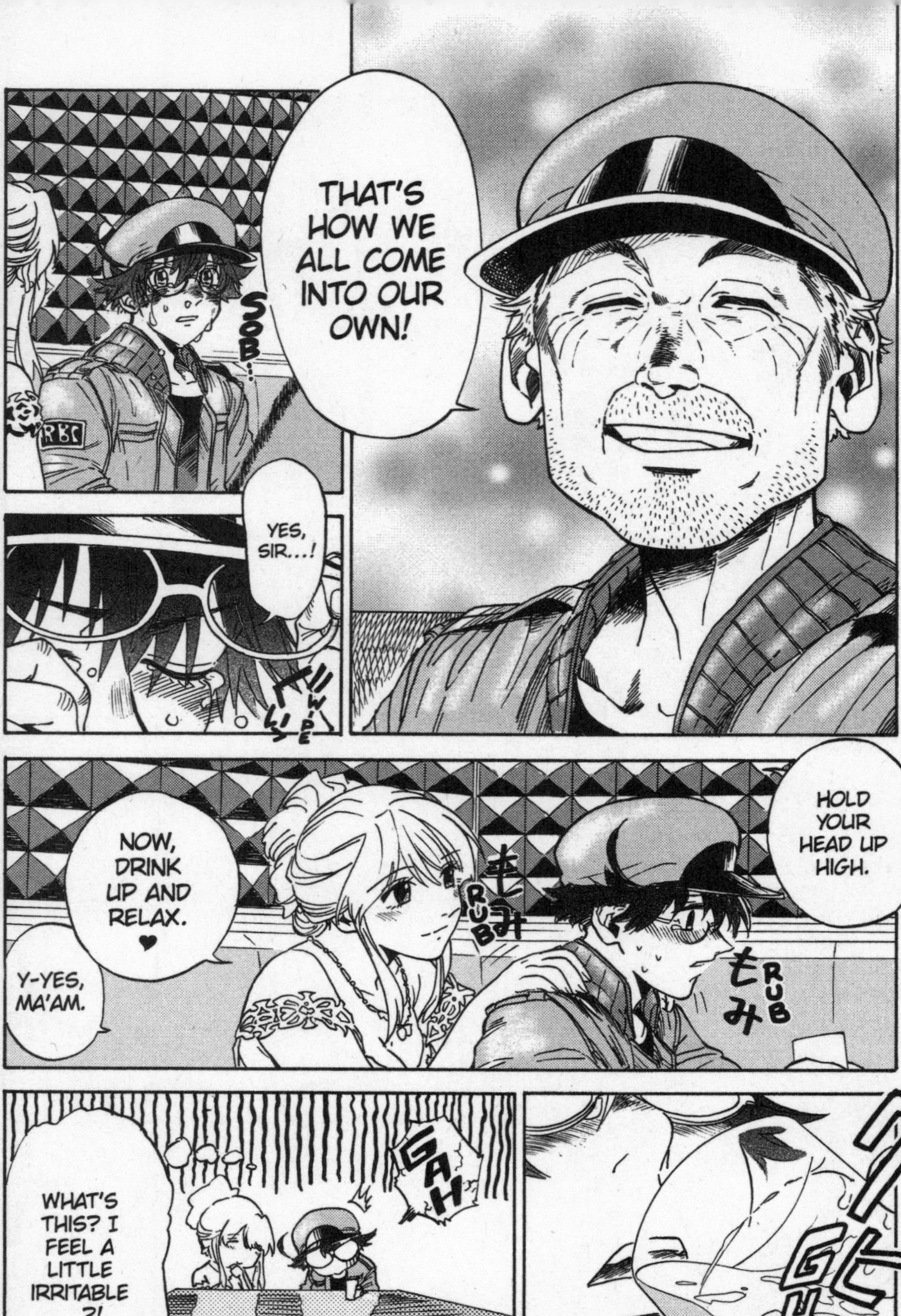

THAT'S HOW WE ALL COME INTO OUR OWN!
SOB...
YES, SIR...!
WIPE
HOLD YOUR HEAD UP HIGH.
もみ RUB
もみ RUB
NOW, DRINK UP AND RELAX. ♥
Y-YES, MA'AM.
GULP
GAH
WHAT'S THIS? I FEEL A LITTLE IRRITABLE ...?!

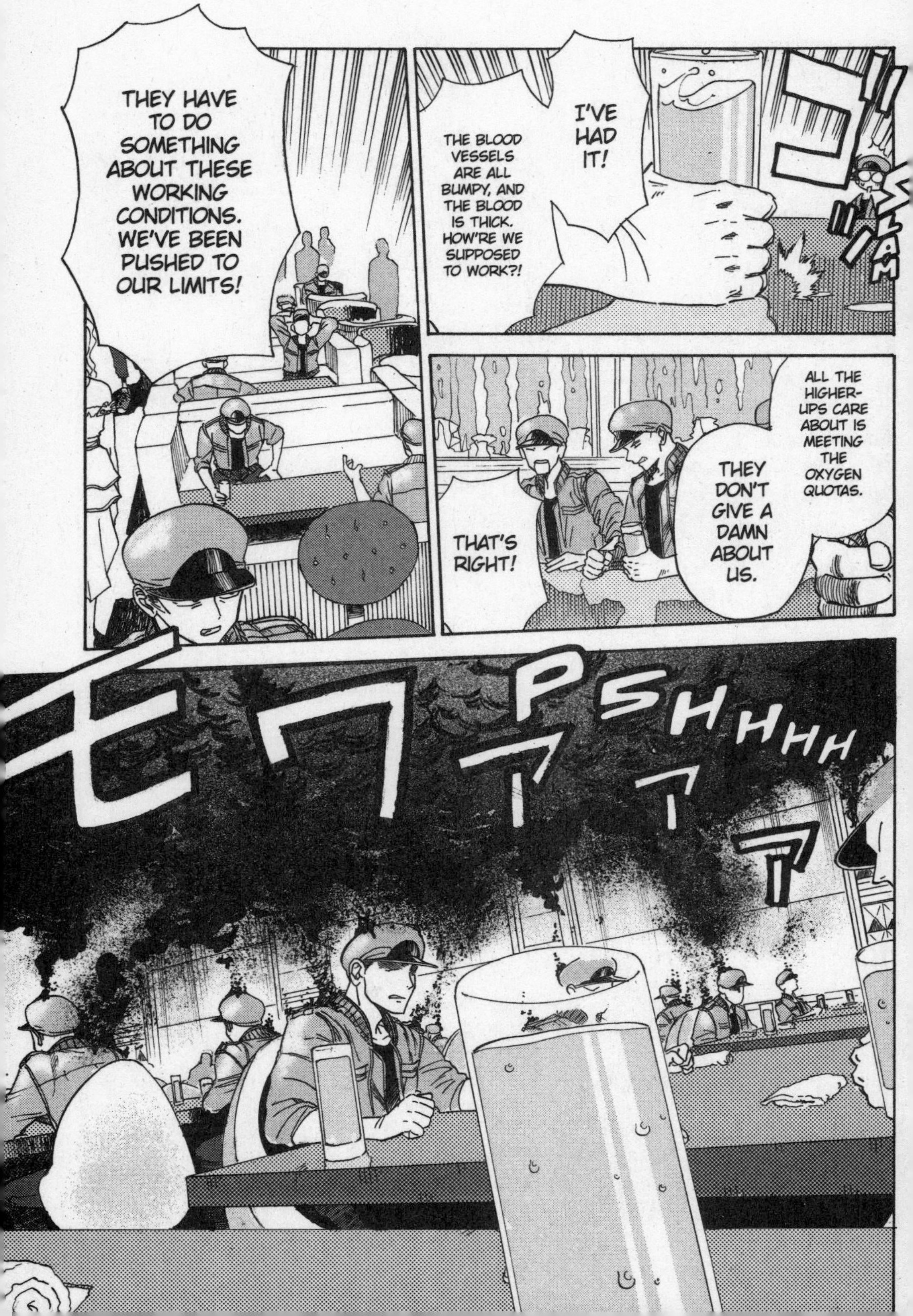
SLAM
I'VE HAD IT!
THE BLOOD VESSELS ARE ALL BUMPY, AND THE BLOOD IS THICK. HOW'RE WE SUPPOSED TO WORK?!
ALL THE HIGHER-UPS CARE ABOUT IS MEETING THE OXYGEN QUOTAS.
THEY DON'T GIVE A DAMN ABOUT US.
THAT'S RIGHT!
THEY HAVE TO DO SOMETHING ABOUT THESE WORKING CONDITIONS. WE'VE BEEN PUSHED TO OUR LIMITS!
PSHHHH

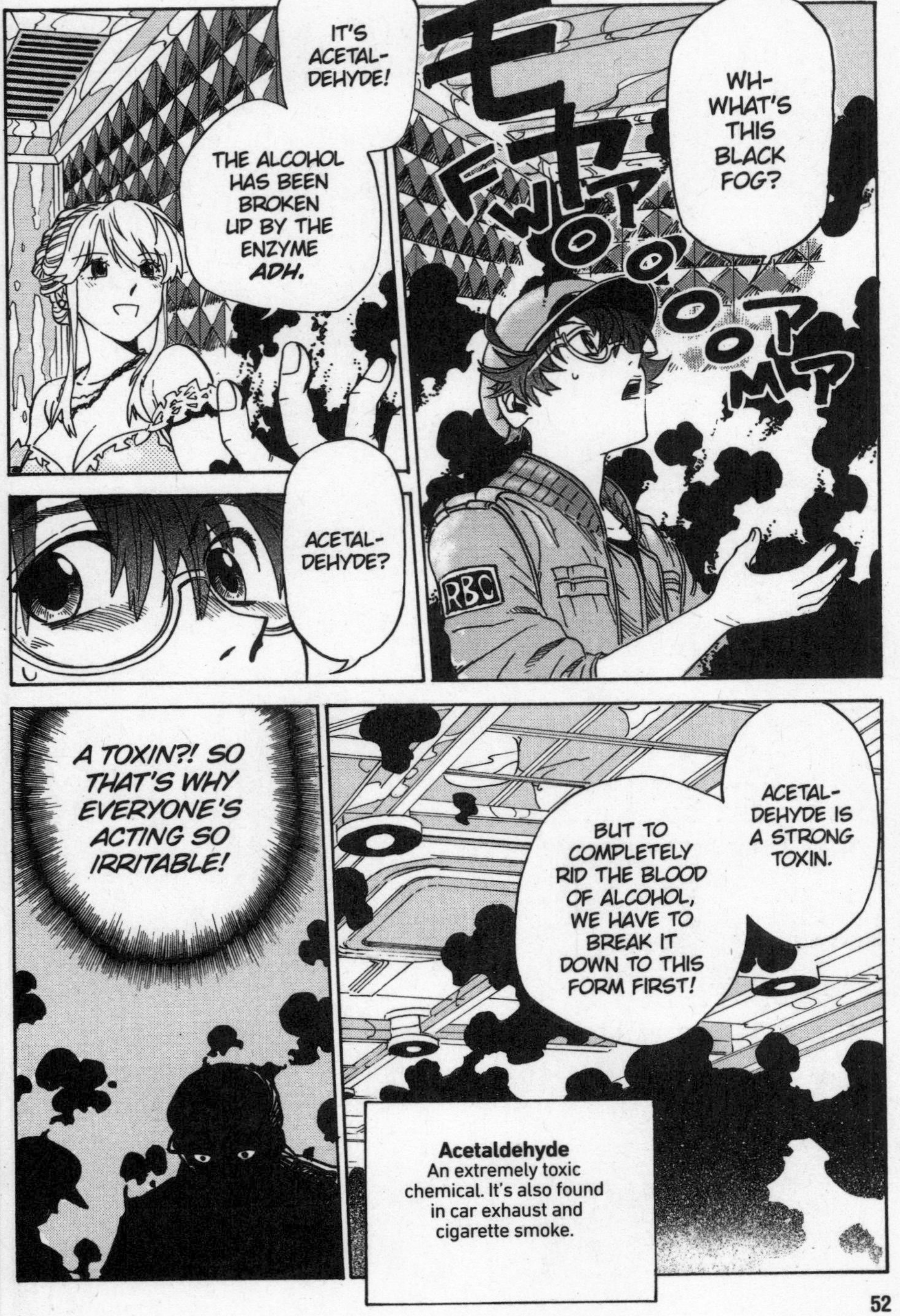
FWOOOOMP
WH-WHAT'S THIS BLACK FOG?
IT'S ACETALDEHYDE!
THE ALCOHOL HAS BEEN BROKEN UP BY THE ENZYME ADH.
ACETALDEHYDE?
ACETALDEHYDE IS A STRONG TOXIN.
BUT TO COMPLETELY RID THE BLOOD OF ALCOHOL, WE HAVE TO BREAK IT DOWN TO THIS FORM FIRST!
Acetaldehyde
An extremely toxic chemical. It's also found in car exhaust and cigarette smoke.
A TOXIN?! SO THAT'S WHY EVERYONE'S ACTING SO IRRITABLE!

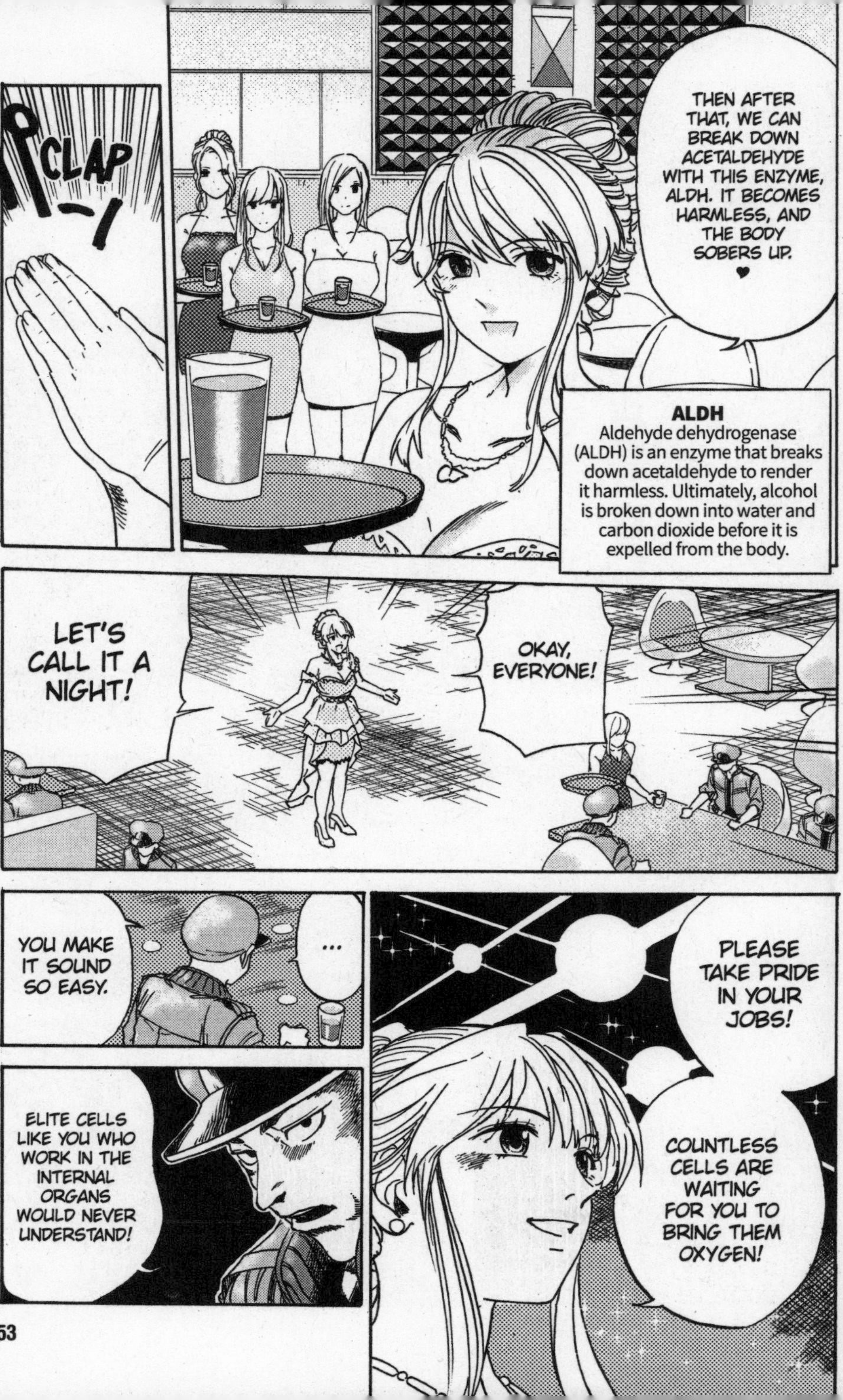
THEN AFTER THAT, WE CAN BREAK DOWN ACETALDEHYDE WITH THIS ENZYME, ALDH. IT BECOMES HARMLESS, AND THE BODY SOBERS UP. ♥
ALDH
Aldehyde dehydrogenase (ALDH) is an enzyme that breaks down acetaldehyde to render it harmless. Ultimately, alcohol is broken down into water and carbon dioxide before it is expelled from the body.
CLAP
OKAY, EVERYONE!
LET'S CALL IT A NIGHT!
PLEASE TAKE PRIDE IN YOUR JOBS!
COUNTLESS CELLS ARE WAITING FOR YOU TO BRING THEM OXYGEN!
...
YOU MAKE IT SOUND SO EASY.
ELITE CELLS LIKE YOU WHO WORK IN THE INTERNAL ORGANS WOULD NEVER UNDERSTAND!

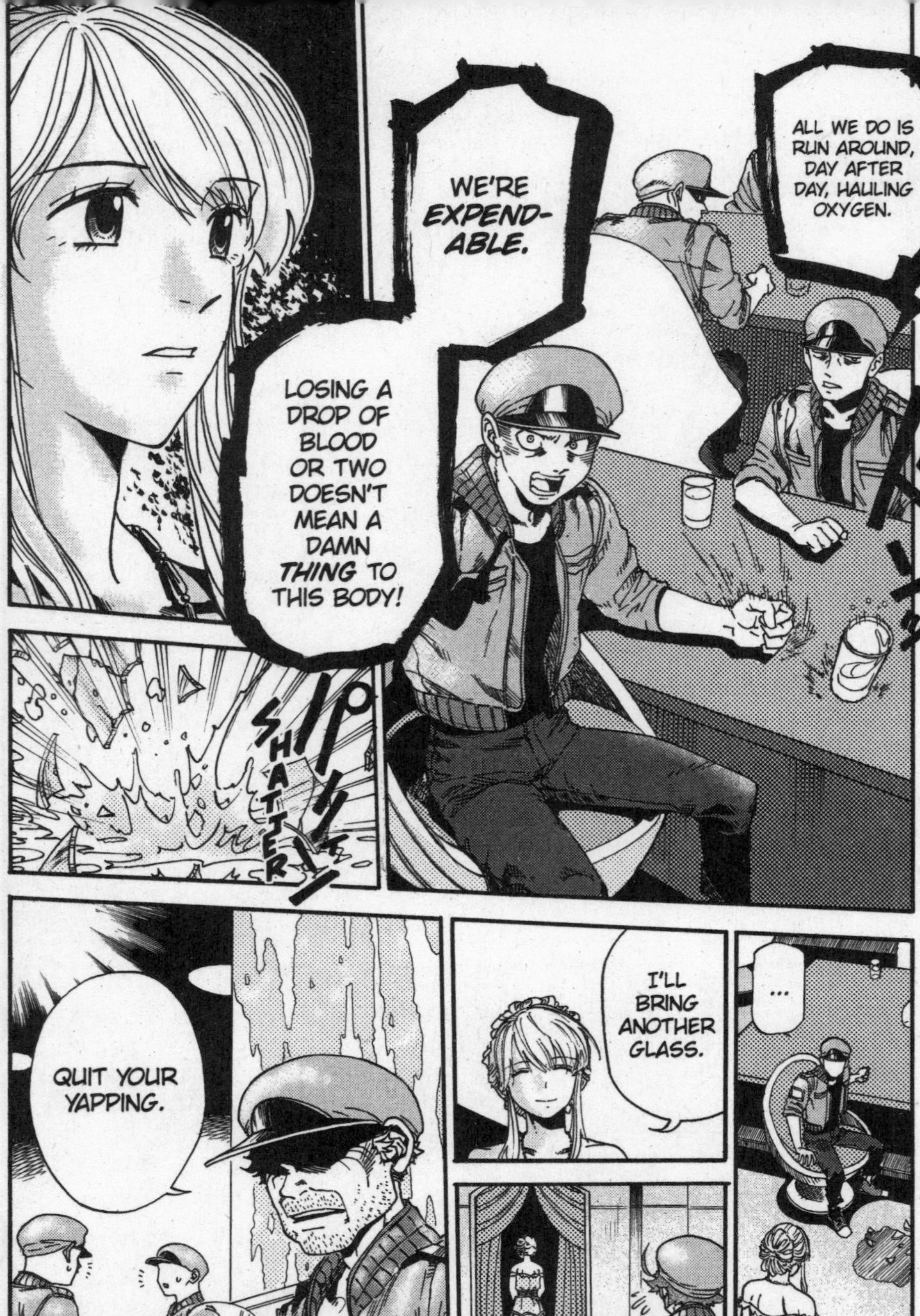
ALL WE DO IS RUN AROUND, DAY AFTER DAY, HAULING OXYGEN.
WE'RE EXPENDABLE.
LOSING A DROP OF BLOOD OR TWO DOESN'T MEAN A DAMN THING TO THIS BODY!
SLAM
SHATTER
...
I'LL BRING ANOTHER GLASS.
QUIT YOUR YAPPING.

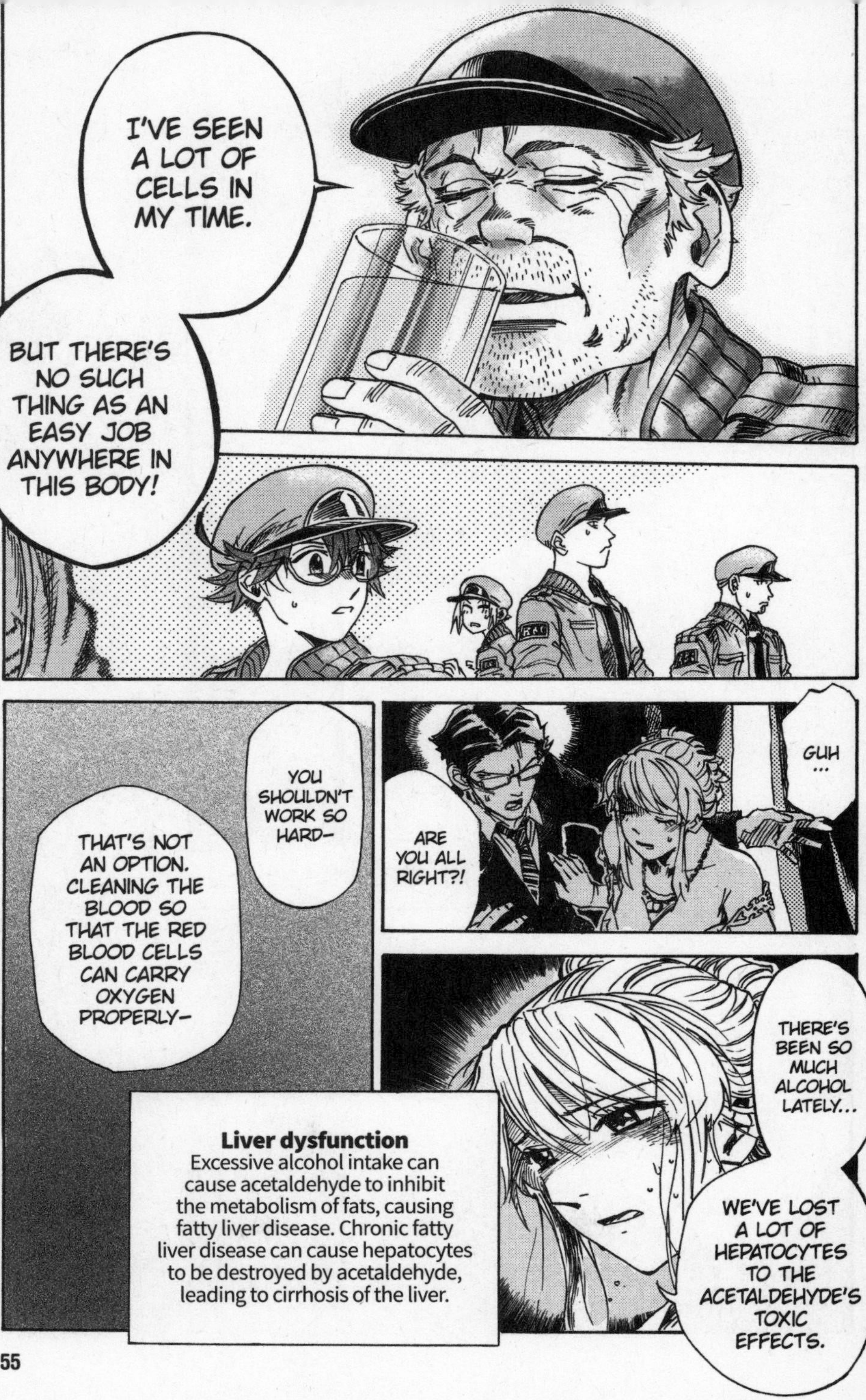
I'VE SEEN A LOT OF CELLS IN MY TIME.
BUT THERE'S NO SUCH THING AS AN EASY JOB ANYWHERE IN THIS BODY!
GUH...
ARE YOU ALL RIGHT?!
THERE'S BEEN SO MUCH ALCOHOL LATELY...
WE'VE LOST A LOT OF HEPATOCYTES TO THE ACETALDEHYDE'S TOXIC EFFECTS.
YOU SHOULDN'T WORK SO HARD–
THAT'S NOT AN OPTION. CLEANING THE BLOOD SO THAT THE RED BLOOD CELLS CAN CARRY OXYGEN PROPERLY–

Liver dysfunction
Excessive alcohol intake can cause acetaldehyde to inhibit the metabolism of fats, causing fatty liver disease. Chronic fatty liver disease can cause hepatocytes to be destroyed by acetaldehyde, leading to cirrhosis of the liver.

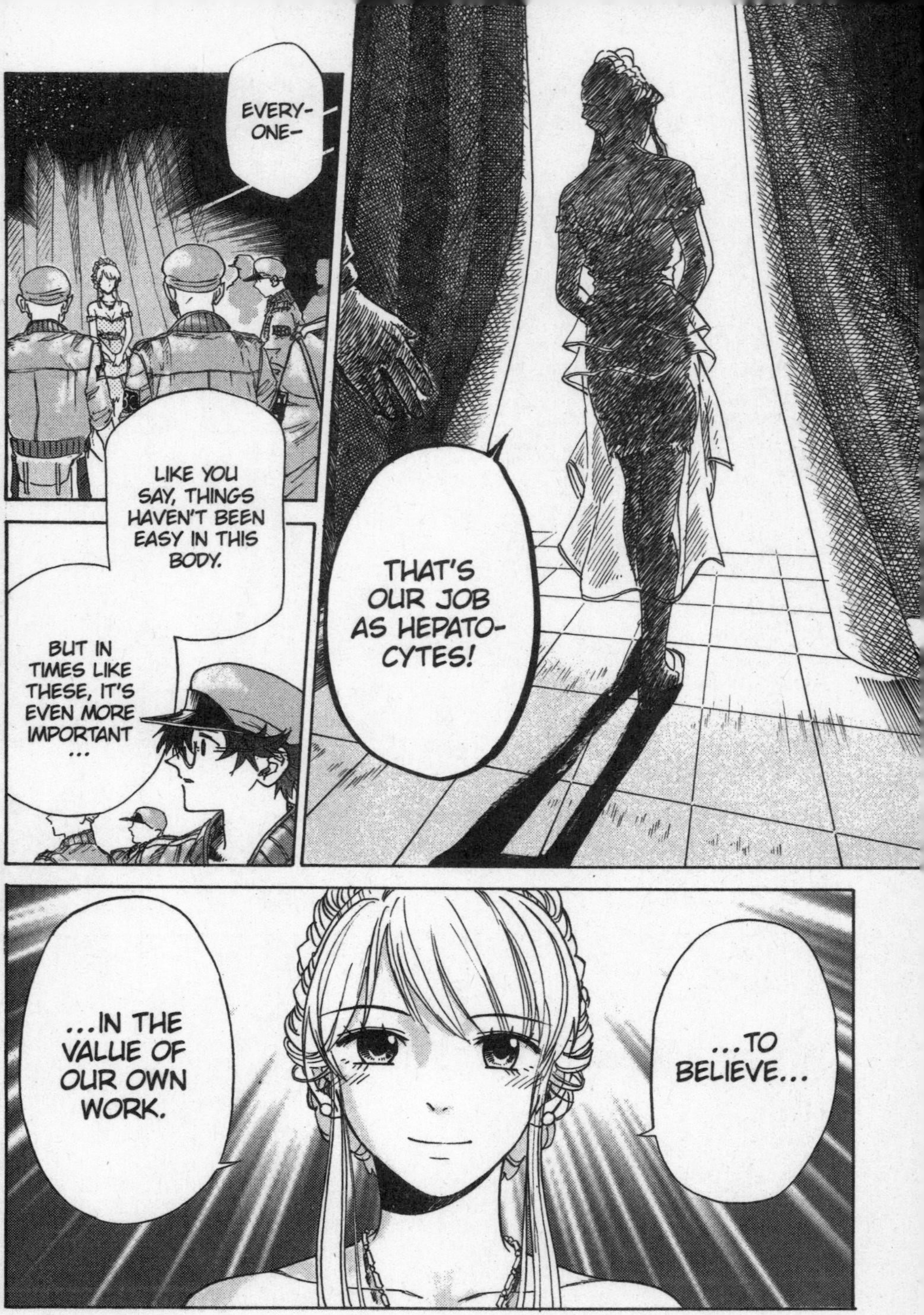
THAT'S OUR JOB AS HEPATO-CYTES!
EVERY-ONE-
LIKE YOU SAY, THINGS HAVEN'T BEEN EASY IN THIS BODY.
BUT IN TIMES LIKE THESE, IT'S EVEN MORE IMPORTANT ...
...TO BELIEVE...
...IN THE VALUE OF OUR OWN WORK.

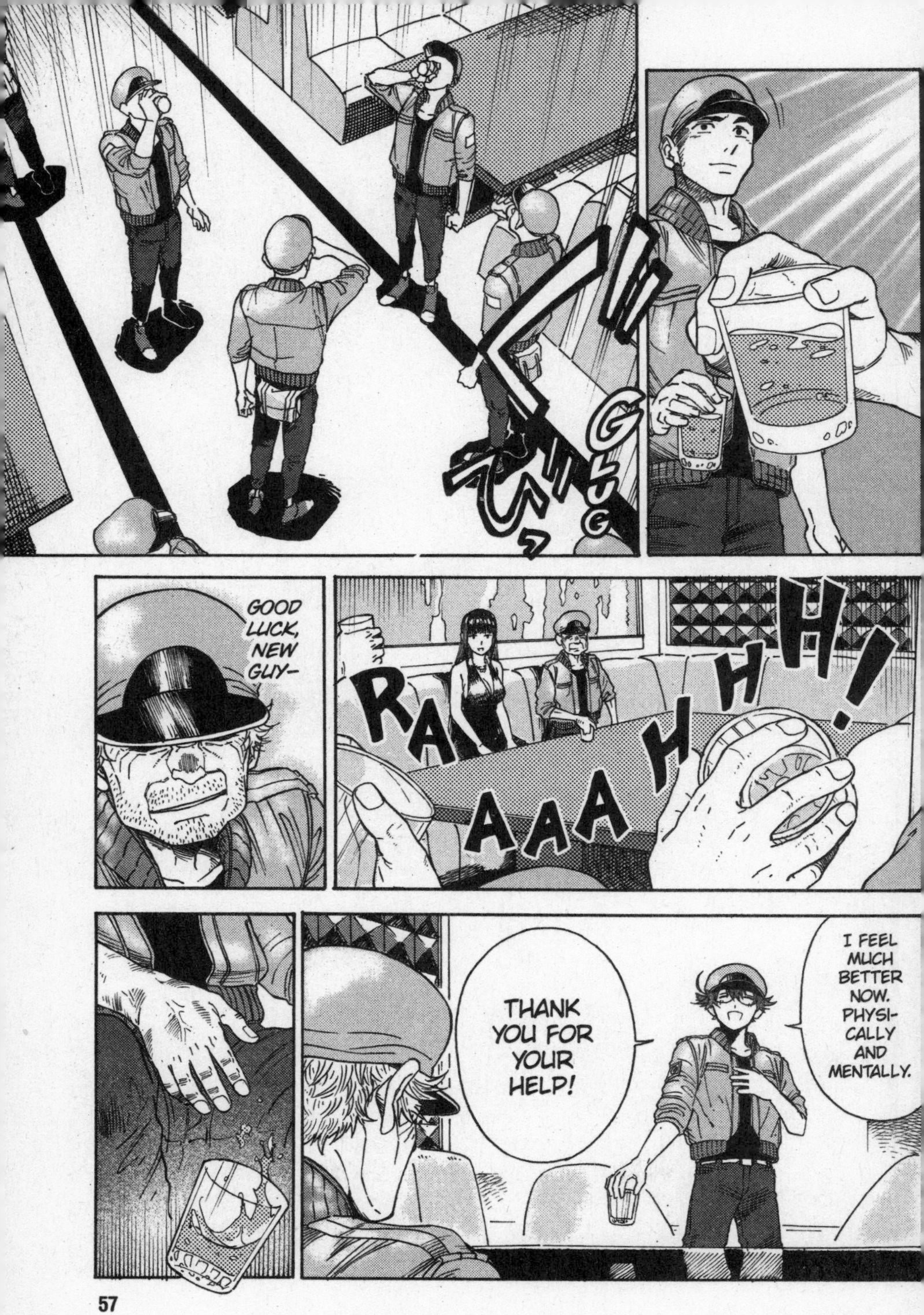
GLUG
RAAAAHHHH!
GOOD LUCK, NEW GUY-
I FEEL MUCH BETTER NOW. PHYSICALLY AND MENTALLY.
THANK YOU FOR YOUR HELP!

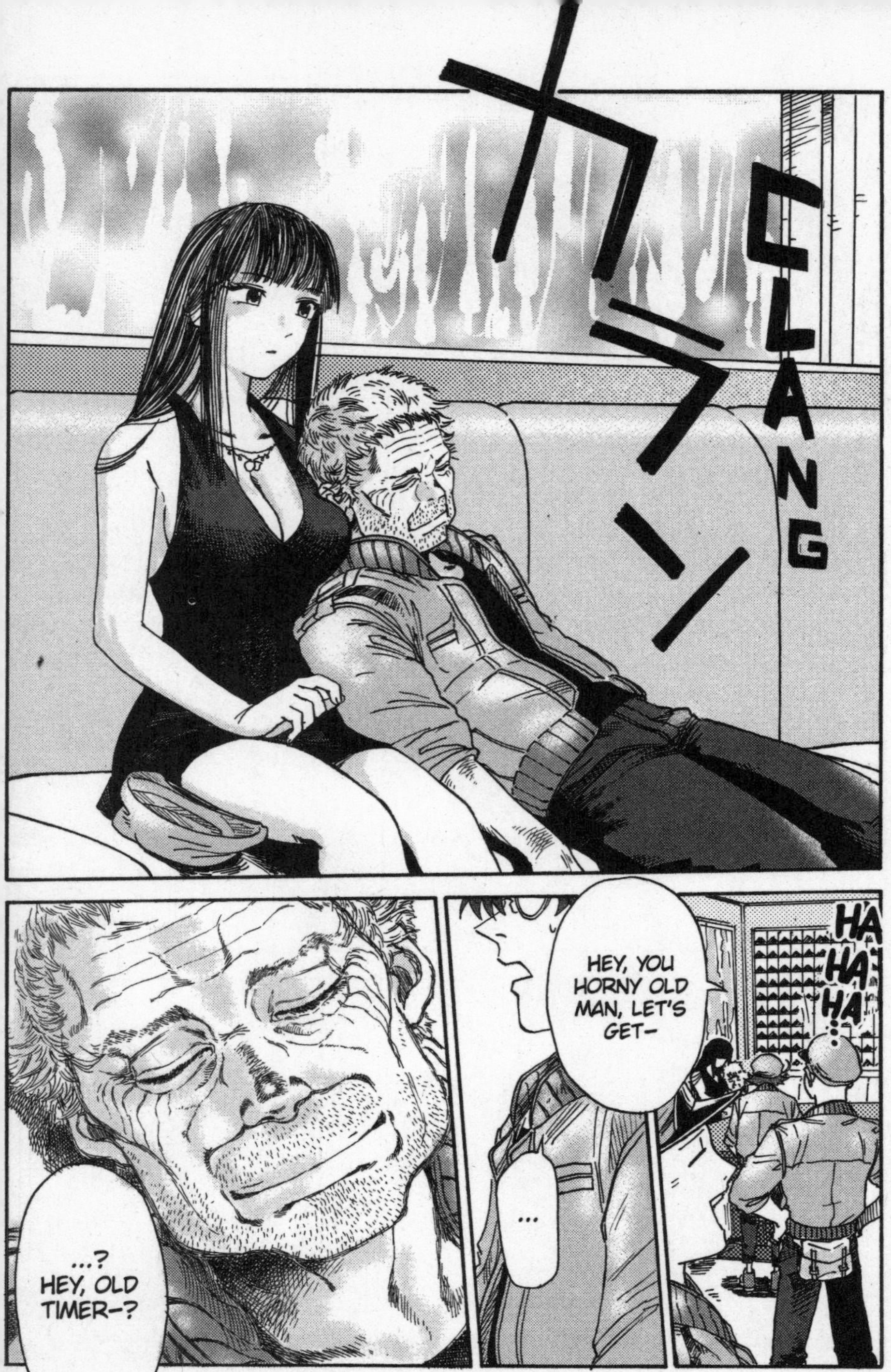
カラーン
CLANG
HEY, YOU HORNY OLD MAN, LET'S GET–
HA HA HA
...
...? HEY, OLD TIMER–?

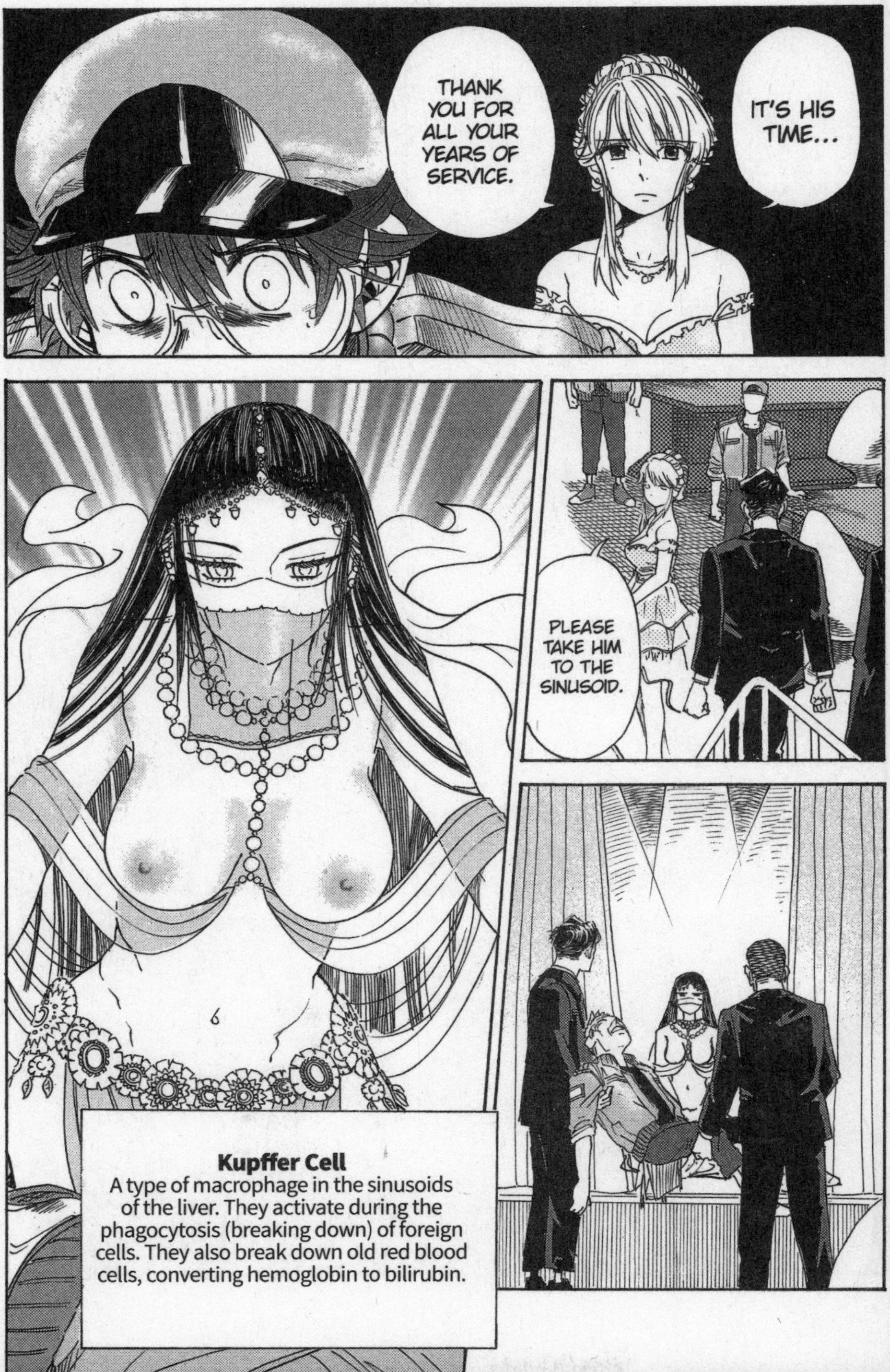
IT'S HIS TIME...
THANK YOU FOR ALL YOUR YEARS OF SERVICE.
PLEASE TAKE HIM TO THE SINUSOID.
Kupffer Cell
A type of macrophage in the sinusoids of the liver. They activate during the phagocytosis (breaking down) of foreign cells. They also break down old red blood cells, converting hemoglobin to bilirubin.

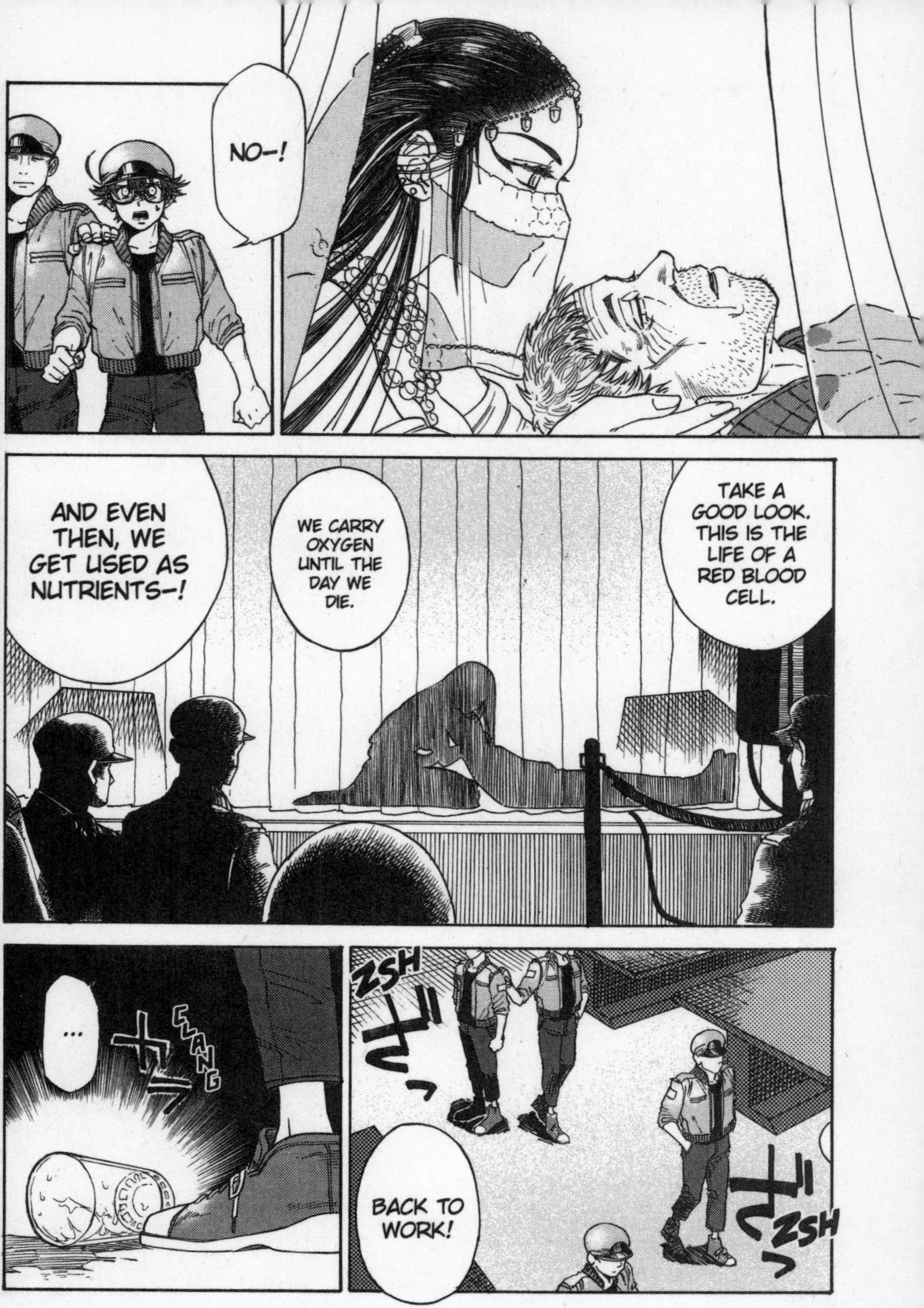
NO-!
TAKE A GOOD LOOK. THIS IS THE LIFE OF A RED BLOOD CELL.
WE CARRY OXYGEN UNTIL THE DAY WE DIE.
AND EVEN THEN, WE GET USED AS NUTRIENTS-!
ZSH
BACK TO WORK!
ZSH
...
CLANG

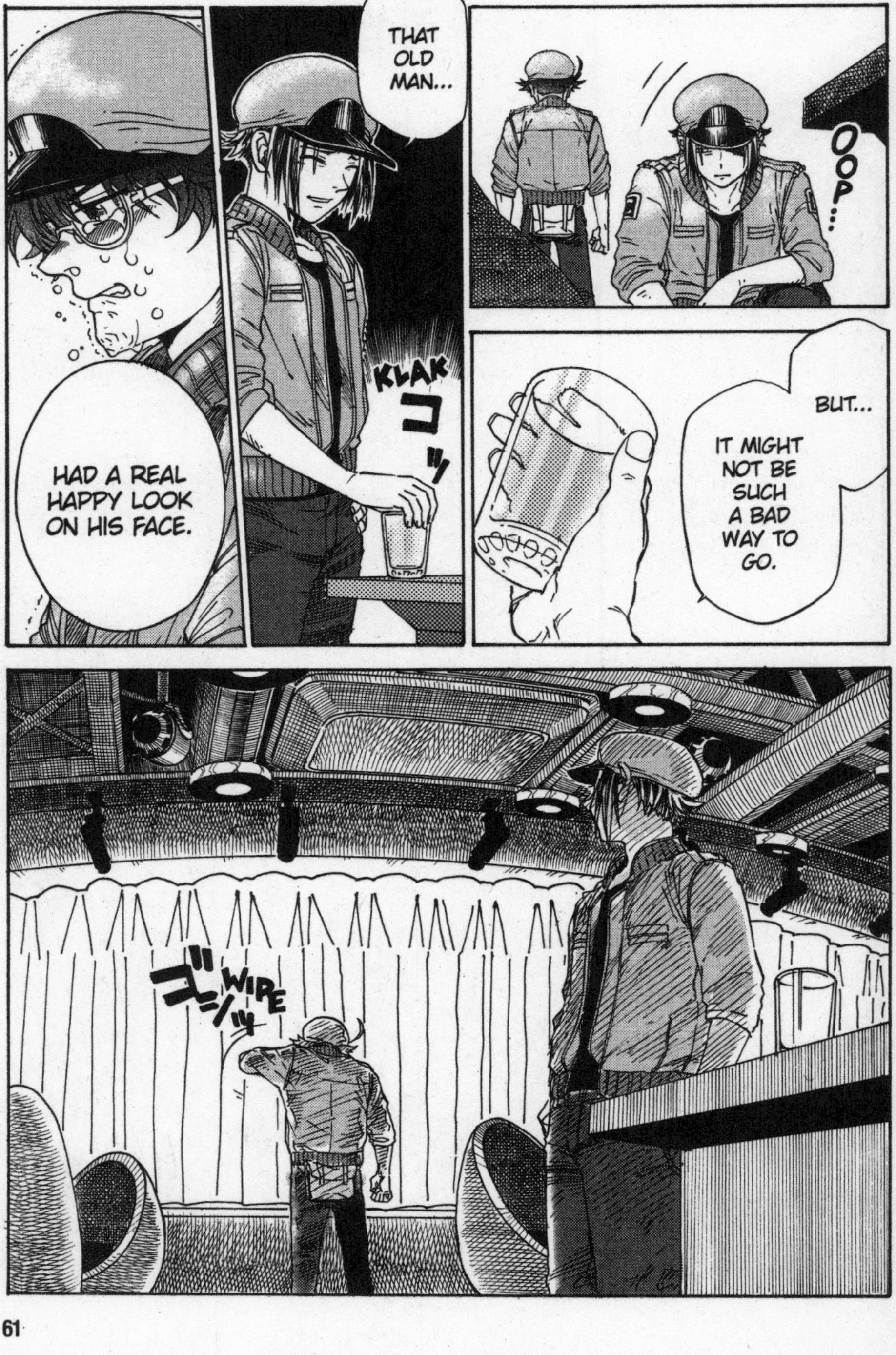
OOP...
BUT...
IT MIGHT NOT BE SUCH A BAD WAY TO GO.
THAT OLD MAN...
KLAK
HAD A REAL HAPPY LOOK ON HIS FACE.
WIPE

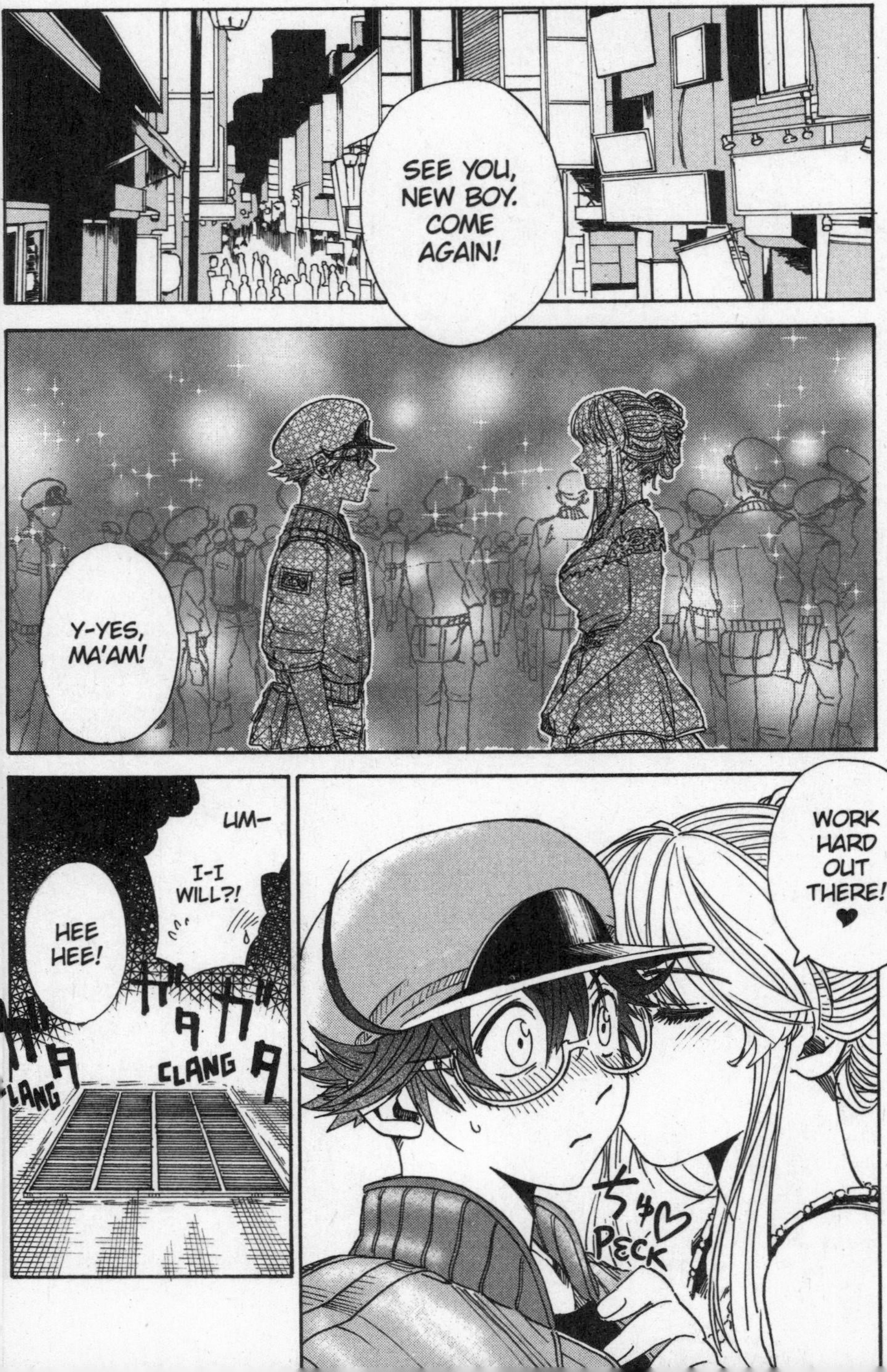
SEE YOU, NEW BOY. COME AGAIN!
Y-YES, MA'AM!
WORK HARD OUT THERE! ♥
PECK
UM-
I-I WILL?!
HEE HEE!
CLANG
CLANG

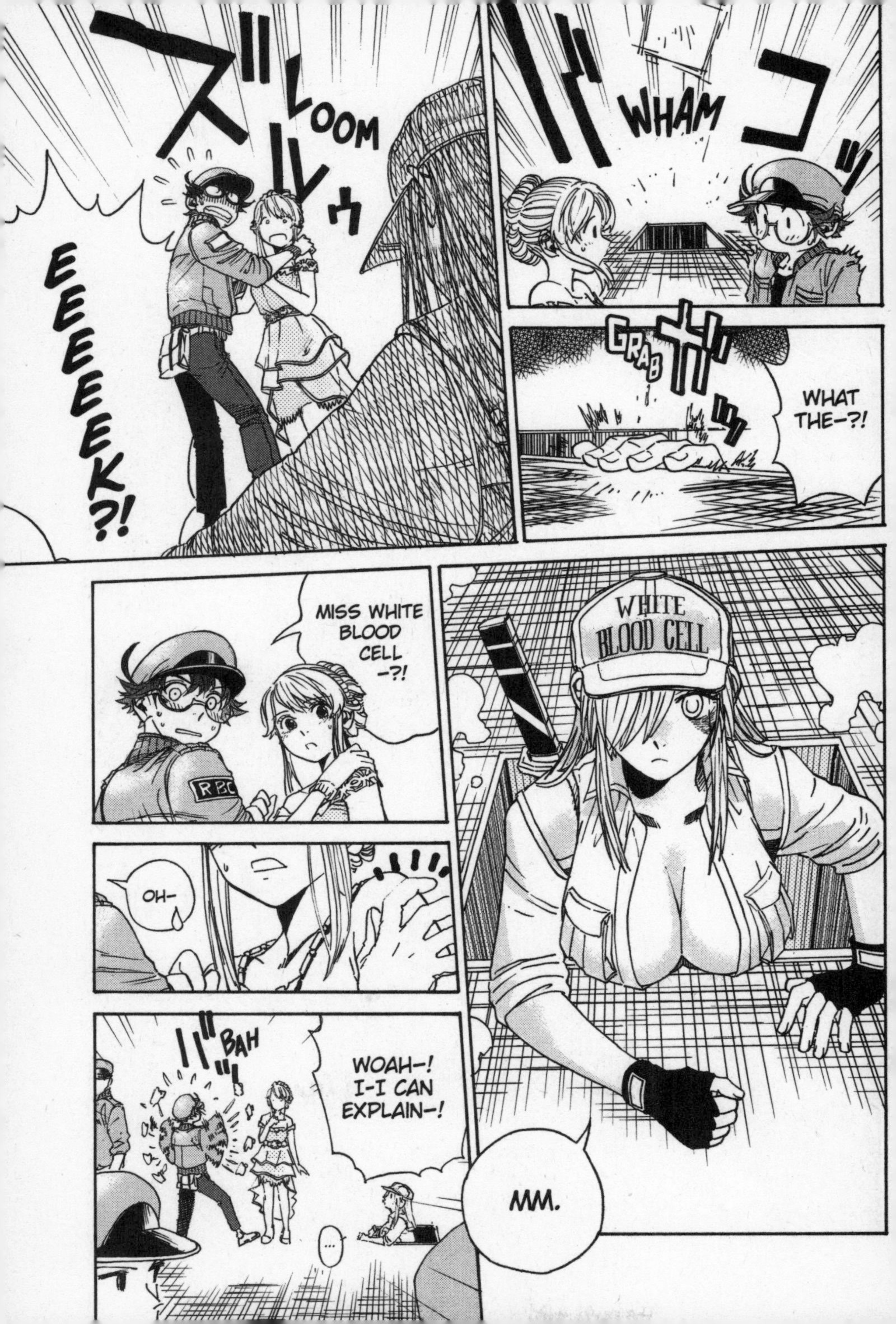
バコッ
WHAM
ガシッ
GRAB
WHAT THE-?!
ズルゥ
LOOM
EEEEEEK?!
WHITE BLOOD CELL
MM.
MISS WHITE BLOOD CELL-?!
OH-
バッ
BAH
WOAH-! I-I CAN EXPLAIN-!
...

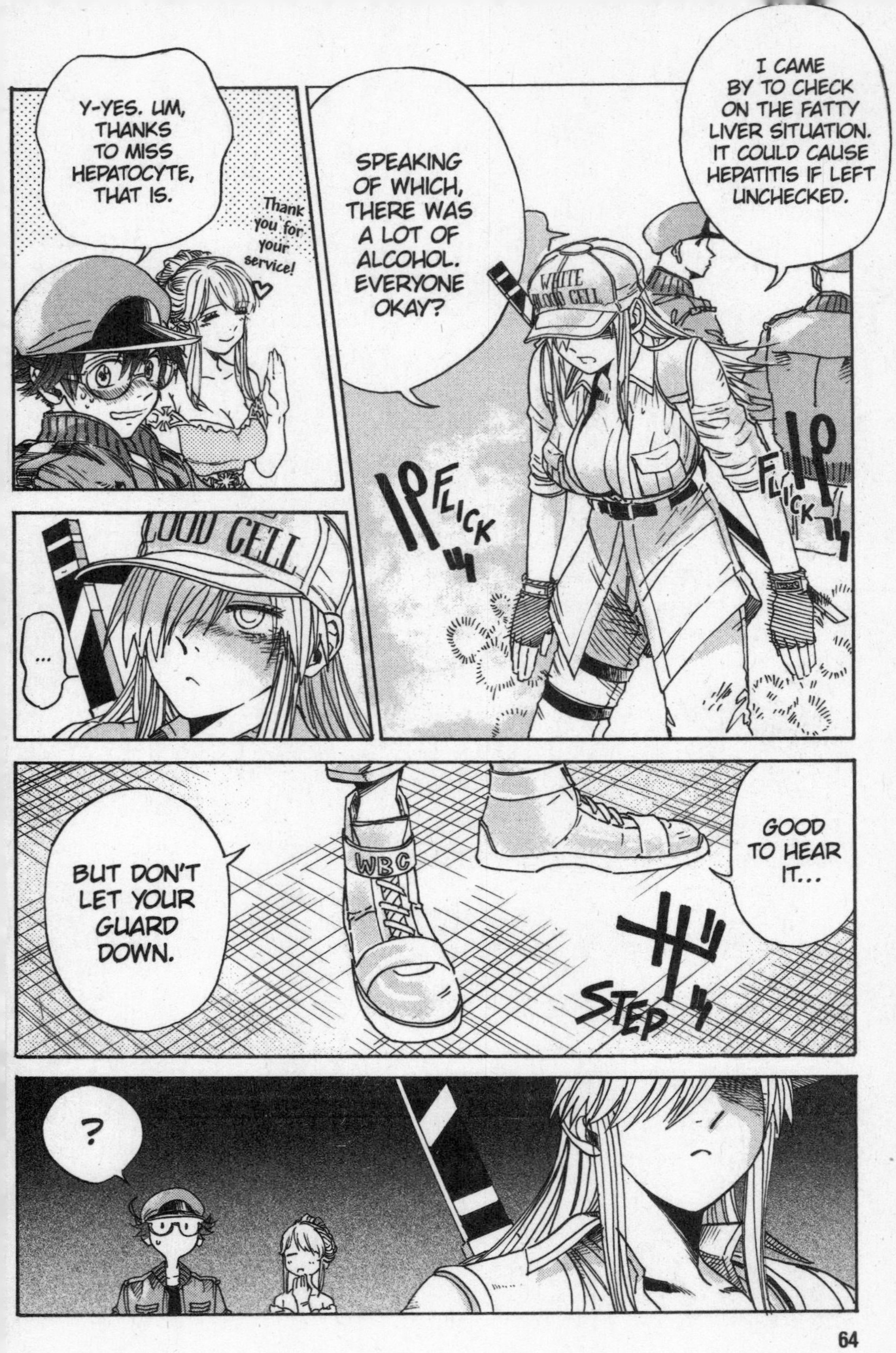
I CAME BY TO CHECK ON THE FATTY LIVER SITUATION. IT COULD CAUSE HEPATITIS IF LEFT UNCHECKED.
SPEAKING OF WHICH, THERE WAS A LOT OF ALCOHOL. EVERYONE OKAY?
FLICK
FLICK
Y-YES. UM, THANKS TO MISS HEPATOCYTE, THAT IS.
Thank you for your service!
...
GOOD TO HEAR IT...
STEP
BUT DON'T LET YOUR GUARD DOWN.
?

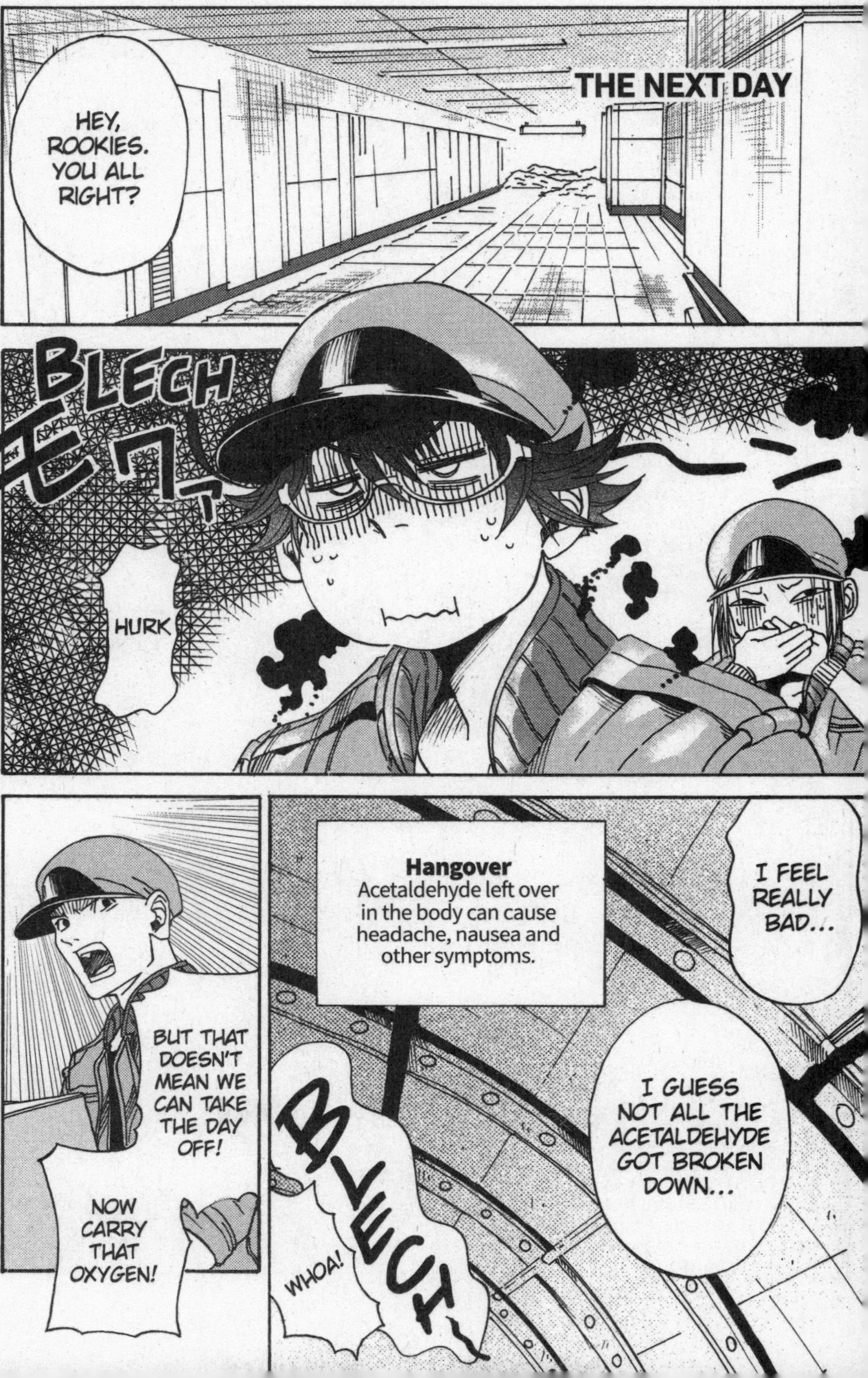
THE NEXT DAY
HEY, ROOKIES. YOU ALL RIGHT?
BLECH
モワァ
HURK
Hangover
Acetaldehyde left over in the body can cause headache, nausea and other symptoms.
I FEEL REALLY BAD...
I GUESS NOT ALL THE ACETALDEHYDE GOT BROKEN DOWN...
BLECH
WHOA!
BUT THAT DOESN'T MEAN WE CAN TAKE THE DAY OFF!
NOW CARRY THAT OXYGEN!

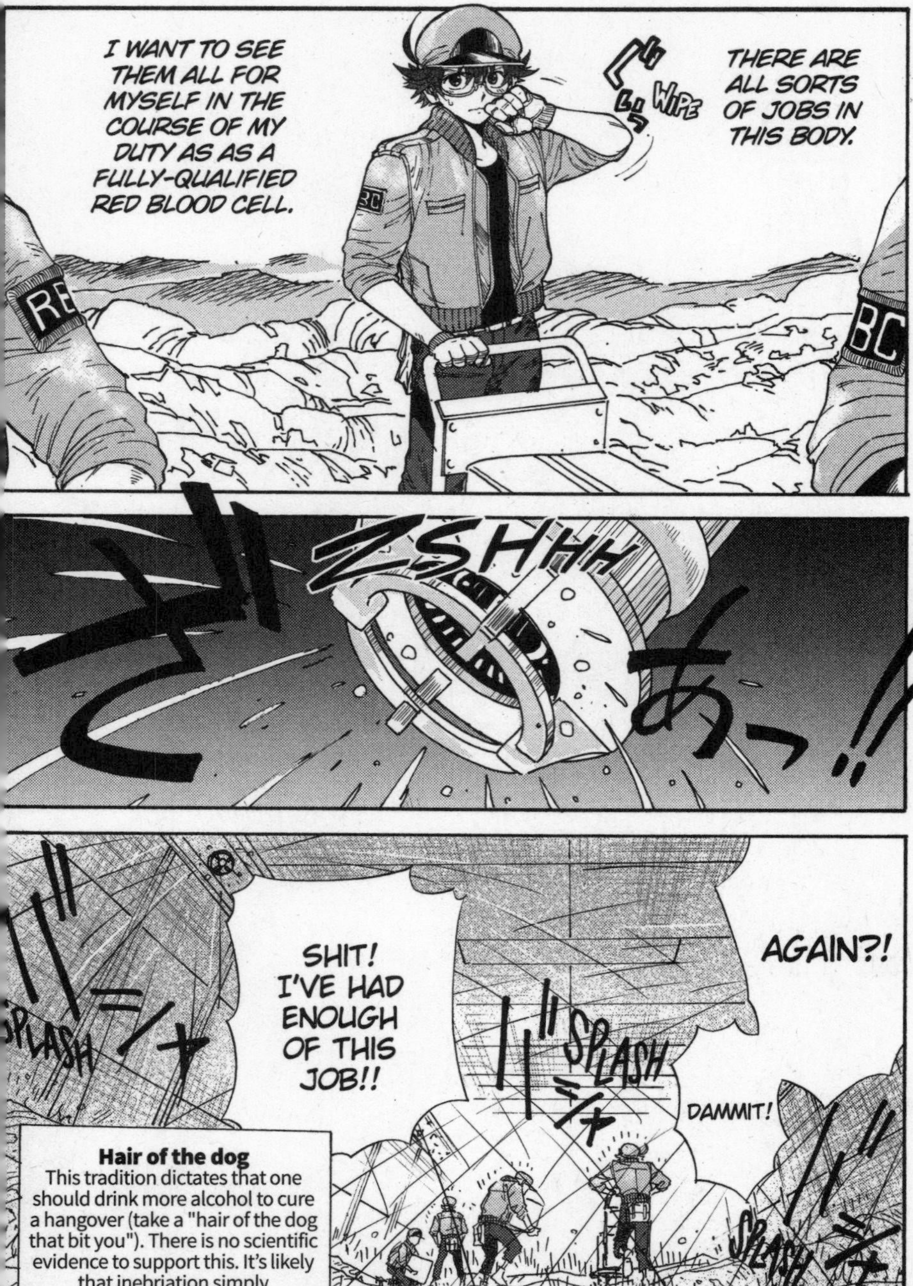
THERE ARE ALL SORTS OF JOBS IN THIS BODY.
WIPE
I WANT TO SEE THEM ALL FOR MYSELF IN THE COURSE OF MY DUTY AS AS A FULLY-QUALIFIED RED BLOOD CELL.
ZSHHH
あっ!!
AGAIN?!
DAMMIT!
SPLASH
SPLASH
SHIT! I'VE HAD ENOUGH OF THIS JOB!!
SPLASH

Hair of the dog
This tradition dictates that one should drink more alcohol to cure a hangover (take a "hair of the dog that bit you"). There is no scientific evidence to support this. It's likely that inebriation simply distracts from the headaches and the nausea.

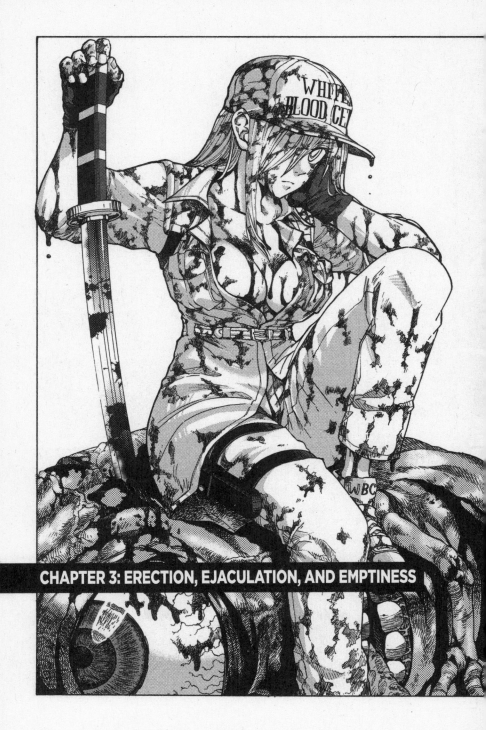

CHAPTER 3: ERECTION, EJACULATION, AND EMPTINESS

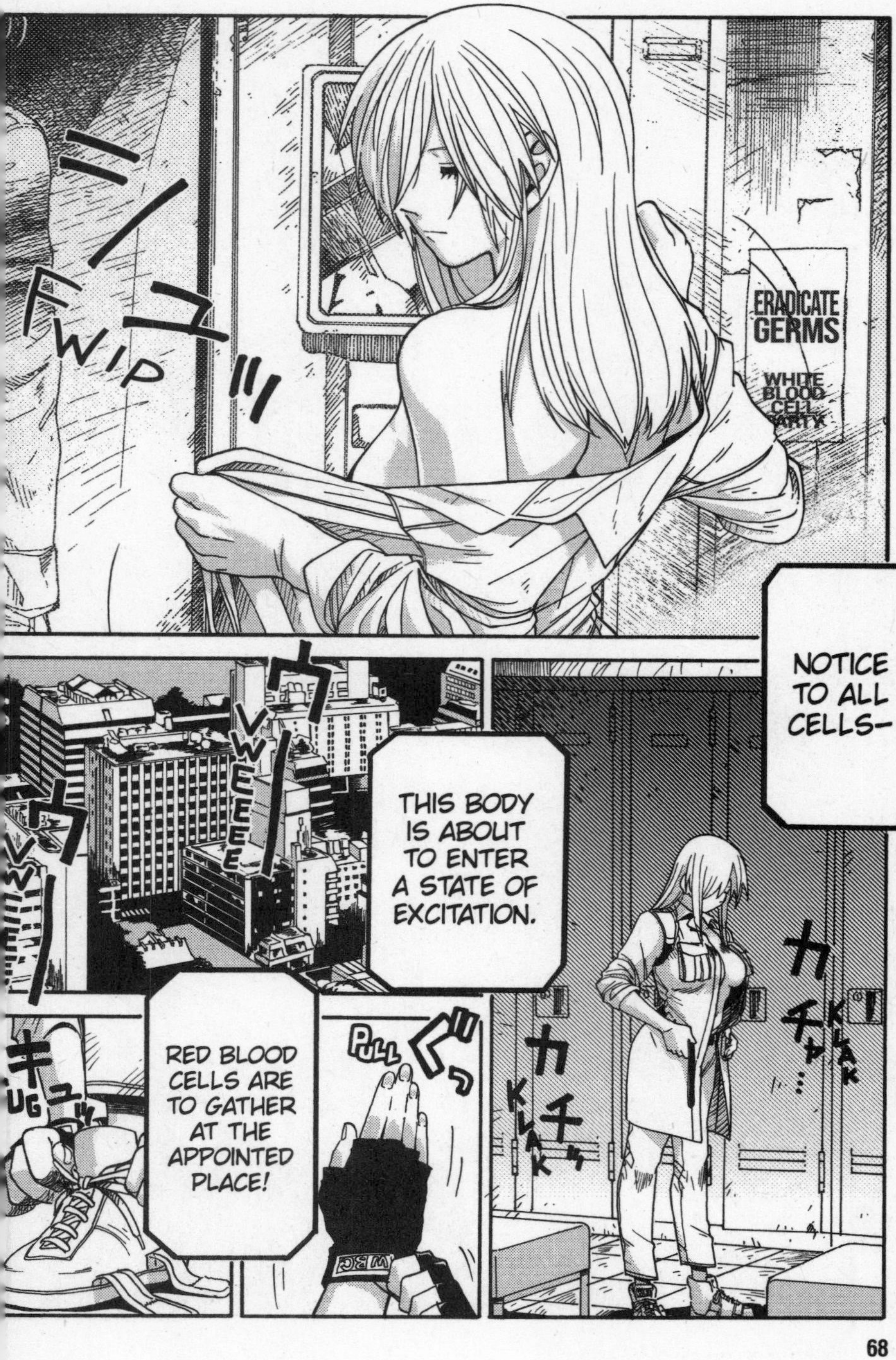
FWIP
ERADICATE GERMS
WHITE BLOOD CELL PARTY
NOTICE TO ALL CELLS-
KLAK
KLAK
THIS BODY IS ABOUT TO ENTER A STATE OF EXCITATION.
VWEEEE
PULL
RED BLOOD CELLS ARE TO GATHER AT THE APPOINTED PLACE!
TUG

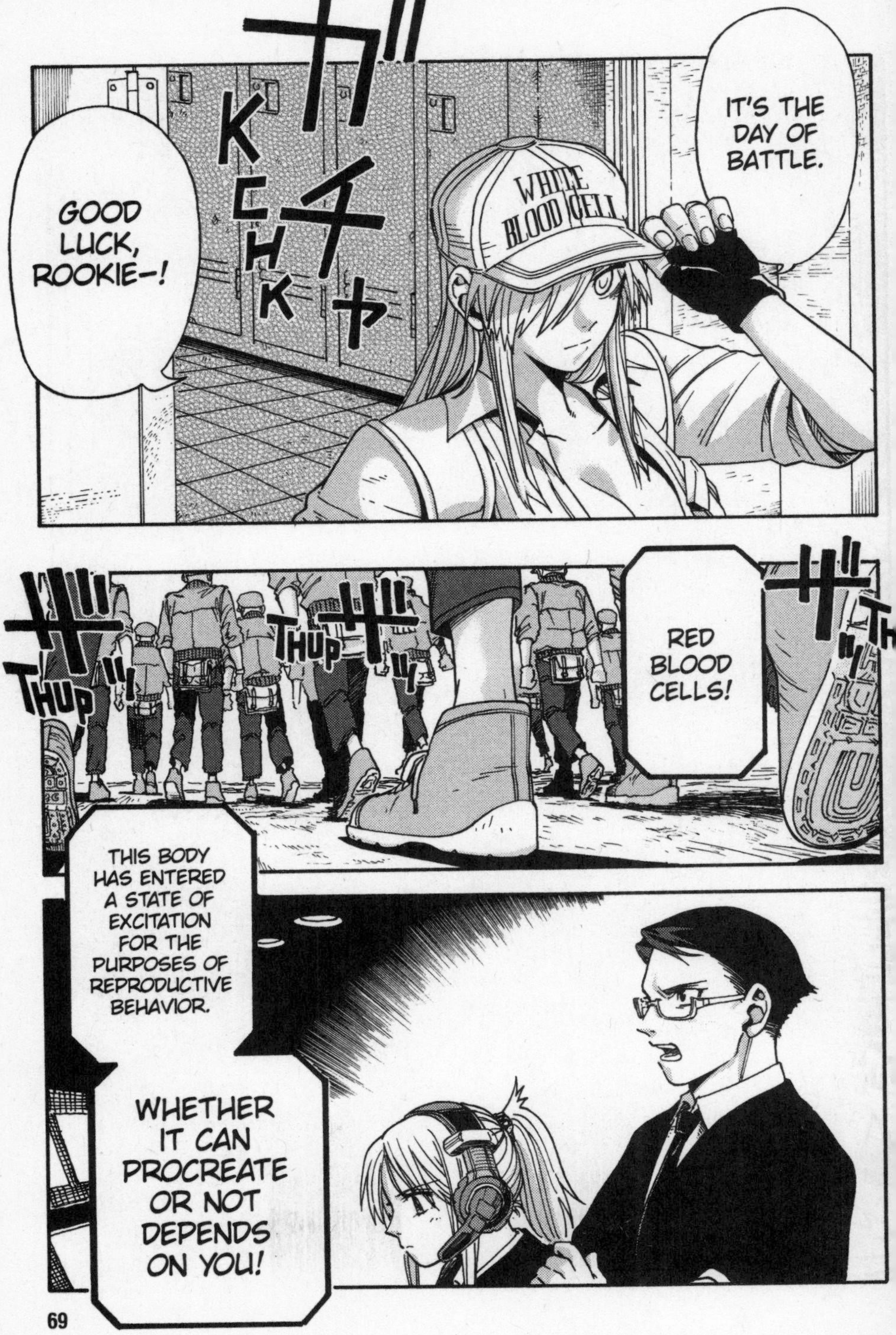
IT'S THE DAY OF BATTLE.
KCHK
GOOD LUCK, ROOKIE-!
RED BLOOD CELLS!
THUP
THUP
THUP
THIS BODY HAS ENTERED A STATE OF EXCITATION FOR THE PURPOSES OF REPRODUCTIVE BEHAVIOR.
WHETHER IT CAN PROCREATE OR NOT DEPENDS ON YOU!

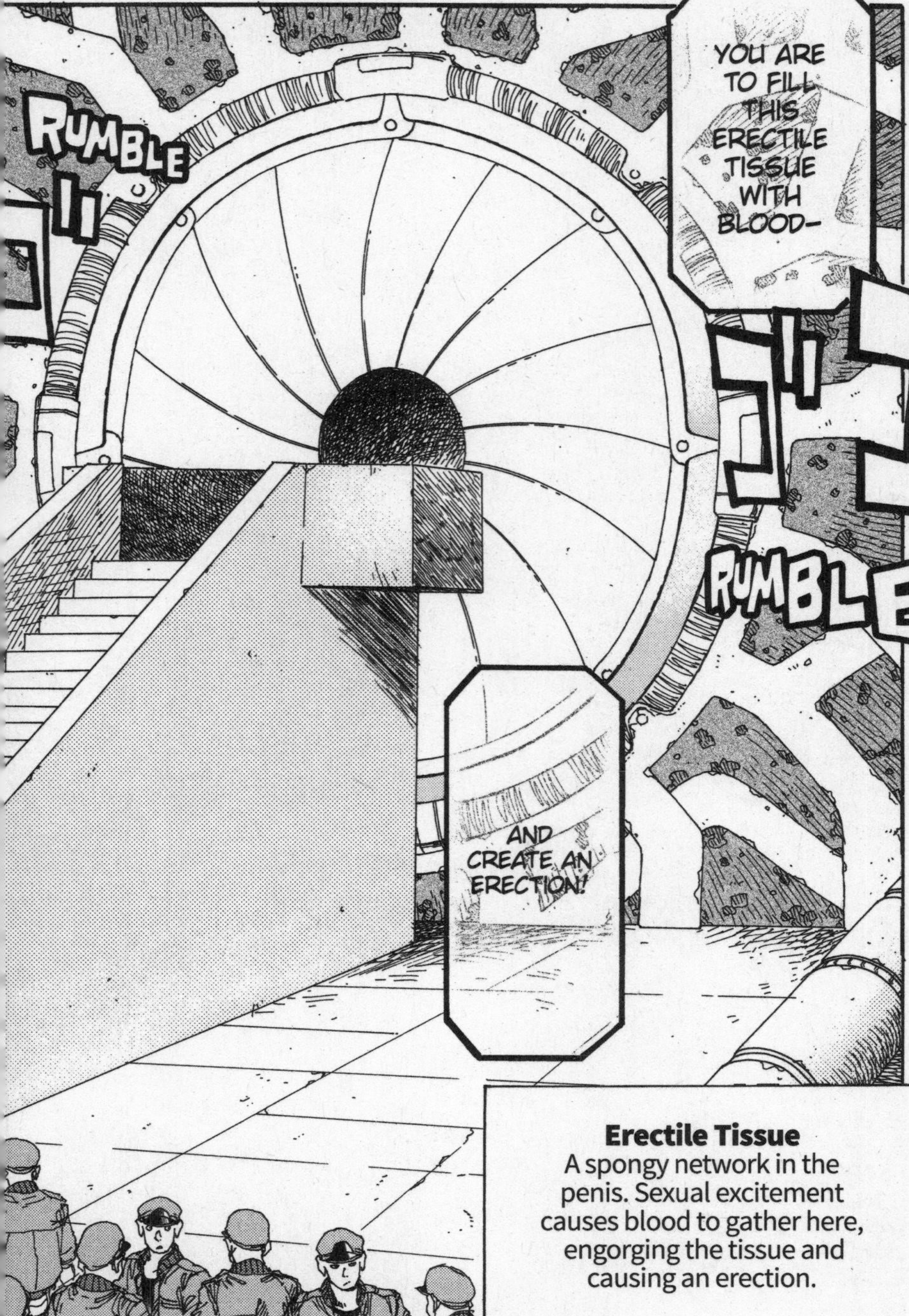
YOU ARE TO FILL THIS ERECTILE TISSUE WITH BLOOD-
ゴゴ
RUMBLE
RUMBLE
AND CREATE AN ERECTION!

Erectile Tissue
A spongy network in the penis. Sexual excitement causes blood to gather here, engorging the tissue and causing an erection.

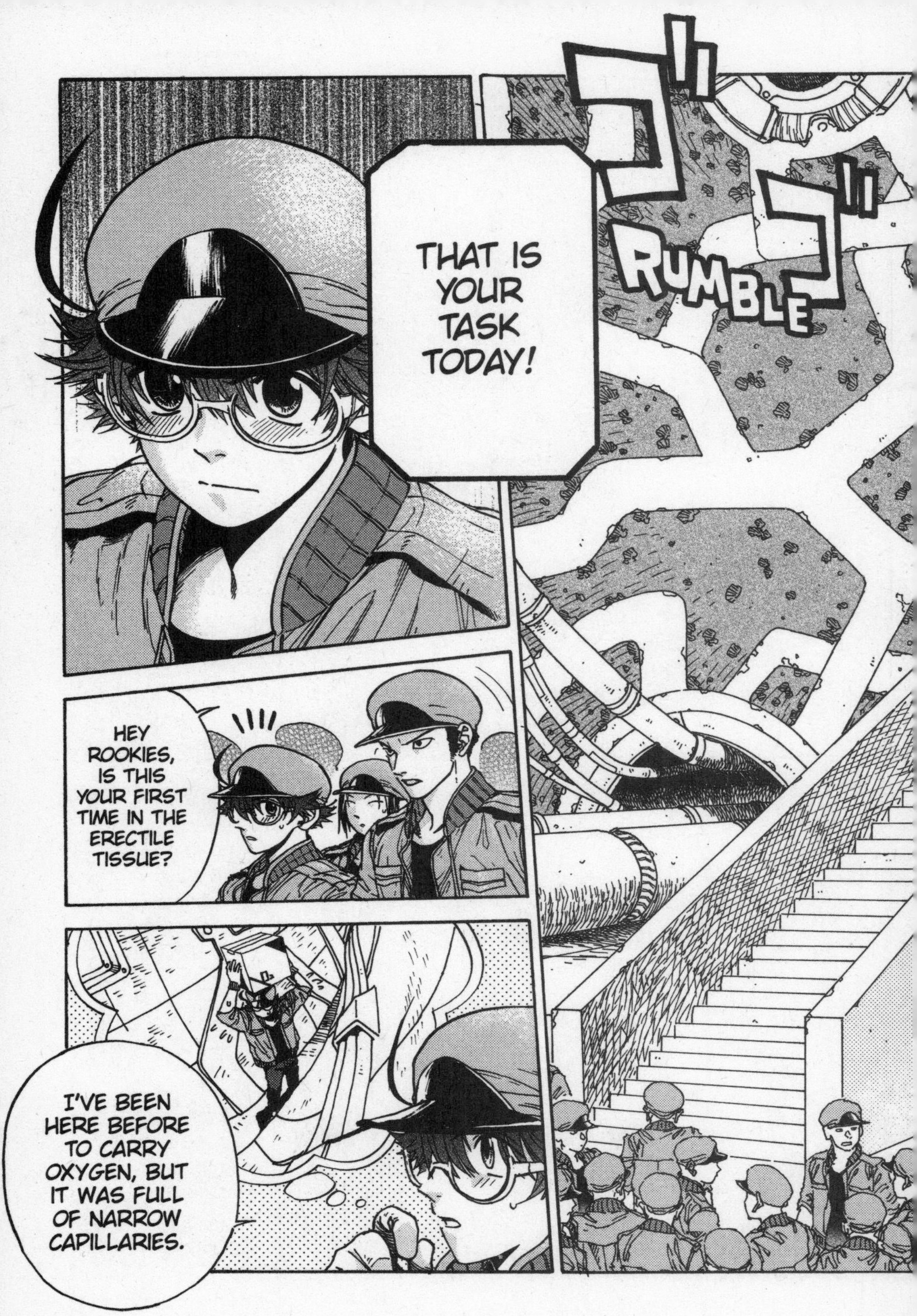
RUMBLE
THAT IS YOUR TASK TODAY!
HEY ROOKIES, IS THIS YOUR FIRST TIME IN THE ERECTILE TISSUE?
I'VE BEEN HERE BEFORE TO CARRY OXYGEN, BUT IT WAS FULL OF NARROW CAPILLARIES.

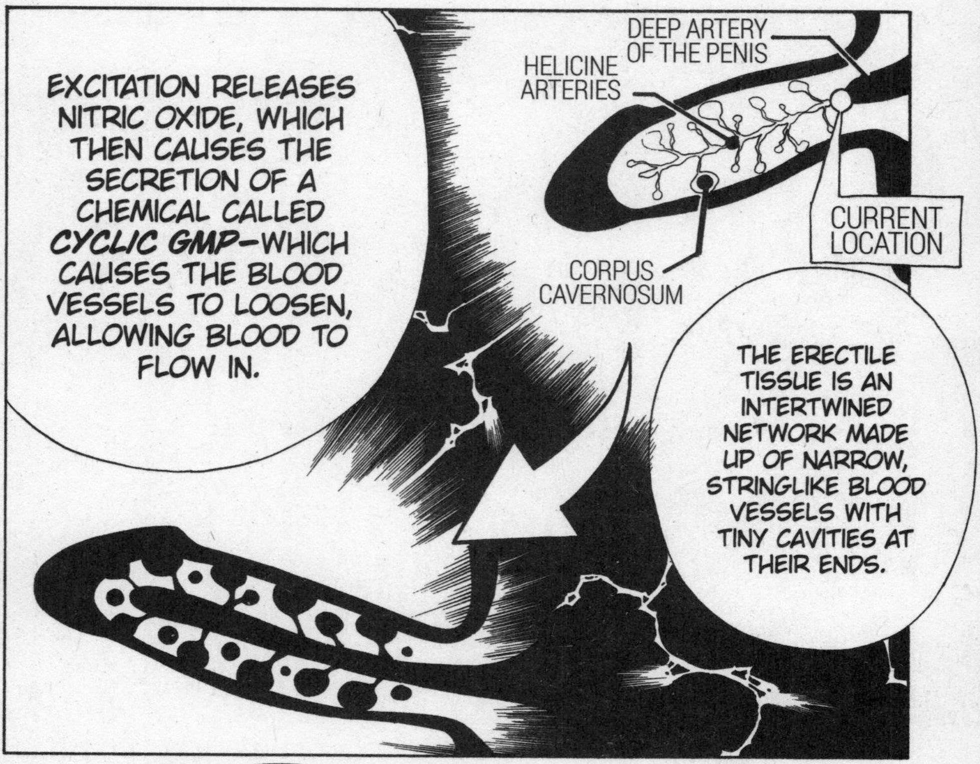
DEEP ARTERY OF THE PENIS
HELICINE ARTERIES
CURRENT LOCATION
CORPUS CAVERNOSUM
THE ERECTILE TISSUE IS AN INTERTWINED NETWORK MADE UP OF NARROW, STRINGLIKE BLOOD VESSELS WITH TINY CAVITIES AT THEIR ENDS.
EXCITATION RELEASES NITRIC OXIDE, WHICH THEN CAUSES THE SECRETION OF A CHEMICAL CALLED *CYCLIC GMP*—WHICH CAUSES THE BLOOD VESSELS TO LOOSEN, ALLOWING BLOOD TO FLOW IN.

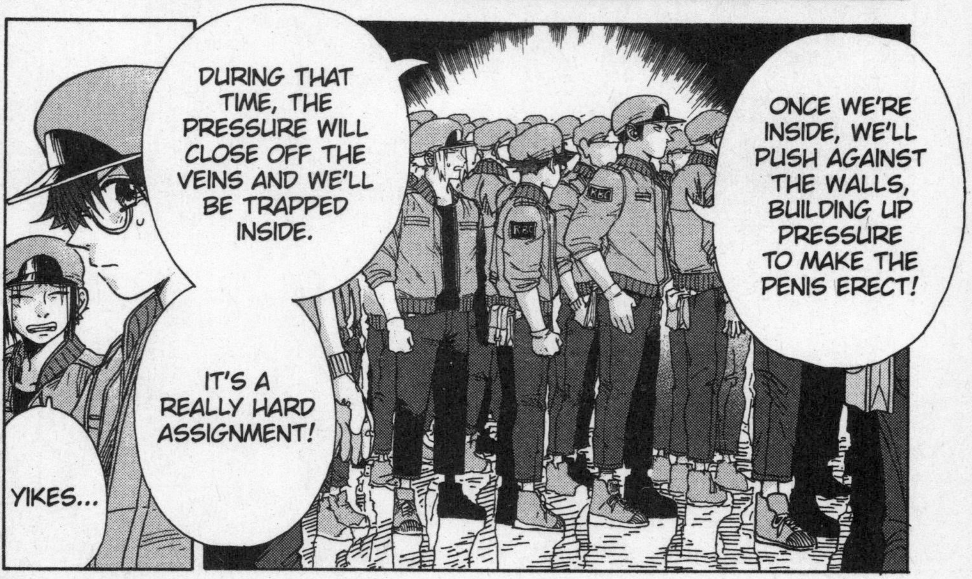
ONCE WE'RE INSIDE, WE'LL PUSH AGAINST THE WALLS, BUILDING UP PRESSURE TO MAKE THE PENIS ERECT!
DURING THAT TIME, THE PRESSURE WILL CLOSE OFF THE VEINS AND WE'LL BE TRAPPED INSIDE.
IT'S A REALLY HARD ASSIGNMENT!
YIKES...

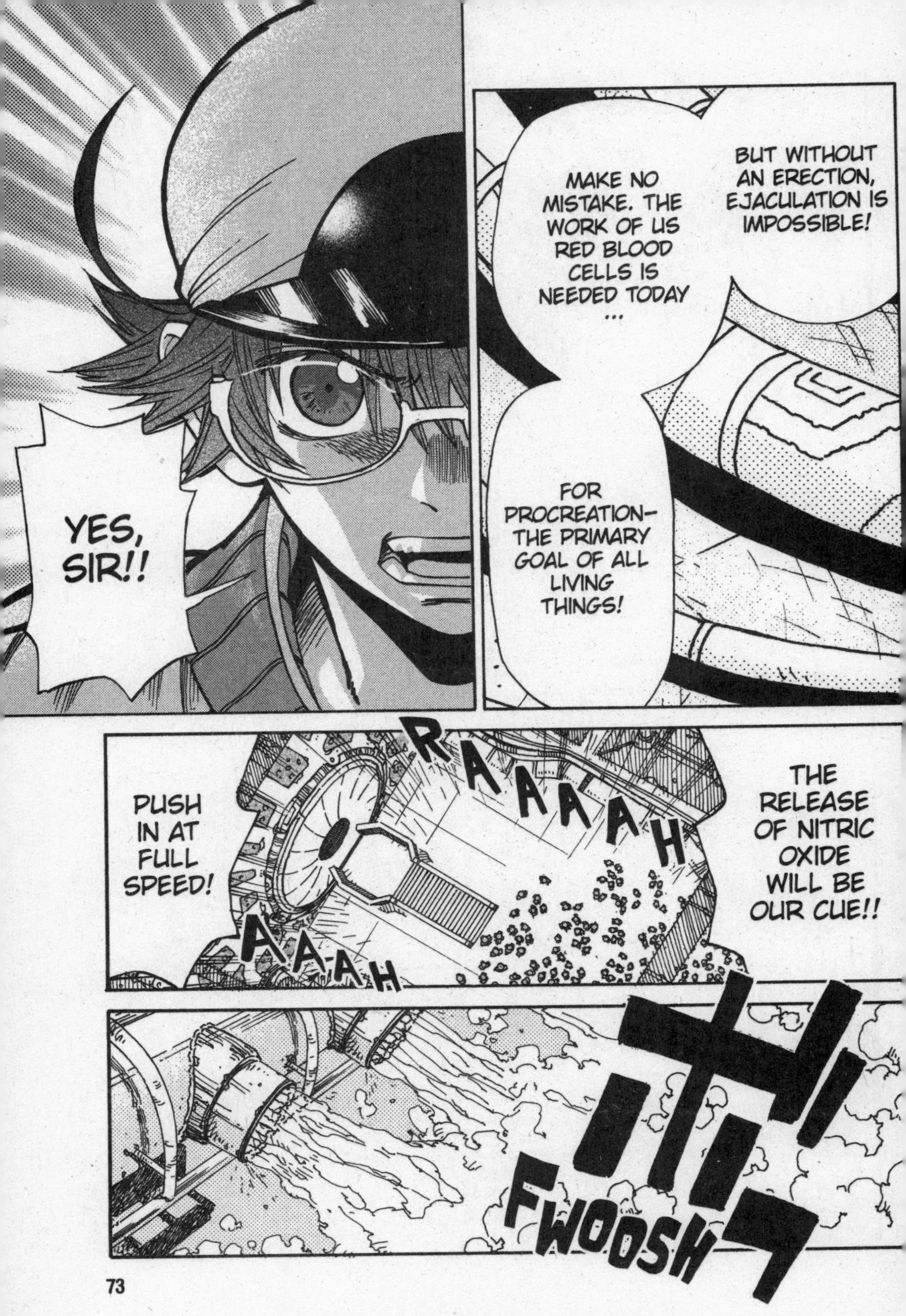
BUT WITHOUT AN ERECTION, EJACULATION IS IMPOSSIBLE!
MAKE NO MISTAKE. THE WORK OF US RED BLOOD CELLS IS NEEDED TODAY ...
FOR PROCREATION– THE PRIMARY GOAL OF ALL LIVING THINGS!
YES, SIR!!
THE RELEASE OF NITRIC OXIDE WILL BE OUR CUE!!
RAAAAH
PUSH IN AT FULL SPEED!
AAAAH
FWOOSH

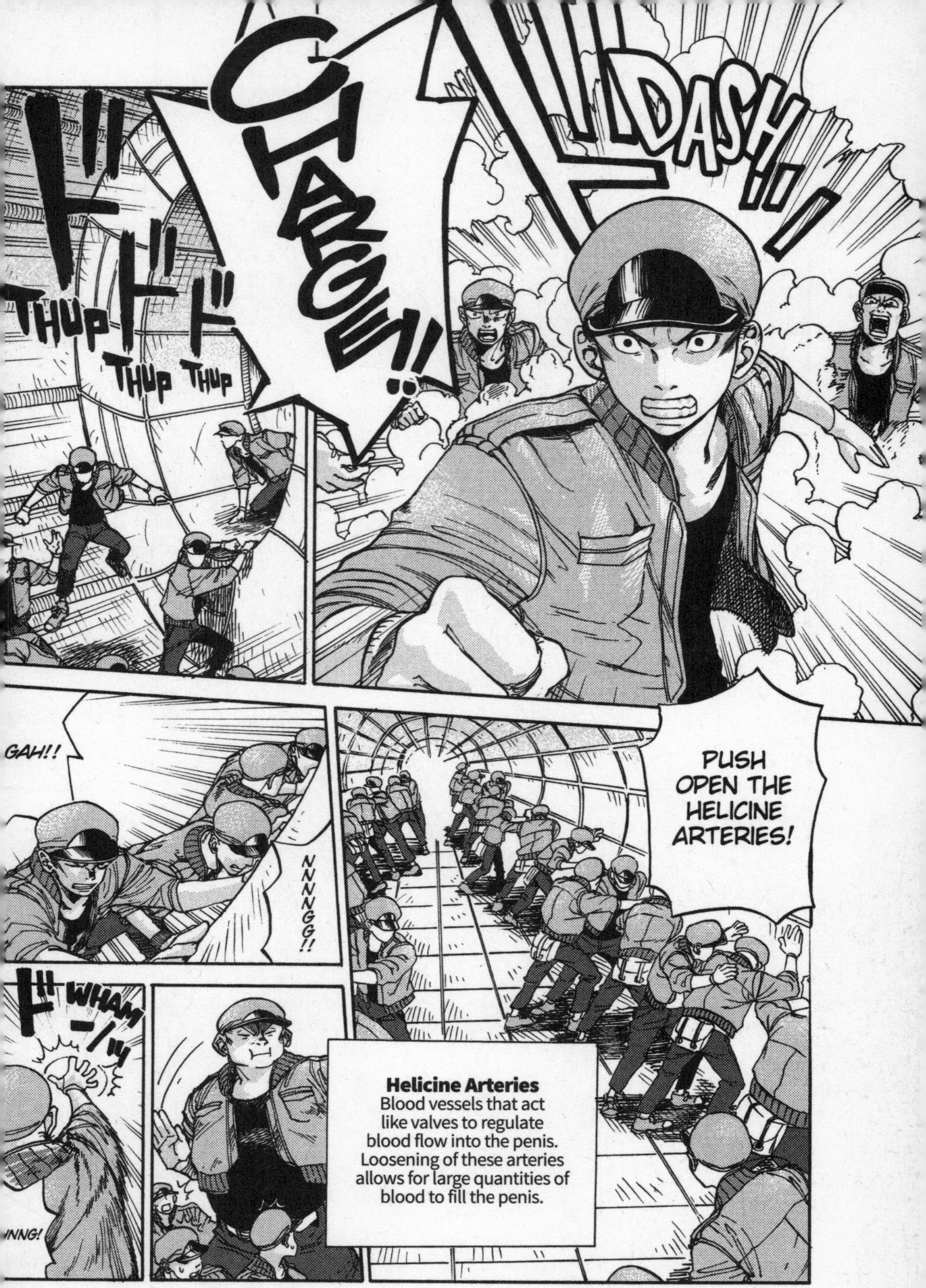
DASH!!
CHARGE!!
ドドド
THUP THUP THUP
PUSH OPEN THE HELICINE ARTERIES!
GAH!!
NNNNGG!!
Helicine Arteries
Blood vessels that act like valves to regulate blood flow into the penis. Loosening of these arteries allows for large quantities of blood to fill the penis.
ド WHAM
NNG!

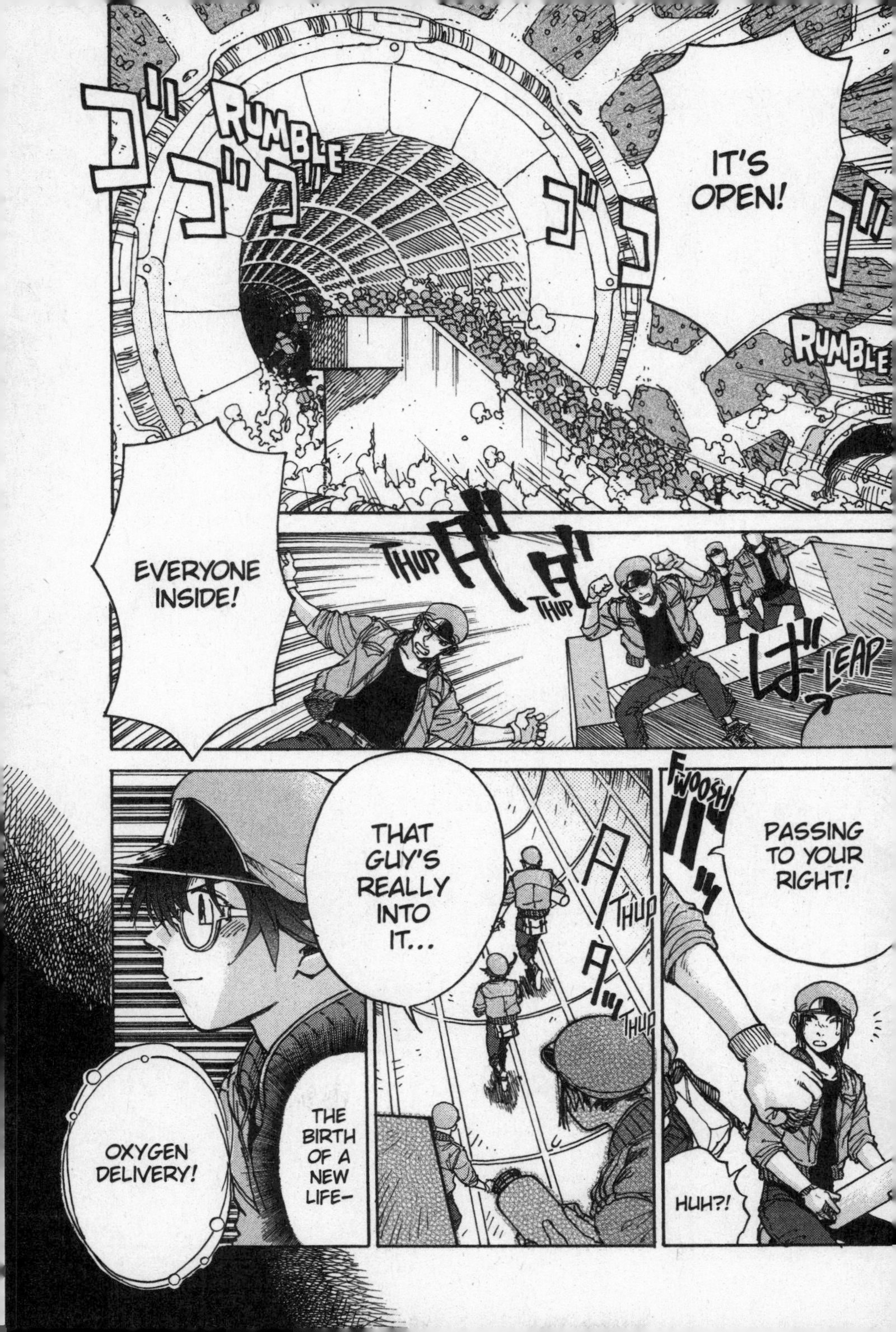
IT'S OPEN!
RUMBLE
RUMBLE
LEAP
THUP
THUP
EVERYONE INSIDE!
FWOOSH
PASSING TO YOUR RIGHT!
HUH?!
THUP
THUP
THAT GUY'S REALLY INTO IT...
THE BIRTH OF A NEW LIFE-
OXYGEN DELIVERY!

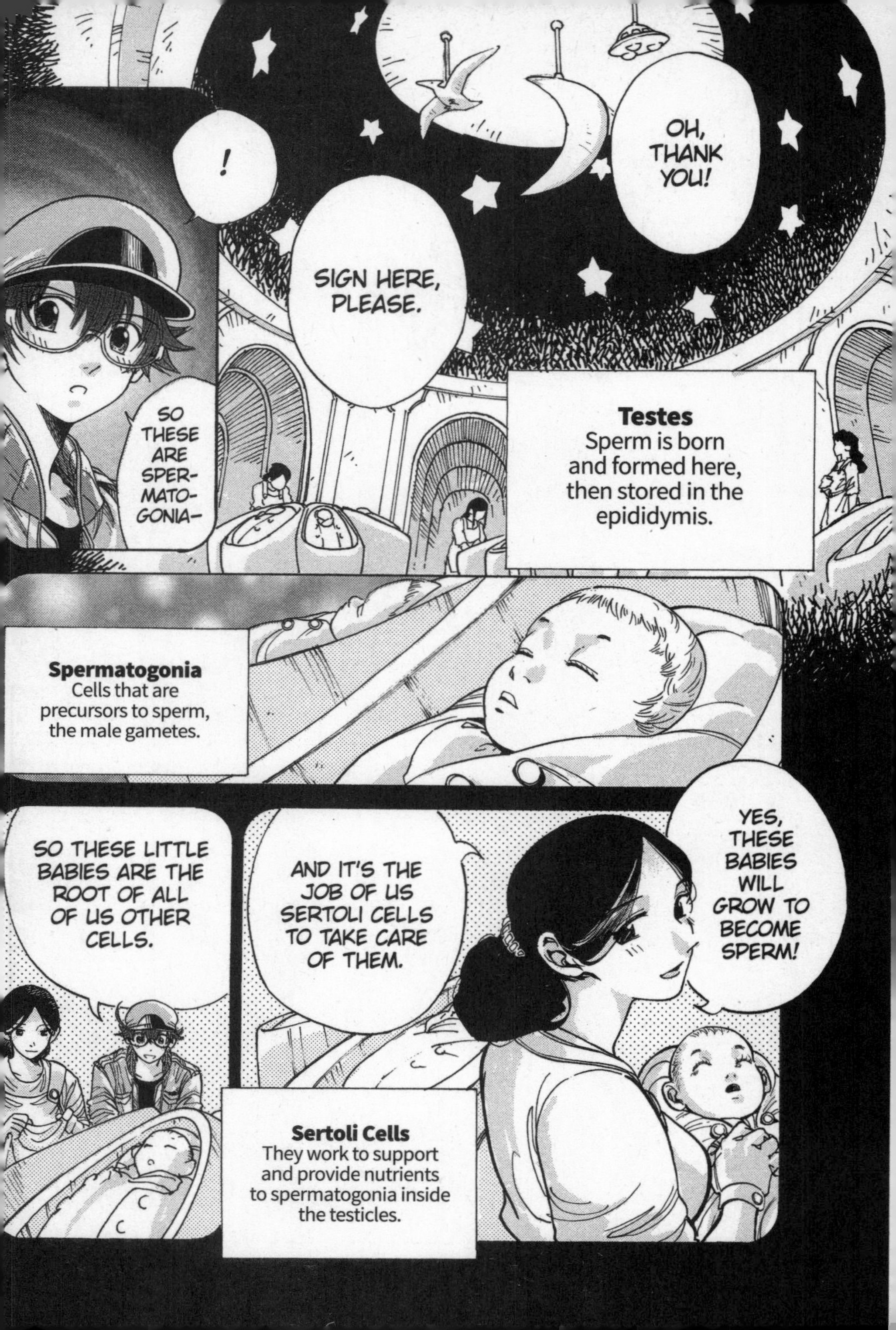
OH, THANK YOU!
SIGN HERE, PLEASE.
Testes
Sperm is born and formed here, then stored in the epididymis.
!
SO THESE ARE SPER-MATO-GONIA—
Spermatogonia
Cells that are precursors to sperm, the male gametes.
YES, THESE BABIES WILL GROW TO BECOME SPERM!
AND IT'S THE JOB OF US SERTOLI CELLS TO TAKE CARE OF THEM.
Sertoli Cells
They work to support and provide nutrients to spermatogonia inside the testicles.
SO THESE LITTLE BABIES ARE THE ROOT OF ALL OF US OTHER CELLS.

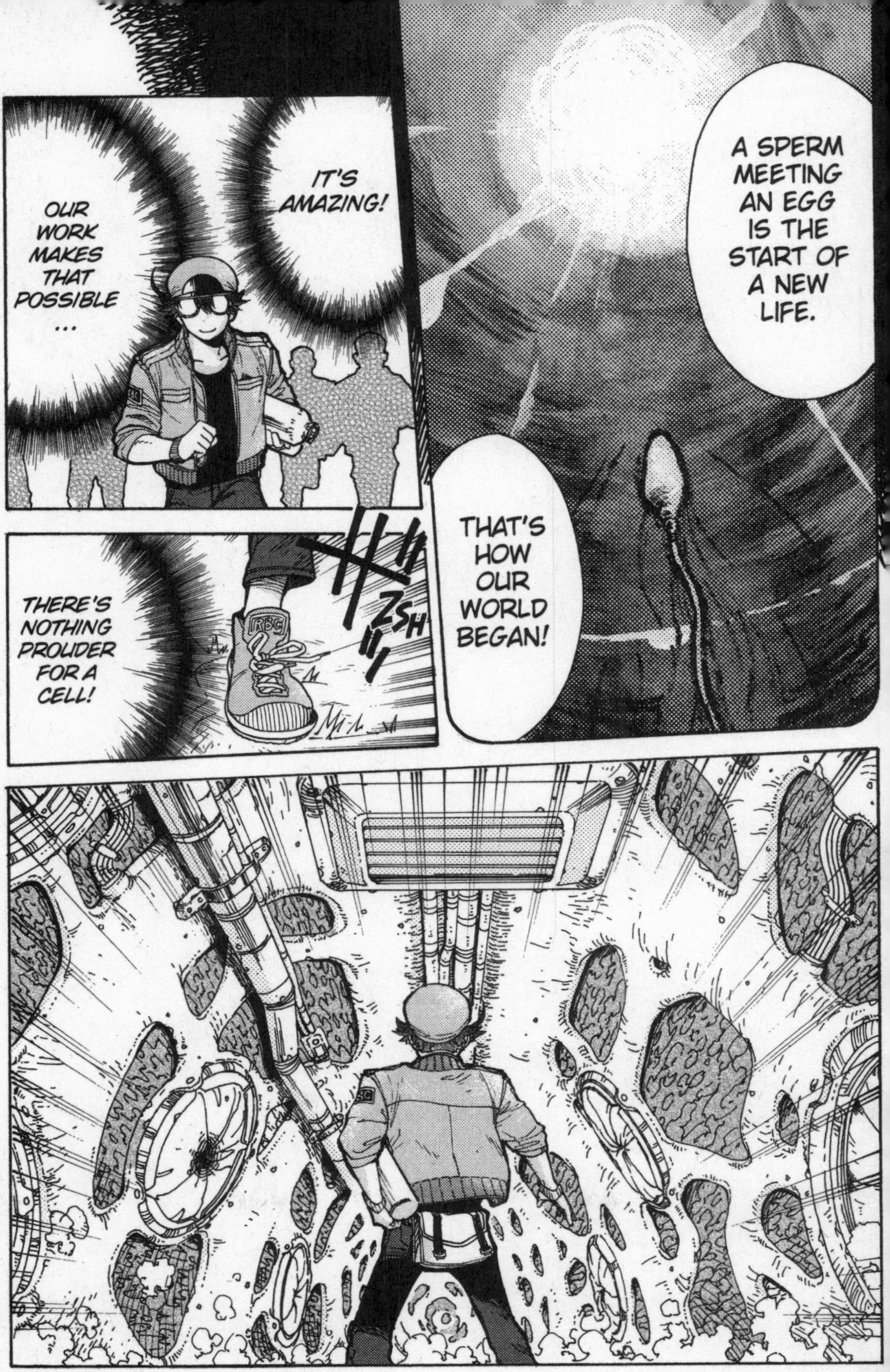
A SPERM MEETING AN EGG IS THE START OF A NEW LIFE.
THAT'S HOW OUR WORLD BEGAN!
IT'S AMAZING!
OUR WORK MAKES THAT POSSIBLE ...
THERE'S NOTHING PROUDER FOR A CELL!
ZSH

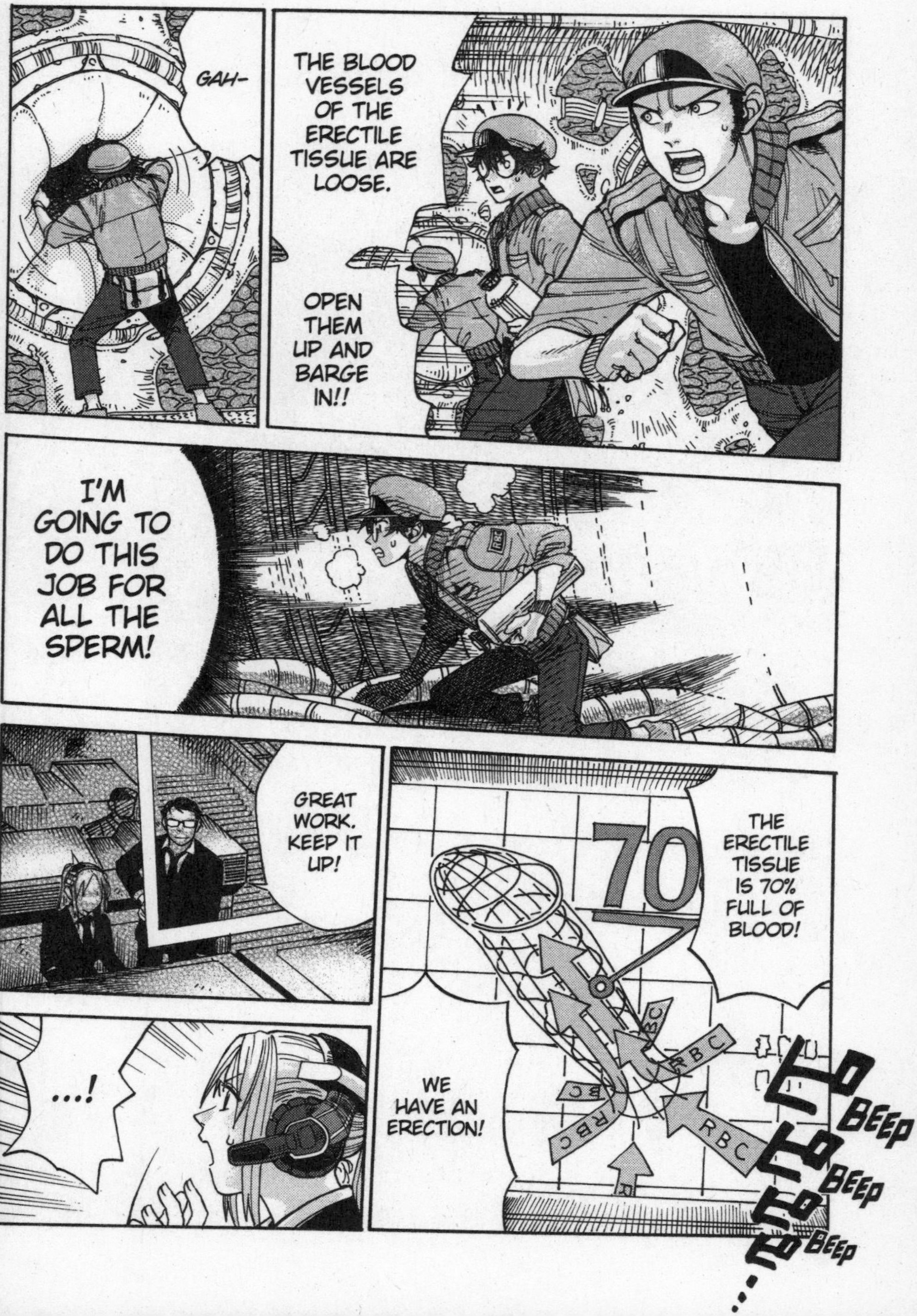
THE BLOOD VESSELS OF THE ERECTILE TISSUE ARE LOOSE.
OPEN THEM UP AND BARGE IN!!
GAH-
I'M GOING TO DO THIS JOB FOR ALL THE SPERM!
THE ERECTILE TISSUE IS 70% FULL OF BLOOD!
70
RBC
WE HAVE AN ERECTION!
BEEP
BEEP
BEEP
GREAT WORK. KEEP IT UP!
...!

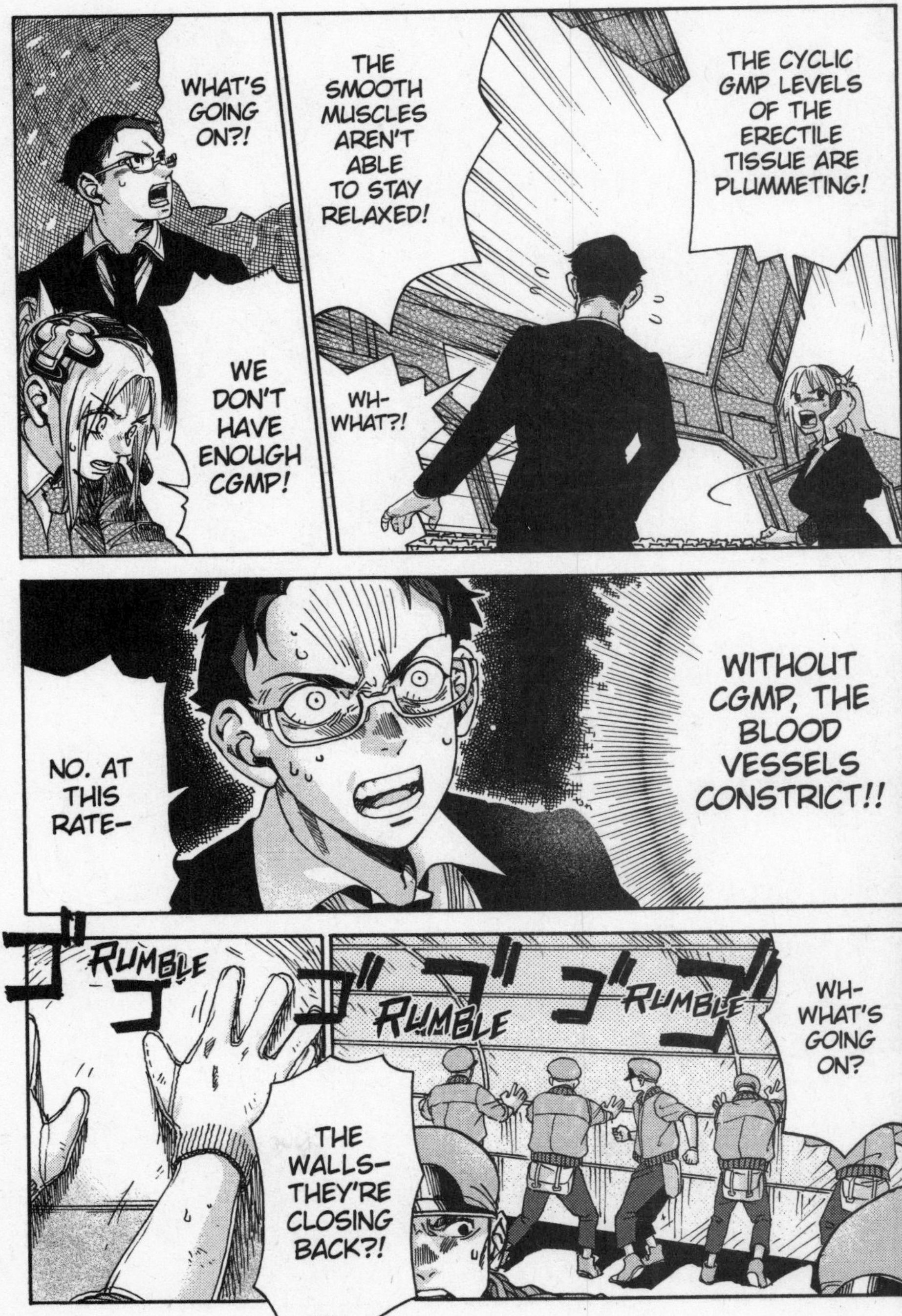
THE CYCLIC GMP LEVELS OF THE ERECTILE TISSUE ARE PLUMMETING!
THE SMOOTH MUSCLES AREN'T ABLE TO STAY RELAXED!
WH- WHAT?!
WHAT'S GOING ON?!
WE DON'T HAVE ENOUGH CGMP!
WITHOUT CGMP, THE BLOOD VESSELS CONSTRICT!!
NO. AT THIS RATE-
ゴ RUMBLE
ゴ RUMBLE
ゴ ゴ RUMBLE
WH- WHAT'S GOING ON?
ゴ ゴ RUMBLE
THE WALLS- THEY'RE CLOSING BACK?!

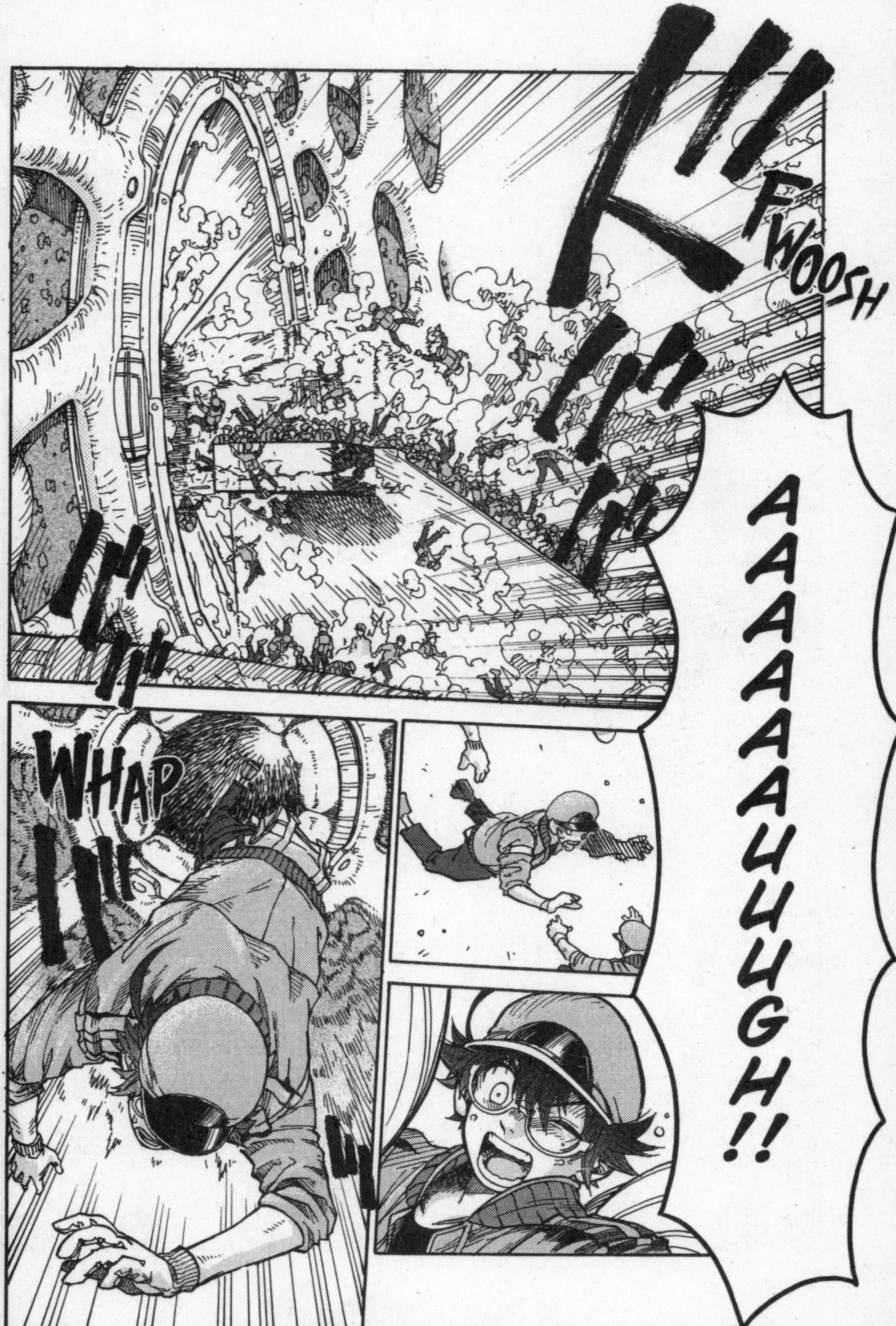
FWOOSH
AAAAAAUUUGH!!
WHAP

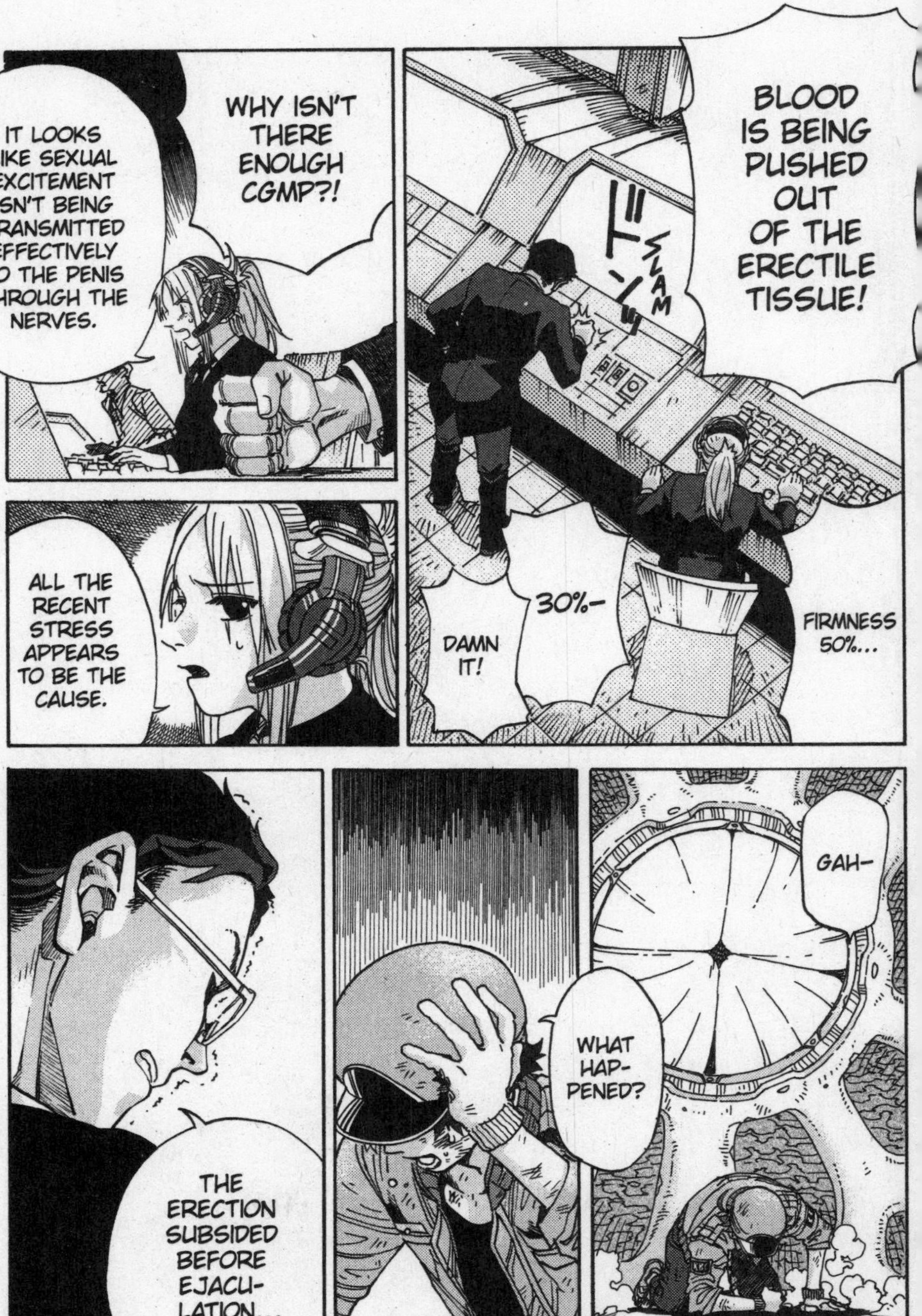
BLOOD IS BEING PUSHED OUT OF THE ERECTILE TISSUE!
SLAM
FIRMNESS 50%...
30%-
DAMN IT!
WHY ISN'T THERE ENOUGH CGMP?!
IT LOOKS LIKE SEXUAL EXCITEMENT ISN'T BEING TRANSMITTED EFFECTIVELY TO THE PENIS THROUGH THE NERVES.
ALL THE RECENT STRESS APPEARS TO BE THE CAUSE.
GAH-
WHAT HAP-PENED?
THE ERECTION SUBSIDED BEFORE EJACU-LATION...

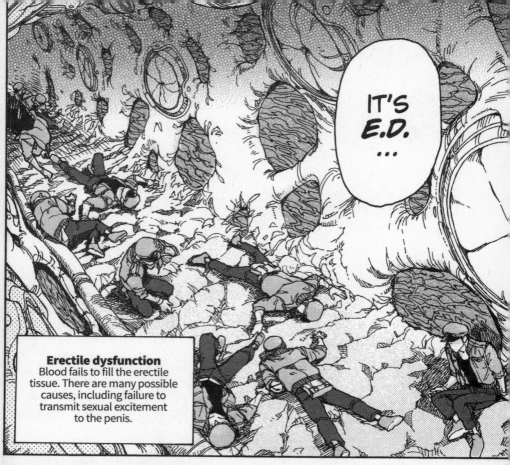

Erectile dysfunction
Blood fails to fill the erectile tissue. There are many possible causes, including failure to transmit sexual excitement to the penis.

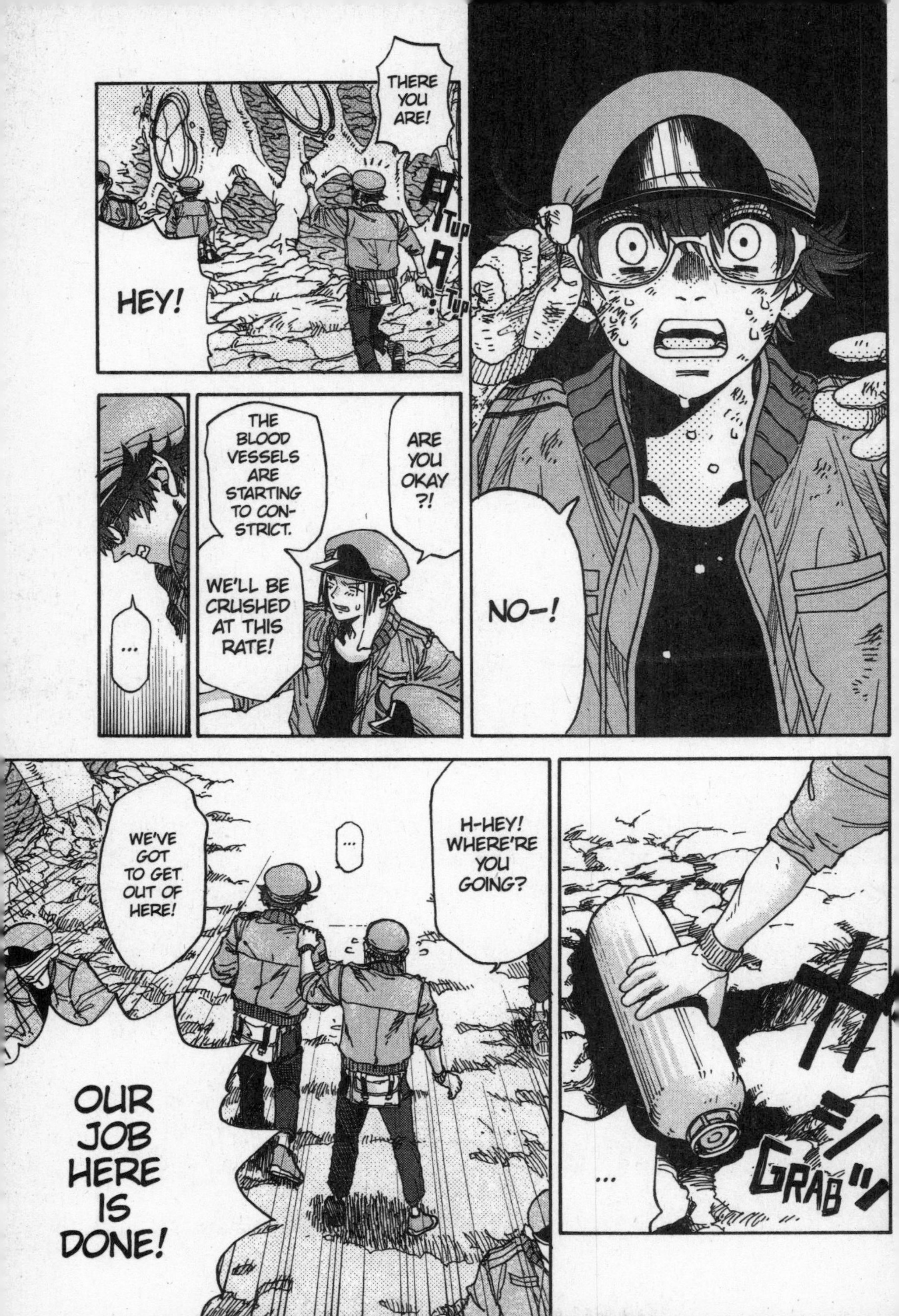
NO--!
THERE YOU ARE!
TUP
TUP
HEY!
ARE YOU OKAY?!
THE BLOOD VESSELS ARE STARTING TO CON-STRICT.
WE'LL BE CRUSHED AT THIS RATE!
...
GRAB
...
H-HEY! WHERE'RE YOU GOING?
...
WE'VE GOT TO GET OUT OF HERE!
OUR JOB HERE IS DONE!

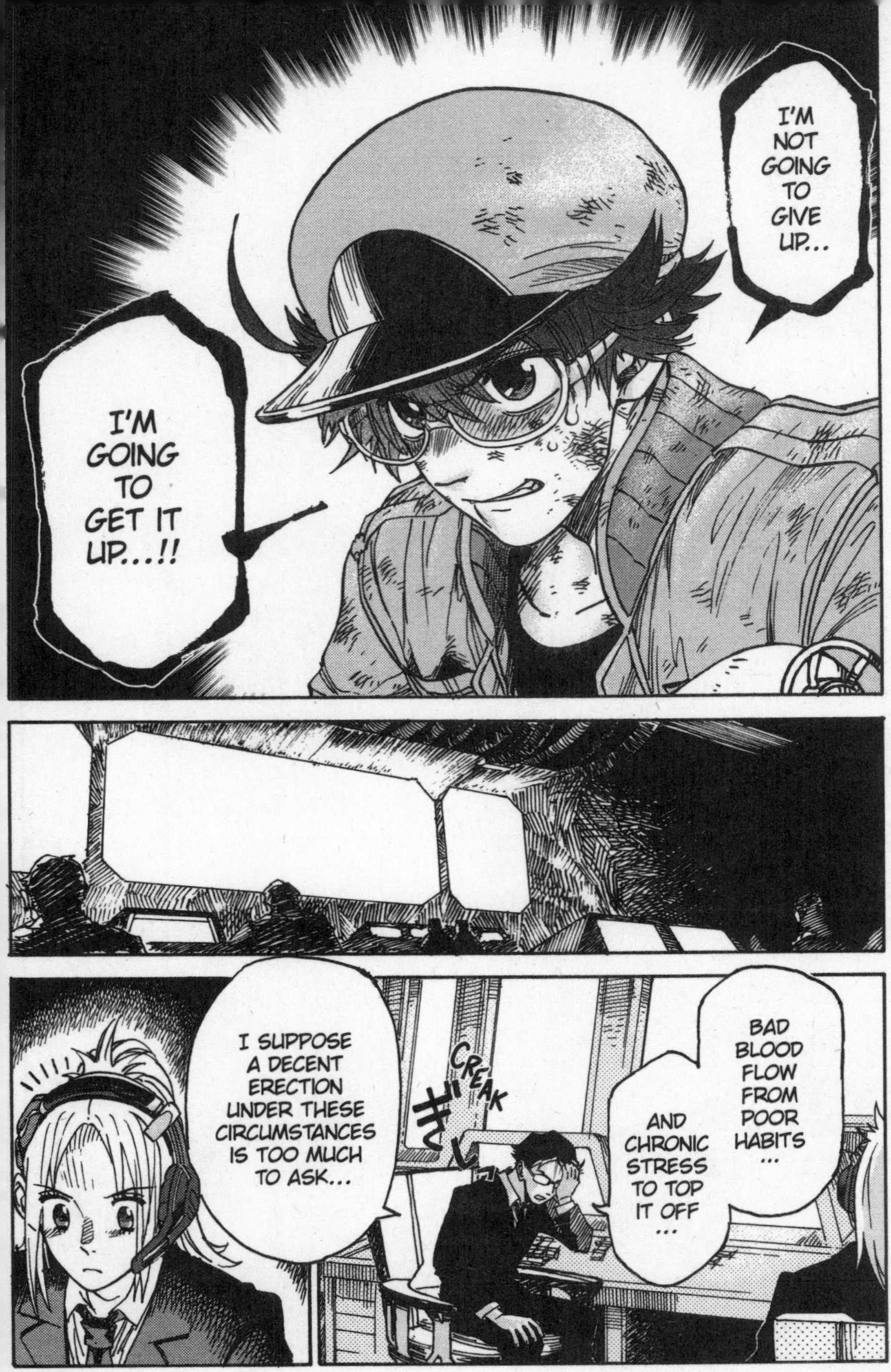
I'M NOT GOING TO GIVE UP...
I'M GOING TO GET IT UP...!!
BAD BLOOD FLOW FROM POOR HABITS ...
AND CHRONIC STRESS TO TOP IT OFF ...
CREAK
ぎし
I SUPPOSE A DECENT ERECTION UNDER THESE CIRCUMSTANCES IS TOO MUCH TO ASK...

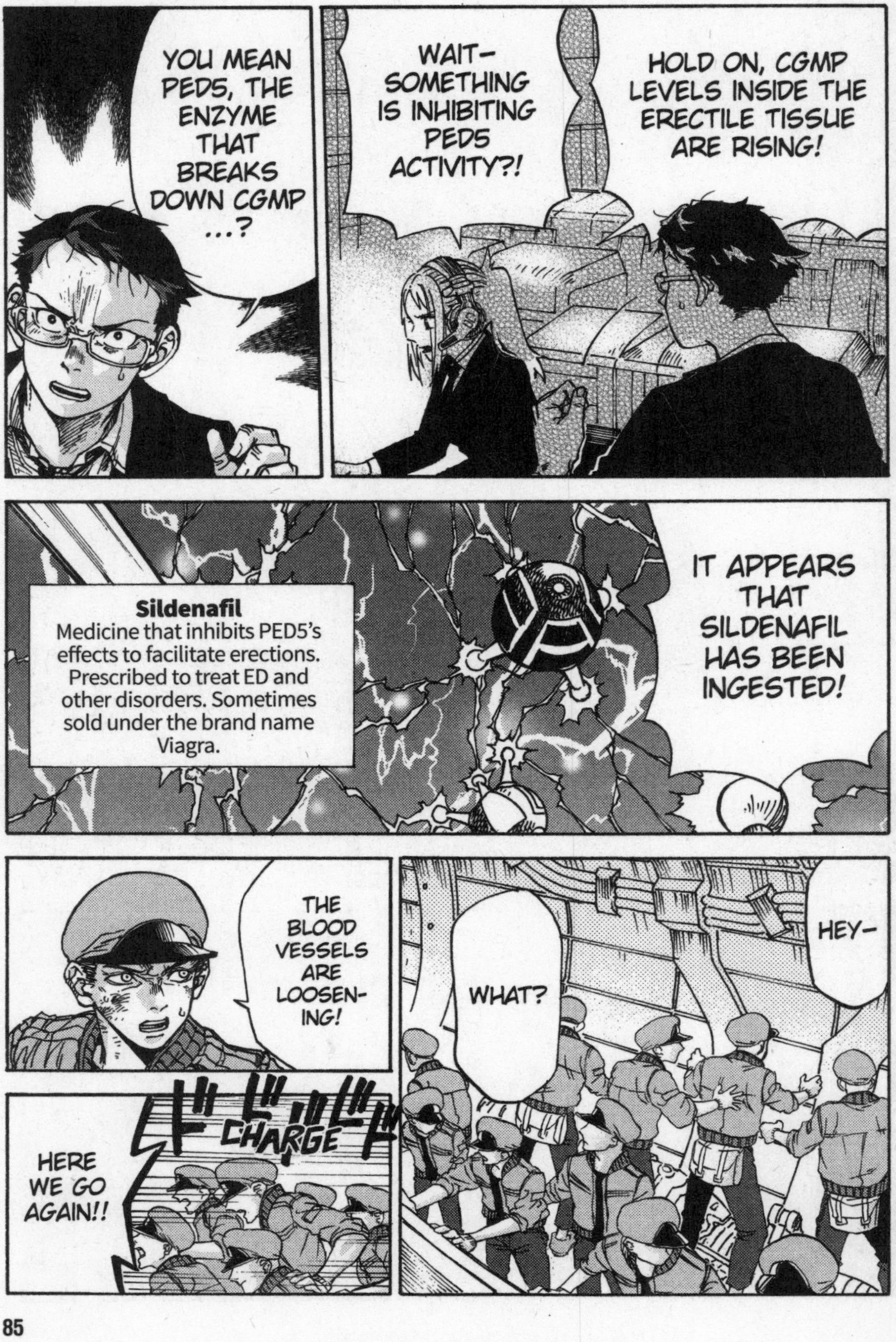
HOLD ON, CGMP LEVELS INSIDE THE ERECTILE TISSUE ARE RISING!
WAIT- SOMETHING IS INHIBITING PED5 ACTIVITY?!
YOU MEAN PED5, THE ENZYME THAT BREAKS DOWN CGMP ...?
IT APPEARS THAT SILDENAFIL HAS BEEN INGESTED!
Sildenafil
Medicine that inhibits PED5's effects to facilitate erections. Prescribed to treat ED and other disorders. Sometimes sold under the brand name Viagra.
HEY-
WHAT?
THE BLOOD VESSELS ARE LOOSEN-ING!
CHARGE
HERE WE GO AGAIN!!

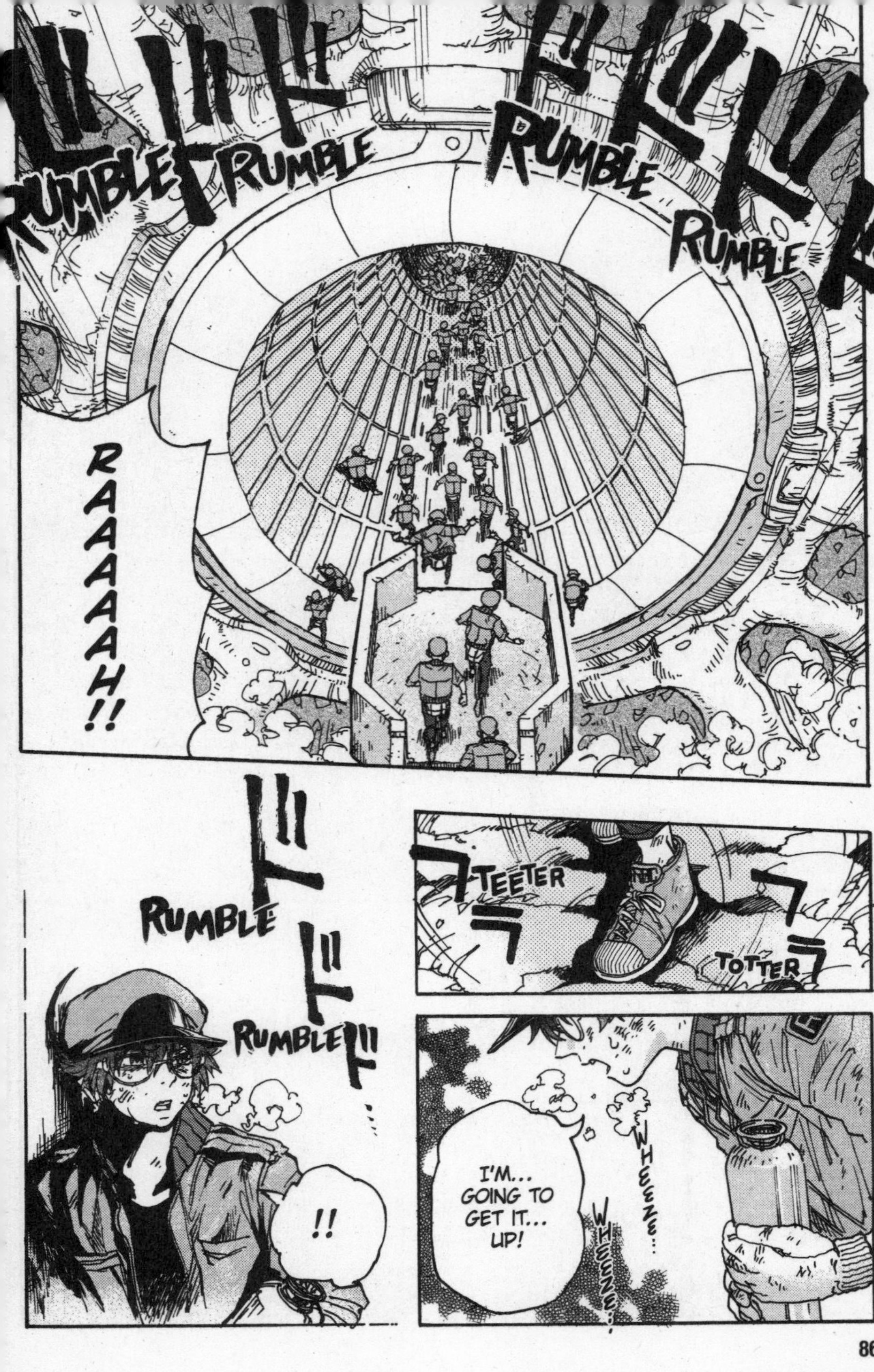
RUMBLE RUMBLE
RUMBLE RUMBLE
RAAAAAAH!!
TEETER
TOTTER
WHEEZE...
WHEEZE...
I'M... GOING TO GET IT... UP!
RUMBLE
RUMBLE!!!
!!

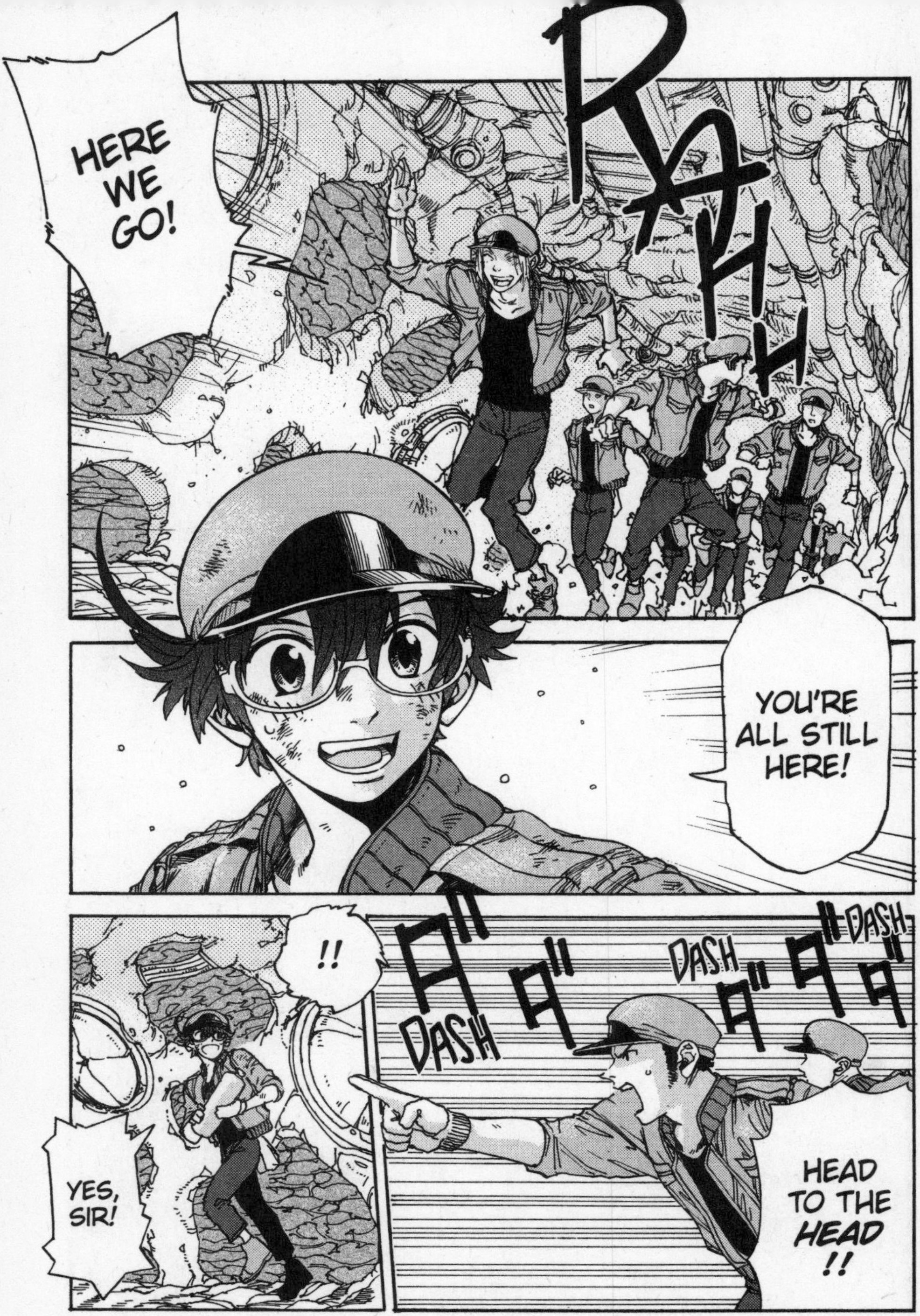
RAHHHH
HERE WE GO!
YOU'RE ALL STILL HERE!
DASH
DASH
DASH
HEAD TO THE HEAD!!
!!
YES, SIR!

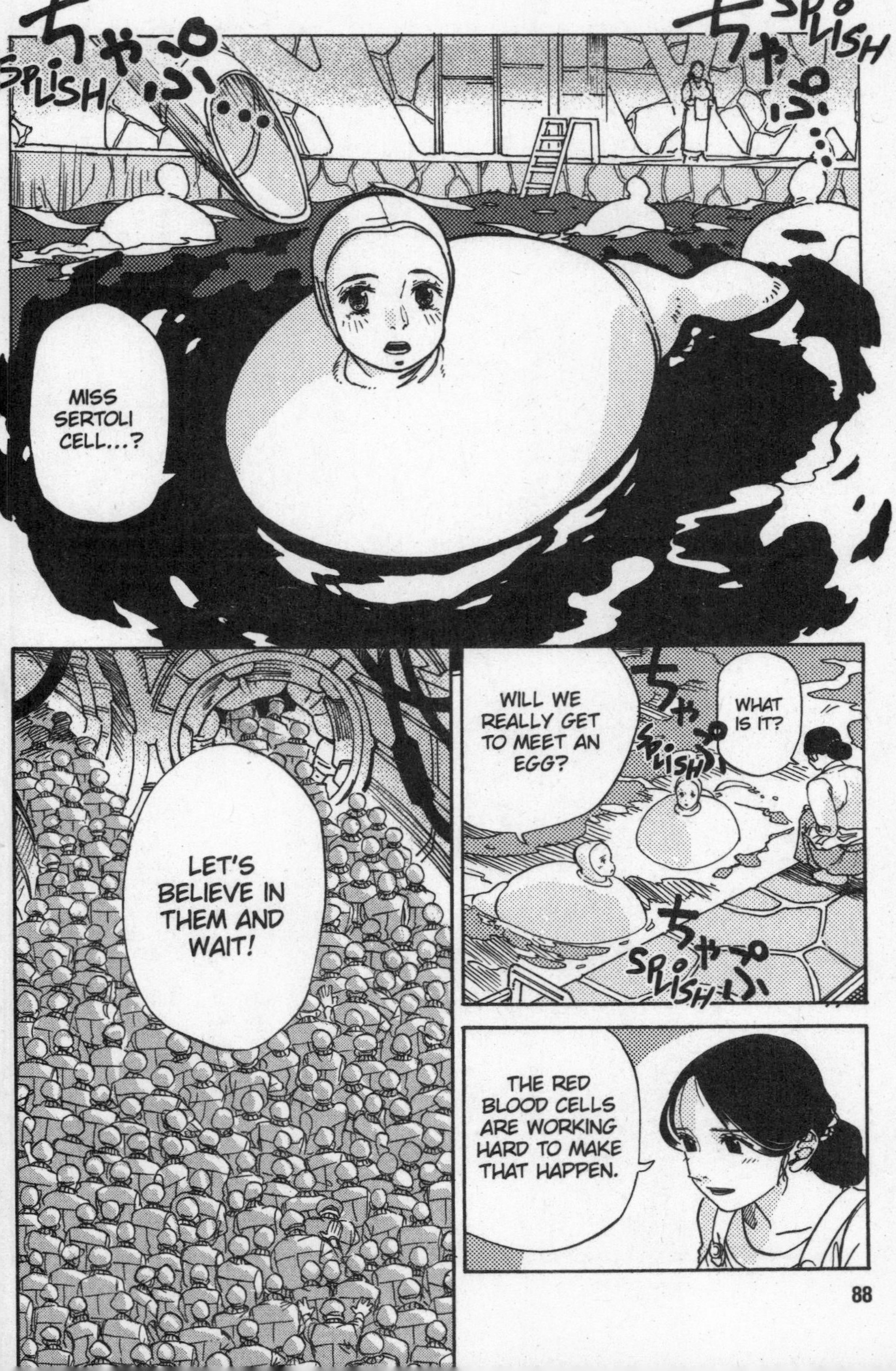
ちゃぷ
SPLISH
...
ちゃぷ
SPLISH
MISS SERTOLI CELL...?
WHAT IS IT?
ちゃぷ
SPLISH
WILL WE REALLY GET TO MEET AN EGG?
ちゃぷ
SPLISH
THE RED BLOOD CELLS ARE WORKING HARD TO MAKE THAT HAPPEN.
LET'S BELIEVE IN THEM AND WAIT!

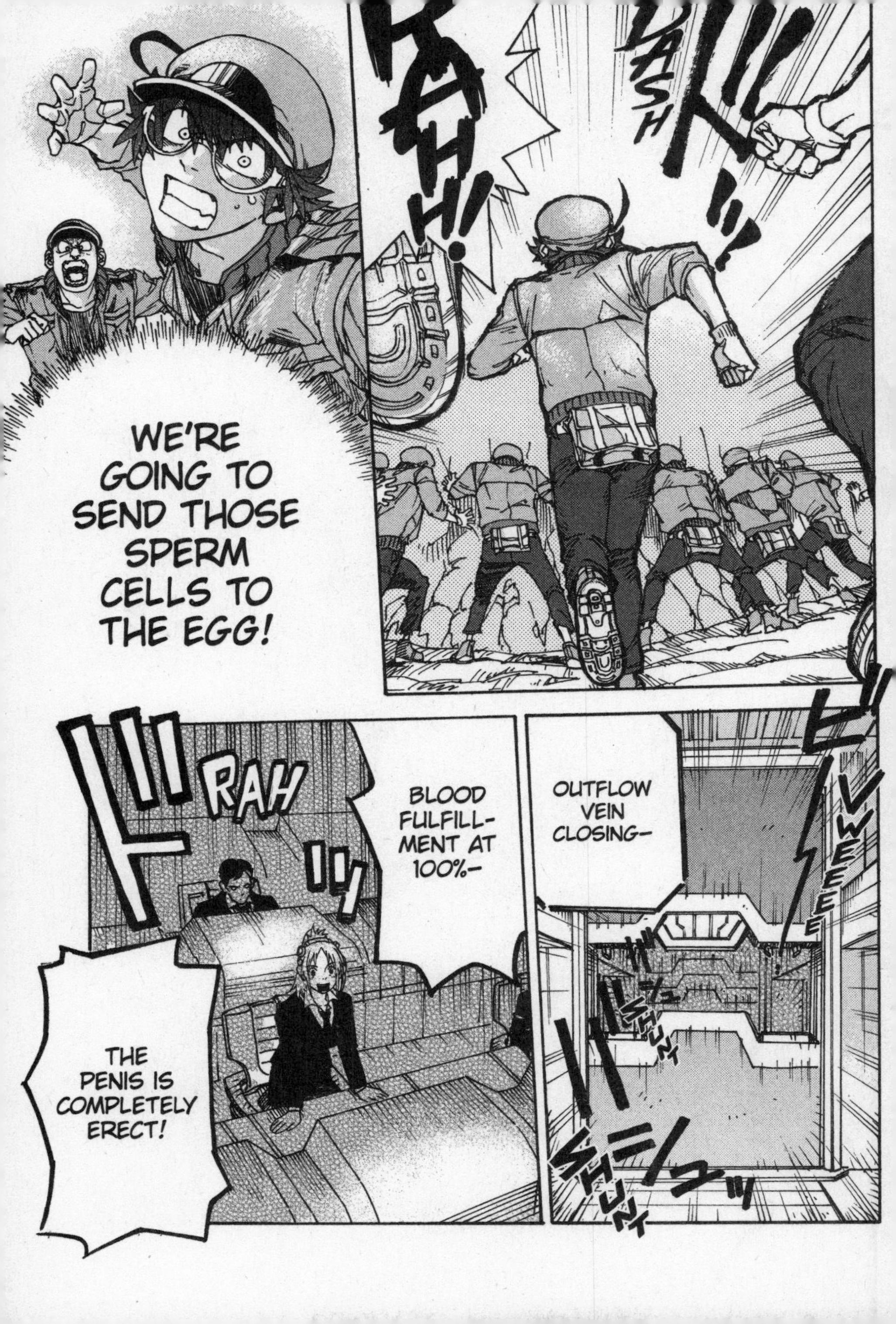
DASH
WAHH!!
WE'RE GOING TO SEND THOSE SPERM CELLS TO THE EGG!
OUTFLOW VEIN CLOSING-
WEEEE
SHUNT
SHUNT
BLOOD FULFILL-MENT AT 100%-
RAH
THE PENIS IS COMPLETELY ERECT!

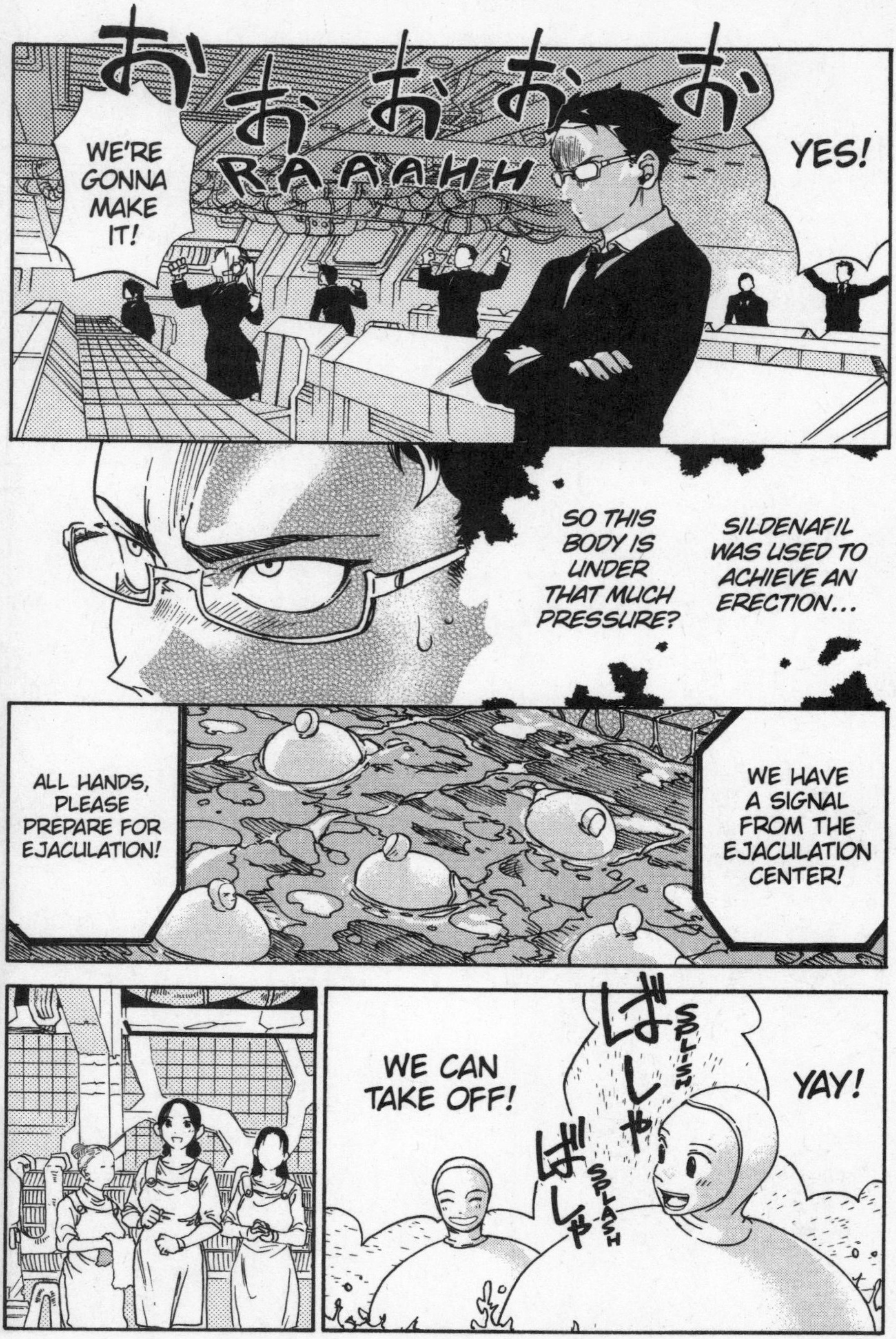
おおおおお
RAAAHH
YES!
WE'RE GONNA MAKE IT!
SILDENAFIL WAS USED TO ACHIEVE AN ERECTION...
SO THIS BODY IS UNDER THAT MUCH PRESSURE?
WE HAVE A SIGNAL FROM THE EJACULATION CENTER!
ALL HANDS, PLEASE PREPARE FOR EJACULATION!
YAY!
ばしゃ
SPLASH
ばしゃ
SPLASH
WE CAN TAKE OFF!

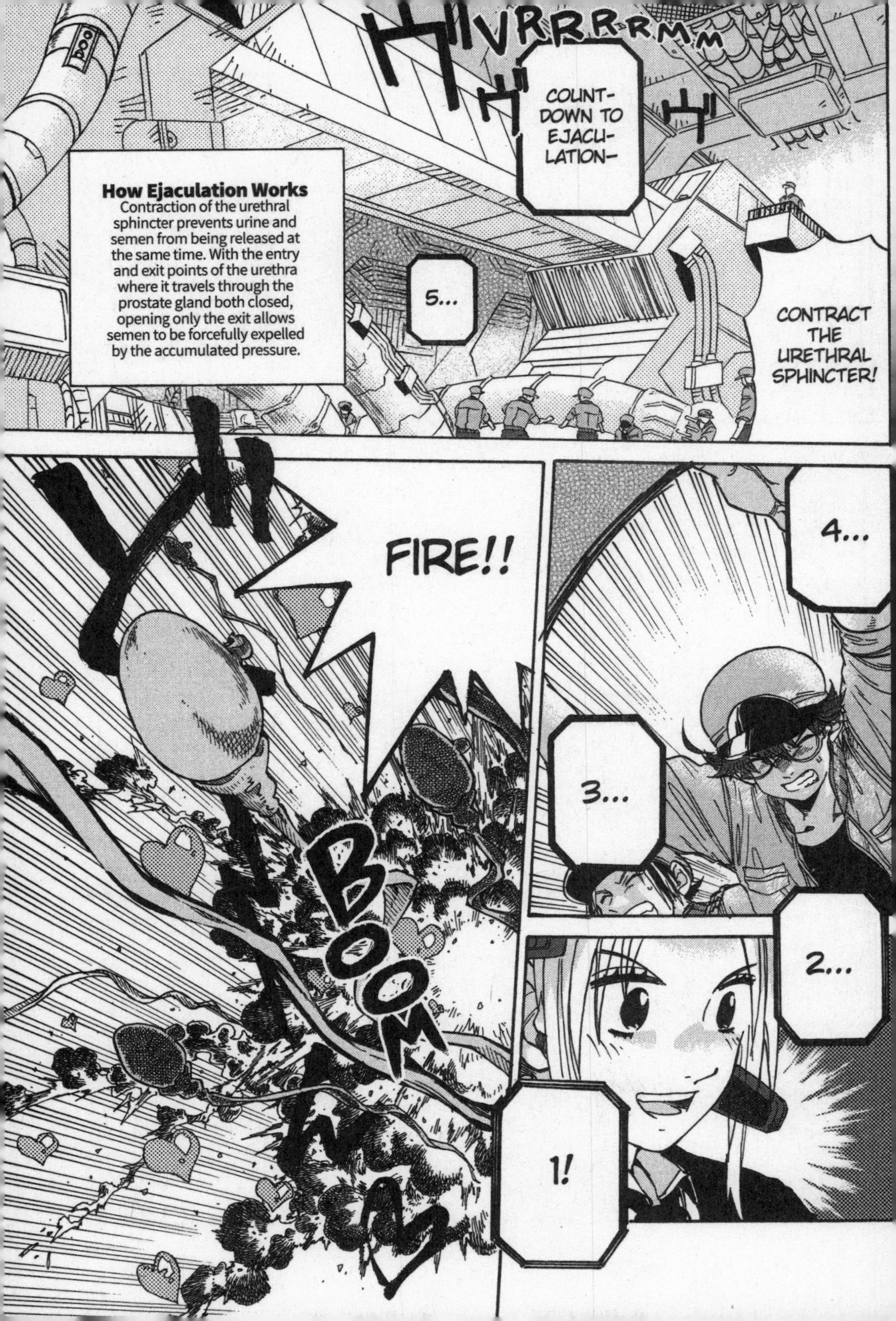
VRRRRRMM
COUNT-DOWN TO EJACULATION-
CONTRACT THE URETHRAL SPHINCTER!
5...
How Ejaculation Works
Contraction of the urethral sphincter prevents urine and semen from being released at the same time. With the entry and exit points of the urethra where it travels through the prostate gland both closed, opening only the exit allows semen to be forcefully expelled by the accumulated pressure.
4...
3...
2...
1!
FIRE!!
BOOM

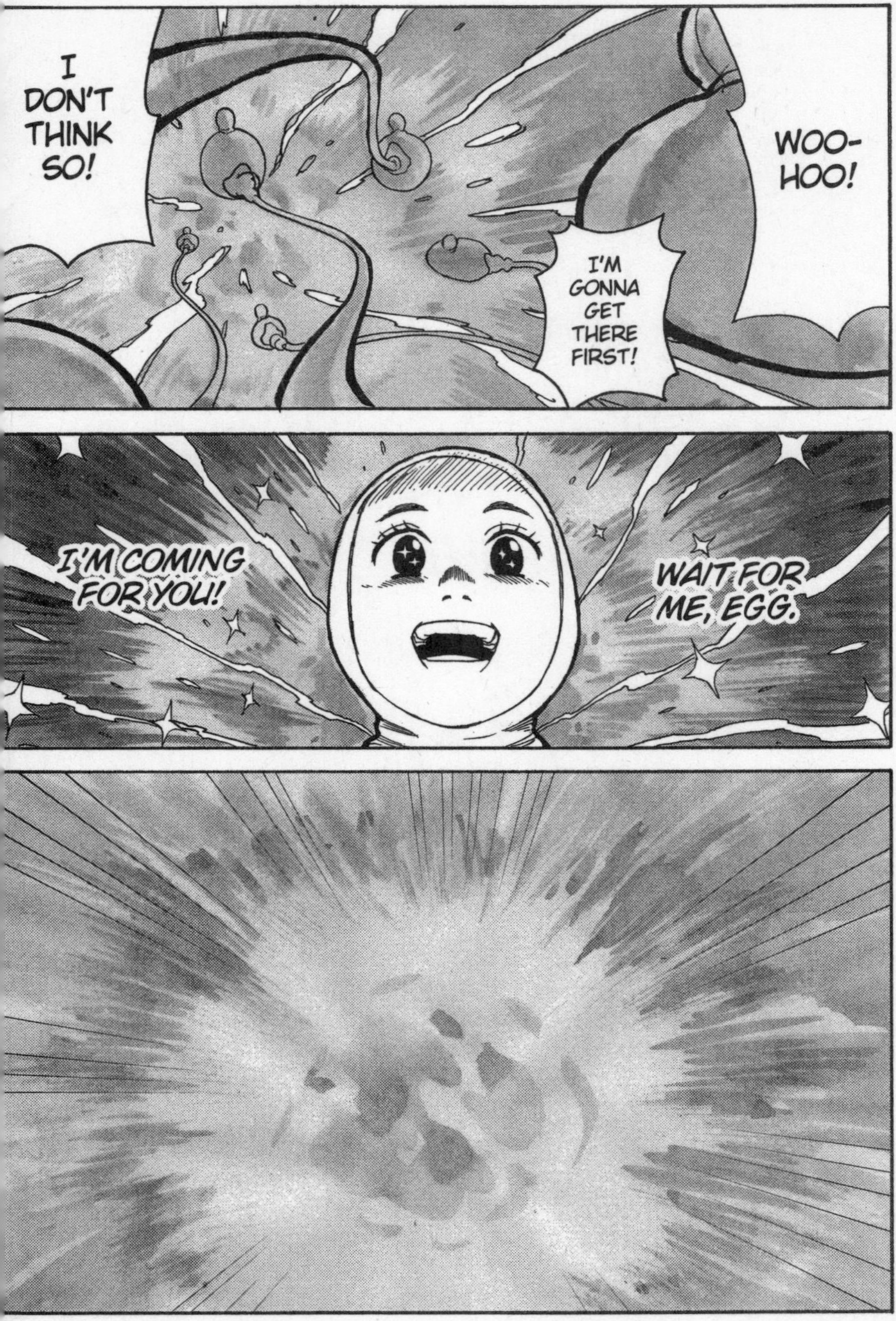
WOO-HOO!
I'M GONNA GET THERE FIRST!
I DON'T THINK SO!
WAIT FOR ME, EGG.
I'M COMING FOR YOU!

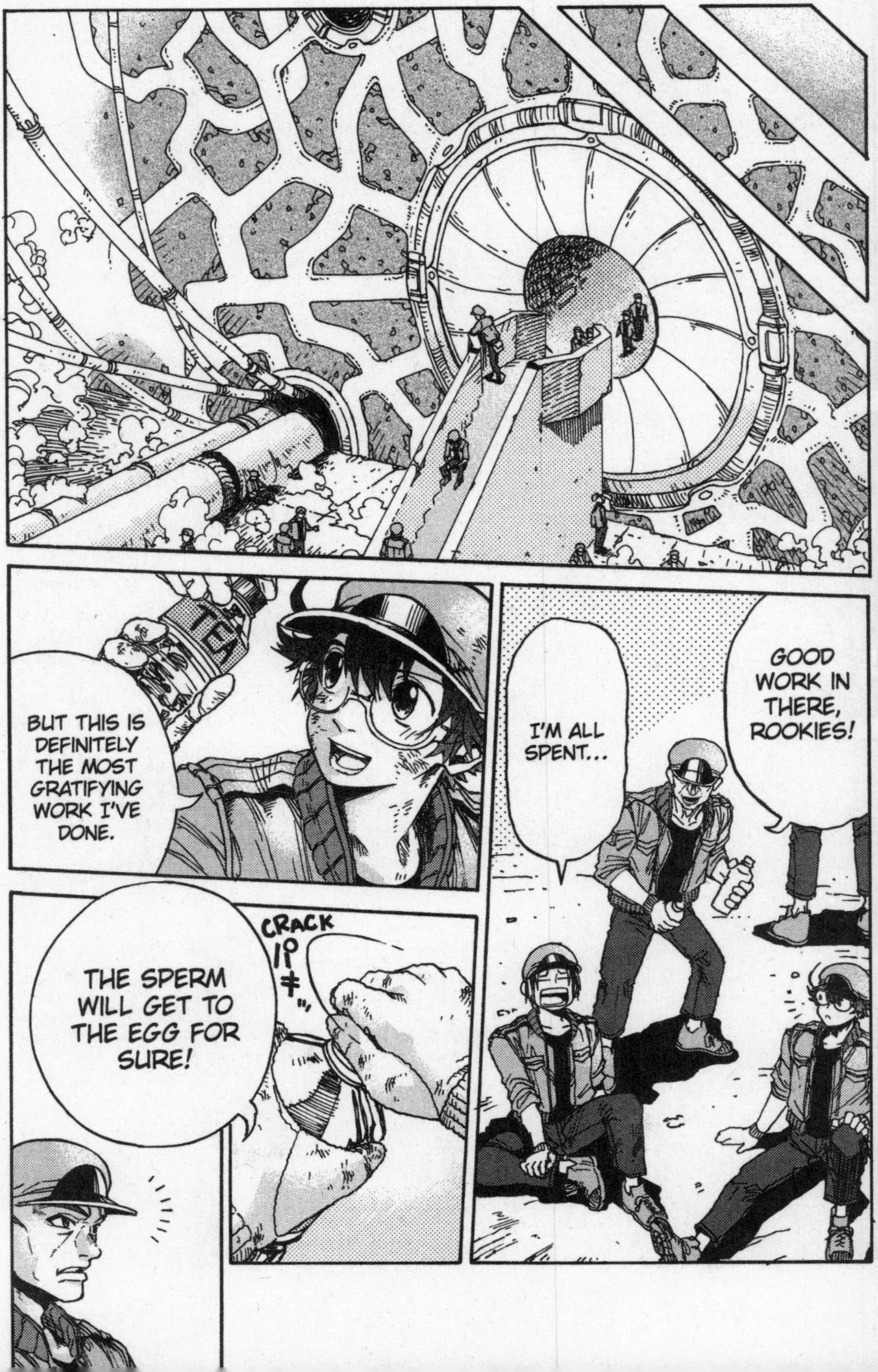
GOOD WORK IN THERE, ROOKIES!
I'M ALL SPENT...
BUT THIS IS DEFINITELY THE MOST GRATIFYING WORK I'VE DONE.
CRACK
THE SPERM WILL GET TO THE EGG FOR SURE!

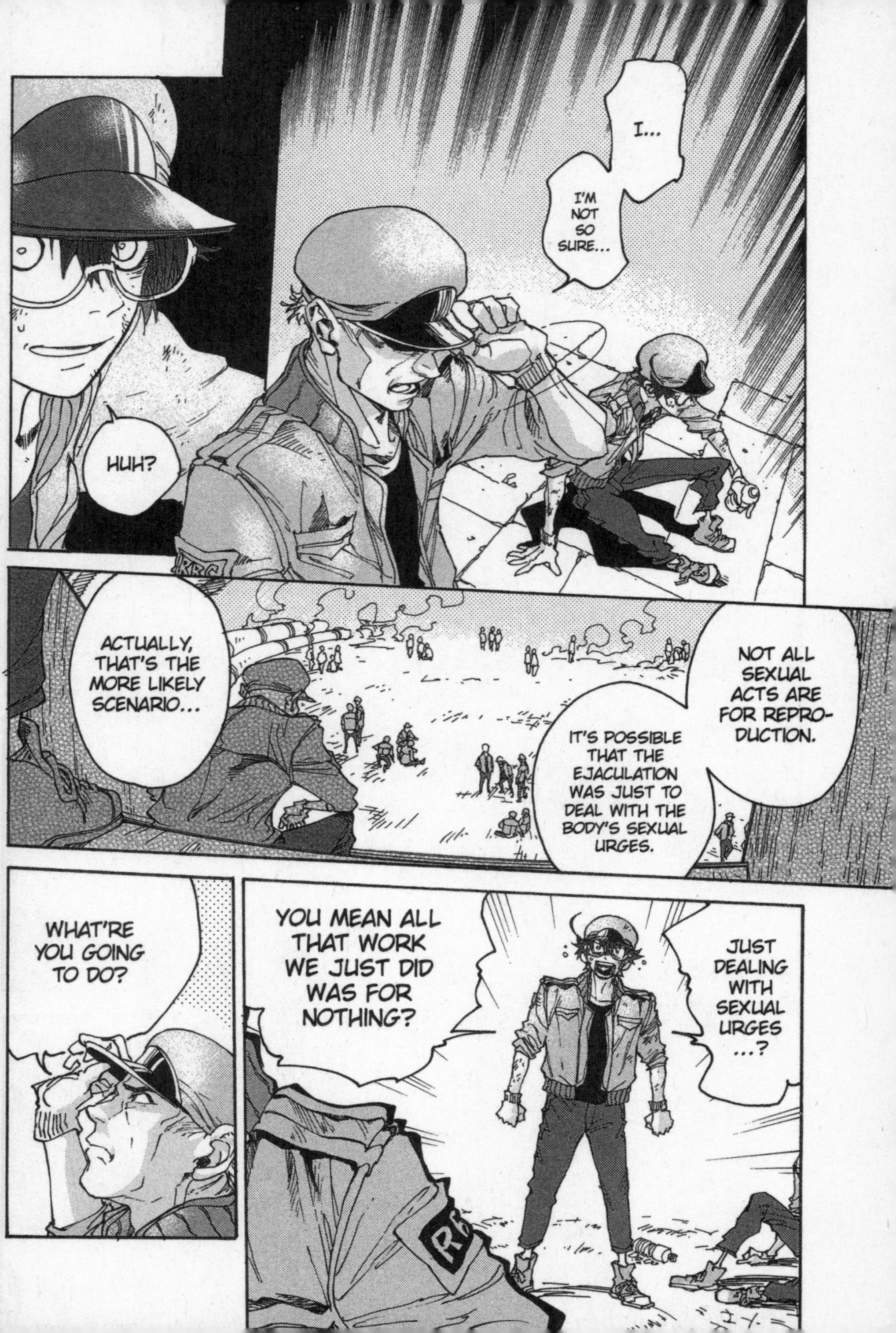
I...
I'M NOT SO SURE...
HUH?
NOT ALL SEXUAL ACTS ARE FOR REPRODUCTION.
IT'S POSSIBLE THAT THE EJACULATION WAS JUST TO DEAL WITH THE BODY'S SEXUAL URGES.
ACTUALLY, THAT'S THE MORE LIKELY SCENARIO...
JUST DEALING WITH SEXUAL URGES ...?
YOU MEAN ALL THAT WORK WE JUST DID WAS FOR NOTHING?
WHAT'RE YOU GOING TO DO?

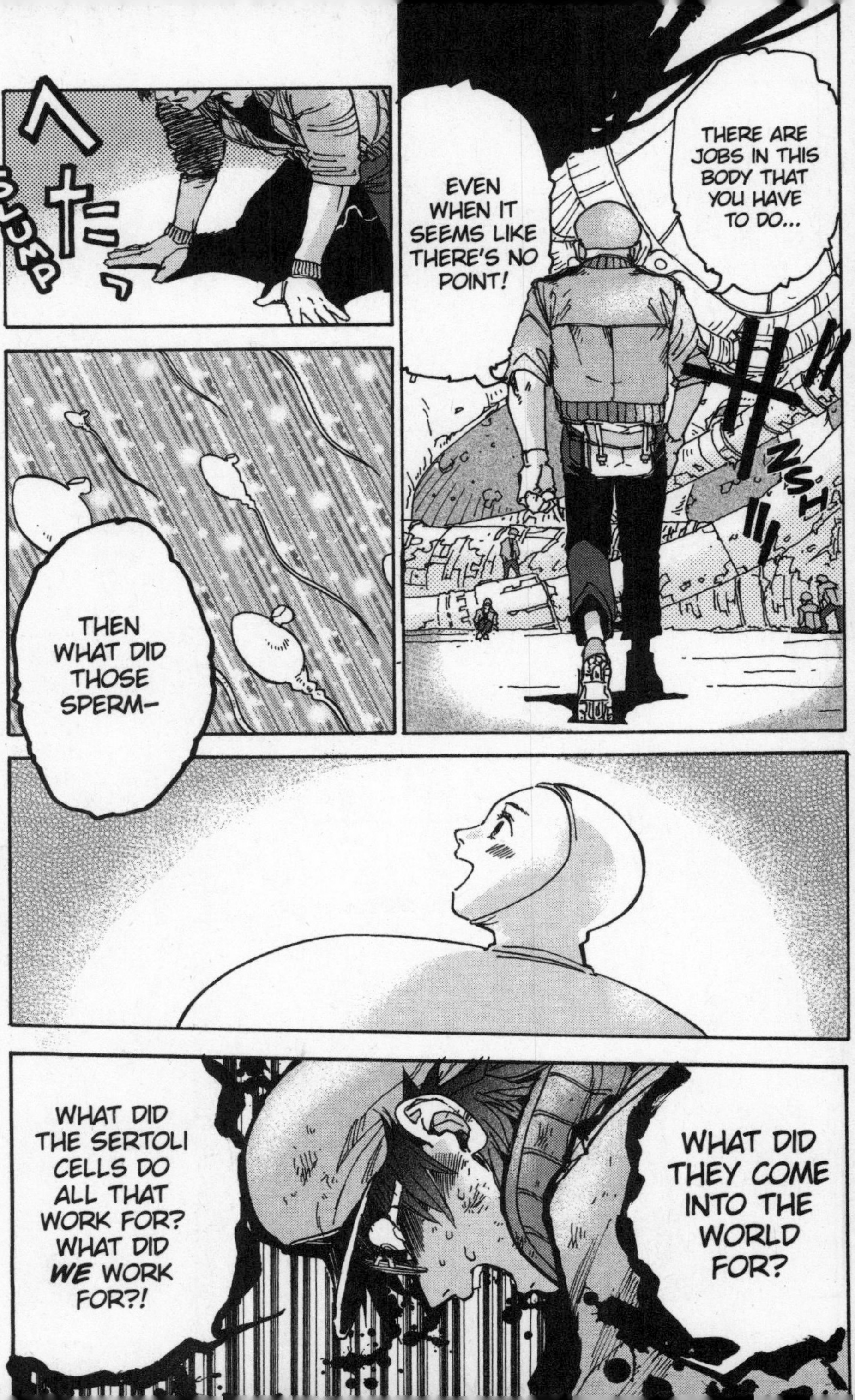
THERE ARE JOBS IN THIS BODY THAT YOU HAVE TO DO...
EVEN WHEN IT SEEMS LIKE THERE'S NO POINT!
ZSH
SLUMP
THEN WHAT DID THOSE SPERM-
WHAT DID THEY COME INTO THE WORLD FOR?
WHAT DID THE SERTOLI CELLS DO ALL THAT WORK FOR? WHAT DID *WE* WORK FOR?!

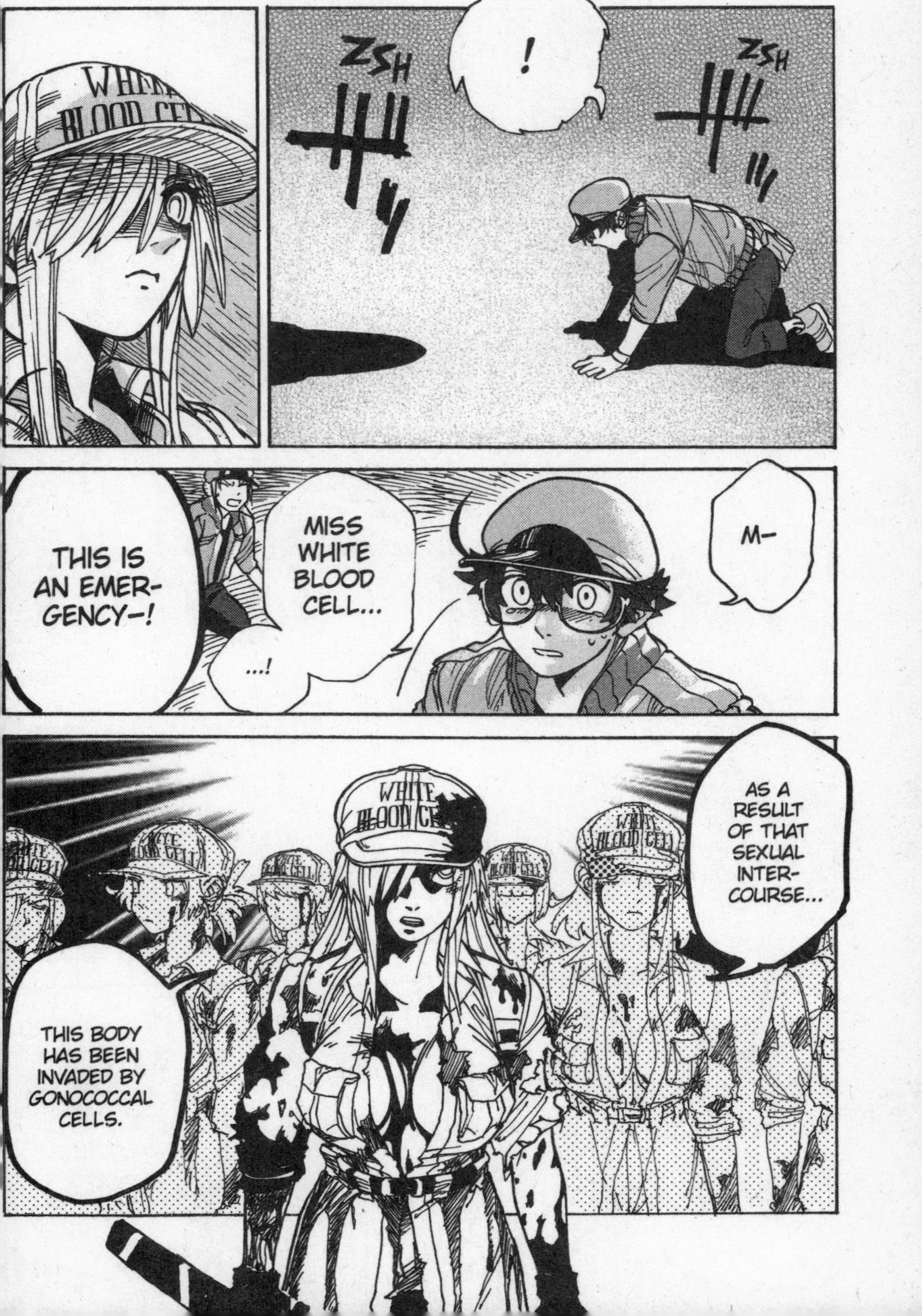
ZSH
!
ZSH
M-
MISS WHITE BLOOD CELL...
...!
THIS IS AN EMERGENCY-!
AS A RESULT OF THAT SEXUAL INTERCOURSE...
THIS BODY HAS BEEN INVADED BY GONOCOCCAL CELLS.

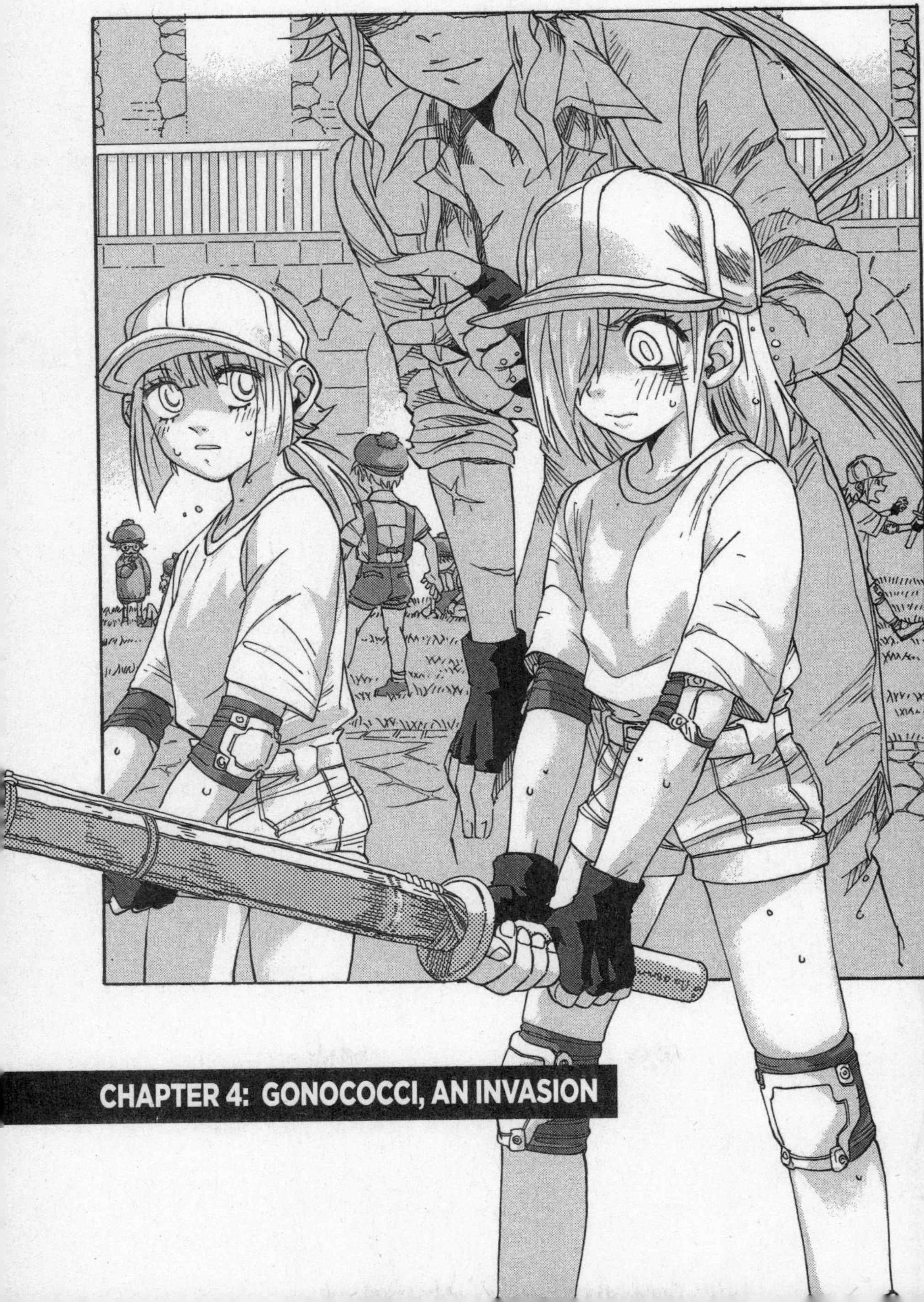
CHAPTER 4: GONOCOCCI, AN INVASION

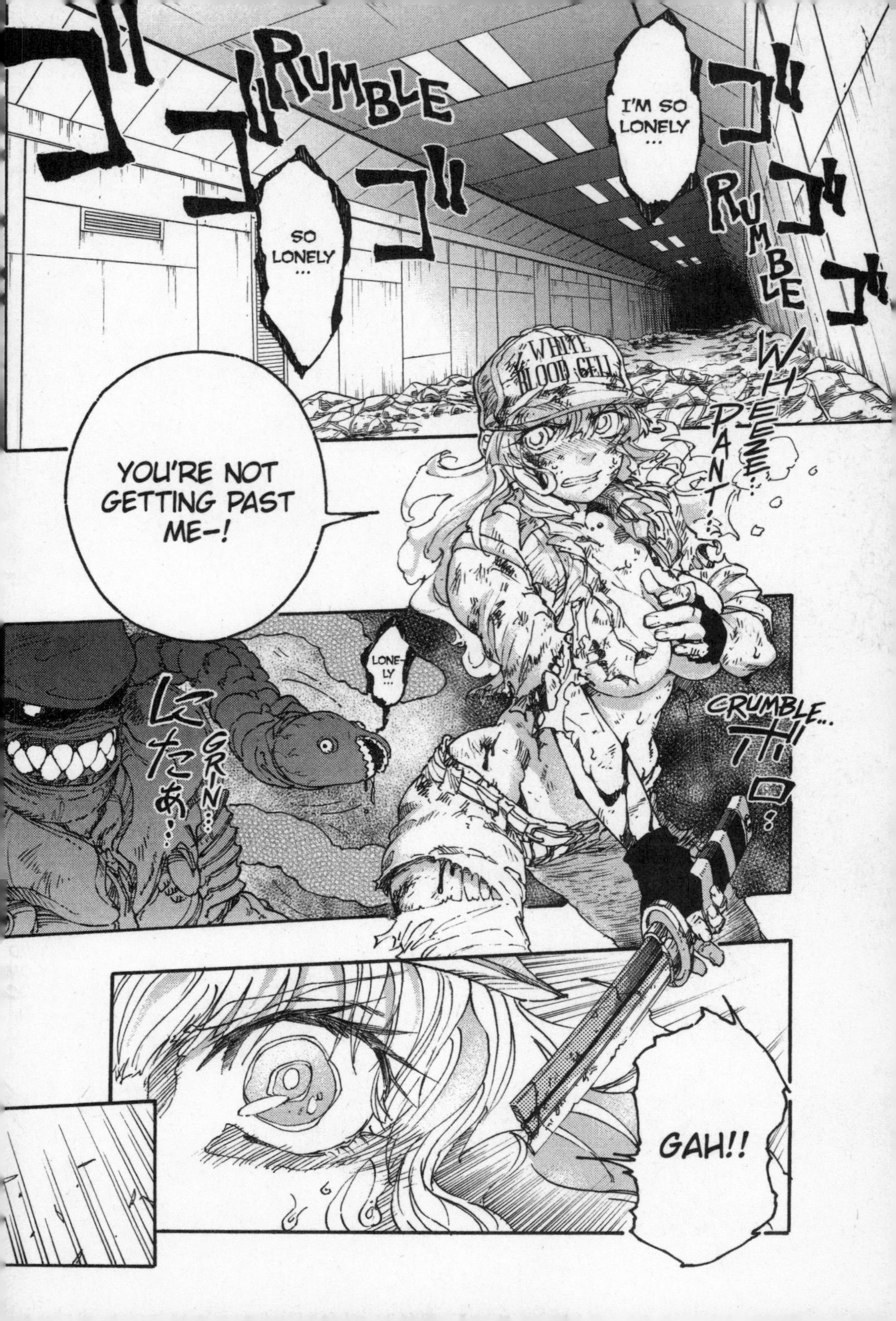
RUMBLE
I'M SO LONELY ...
RUMBLE
SO LONELY ...
WHEEZE...
PANT...
YOU'RE NOT GETTING PAST ME-!
CRUMBLE...
LONE-LY ...
GRIN...
にたぁ…
GAH!!

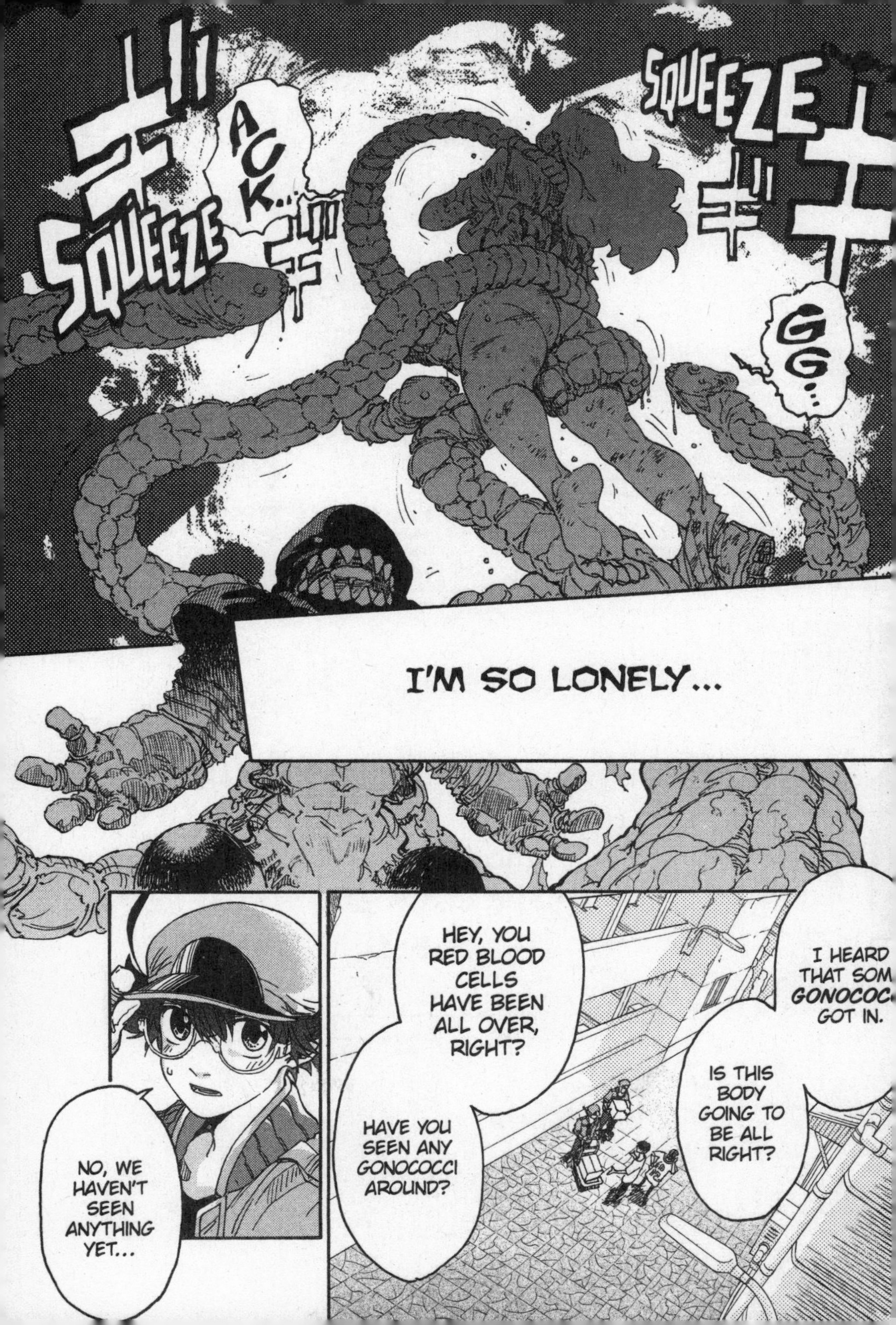
SQUEEZE
GG...
SQUEEZE
ACK...
I'M SO LONELY...
I HEARD THAT SOM GONOCOC GOT IN.
IS THIS BODY GOING TO BE ALL RIGHT?
HEY, YOU RED BLOOD CELLS HAVE BEEN ALL OVER, RIGHT?
HAVE YOU SEEN ANY GONOCOCCI AROUND?
NO, WE HAVEN'T SEEN ANYTHING YET...

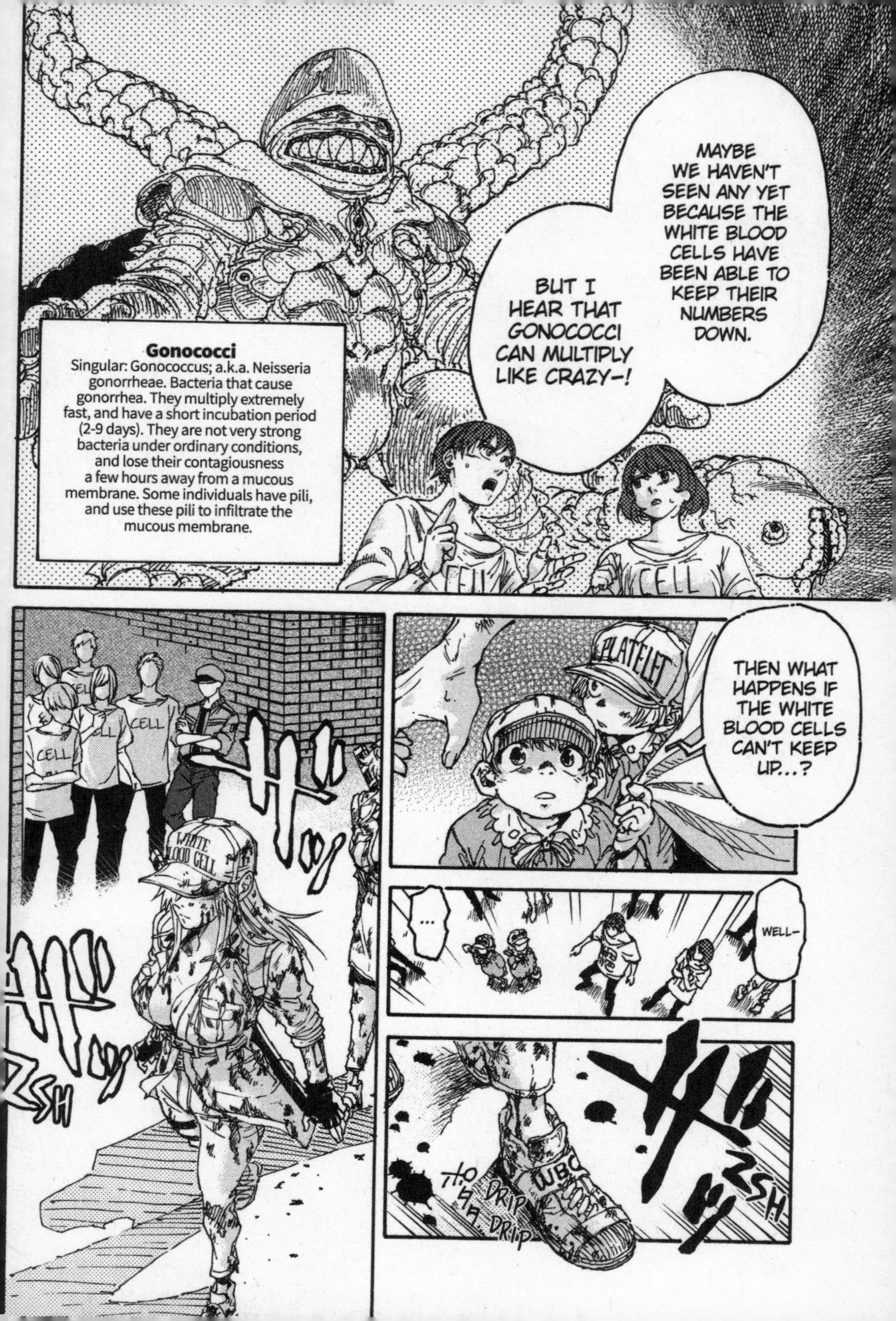
MAYBE WE HAVEN'T SEEN ANY YET BECAUSE THE WHITE BLOOD CELLS HAVE BEEN ABLE TO KEEP THEIR NUMBERS DOWN.
BUT I HEAR THAT GONOCOCCI CAN MULTIPLY LIKE CRAZY–!
Gonococci
Singular: Gonococcus; a.k.a. Neisseria gonorrheae. Bacteria that cause gonorrhea. They multiply extremely fast, and have a short incubation period (2-9 days). They are not very strong bacteria under ordinary conditions, and lose their contagiousness a few hours away from a mucous membrane. Some individuals have pili, and use these pili to infiltrate the mucous membrane.
CELL
CELL
PLATELET
THEN WHAT HAPPENS IF THE WHITE BLOOD CELLS CAN'T KEEP UP...?
WELL–
...
ZSH
DRIP
DRIP
WBC
WHITE BLOOD CELL
CELL
CELL
CELL
ZSH

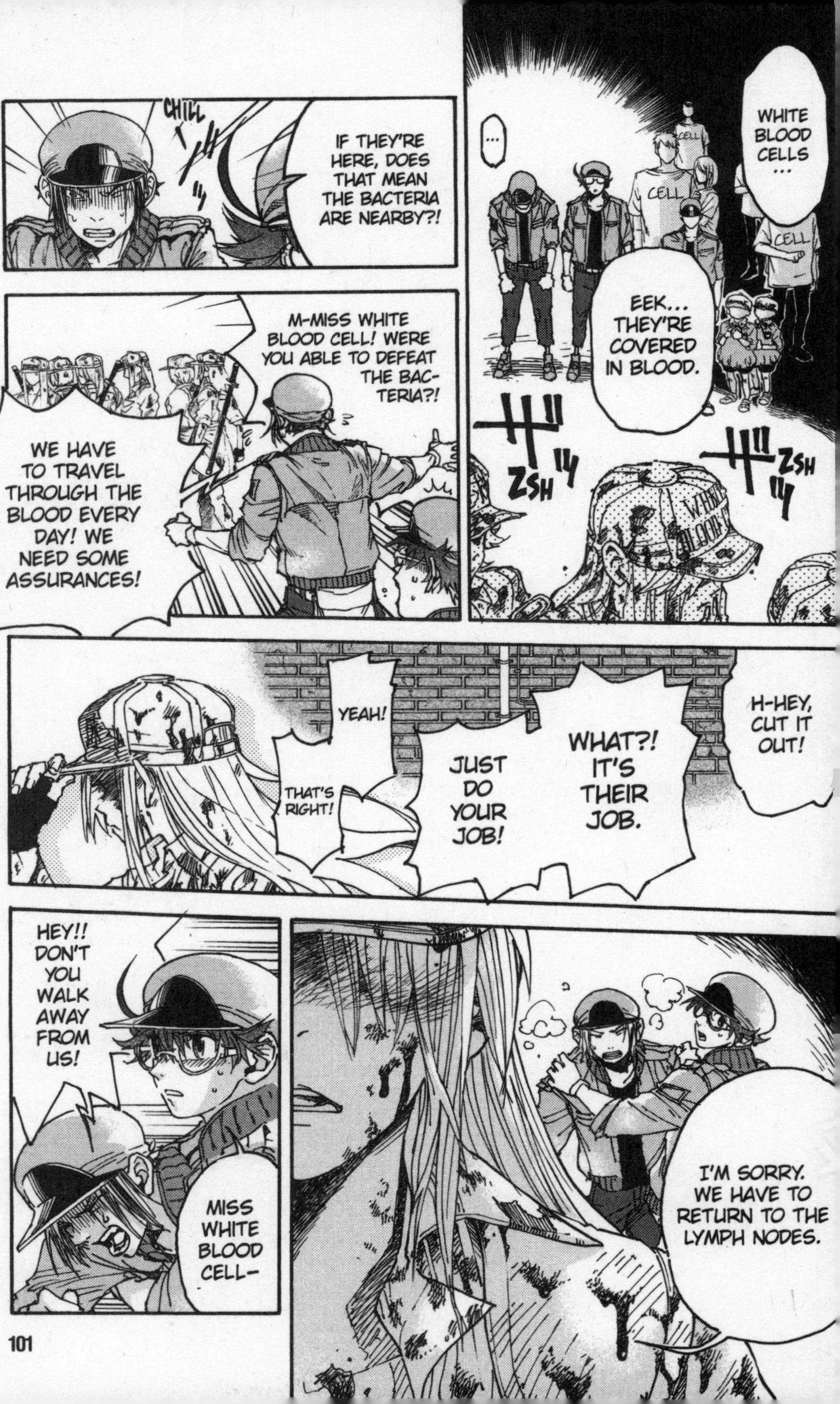
WHITE BLOOD CELLS ...
...
EEK... THEY'RE COVERED IN BLOOD.
ZSH
ZSH
CHILL
IF THEY'RE HERE, DOES THAT MEAN THE BACTERIA ARE NEARBY?!
M-MISS WHITE BLOOD CELL! WERE YOU ABLE TO DEFEAT THE BAC-TERIA?!
WE HAVE TO TRAVEL THROUGH THE BLOOD EVERY DAY! WE NEED SOME ASSURANCES!
H-HEY, CUT IT OUT!
WHAT?! IT'S THEIR JOB.
JUST DO YOUR JOB!
YEAH!
THAT'S RIGHT!
I'M SORRY. WE HAVE TO RETURN TO THE LYMPH NODES.
HEY!! DON'T YOU WALK AWAY FROM US!
MISS WHITE BLOOD CELL-

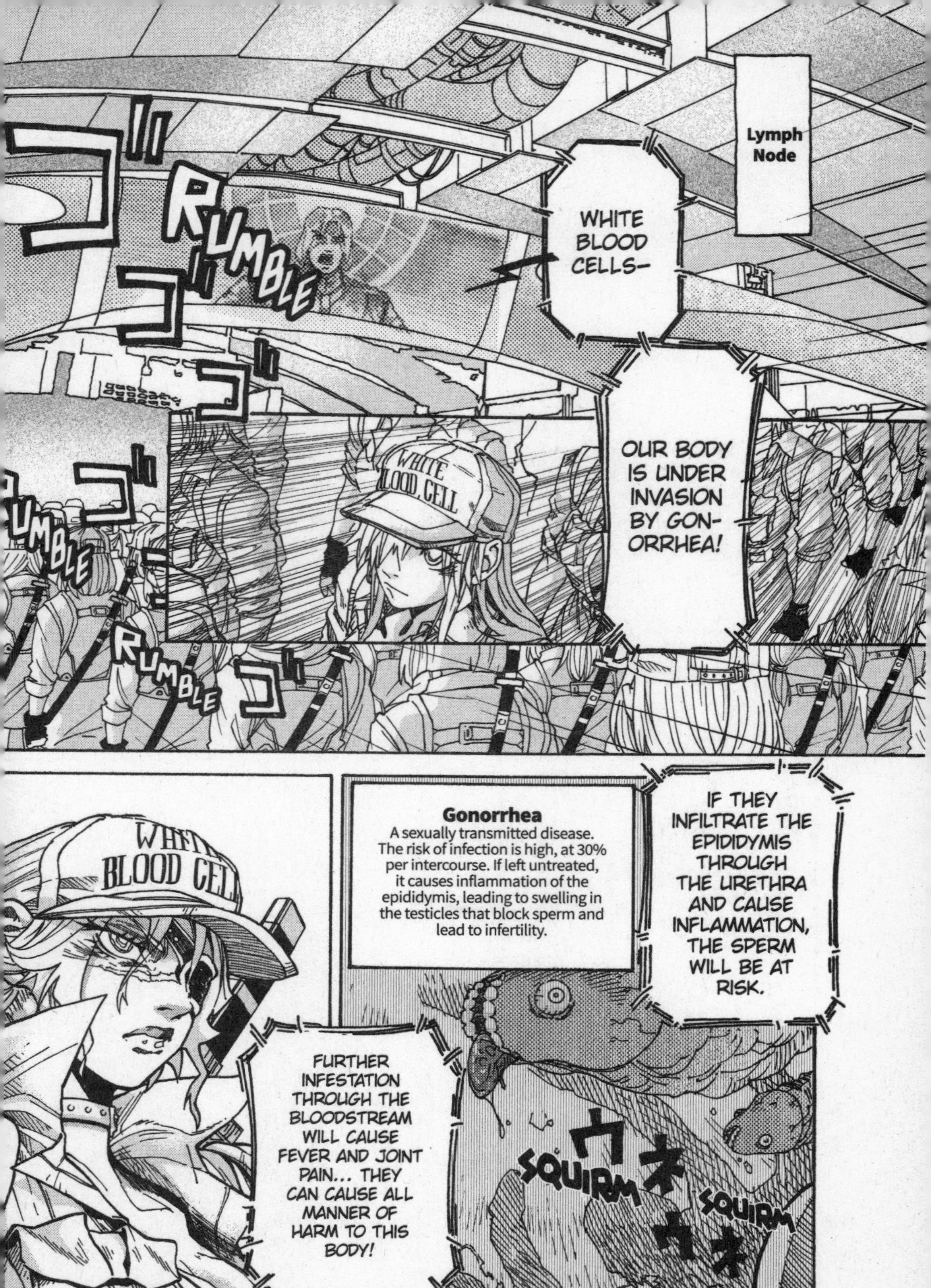

Lymph Node
WHITE BLOOD CELLS-
RUMBLE
RUMBLE
RUMBLE
OUR BODY IS UNDER INVASION BY GON-ORRHEA!
Gonorrhea
A sexually transmitted disease. The risk of infection is high, at 30% per intercourse. If left untreated, it causes inflammation of the epididymis, leading to swelling in the testicles that block sperm and lead to infertility.
IF THEY INFILTRATE THE EPIDIDYMIS THROUGH THE URETHRA AND CAUSE INFLAMMATION, THE SPERM WILL BE AT RISK.
SQUIRM
SQUIRM
FURTHER INFESTATION THROUGH THE BLOODSTREAM WILL CAUSE FEVER AND JOINT PAIN... THEY CAN CAUSE ALL MANNER OF HARM TO THIS BODY!

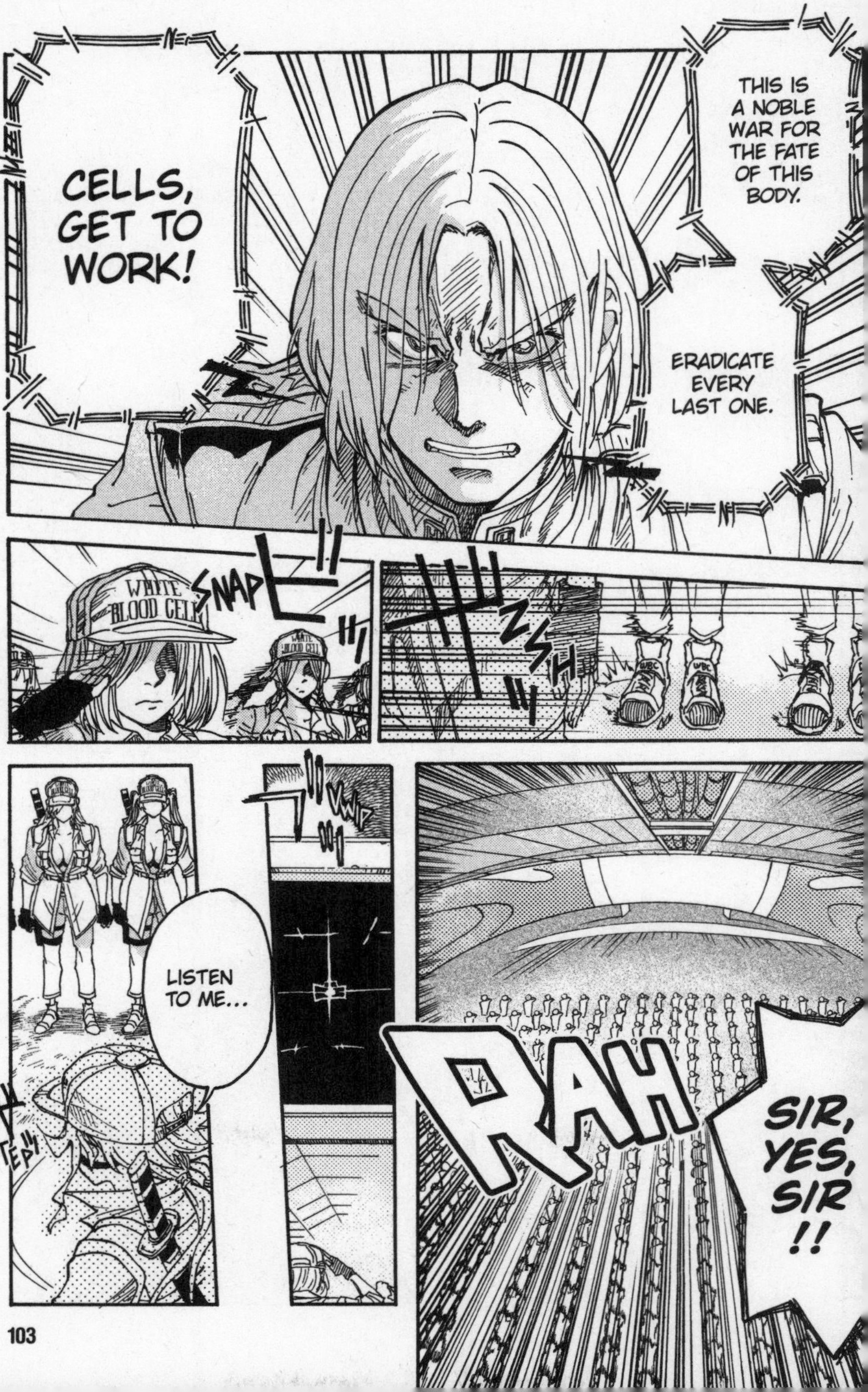
THIS IS A NOBLE WAR FOR THE FATE OF THIS BODY.
ERADICATE EVERY LAST ONE.
CELLS, GET TO WORK!
ZSH
WBC
WBC
SNAP
WHITE BLOOD CELL
WHITE BLOOD CELL
RAH
SIR, YES, SIR!!
VWIP
LISTEN TO ME...
STEP

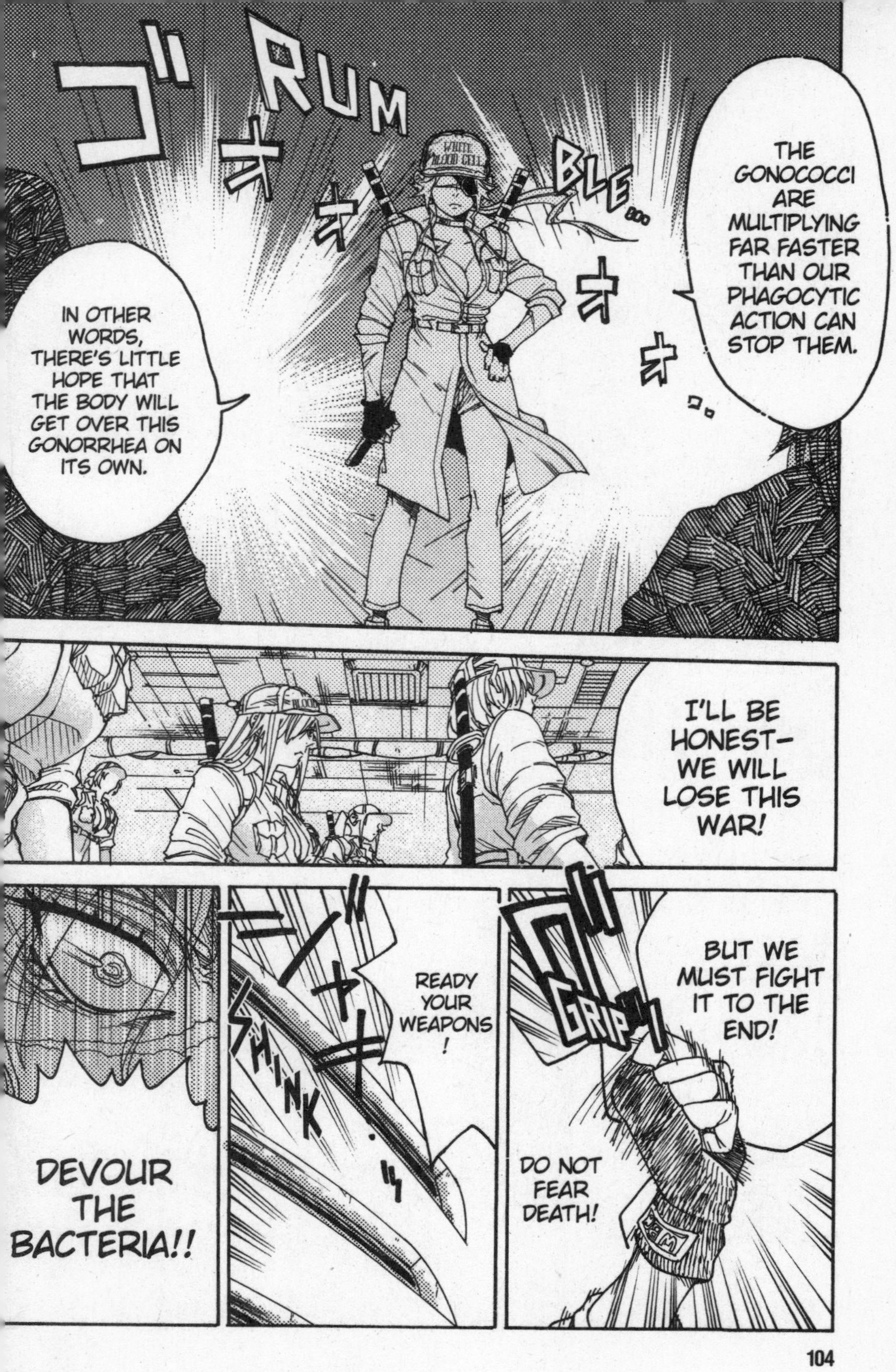
RUMBLE...
THE GONOCOCCI ARE MULTIPLYING FAR FASTER THAN OUR PHAGOCYTIC ACTION CAN STOP THEM.
IN OTHER WORDS, THERE'S LITTLE HOPE THAT THE BODY WILL GET OVER THIS GONORRHEA ON ITS OWN.
I'LL BE HONEST- WE WILL LOSE THIS WAR!
GRIP
BUT WE MUST FIGHT IT TO THE END!
DO NOT FEAR DEATH!
SHINK
READY YOUR WEAPONS!
DEVOUR THE BACTERIA!!

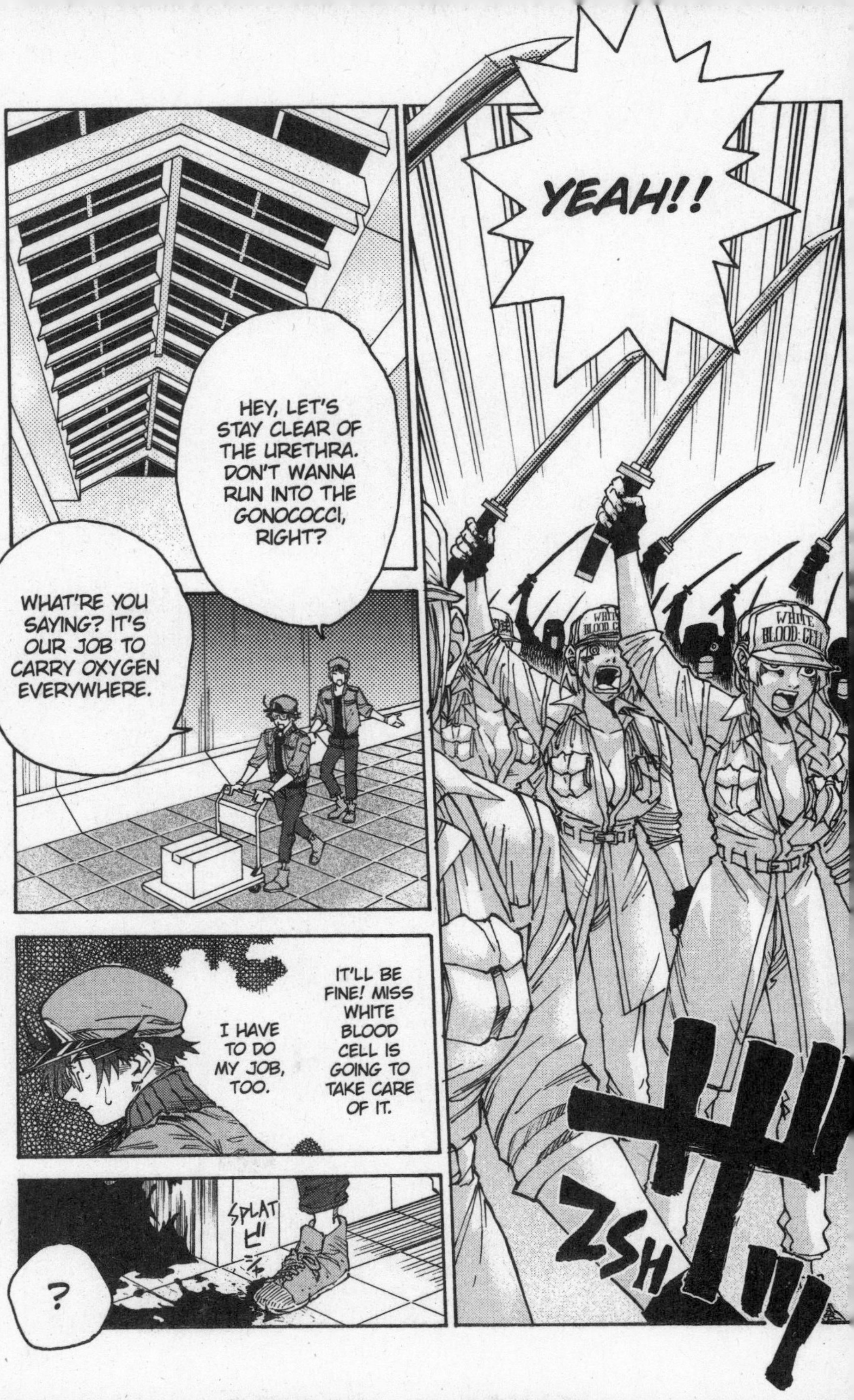
YEAH!!
ZSH!!!
HEY, LET'S STAY CLEAR OF THE URETHRA. DON'T WANNA RUN INTO THE GONOCOCCI, RIGHT?
WHAT'RE YOU SAYING? IT'S OUR JOB TO CARRY OXYGEN EVERYWHERE.
IT'LL BE FINE! MISS WHITE BLOOD CELL IS GOING TO TAKE CARE OF IT.
I HAVE TO DO MY JOB, TOO.
SPLAT
?

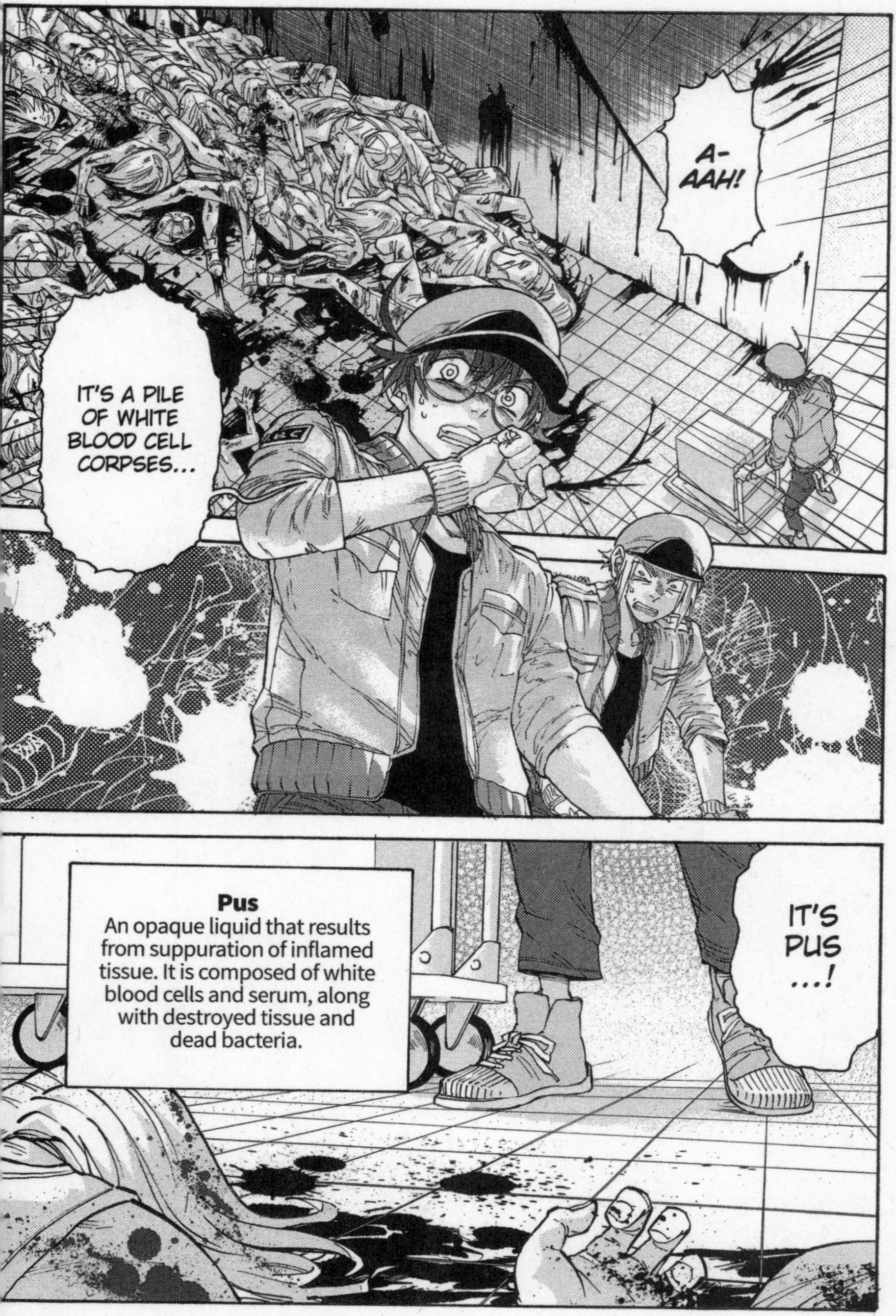
A-AAH!
IT'S A PILE OF WHITE BLOOD CELL CORPSES...
IT'S PUS ...!
Pus
An opaque liquid that results from suppuration of inflamed tissue. It is composed of white blood cells and serum, along with destroyed tissue and dead bacteria.

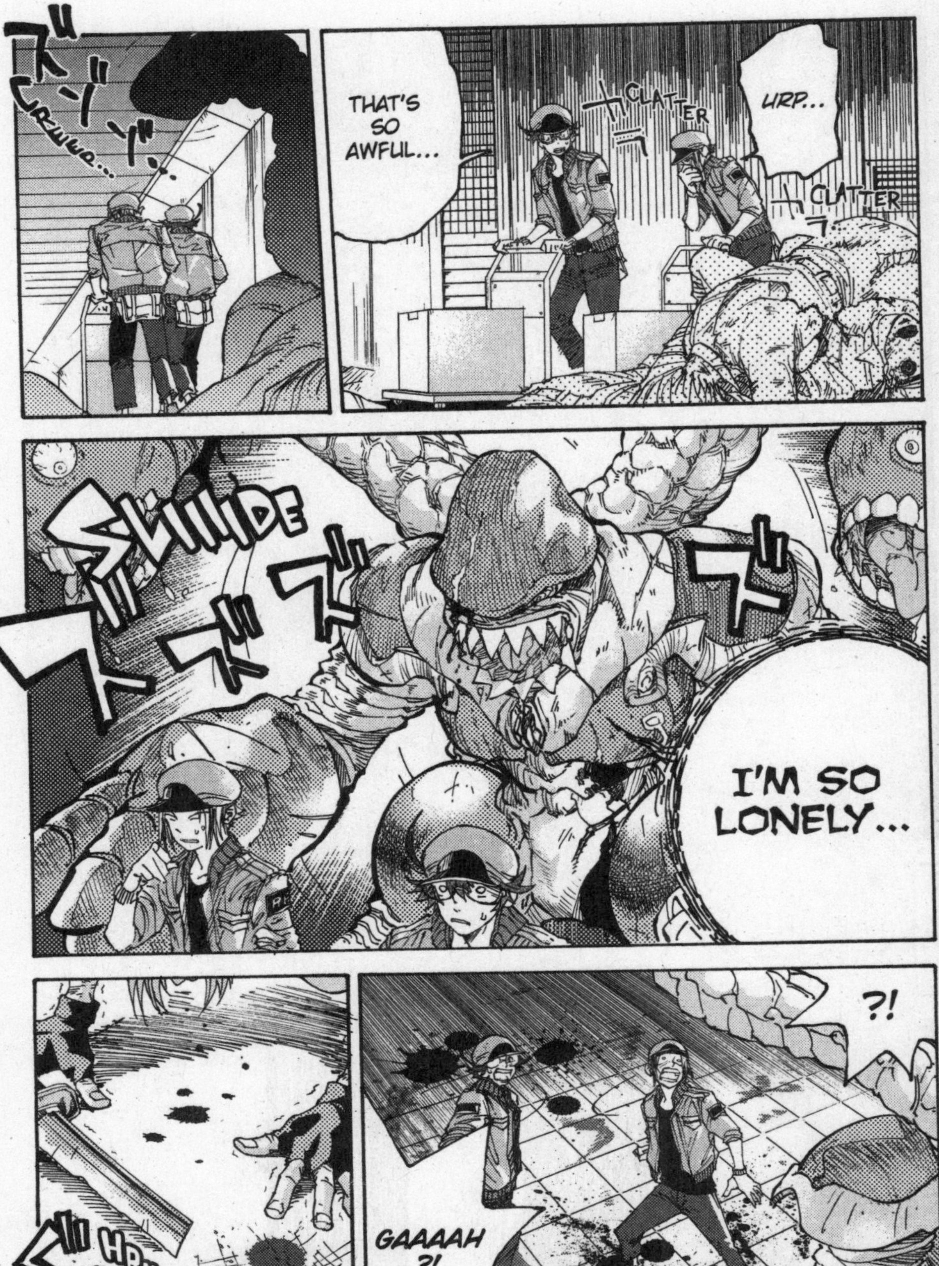
URP...
CLATTER
THAT'S SO AWFUL...
CLATTER
SLIIIIDE
I'M SO LONELY...
?!
GAAAAH ?!
HRNGH

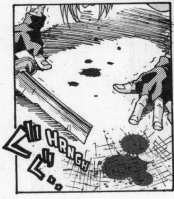

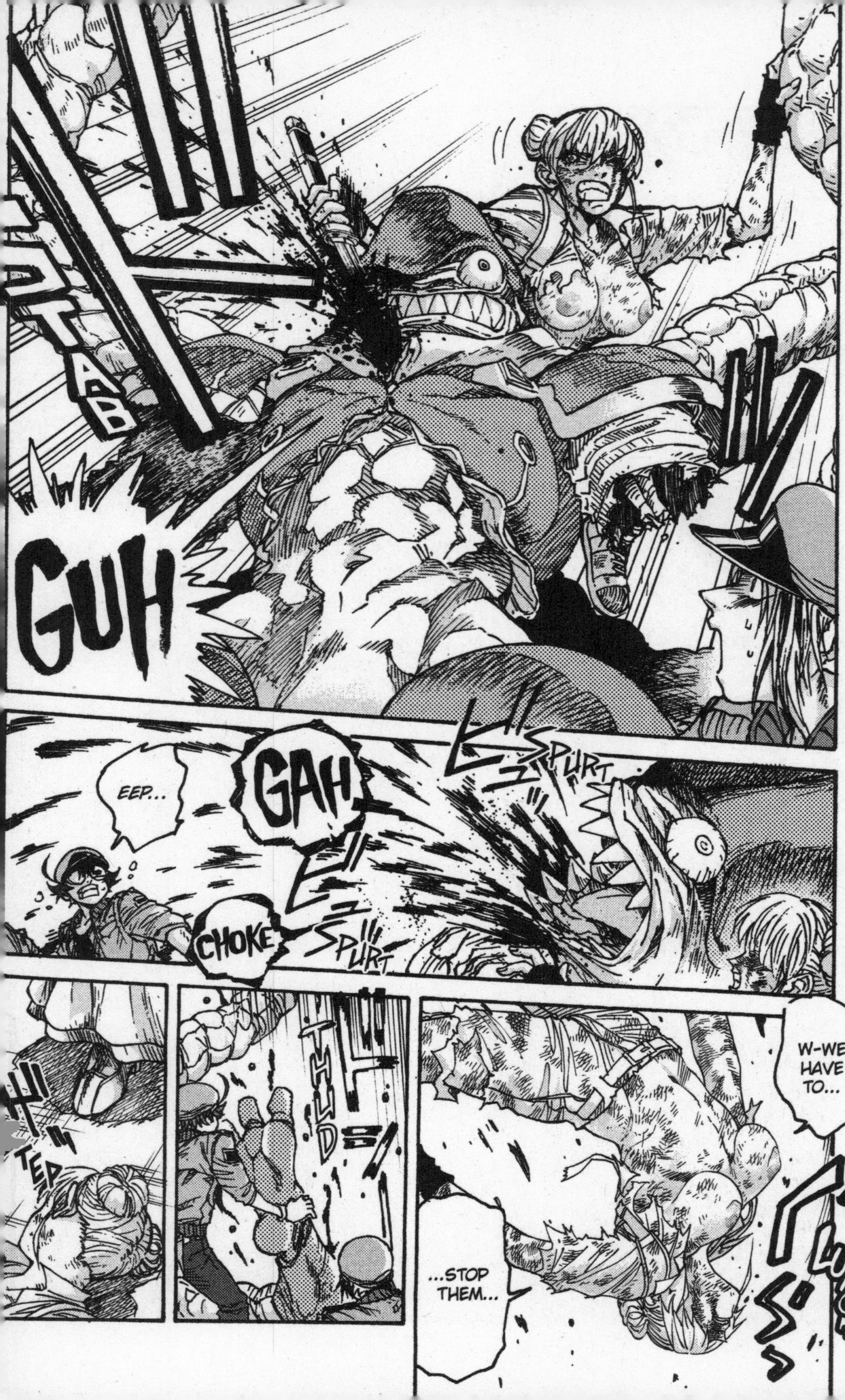
STABB
GUH
SPURT
GAH
EEP...
CHOKE
SPURT
W-WE HAVE TO...
LURCH
...STOP THEM...
THUD
TEP

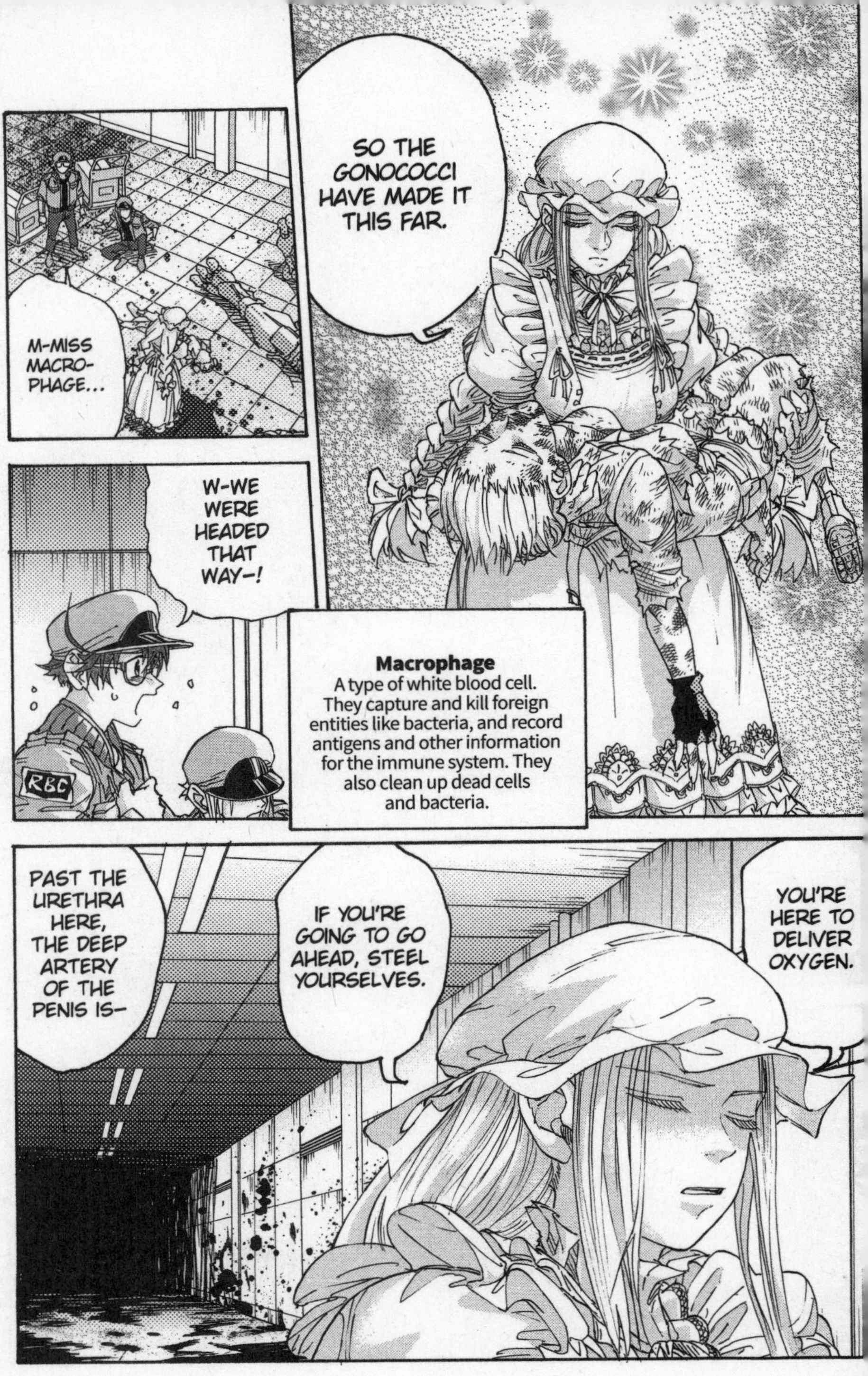
SO THE GONOCOCCI HAVE MADE IT THIS FAR.
M-MISS MACRO-PHAGE...
W-WE WERE HEADED THAT WAY-!
RBC
Macrophage
A type of white blood cell. They capture and kill foreign entities like bacteria, and record antigens and other information for the immune system. They also clean up dead cells and bacteria.
YOU'RE HERE TO DELIVER OXYGEN.
IF YOU'RE GOING TO GO AHEAD, STEEL YOURSELVES.
PAST THE URETHRA HERE, THE DEEP ARTERY OF THE PENIS IS-

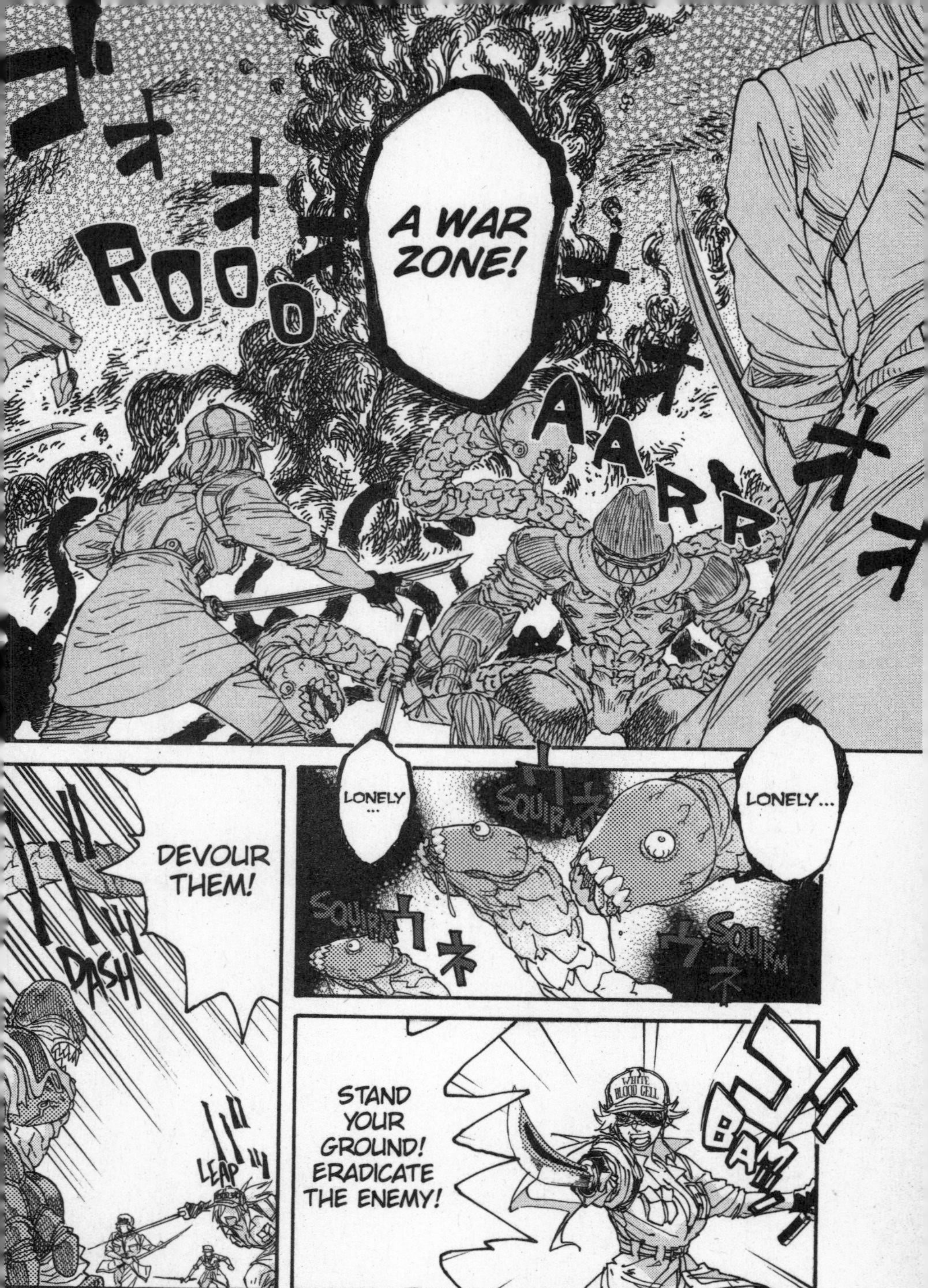
A WAR ZONE!
ROOO
AARRR
LONELY...
LONELY...
SQUIRM
SQUIRM
SQUIRM
BAM
STAND YOUR GROUND! ERADICATE THE ENEMY!
DEVOUR THEM!
DASH
LEAP

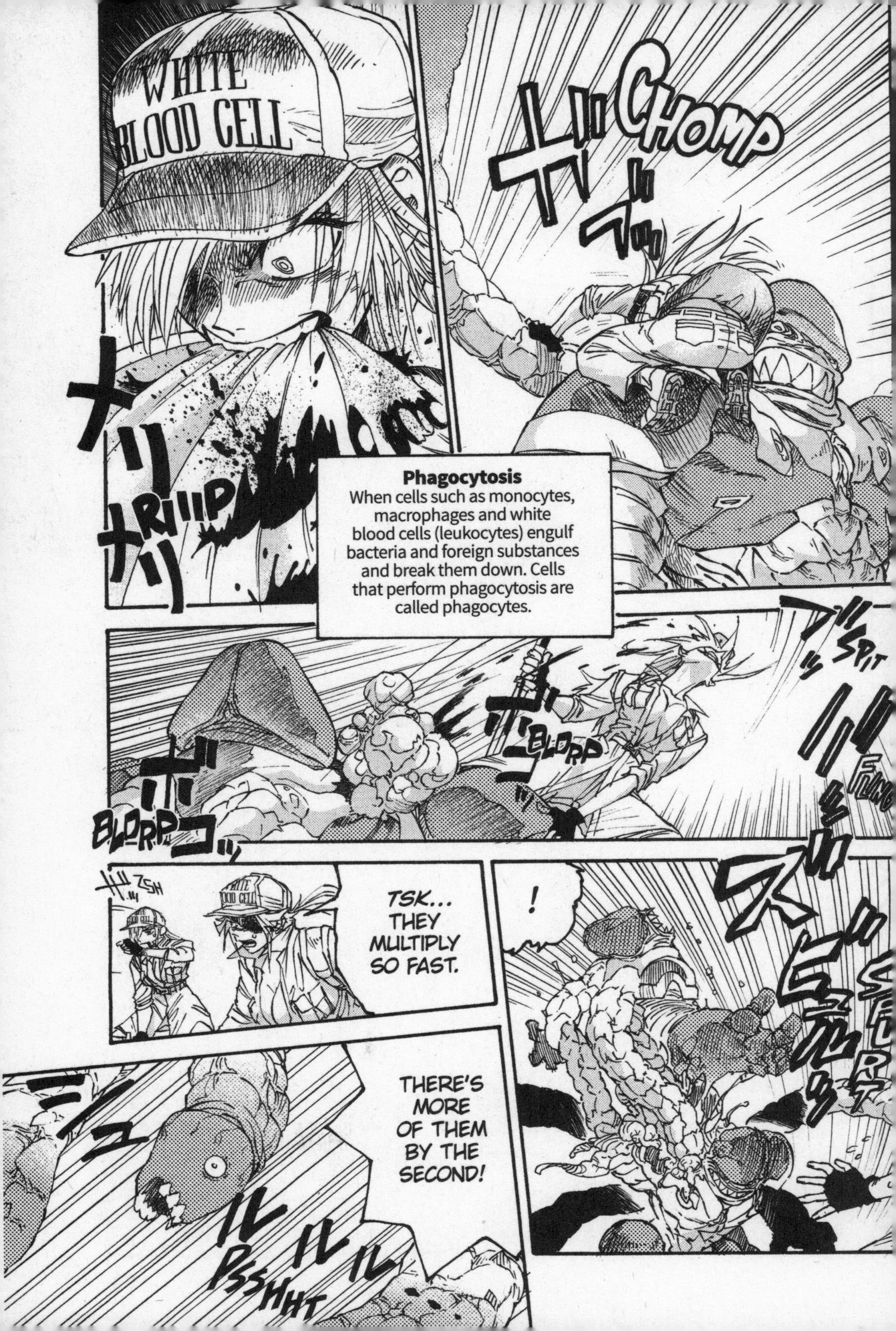
CHOMP
RIIIP
Phagocytosis
When cells such as monocytes, macrophages and white blood cells (leukocytes) engulf bacteria and foreign substances and break them down. Cells that perform phagocytosis are called phagocytes.
SPIT
BLORP
BLORP
SPLURT
!
ZSH
TSK... THEY MULTIPLY SO FAST.
THERE'S MORE OF THEM BY THE SECOND!
PSSSHHHT

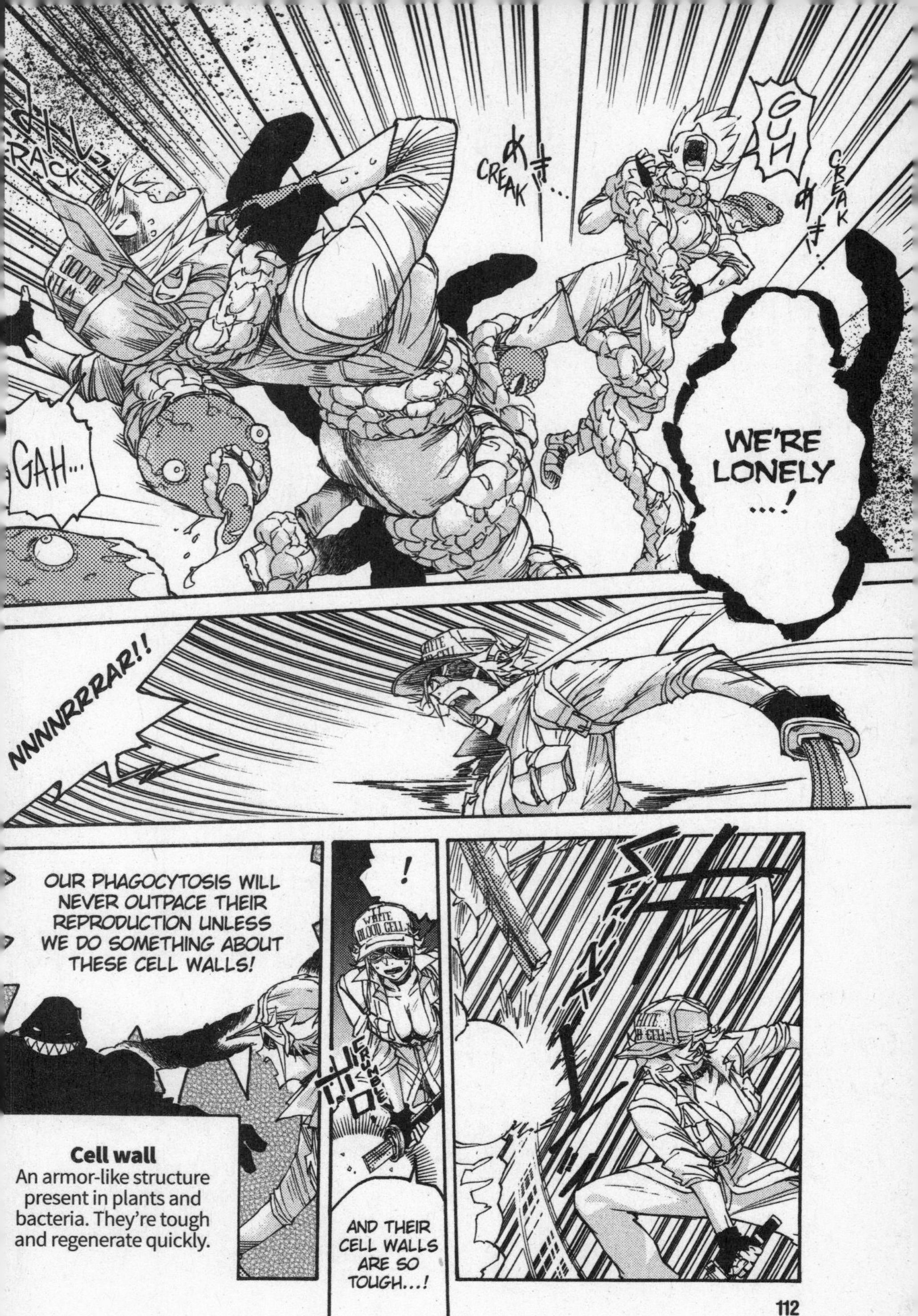
GUH
CREAK
CREAK
WE'RE LONELY...!
CRACK
GAH...
NNNNRRRAR!!
!
CRUMBLE
AND THEIR CELL WALLS ARE SO TOUGH...!
OUR PHAGOCYTOSIS WILL NEVER OUTPACE THEIR REPRODUCTION UNLESS WE DO SOMETHING ABOUT THESE CELL WALLS!
Cell wall
An armor-like structure present in plants and bacteria. They're tough and regenerate quickly.

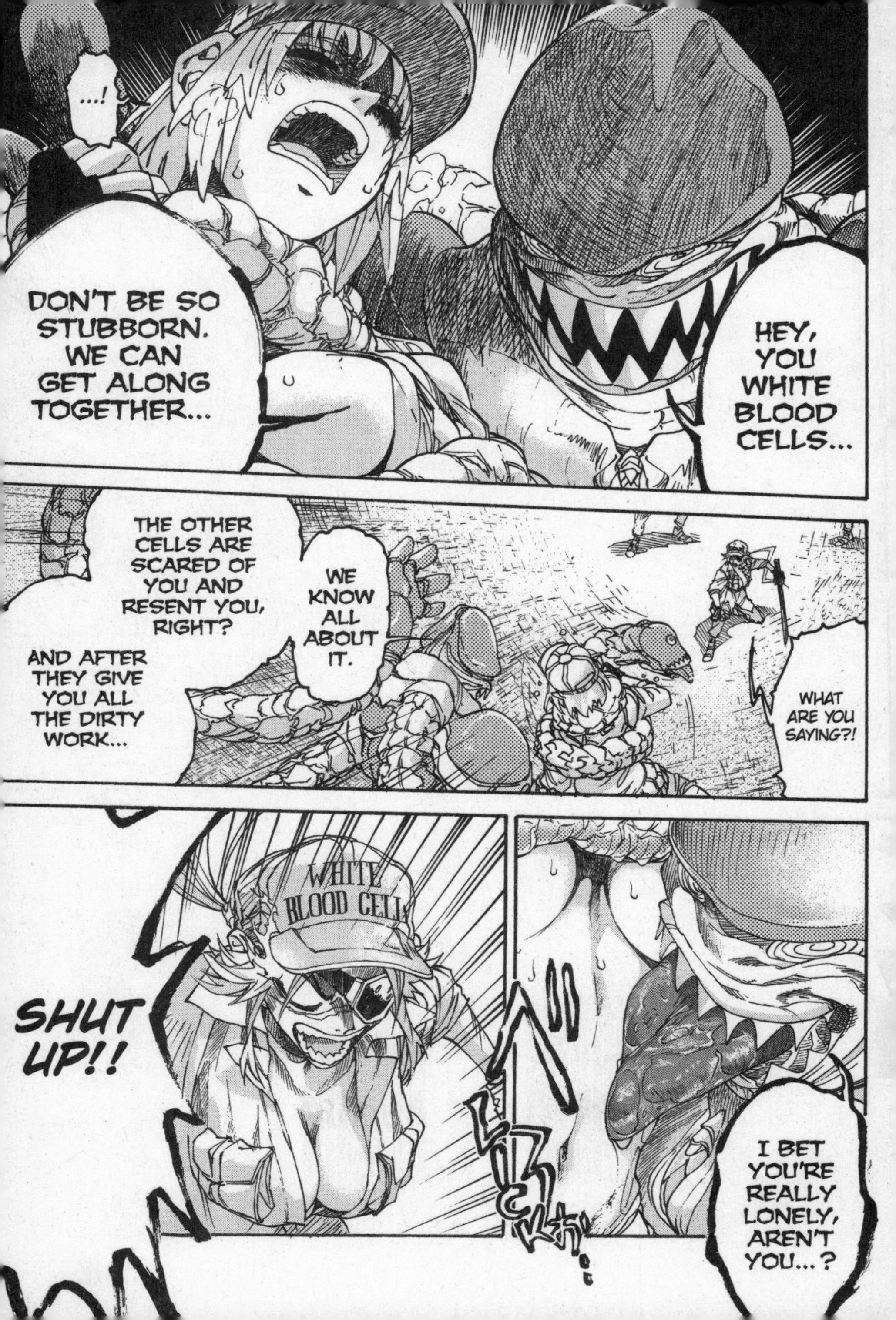
HEY, YOU WHITE BLOOD CELLS...
...!
DON'T BE SO STUBBORN. WE CAN GET ALONG TOGETHER...
WHAT ARE YOU SAYING?!
WE KNOW ALL ABOUT IT.
THE OTHER CELLS ARE SCARED OF YOU AND RESENT YOU, RIGHT?
AND AFTER THEY GIVE YOU ALL THE DIRTY WORK...
I BET YOU'RE REALLY LONELY, AREN'T YOU...?
WHITE BLOOD CELL
SHUT UP!!

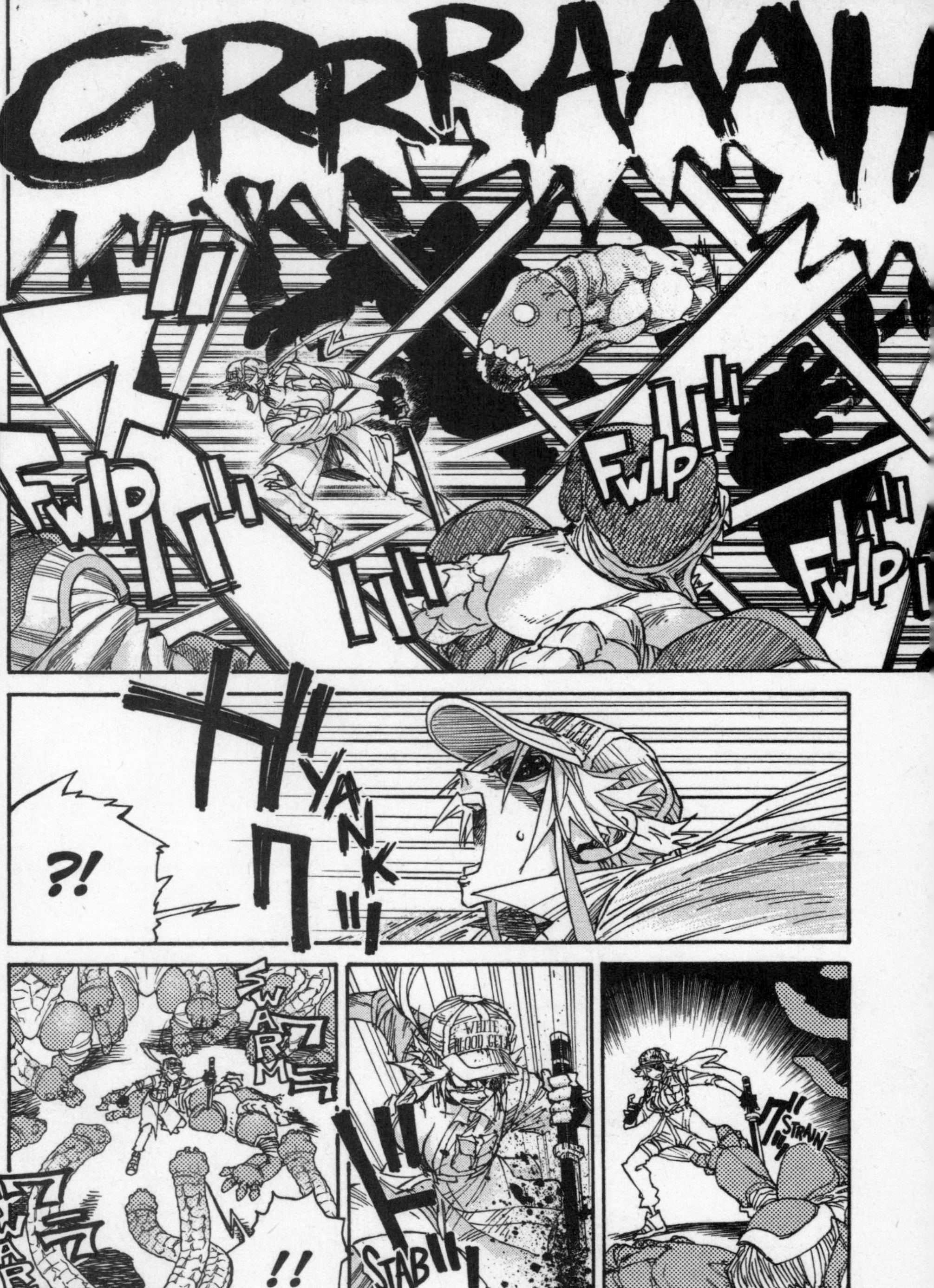
GRRRAAAH
FWIP
FWIP
FWIP
YANK
?!
STRAIN
WHITE BLOOD CELL
STAB
SWARM
SWARM
!!

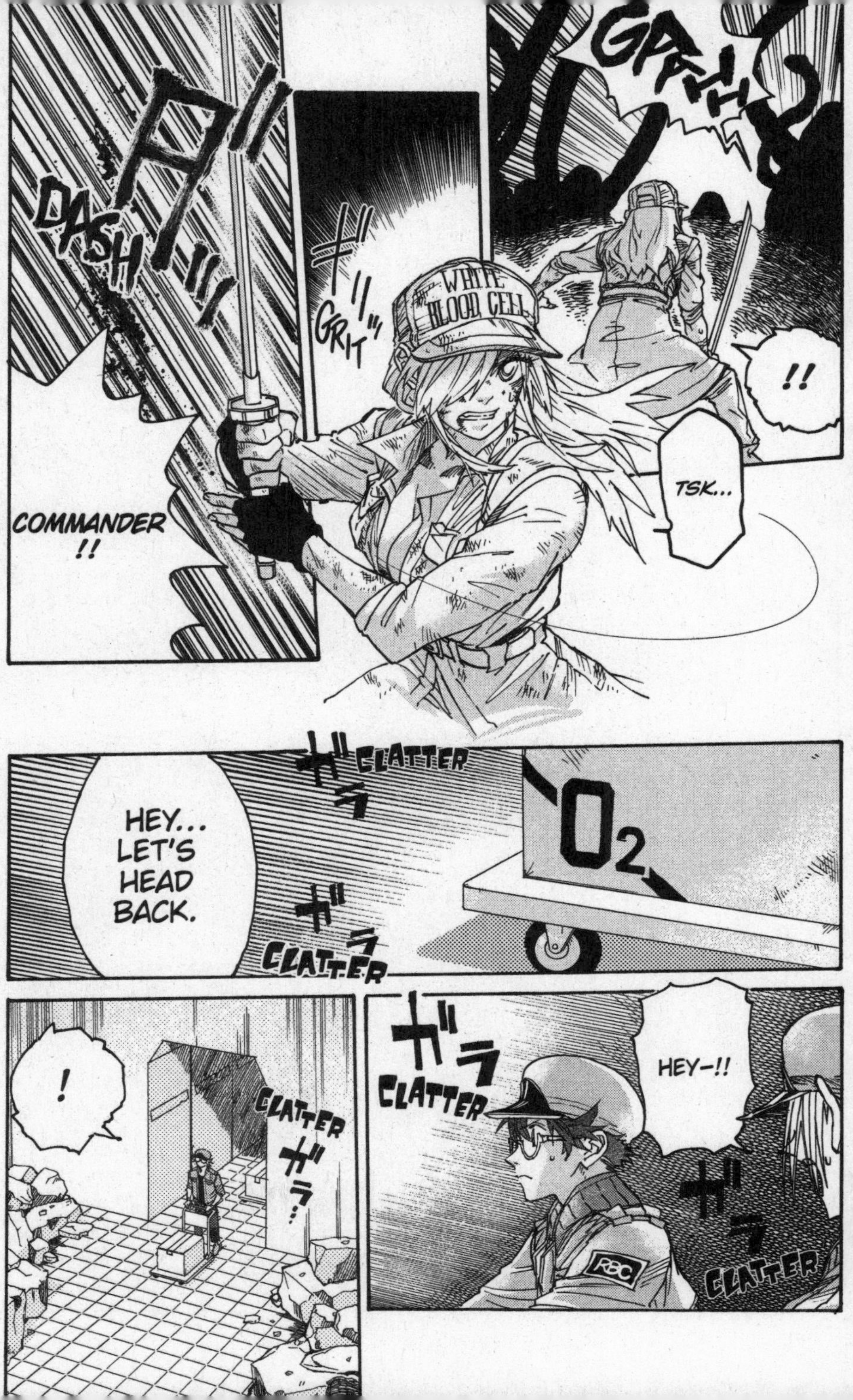
GRAHH
!!
TSK...
GRIT
DASH
COMMANDER!!
CLATTER
HEY... LET'S HEAD BACK.
CLATTER
CLATTER
HEY–!!
CLATTER
!
CLATTER

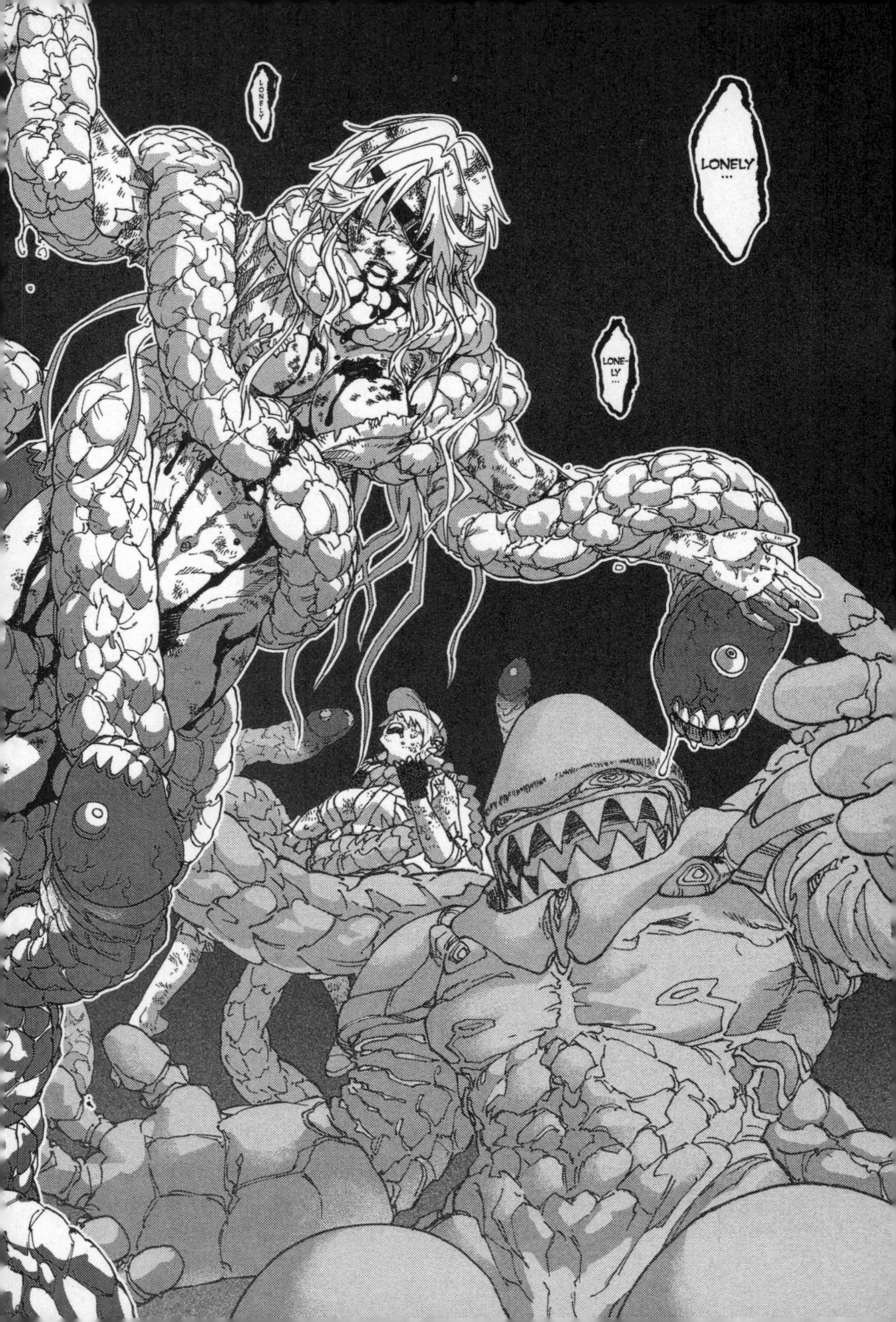
LONELY
...
LONE-
LY
...
LONELY

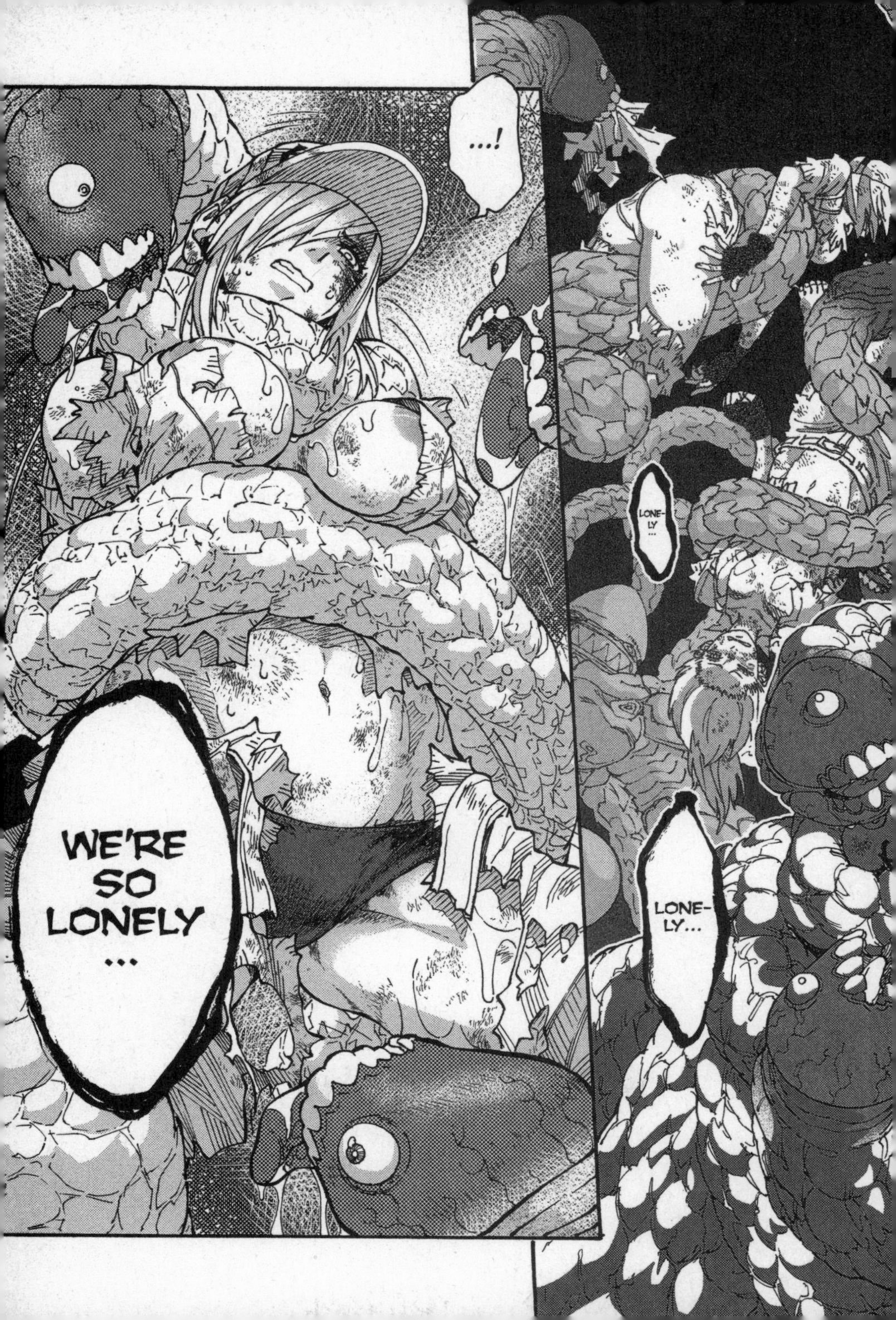
LONE-LY...
LONE-LY...
...!
WE'RE SO LONELY...

M-MISS WHITE BLOOD CELL!

BUCKLE

EEP...

BUCKLE

SPLAT

WHAT DID YOU COME HERE FOR...?

BWA HA HA—

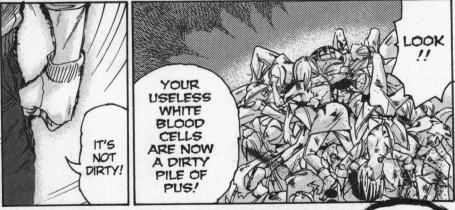

IT'S NOT DIRTY!

YOUR USELESS WHITE BLOOD CELLS ARE NOW A DIRTY PILE OF PUS!

LOOK!!

PUS IS PROOF THAT THE WHITE BLOOD CELLS FOUGHT WITH THEIR LIVES!

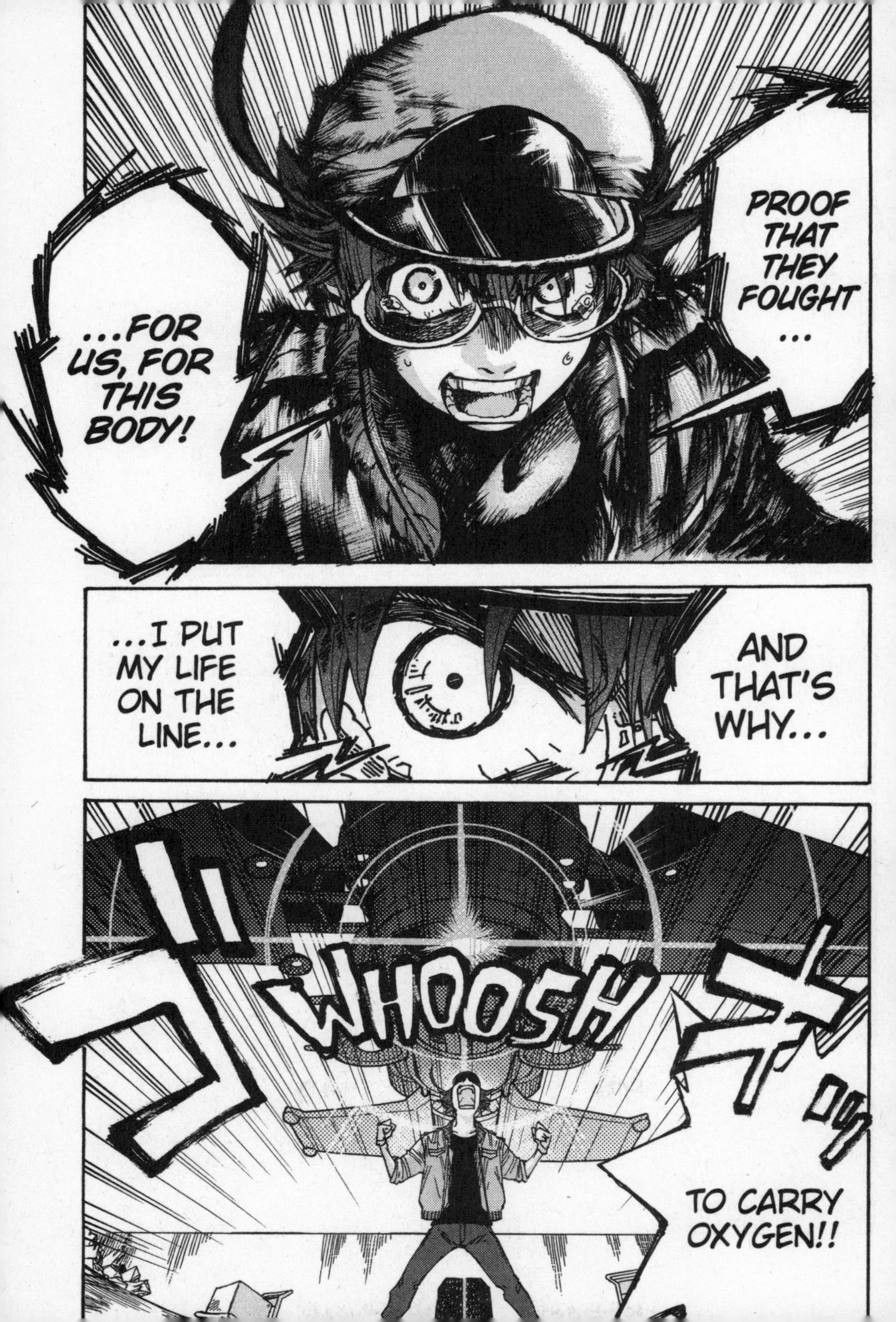
PROOF THAT THEY FOUGHT...
...FOR US, FOR THIS BODY!
AND THAT'S WHY...
...I PUT MY LIFE ON THE LINE...
WHOOSH
TO CARRY OXYGEN!!

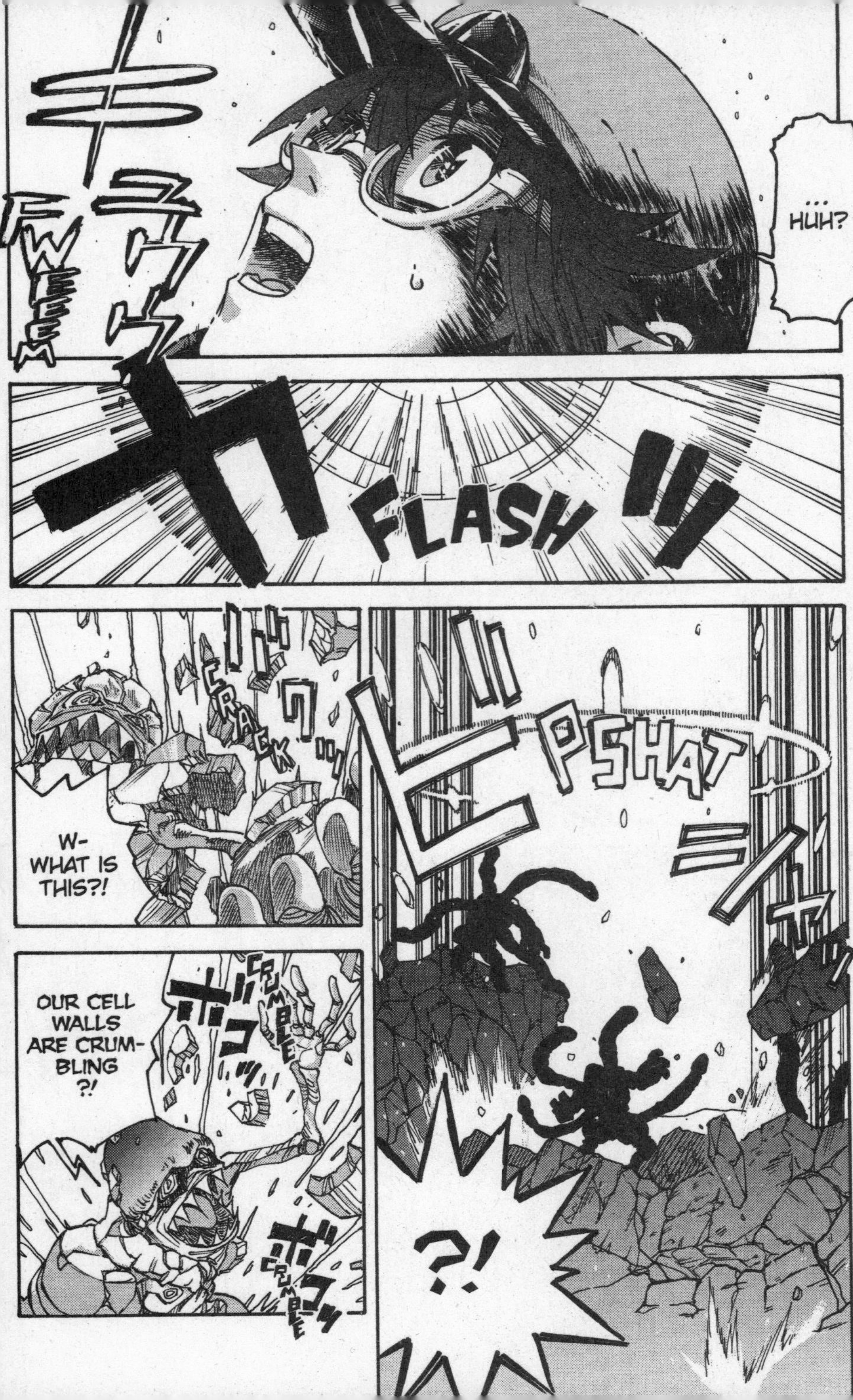
...HÜH?
FWEEEM
FLASH
PSHAT
?!
W-WHAT IS THIS?!
CRACK
OUR CELL WALLS ARE CRUM-BLING?!
CRUMBLE
CRUMBLE

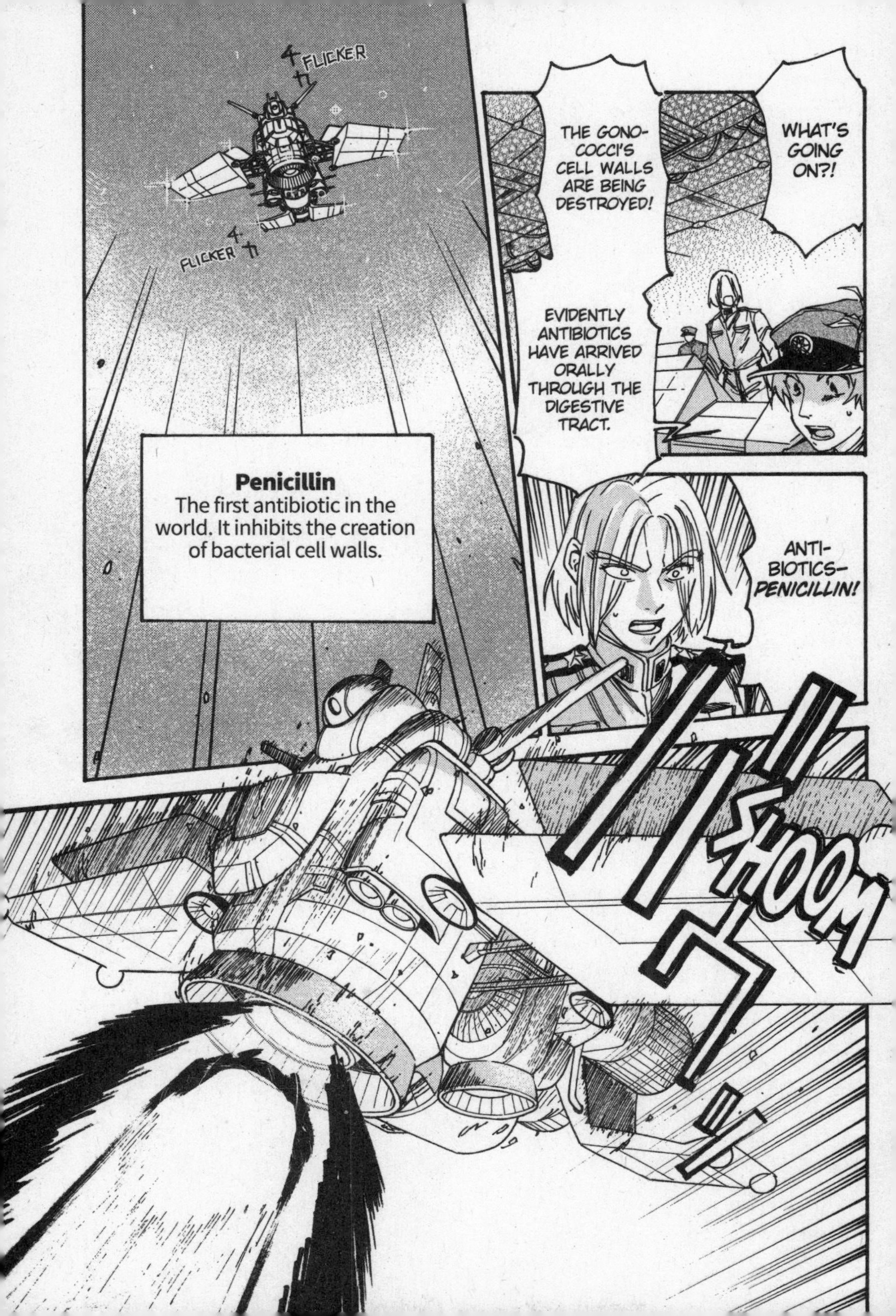
WHAT'S GOING ON?!
THE GONO-COCCI'S CELL WALLS ARE BEING DESTROYED!
EVIDENTLY ANTIBIOTICS HAVE ARRIVED ORALLY THROUGH THE DIGESTIVE TRACT.
ANTI-BIOTICS—PENICILLIN!
FLICKER
FLICKER
Penicillin
The first antibiotic in the world. It inhibits the creation of bacterial cell walls.
SHOOM

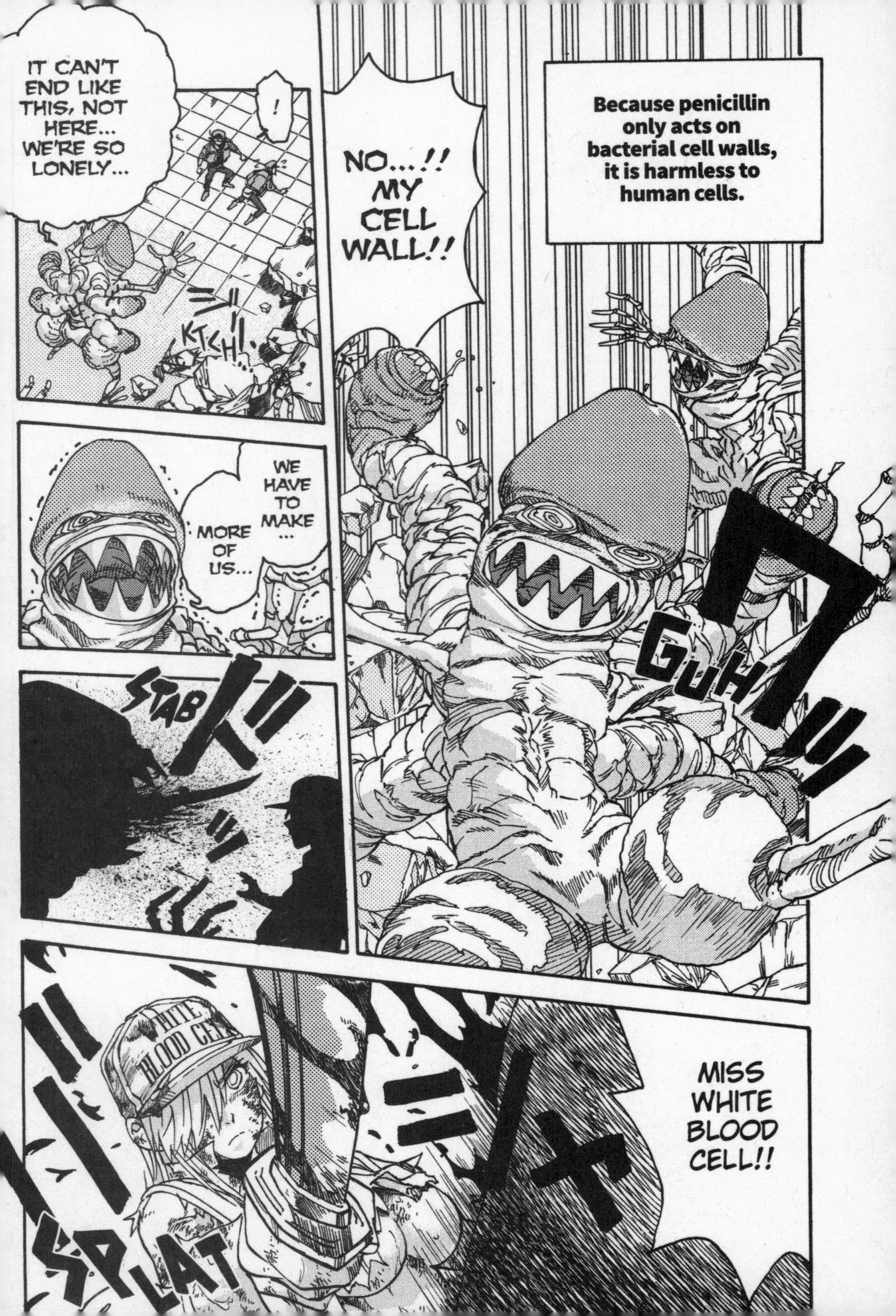

Because penicillin only acts on bacterial cell walls, it is harmless to human cells.
NO...!! MY CELL WALL!!
GUH
IT CAN'T END LIKE THIS, NOT HERE... WE'RE SO LONELY...
!
KTCH
WE HAVE TO MAKE...
MORE OF US...
STAB
MISS WHITE BLOOD CELL!!
SPLAT

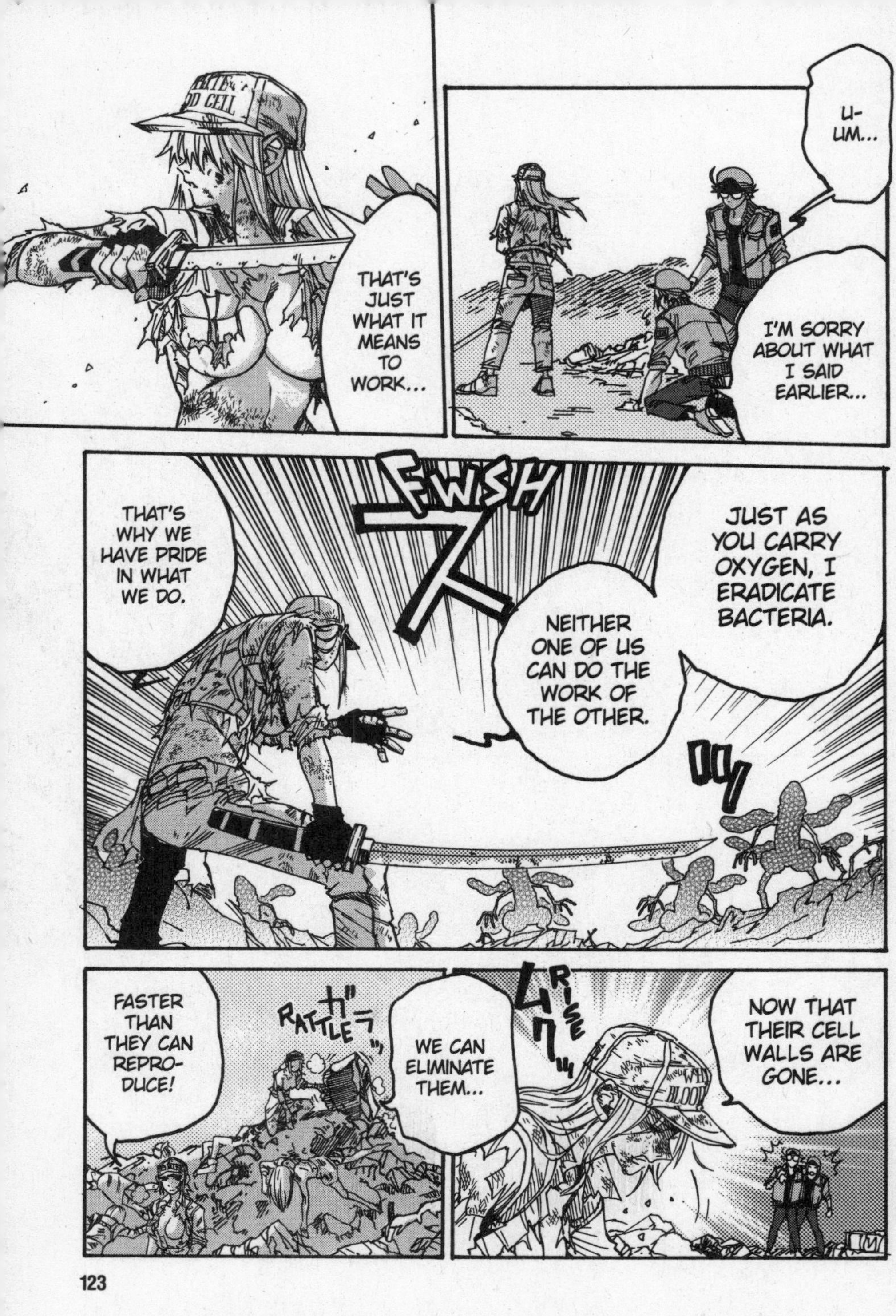
U-UM...
I'M SORRY ABOUT WHAT I SAID EARLIER...
THAT'S JUST WHAT IT MEANS TO WORK...
JUST AS YOU CARRY OXYGEN, I ERADICATE BACTERIA.
NEITHER ONE OF US CAN DO THE WORK OF THE OTHER.
FWSH
THAT'S WHY WE HAVE PRIDE IN WHAT WE DO.
NOW THAT THEIR CELL WALLS ARE GONE...
RISE
WE CAN ELIMINATE THEM...
RATTLE
FASTER THAN THEY CAN REPRO-DUCE!

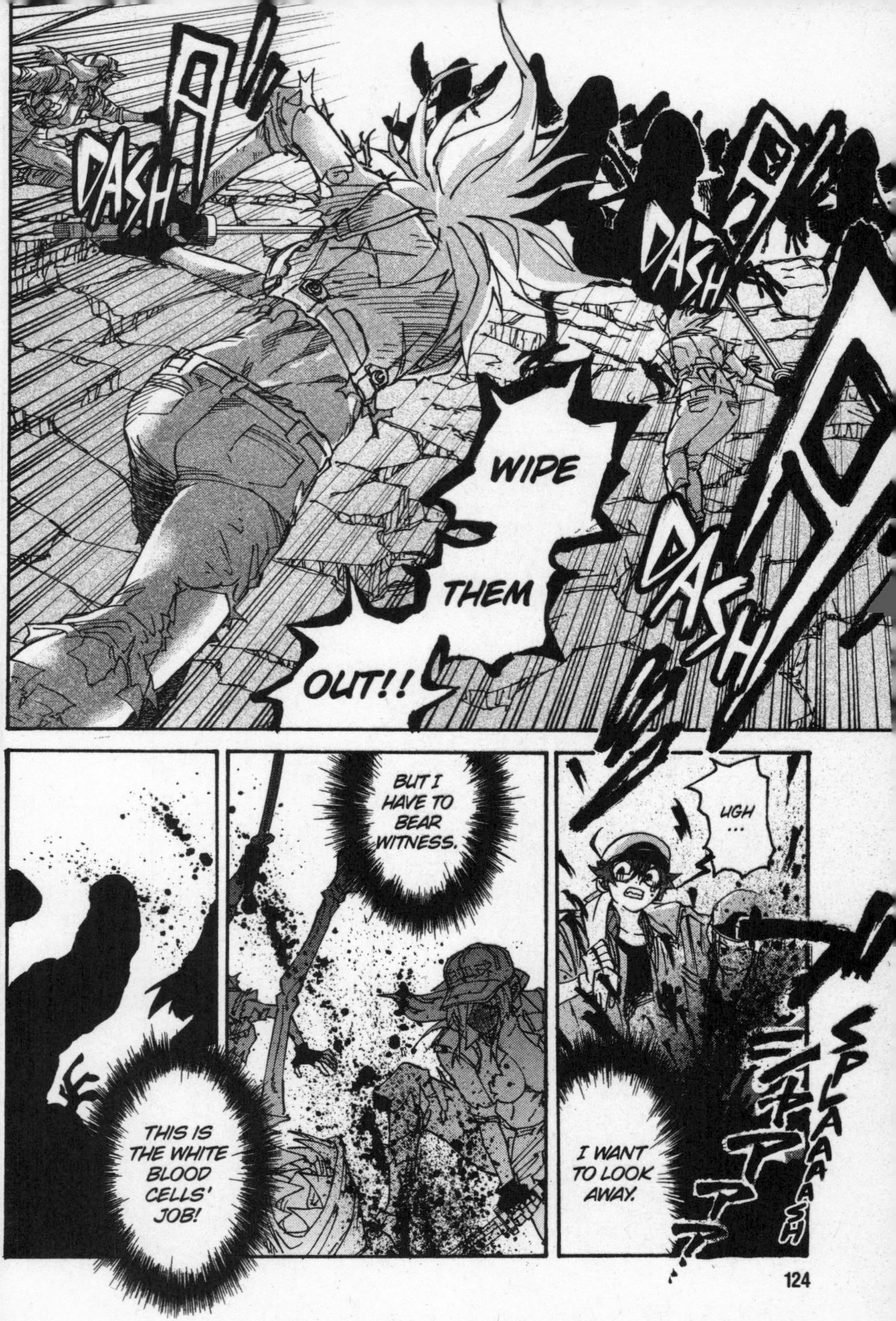
DASH
DASH
DASH
WIPE THEM OUT!!
UGH...
I WANT TO LOOK AWAY.
SPLAAAASH
BUT I HAVE TO BEAR WITNESS.
THIS IS THE WHITE BLOOD CELLS' JOB!

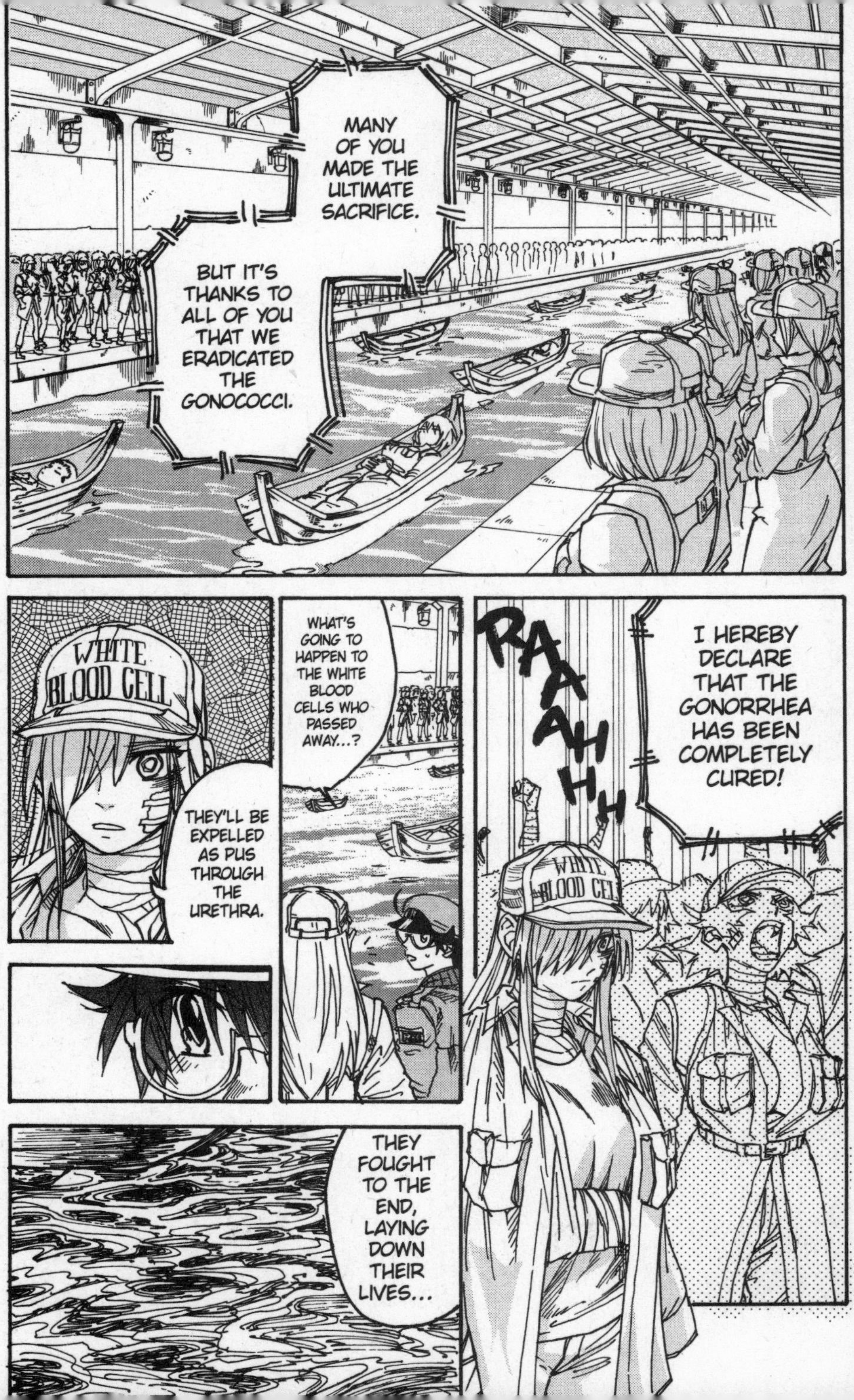
MANY OF YOU MADE THE ULTIMATE SACRIFICE.
BUT IT'S THANKS TO ALL OF YOU THAT WE ERADICATED THE GONOCOCCI.
RAAAHHH
I HEREBY DECLARE THAT THE GONORRHEA HAS BEEN COMPLETELY CURED!
WHITE BLOOD CELL
WHAT'S GOING TO HAPPEN TO THE WHITE BLOOD CELLS WHO PASSED AWAY...?
WHITE BLOOD CELL
THEY'LL BE EXPELLED AS PUS THROUGH THE URETHRA.
THEY FOUGHT TO THE END, LAYING DOWN THEIR LIVES...

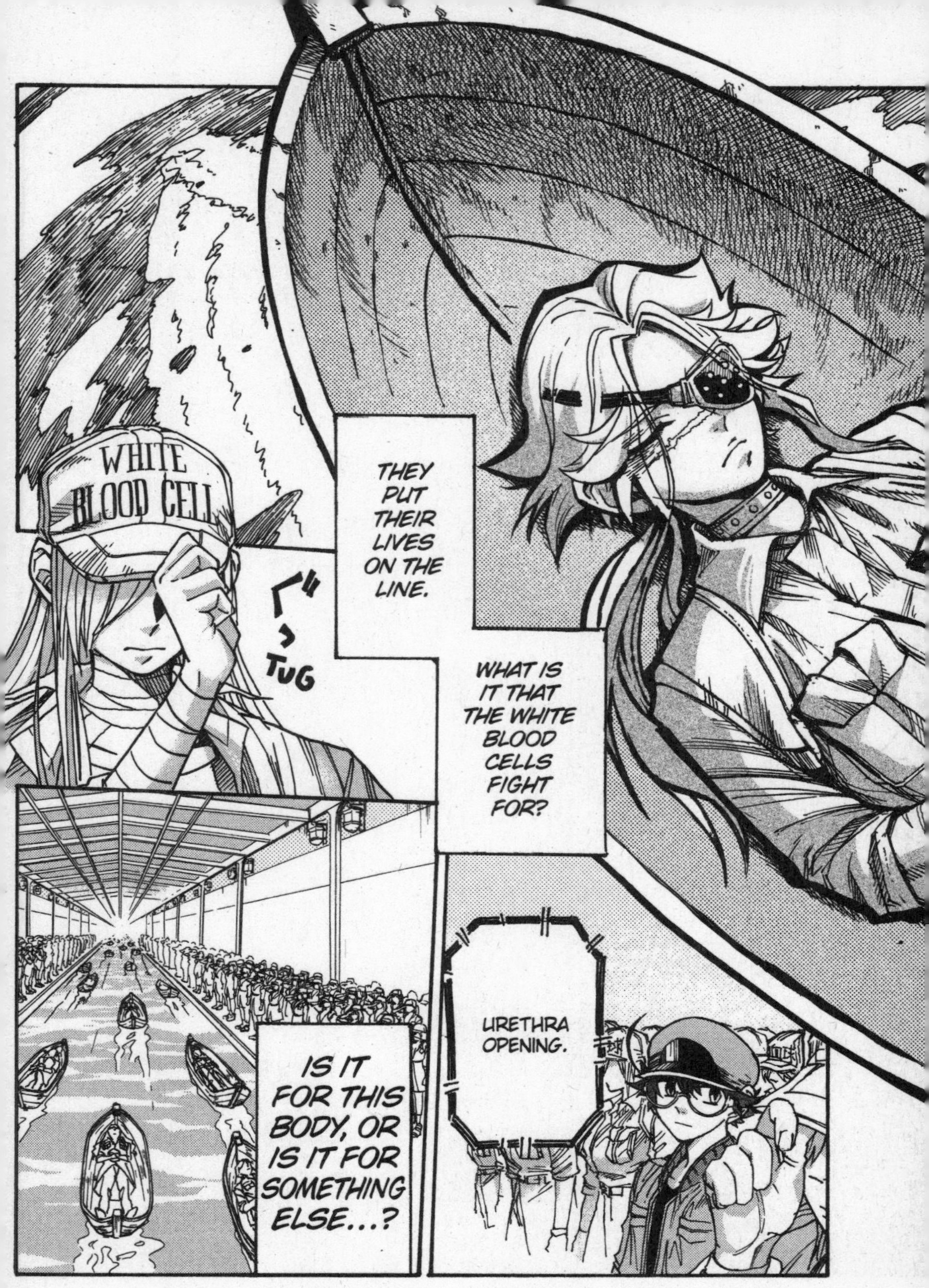
THEY PUT THEIR LIVES ON THE LINE.
WHAT IS IT THAT THE WHITE BLOOD CELLS FIGHT FOR?
WHITE BLOOD CELL
TUG
URETHRA OPENING.
IS IT FOR THIS BODY, OR IS IT FOR SOMETHING ELSE...?

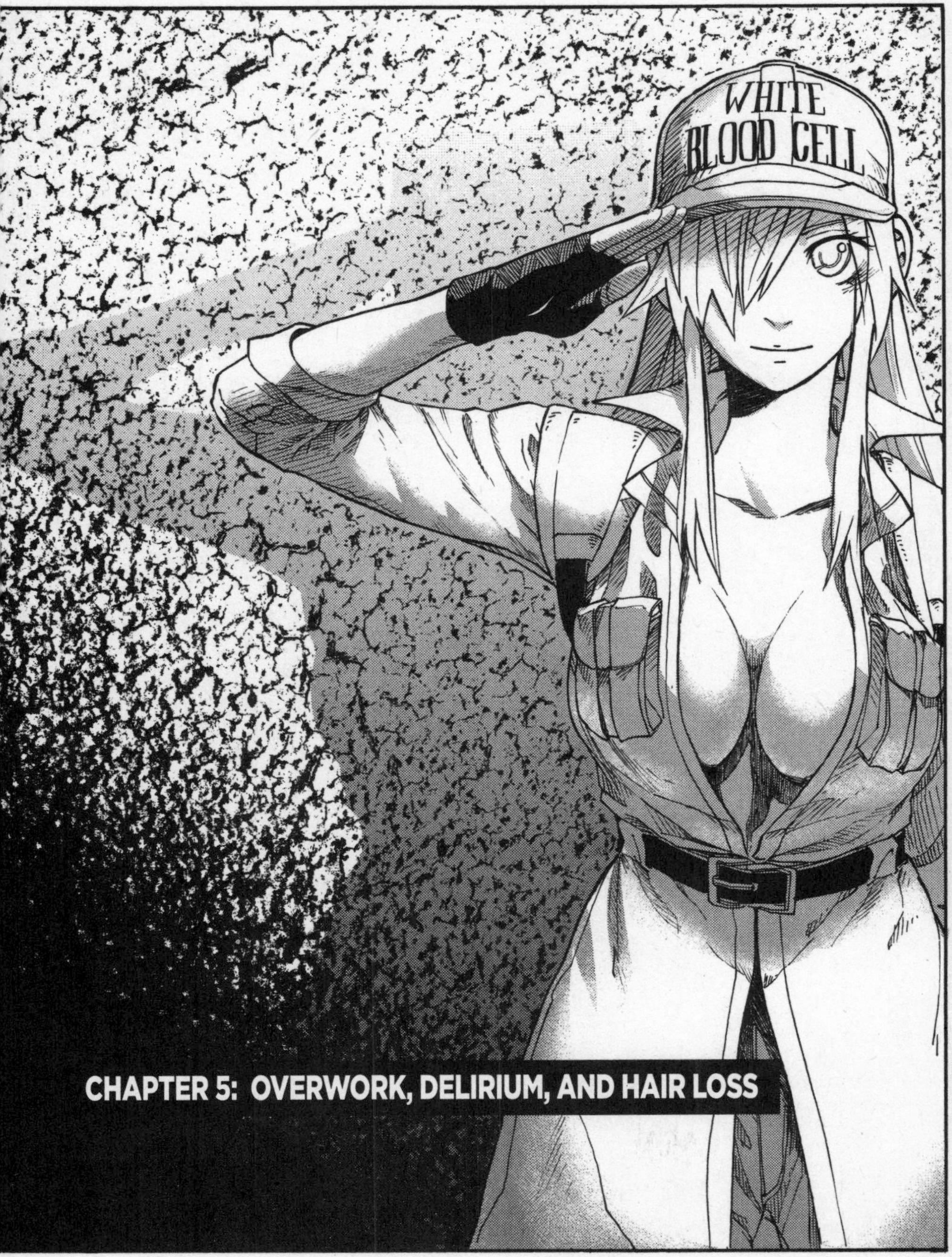
WHITE
BLOOD CELL

CHAPTER 5: OVERWORK, DELIRIUM, AND HAIR LOSS

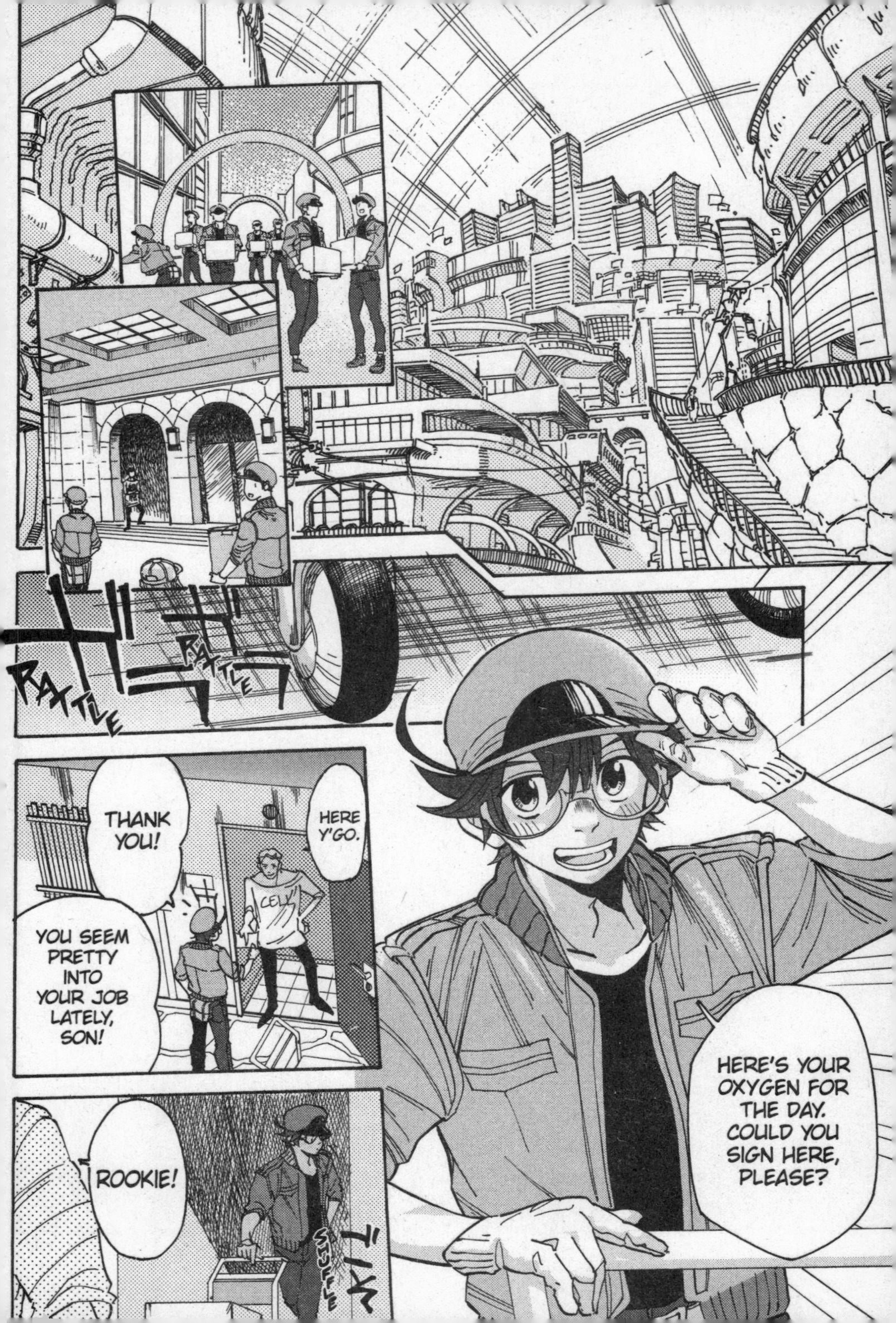
RATTLE
RATTLE
HERE'S YOUR OXYGEN FOR THE DAY. COULD YOU SIGN HERE, PLEASE?
HERE Y'GO.
THANK YOU!
YOU SEEM PRETTY INTO YOUR JOB LATELY, SON!
CELL
ROOKIE!
SHUFFLE

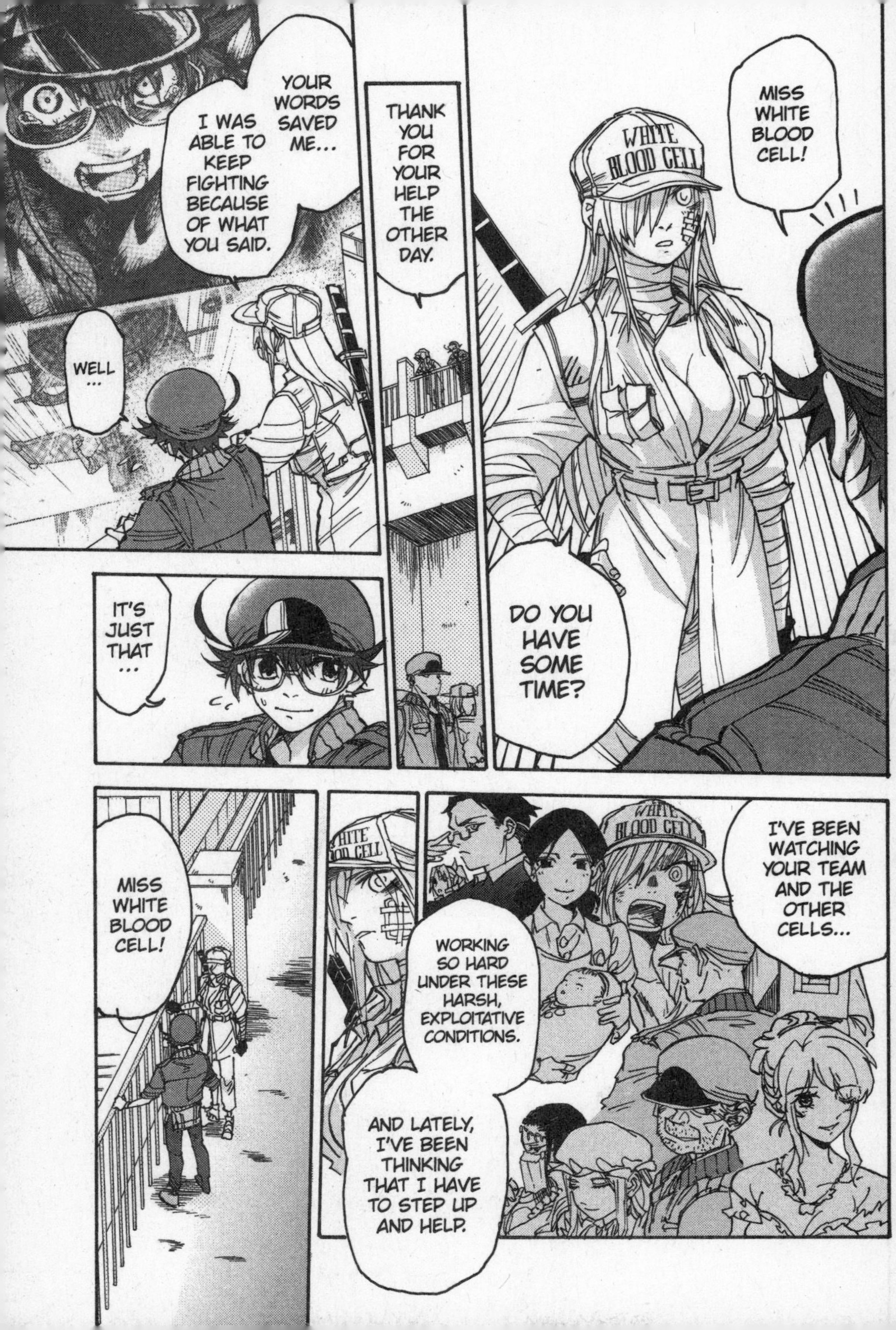
MISS WHITE BLOOD CELL!
WHITE BLOOD CELL
DO YOU HAVE SOME TIME?
THANK YOU FOR YOUR HELP THE OTHER DAY.
YOUR WORDS SAVED ME...
I WAS ABLE TO KEEP FIGHTING BECAUSE OF WHAT YOU SAID.
WELL...
IT'S JUST THAT...
I'VE BEEN WATCHING YOUR TEAM AND THE OTHER CELLS...
WORKING SO HARD UNDER THESE HARSH, EXPLOITATIVE CONDITIONS.
AND LATELY, I'VE BEEN THINKING THAT I HAVE TO STEP UP AND HELP.
MISS WHITE BLOOD CELL!

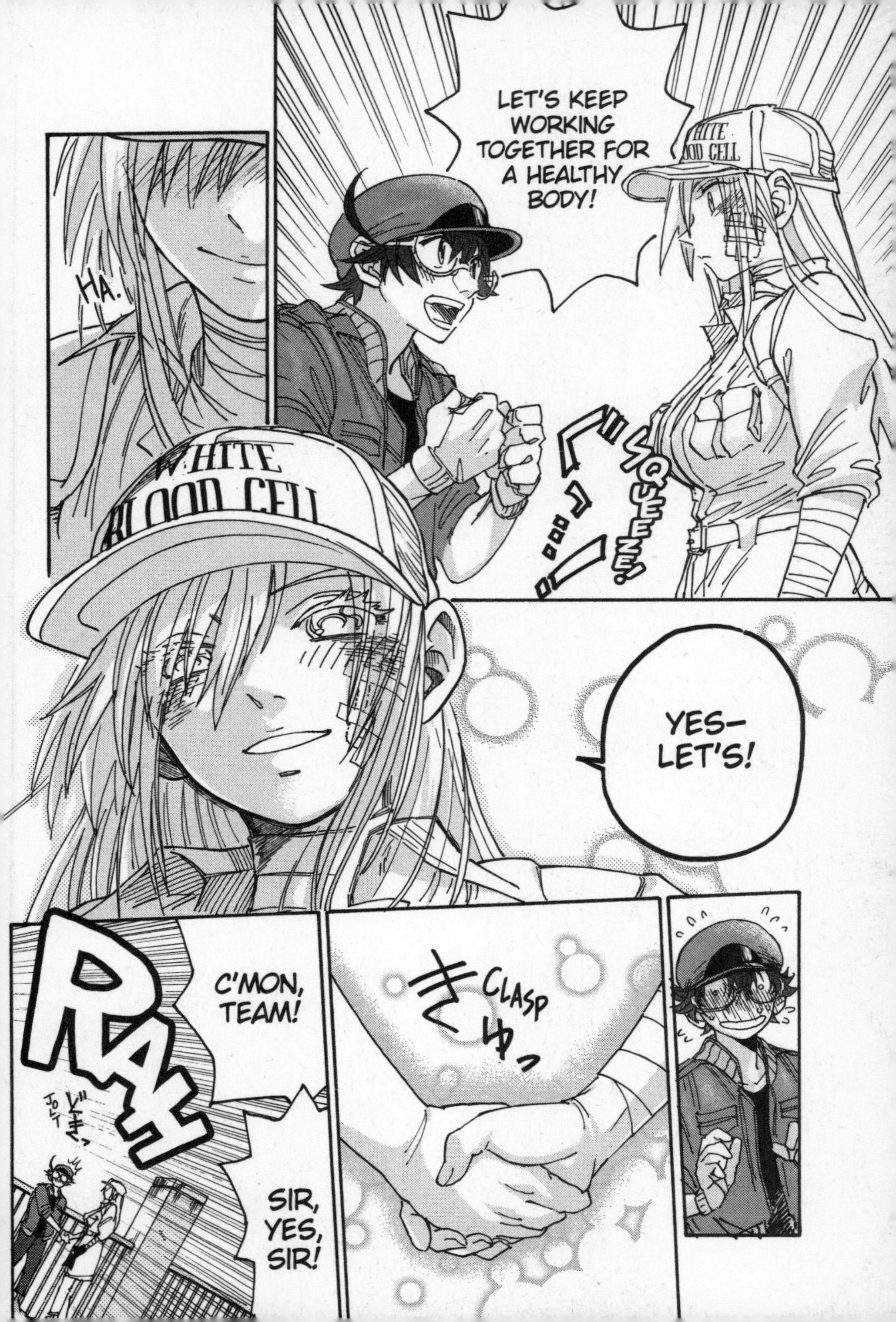

LET'S KEEP WORKING TOGETHER FOR A HEALTHY BODY!
SQUEEZE!
HA.
YES— LET'S!
CLASP
きゅっ
C'MON, TEAM!
RAH
JOLT
SIR, YES, SIR!

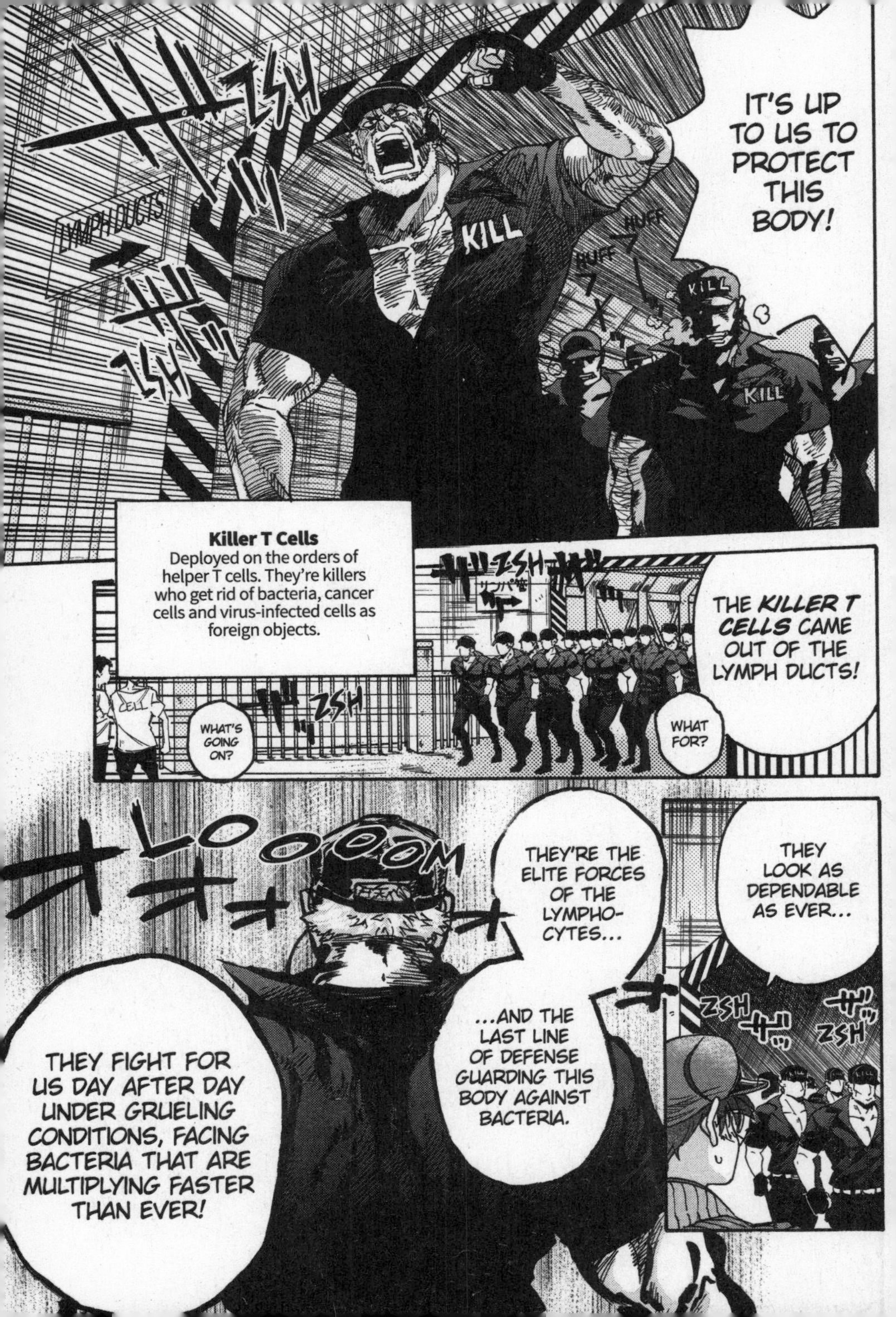
IT'S UP TO US TO PROTECT THIS BODY!
HUFF
HUFF
ZSH
LYMPH DUCTS
KILL
ZSH
KILL
KILL
THE KILLER T CELLS CAME OUT OF THE LYMPH DUCTS!
ZSH
WHAT FOR?
ZSH
WHAT'S GOING ON?
CELL
Killer T Cells
Deployed on the orders of helper T cells. They're killers who get rid of bacteria, cancer cells and virus-infected cells as foreign objects.
THEY LOOK AS DEPENDABLE AS EVER...
ZSH
ZSH
THEY'RE THE ELITE FORCES OF THE LYMPHO-CYTES...
...AND THE LAST LINE OF DEFENSE GUARDING THIS BODY AGAINST BACTERIA.
LOOOOOM
THEY FIGHT FOR US DAY AFTER DAY UNDER GRUELING CONDITIONS, FACING BACTERIA THAT ARE MULTIPLYING FASTER THAN EVER!

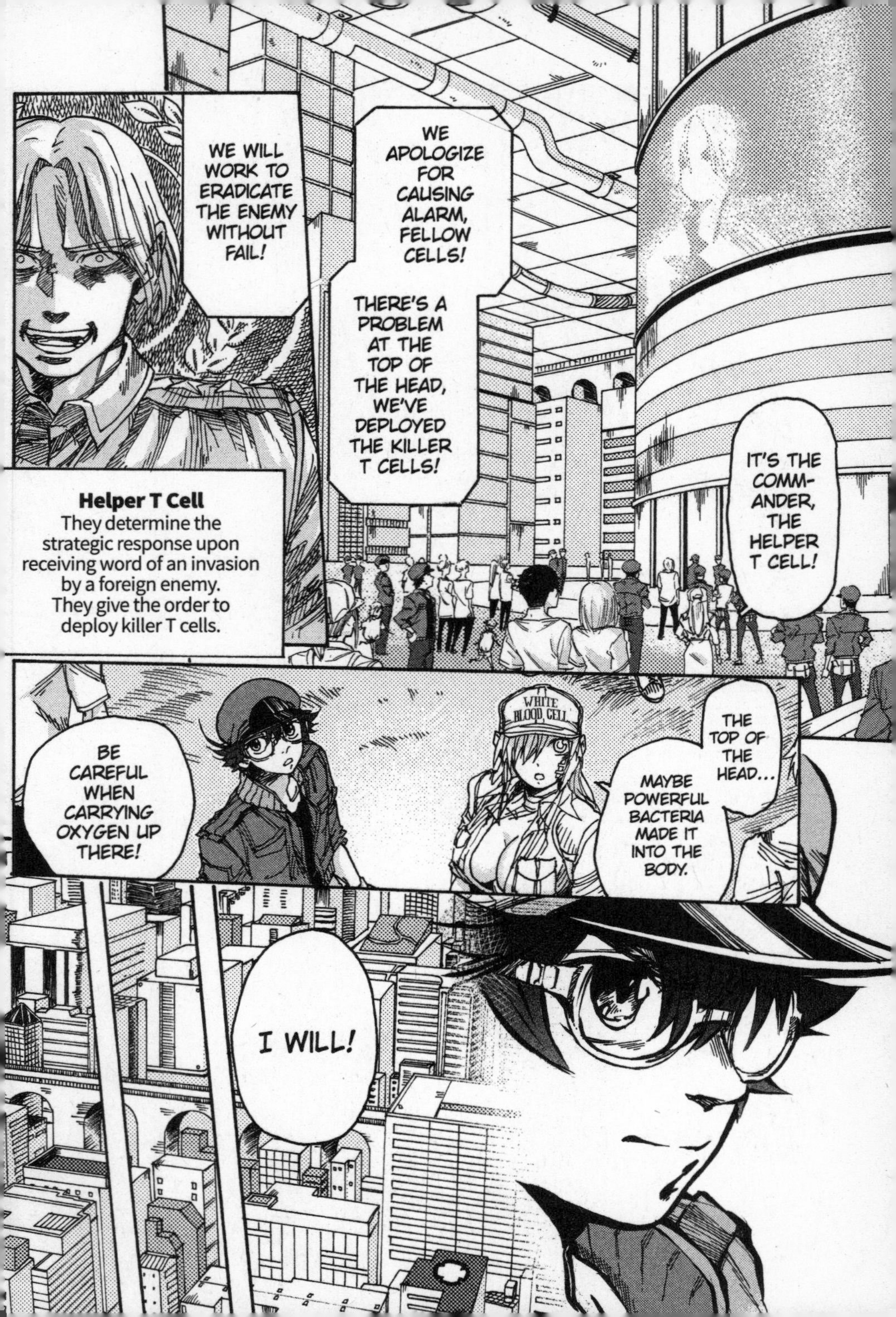
IT'S THE COMMANDER, THE HELPER T CELL!
WE APOLOGIZE FOR CAUSING ALARM, FELLOW CELLS!
THERE'S A PROBLEM AT THE TOP OF THE HEAD, WE'VE DEPLOYED THE KILLER T CELLS!
WE WILL WORK TO ERADICATE THE ENEMY WITHOUT FAIL!
Helper T Cell
They determine the strategic response upon receiving word of an invasion by a foreign enemy. They give the order to deploy killer T cells.
WHITE BLOOD CELL
THE TOP OF THE HEAD...
MAYBE POWERFUL BACTERIA MADE IT INTO THE BODY.
BE CAREFUL WHEN CARRYING OXYGEN UP THERE!
I WILL!

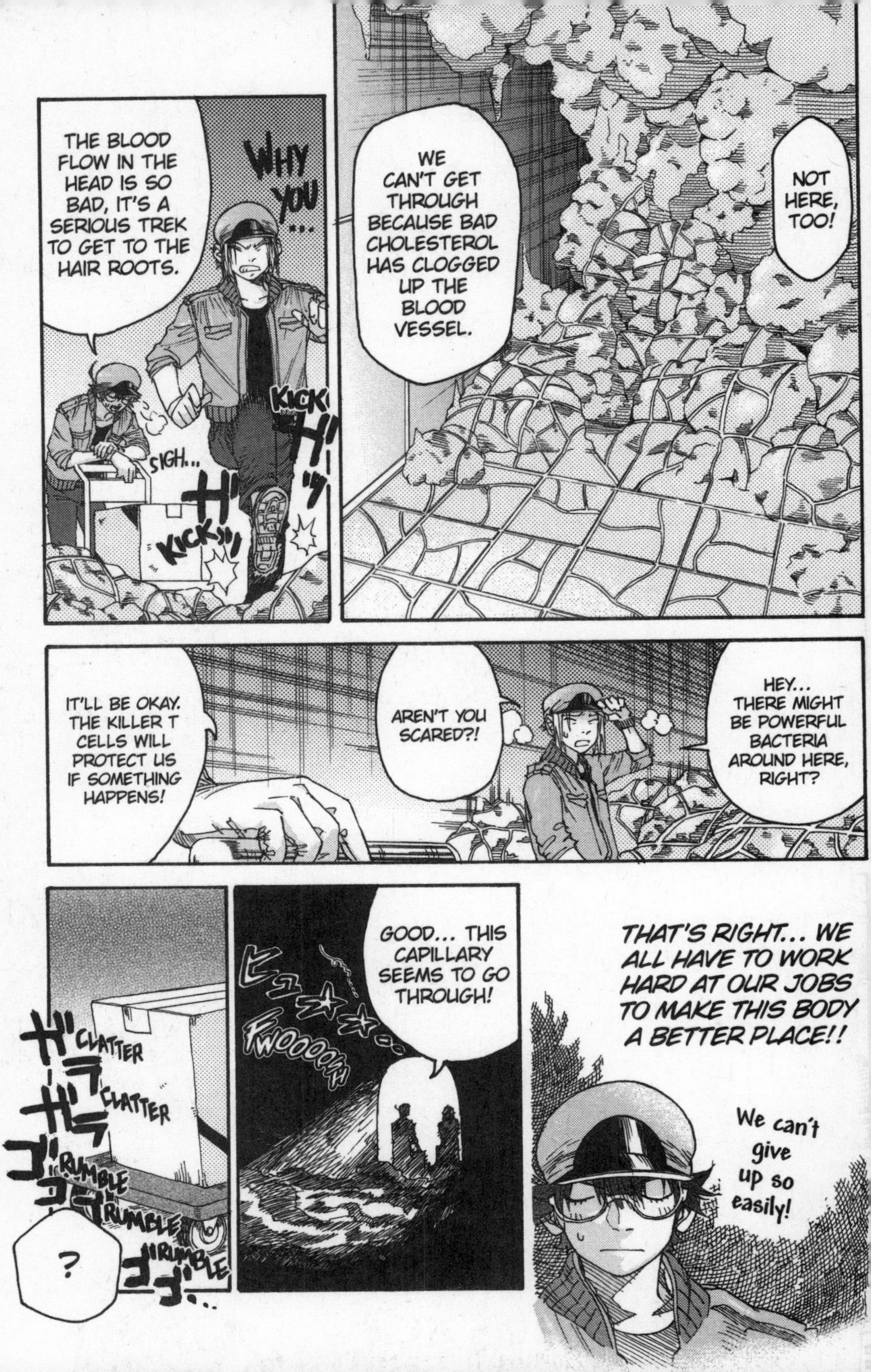
NOT HERE, TOO!
WE CAN'T GET THROUGH BECAUSE BAD CHOLESTEROL HAS CLOGGED UP THE BLOOD VESSEL.
WHY YOU...
THE BLOOD FLOW IN THE HEAD IS SO BAD, IT'S A SERIOUS TREK TO GET TO THE HAIR ROOTS.
KICK
SIGH...
KICK
HEY... THERE MIGHT BE POWERFUL BACTERIA AROUND HERE, RIGHT?
AREN'T YOU SCARED?!
IT'LL BE OKAY. THE KILLER T CELLS WILL PROTECT US IF SOMETHING HAPPENS!
THAT'S RIGHT... WE ALL HAVE TO WORK HARD AT OUR JOBS TO MAKE THIS BODY A BETTER PLACE!!
We can't give up so easily!
GOOD... THIS CAPILLARY SEEMS TO GO THROUGH!
FWOOOOH
CLATTER
CLATTER
RUMBLE
RUMBLE
RUMBLE
?

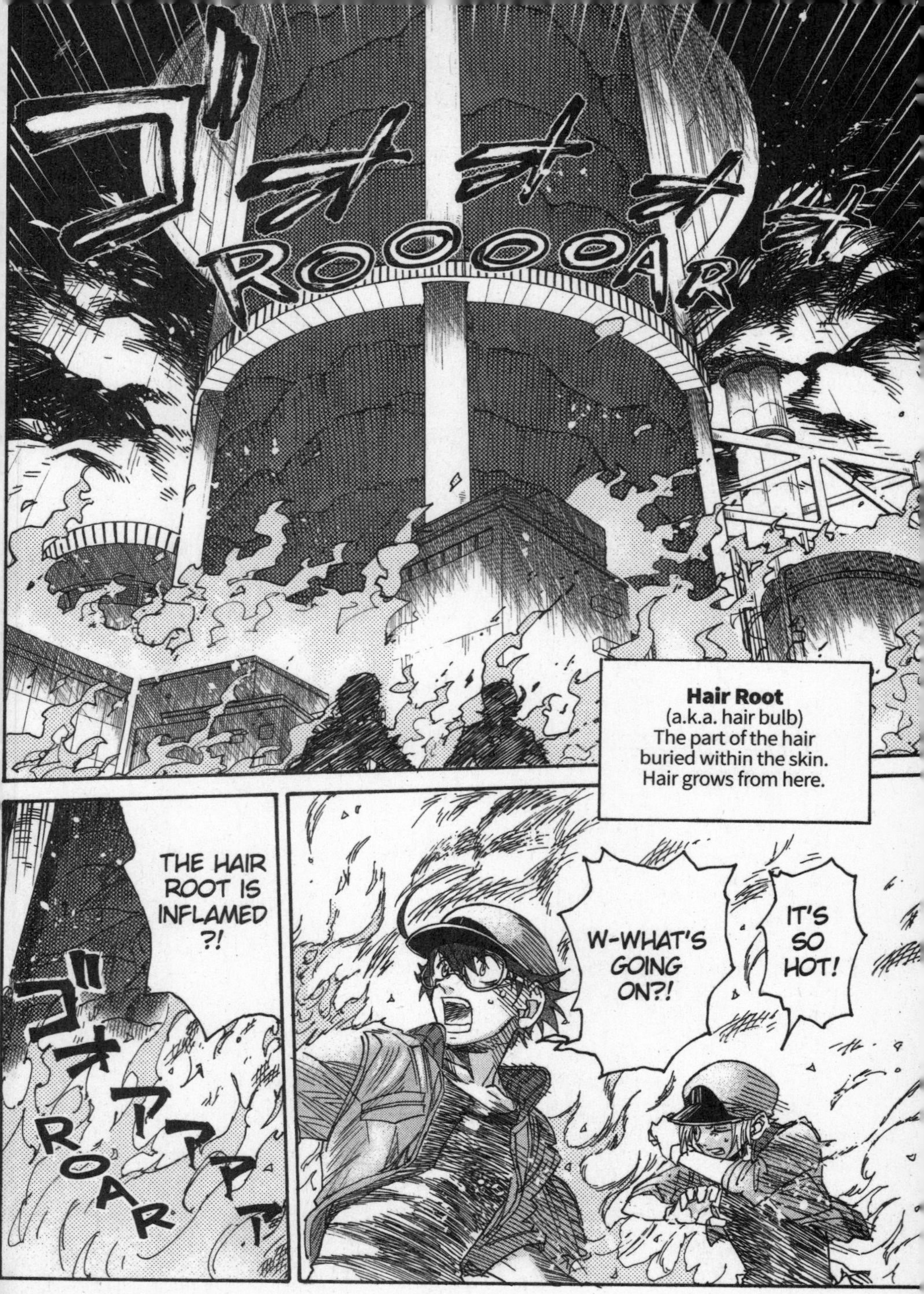
ROOOOAR
Hair Root
(a.k.a. hair bulb)
The part of the hair buried within the skin. Hair grows from here.
IT'S SO HOT!
W-WHAT'S GOING ON?!
THE HAIR ROOT IS INFLAMED ?!
ROAR

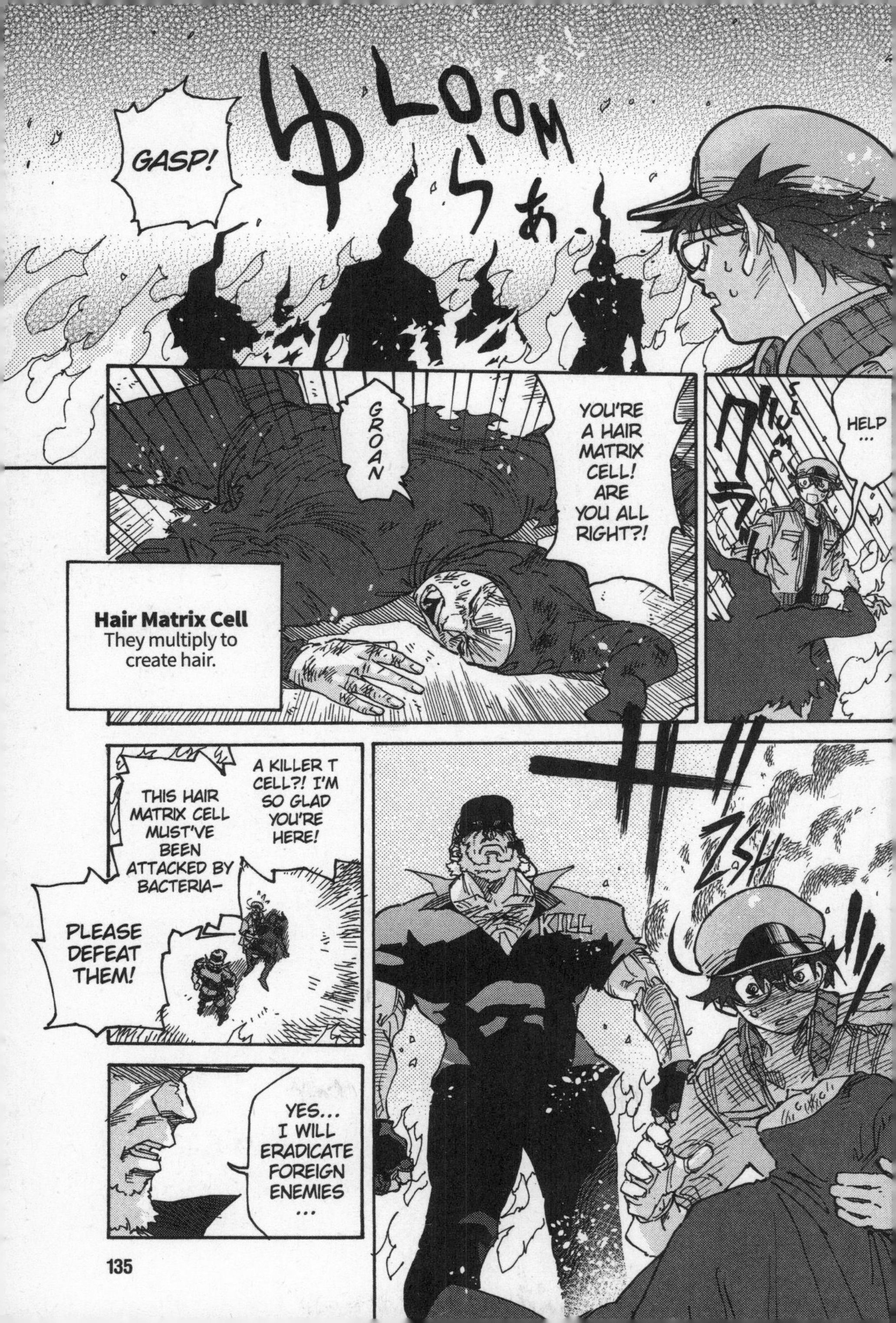
GASP!
ゆ LOOM らぁ
HELP ...
SLUMP
グラ
YOU'RE A HAIR MATRIX CELL! ARE YOU ALL RIGHT?!
GROAN
Hair Matrix Cell
They multiply to create hair.
ZSH
A KILLER T CELL?! I'M SO GLAD YOU'RE HERE!
THIS HAIR MATRIX CELL MUST'VE BEEN ATTACKED BY BACTERIA—
PLEASE DEFEAT THEM!
YES... I WILL ERADICATE FOREIGN ENEMIES ...
KILL

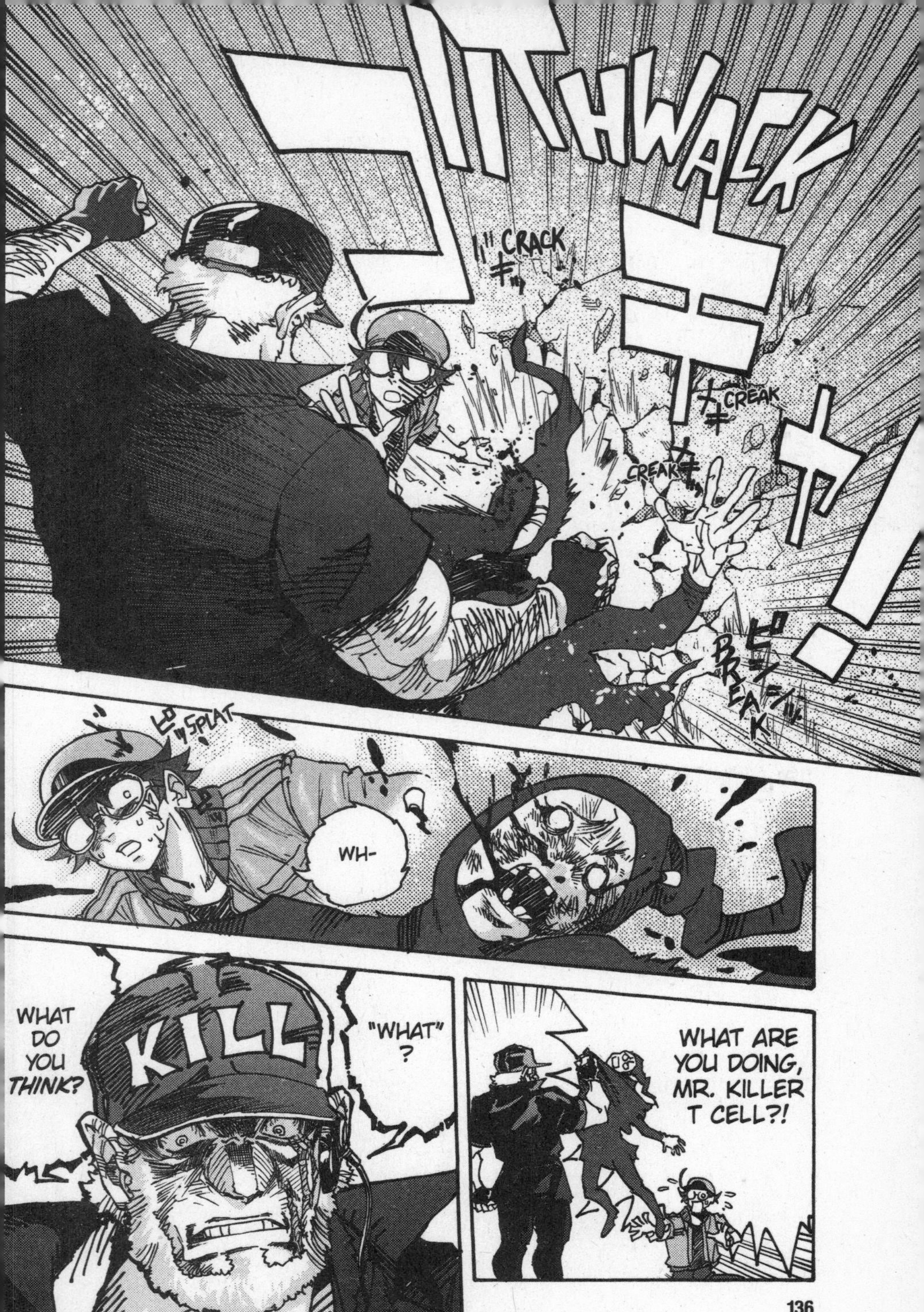
WHACK
CRACK
CREAK
CREAK
BREAK
SPLAT
WH-
WHAT ARE YOU DOING, MR. KILLER T CELL?!
"WHAT"?
WHAT DO YOU THINK?
KILL

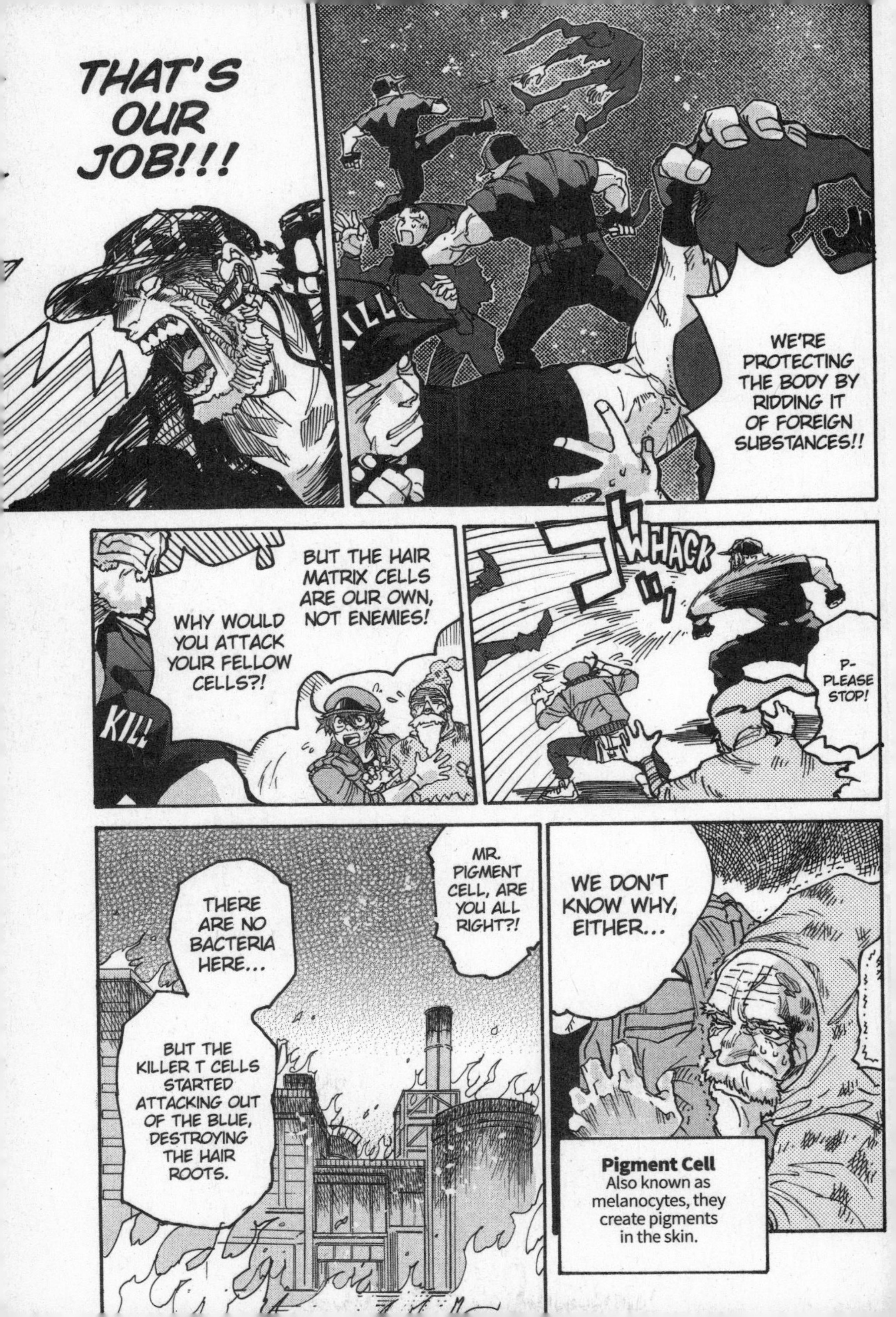
WE'RE PROTECTING THE BODY BY RIDDING IT OF FOREIGN SUBSTANCES!!
THAT'S OUR JOB!!!
WHACK
P- PLEASE STOP!
BUT THE HAIR MATRIX CELLS ARE OUR OWN, NOT ENEMIES!
WHY WOULD YOU ATTACK YOUR FELLOW CELLS?!
WE DON'T KNOW WHY, EITHER...
Pigment Cell
Also known as melanocytes, they create pigments in the skin.
MR. PIGMENT CELL, ARE YOU ALL RIGHT?!
THERE ARE NO BACTERIA HERE...
BUT THE KILLER T CELLS STARTED ATTACKING OUT OF THE BLUE, DESTROYING THE HAIR ROOTS.

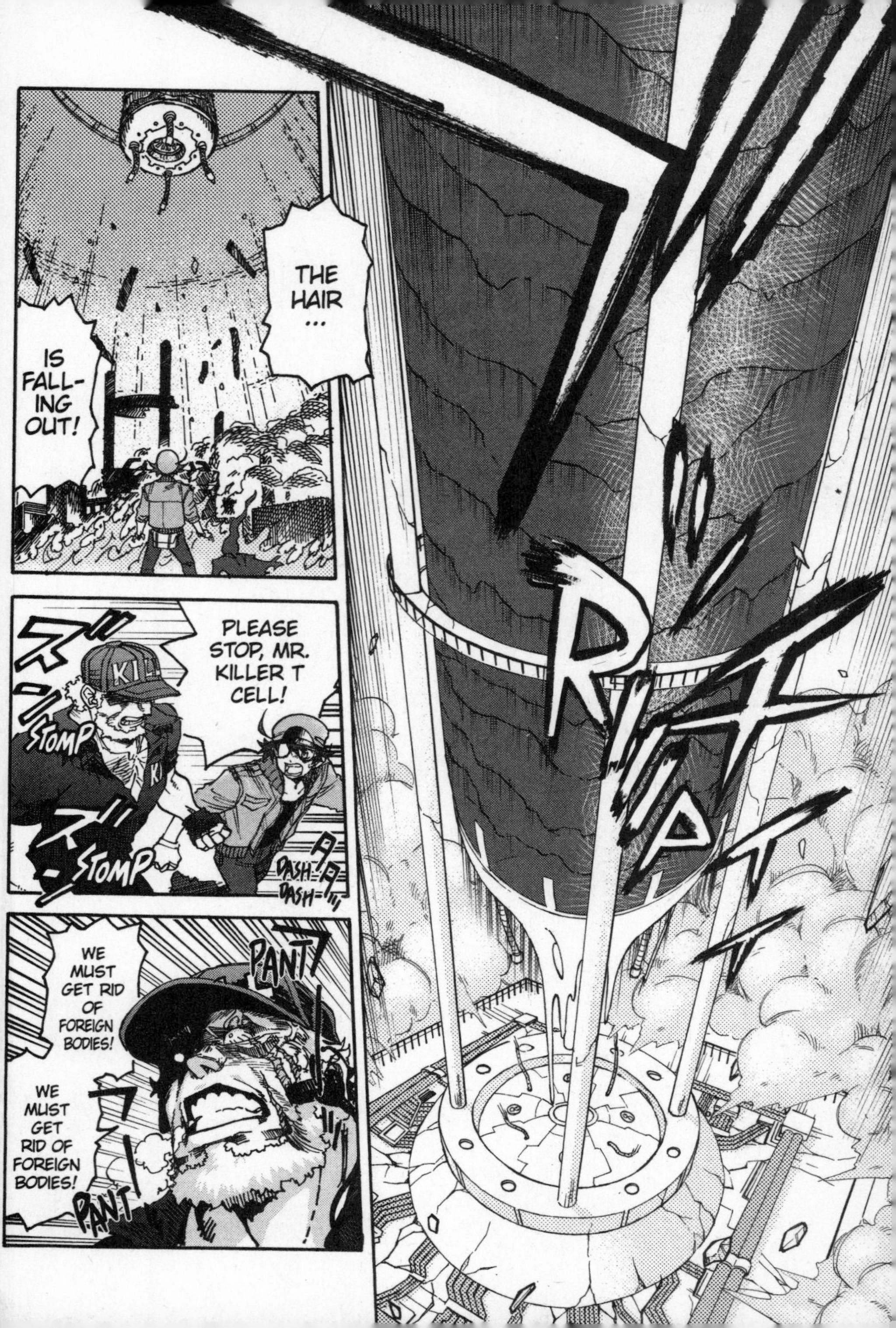
RIP
THE HAIR ...
IS FALLING OUT!
PLEASE STOP, MR. KILLER T CELL!
STOMP
STOMP
DASH DASH
WE MUST GET RID OF FOREIGN BODIES!
WE MUST GET RID OF FOREIGN BODIES!
PANT
PANT

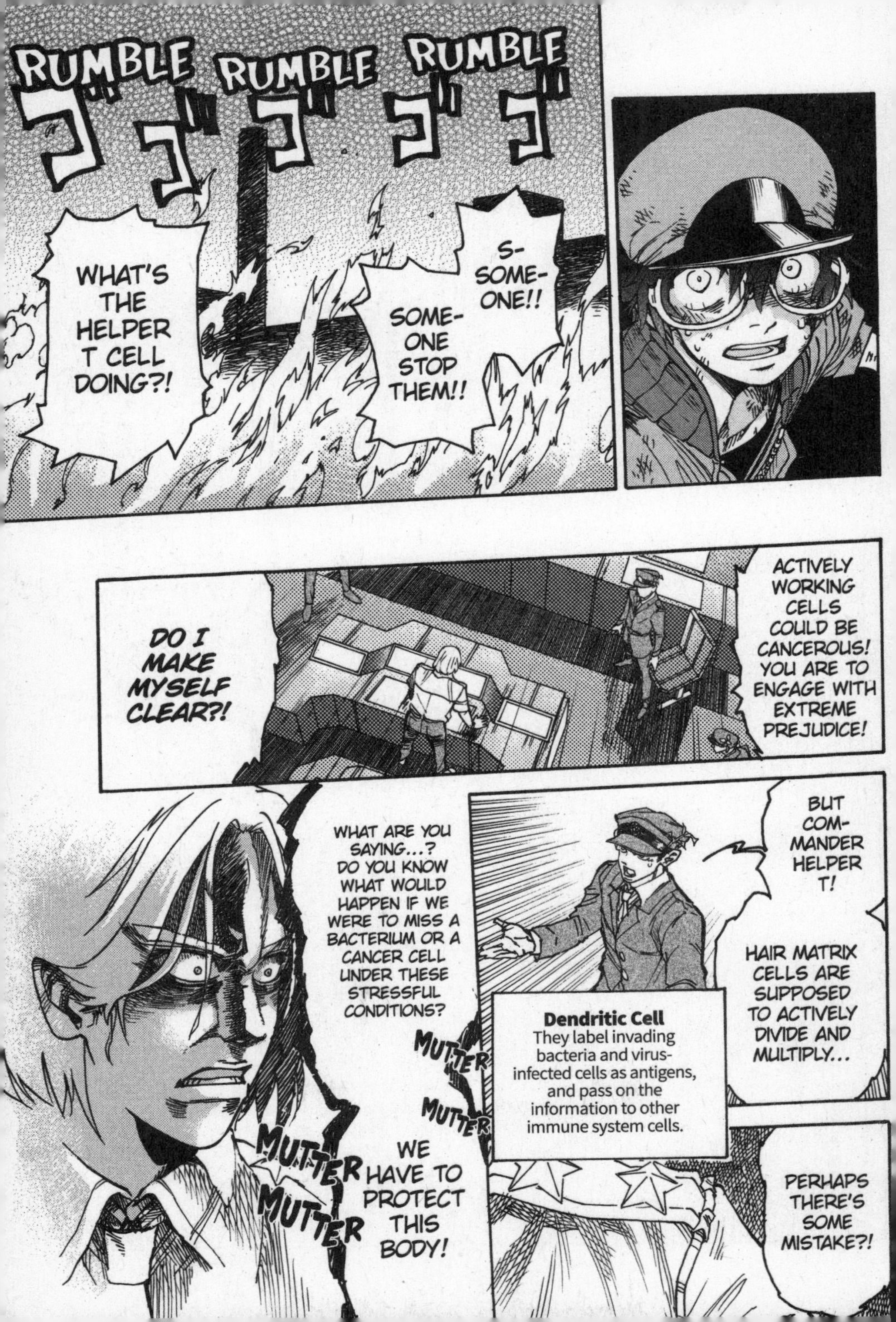
RUMBLE RUMBLE RUMBLE
S-SOME-ONE!!
SOME-ONE STOP THEM!!
WHAT'S THE HELPER T CELL DOING?!
ACTIVELY WORKING CELLS COULD BE CANCEROUS! YOU ARE TO ENGAGE WITH EXTREME PREJUDICE!
DO I MAKE MYSELF CLEAR?!
BUT COM-MANDER HELPER T!
HAIR MATRIX CELLS ARE SUPPOSED TO ACTIVELY DIVIDE AND MULTIPLY...
Dendritic Cell
They label invading bacteria and virus-infected cells as antigens, and pass on the information to other immune system cells.
PERHAPS THERE'S SOME MISTAKE?!
WHAT ARE YOU SAYING...? DO YOU KNOW WHAT WOULD HAPPEN IF WE WERE TO MISS A BACTERIUM OR A CANCER CELL UNDER THESE STRESSFUL CONDITIONS?
MUTTER
MUTTER
WE HAVE TO PROTECT THIS BODY!
MUTTER
MUTTER

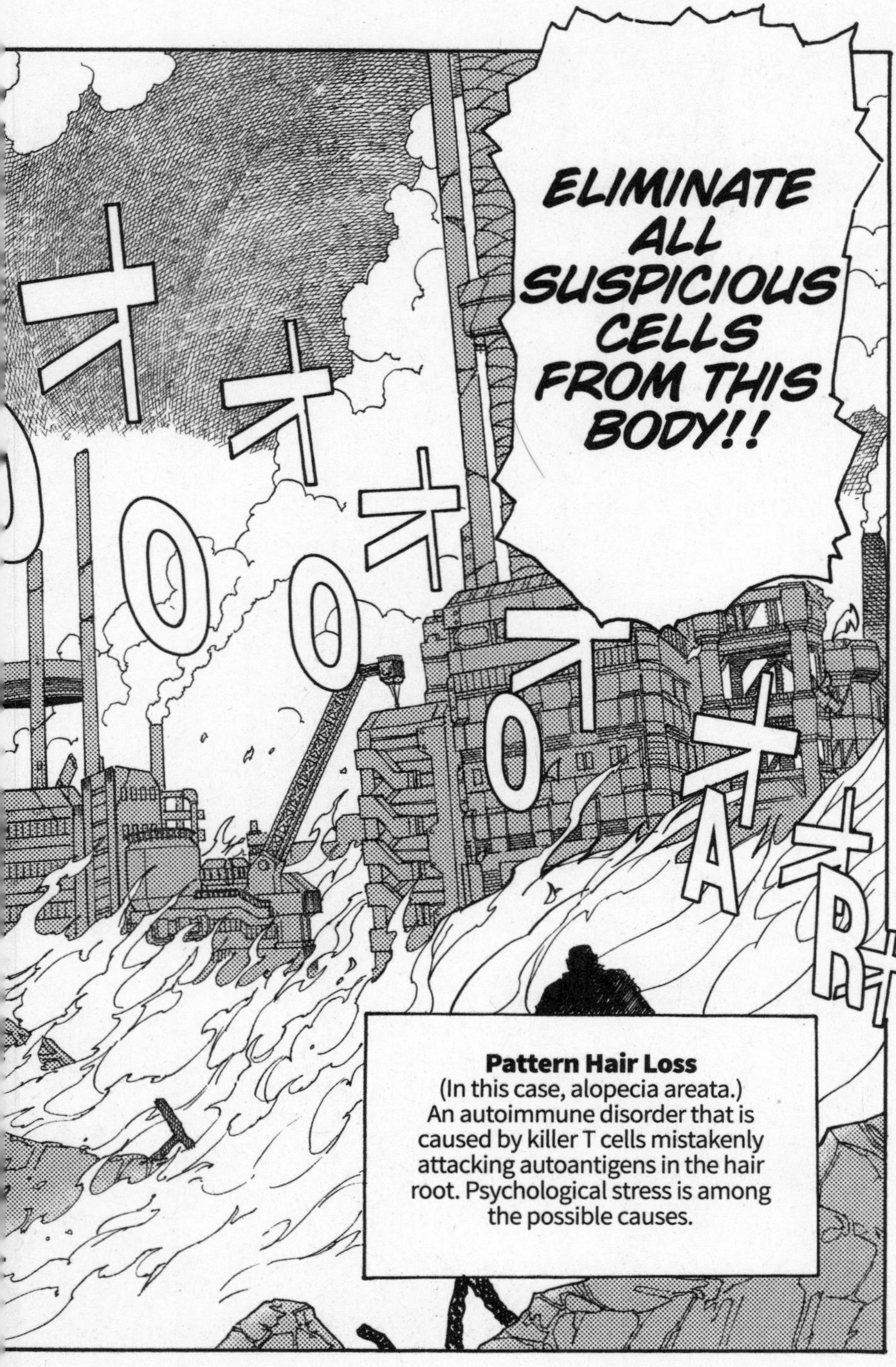
ELIMINATE ALL SUSPICIOUS CELLS FROM THIS BODY!!
OOOAR
Pattern Hair Loss
(In this case, alopecia areata.)
An autoimmune disorder that is caused by killer T cells mistakenly attacking autoantigens in the hair root. Psychological stress is among the possible causes.

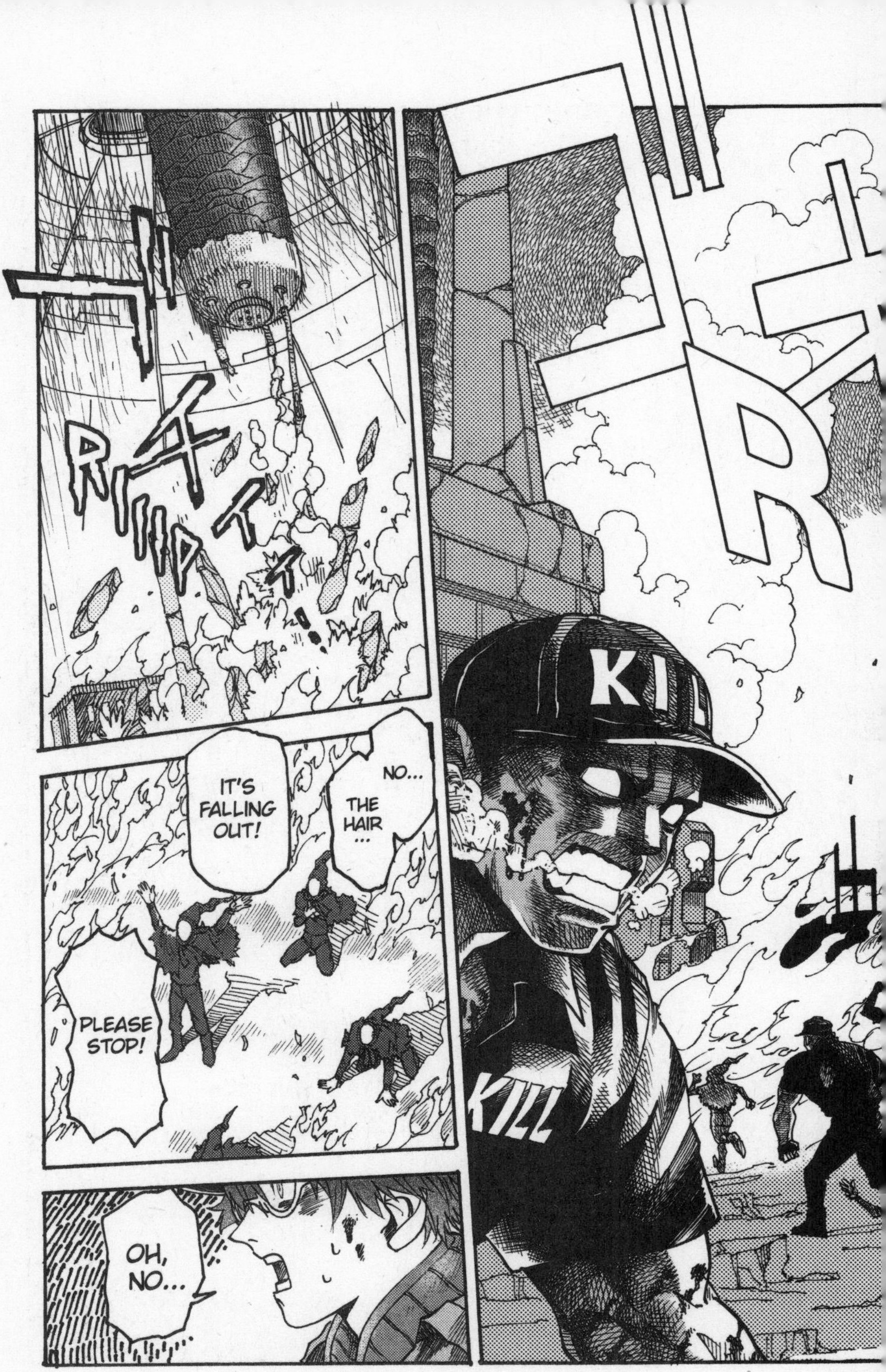
KILL
RIIIP
NO... THE HAIR ...
IT'S FALLING OUT!
PLEASE STOP!
OH, NO...

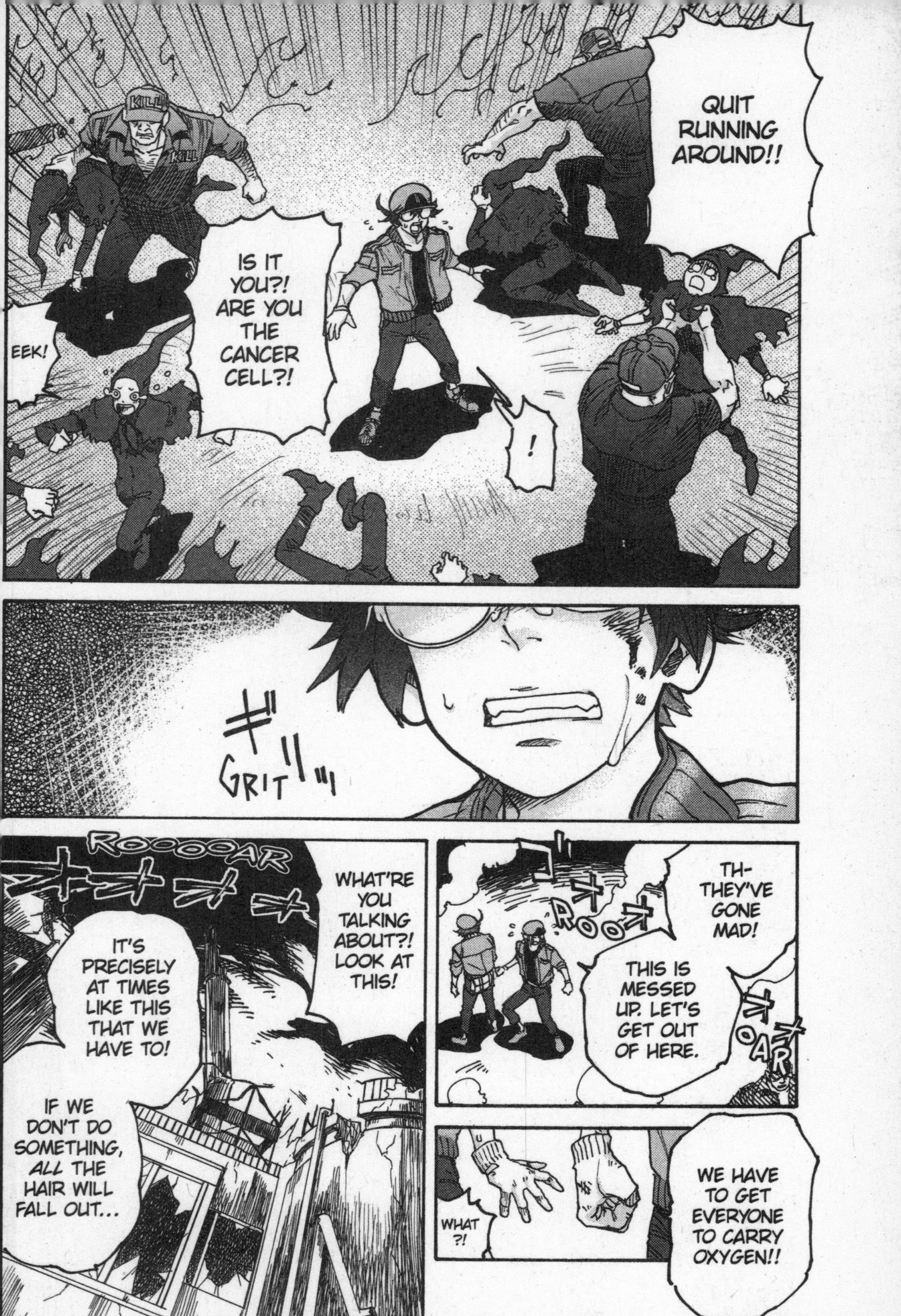
QUIT RUNNING AROUND!!
IS IT YOU?! ARE YOU THE CANCER CELL?!
!
EEK!
GRIT
TH- THEY'VE GONE MAD!
ROOAR
THIS IS MESSED UP. LET'S GET OUT OF HERE.
OAR
WE HAVE TO GET EVERYONE TO CARRY OXYGEN!!
WHAT ?!
ROOOOAR
WHAT'RE YOU TALKING ABOUT?! LOOK AT THIS!
IT'S PRECISELY AT TIMES LIKE THIS THAT WE HAVE TO!
IF WE DON'T DO SOMETHING, *ALL* THE HAIR WILL FALL OUT...

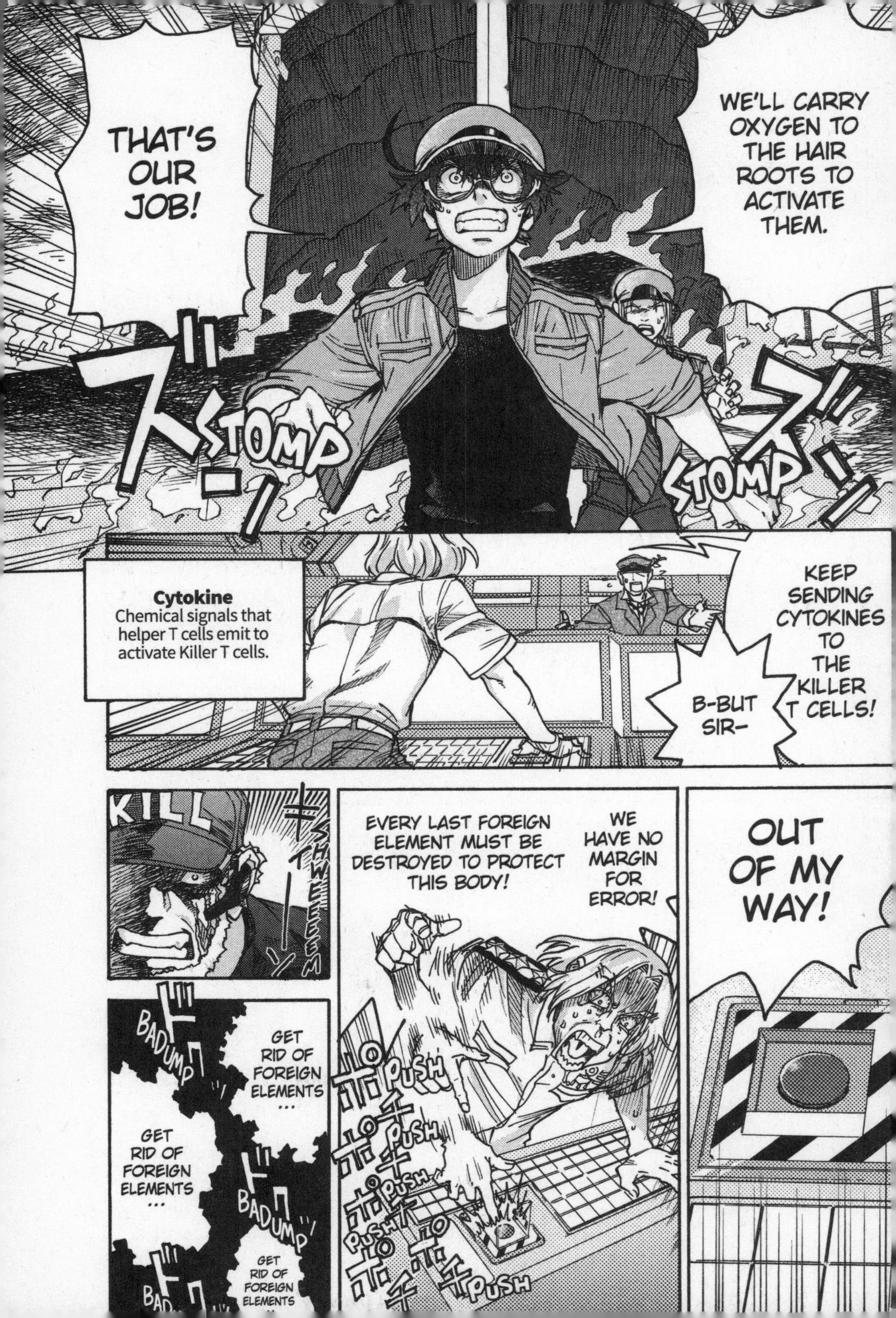
WE'LL CARRY OXYGEN TO THE HAIR ROOTS TO ACTIVATE THEM.
THAT'S OUR JOB!
STOMP
STOMP
KEEP SENDING CYTOKINES TO THE KILLER T CELLS!
B-BUT SIR-
Cytokine
Chemical signals that helper T cells emit to activate Killer T cells.
OUT OF MY WAY!
WE HAVE NO MARGIN FOR ERROR!
EVERY LAST FOREIGN ELEMENT MUST BE DESTROYED TO PROTECT THIS BODY!
PUSH
PUSH
PUSH
PUSH
PUSH
KILL
SHWEEEEM
GET RID OF FOREIGN ELEMENTS...
BADUMP
GET RID OF FOREIGN ELEMENTS...
BADUMP
GET RID OF FOREIGN ELEMENTS
BAD

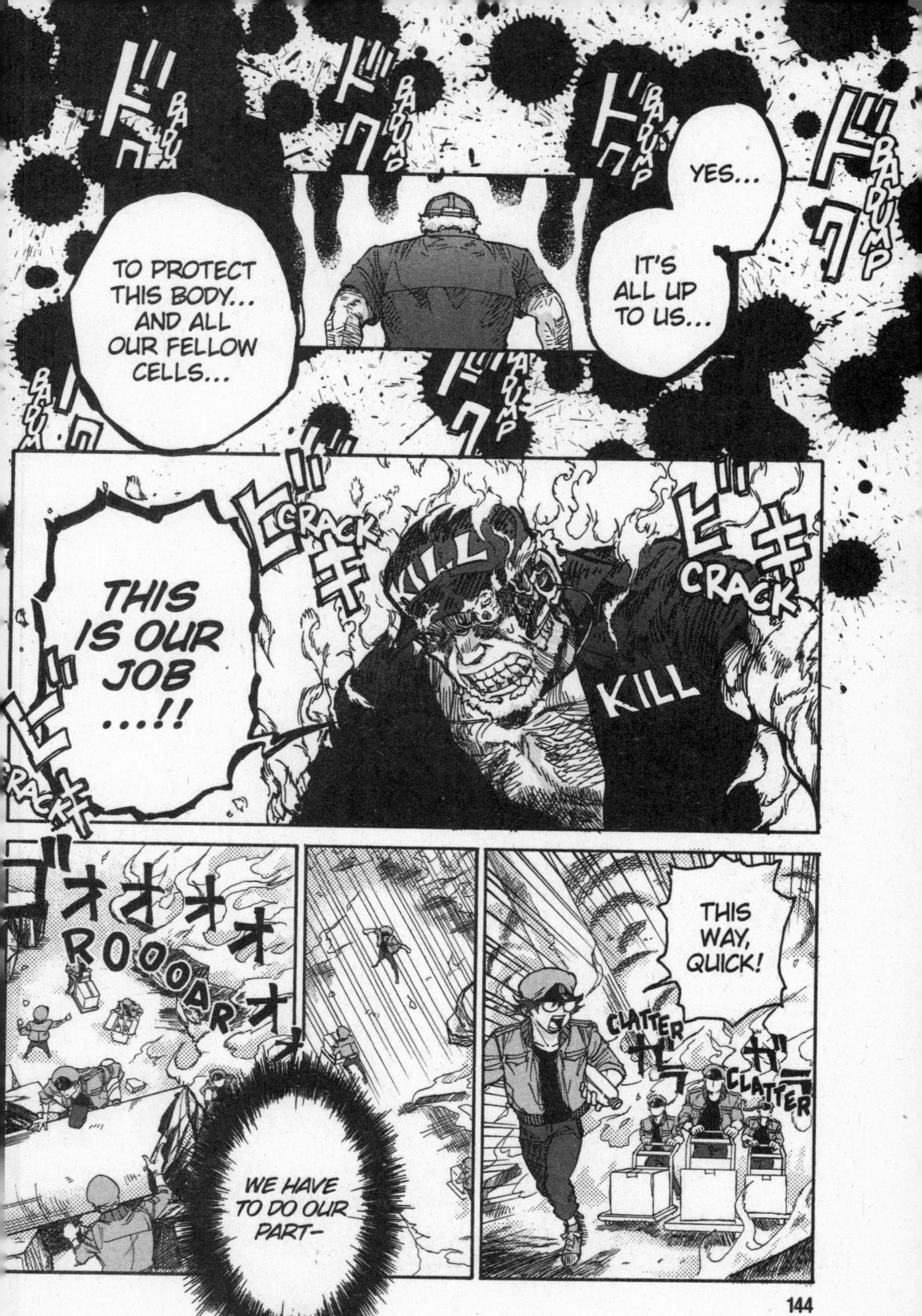

BADUMP
YES...
IT'S ALL UP TO US...
BADUMP
BADUMP
TO PROTECT THIS BODY... AND ALL OUR FELLOW CELLS...
BADUMP
BADUMP
CRACK
CRACK
THIS IS OUR JOB ...!!
CRACK
THIS WAY, QUICK!
CLATTER
CLATTER
ROOOOAR
WE HAVE TO DO OUR PART-

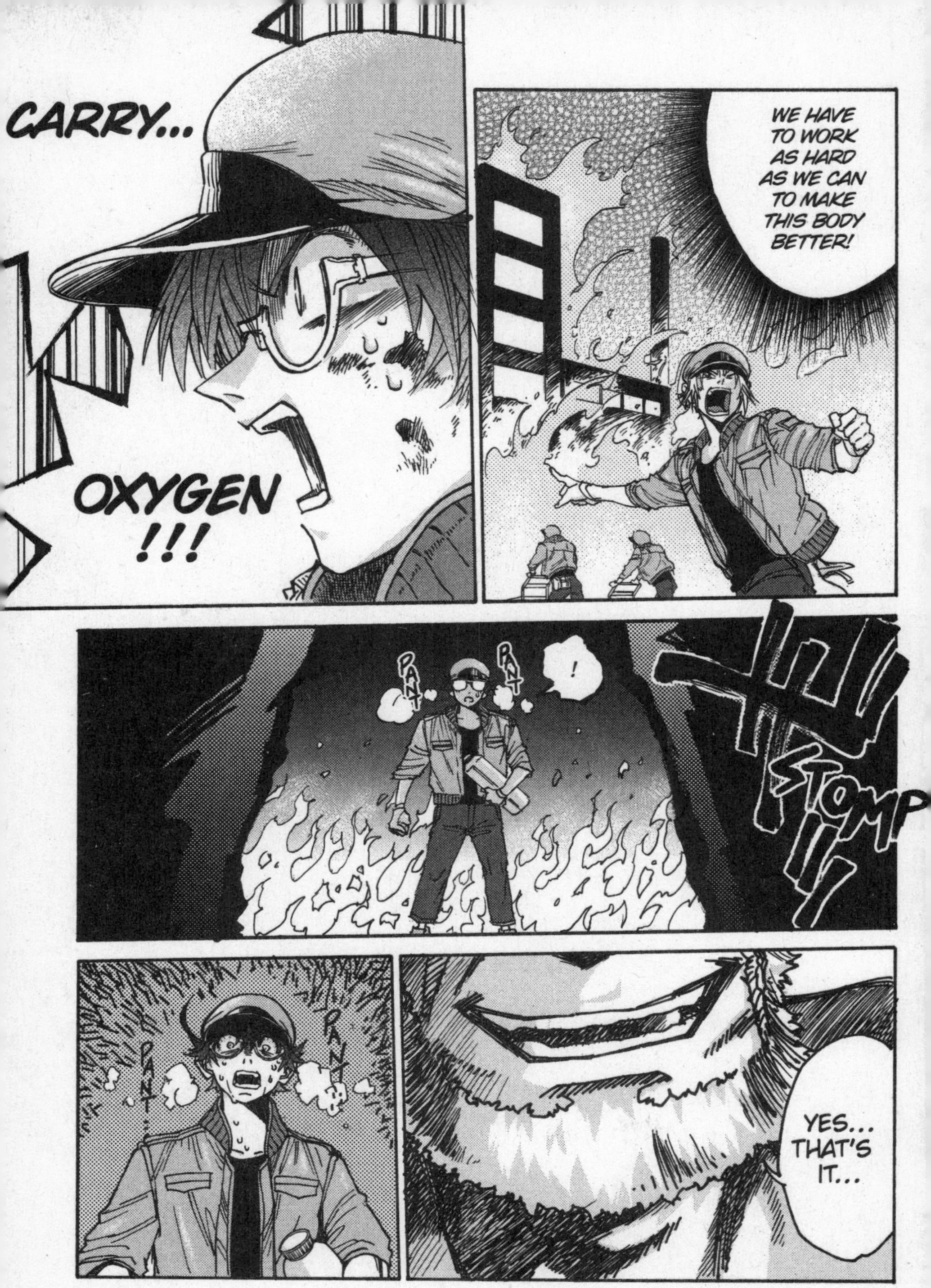
WE HAVE TO WORK AS HARD AS WE CAN TO MAKE THIS BODY BETTER!
CARRY...
OXYGEN !!!
STOMP
PANT
PANT
!
YES... THAT'S IT...
PANT
PANT...

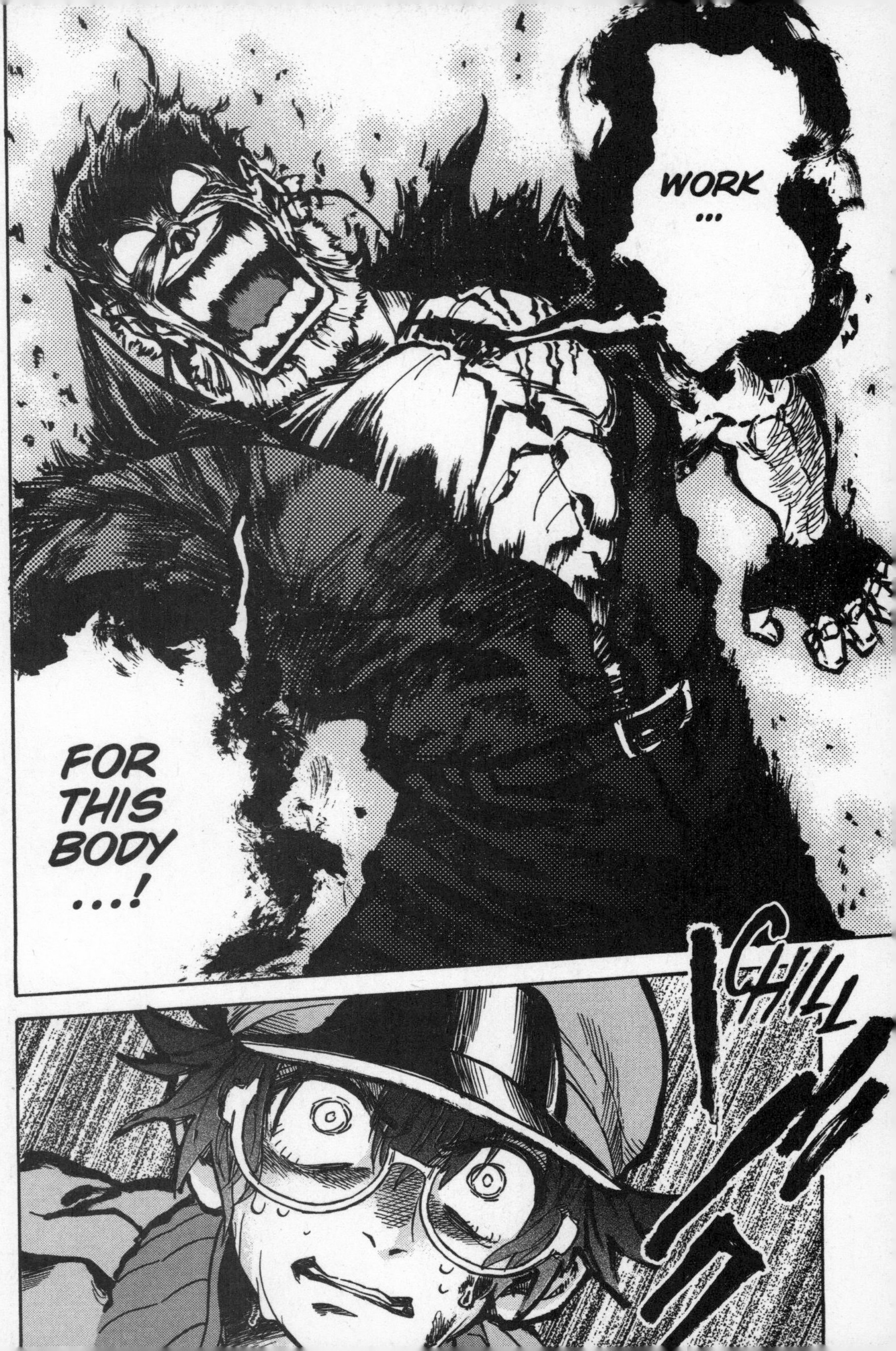
WORK ...
FOR THIS BODY ...!
CHILL

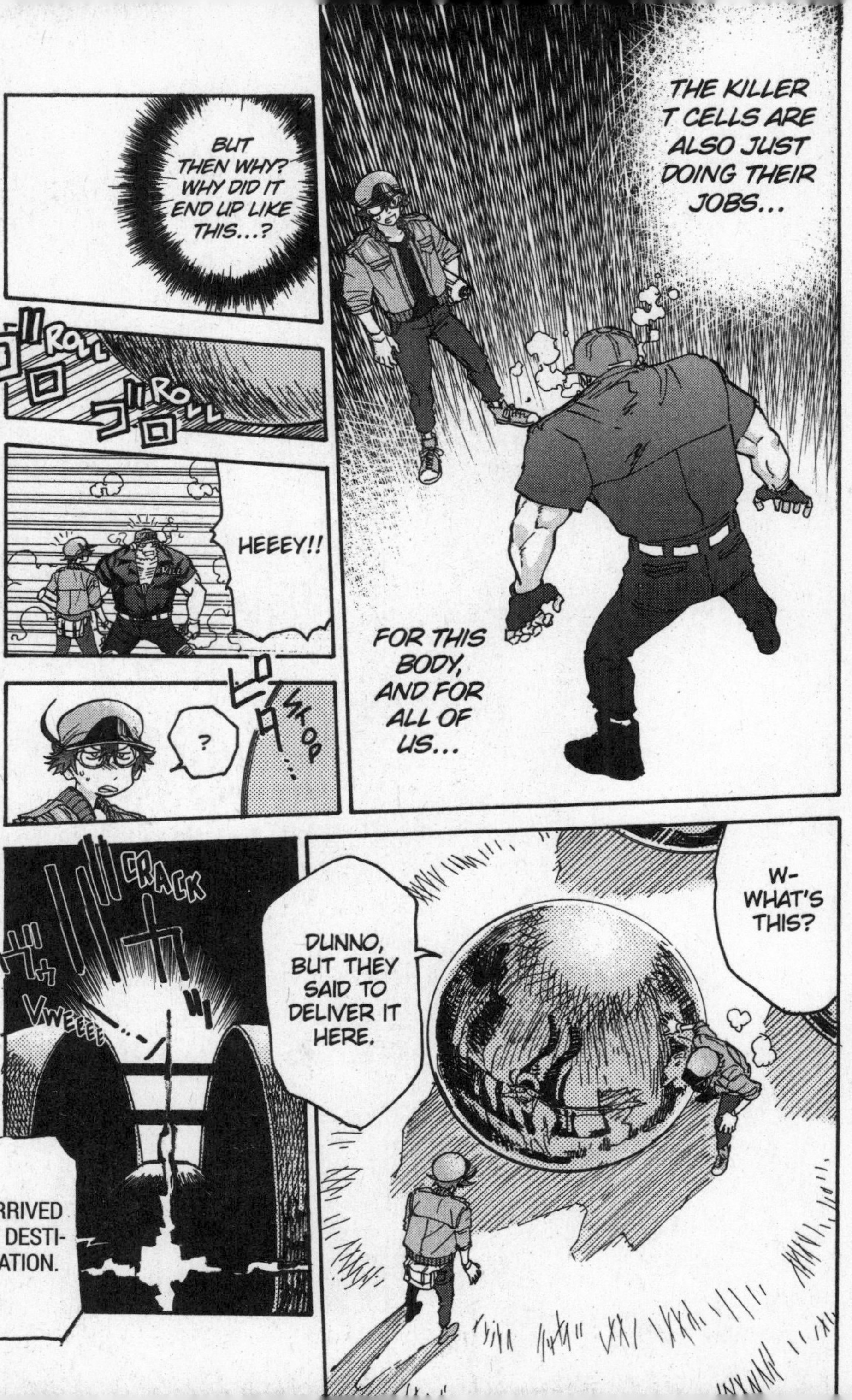
THE KILLER T CELLS ARE ALSO JUST DOING THEIR JOBS...
FOR THIS BODY, AND FOR ALL OF US...
BUT THEN WHY? WHY DID IT END UP LIKE THIS...?
ゴロ ROLL
ゴロ ROLL
HEEEY!!
?
ピタ STOP...
W-WHAT'S THIS?
DUNNO, BUT THEY SAID TO DELIVER IT HERE.
CRACK
VWEEEE
ARRIVED AT DESTINATION.

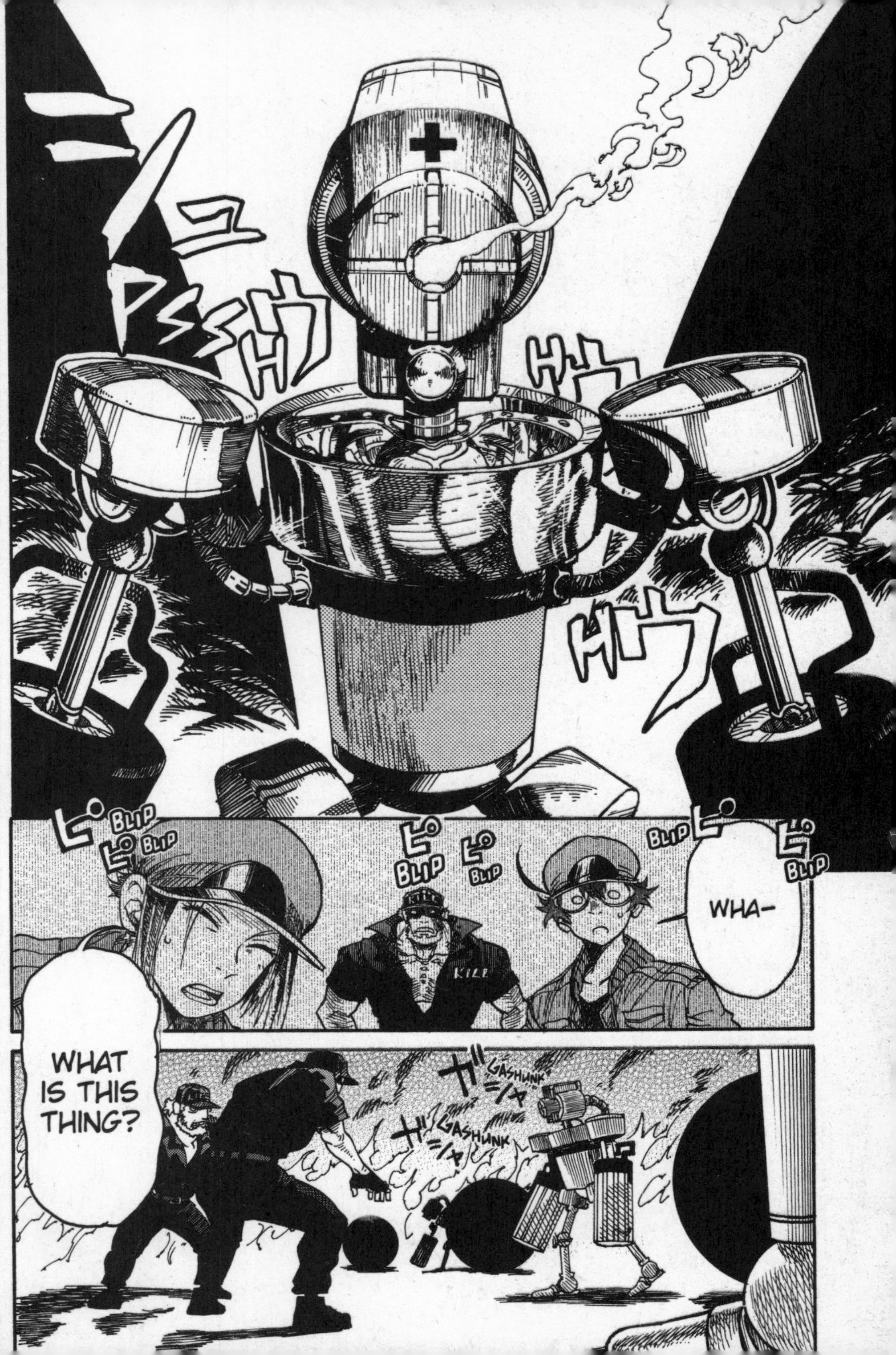
PSSH
BLIP
BLIP
WHA-
BLIP
BLIP
BLIP
BLIP
WHAT IS THIS THING?
GASHUNK
GASHUNK

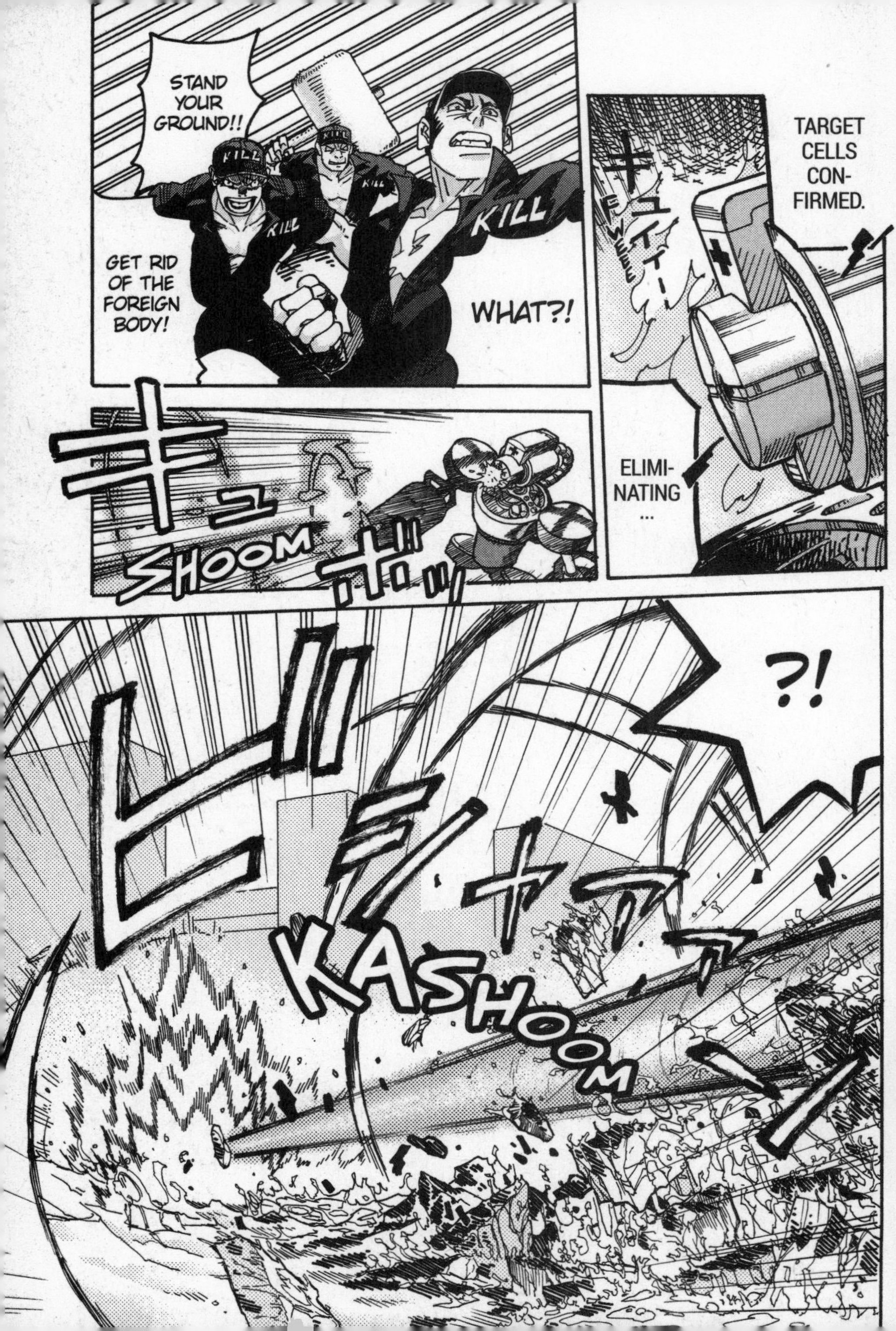
TARGET CELLS CON-FIRMED.
FWEE
ELIMI-NATING ...
STAND YOUR GROUND!!
WHAT?!
GET RID OF THE FOREIGN BODY!
SHOOM
?!
KASHOOM

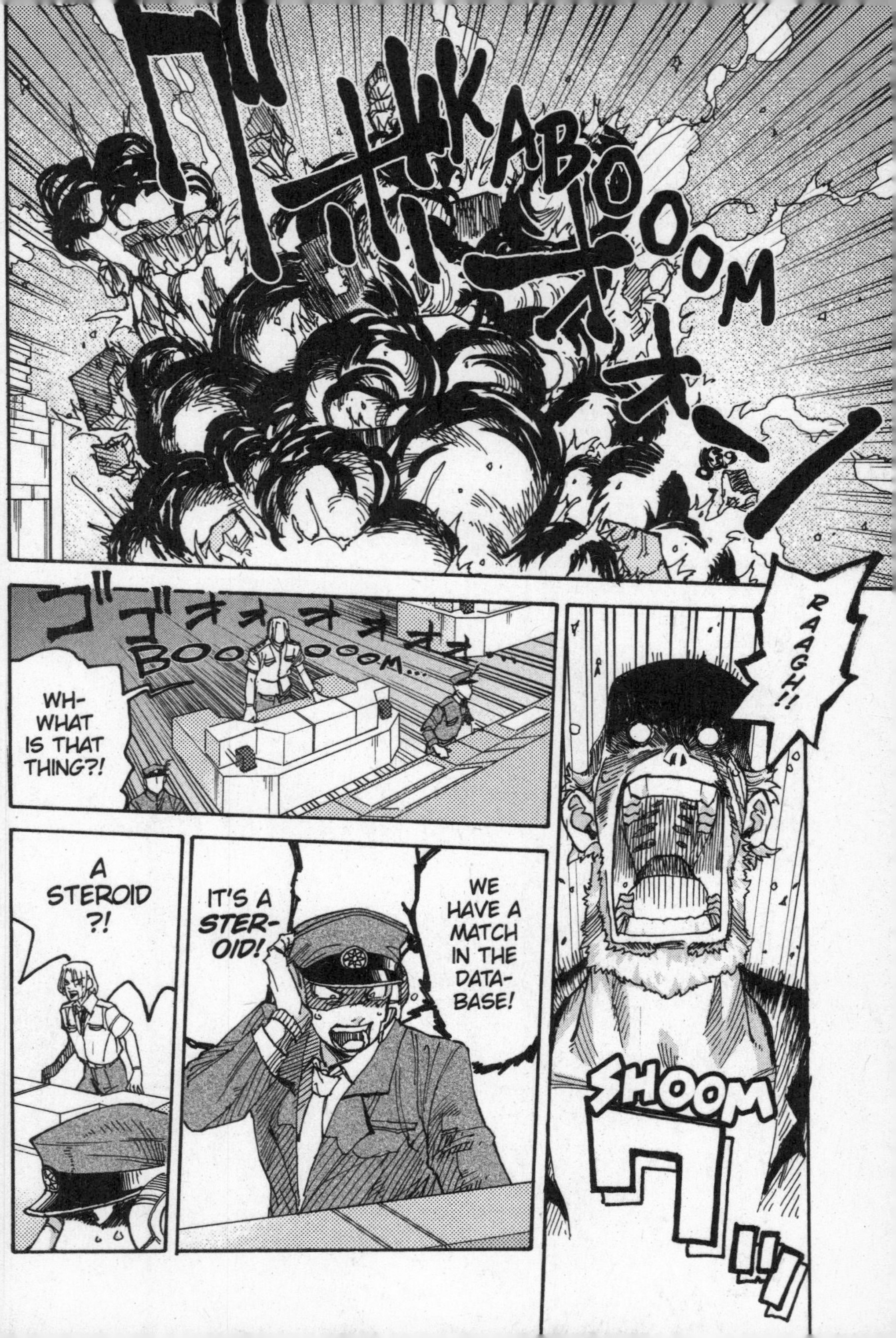
KABOOOOM
RAAGH!!
SHOOM
BOOOOOOOM...
WH-WHAT IS THAT THING?!
WE HAVE A MATCH IN THE DATA-BASE!
IT'S A STER-OID!
A STEROID ?!

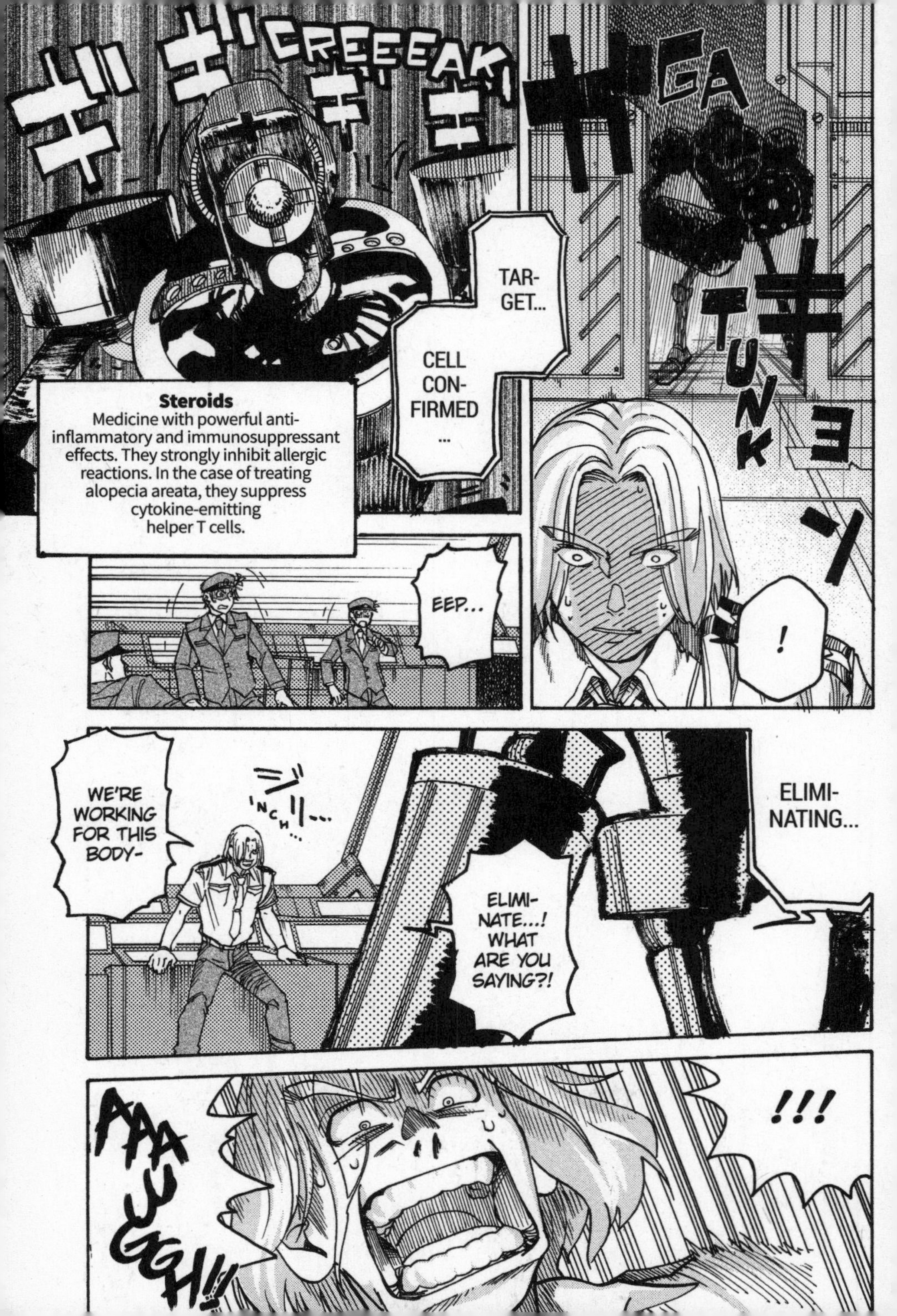
GA
TUNK
CREEEAK!
TARGET...
CELL CONFIRMED...
Steroids
Medicine with powerful anti-inflammatory and immunosuppressant effects. They strongly inhibit allergic reactions. In the case of treating alopecia areata, they suppress cytokine-emitting helper T cells.
!
EEP...
ELIMINATING...
ELIMINATE...! WHAT ARE YOU SAYING?!
WE'RE WORKING FOR THIS BODY-
INCH...
!!!
AAAUUGGH!!

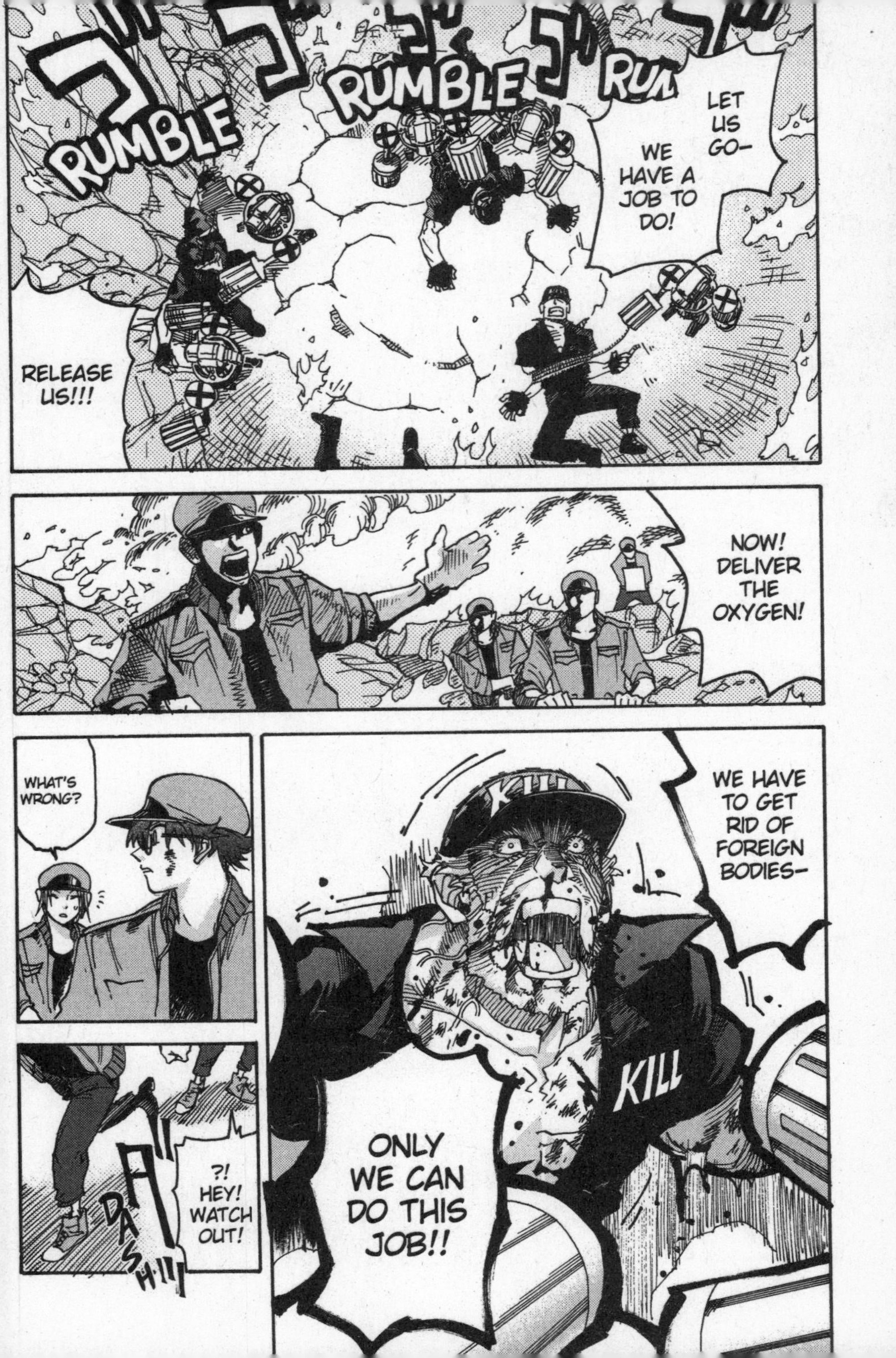
RUMBLE
RUMBLE
RUM
LET US GO—
WE HAVE A JOB TO DO!
RELEASE US!!!
NOW! DELIVER THE OXYGEN!
WE HAVE TO GET RID OF FOREIGN BODIES—
KILL
KILL
ONLY WE CAN DO THIS JOB!!
WHAT'S WRONG?
?! HEY! WATCH OUT!
DASH!!!

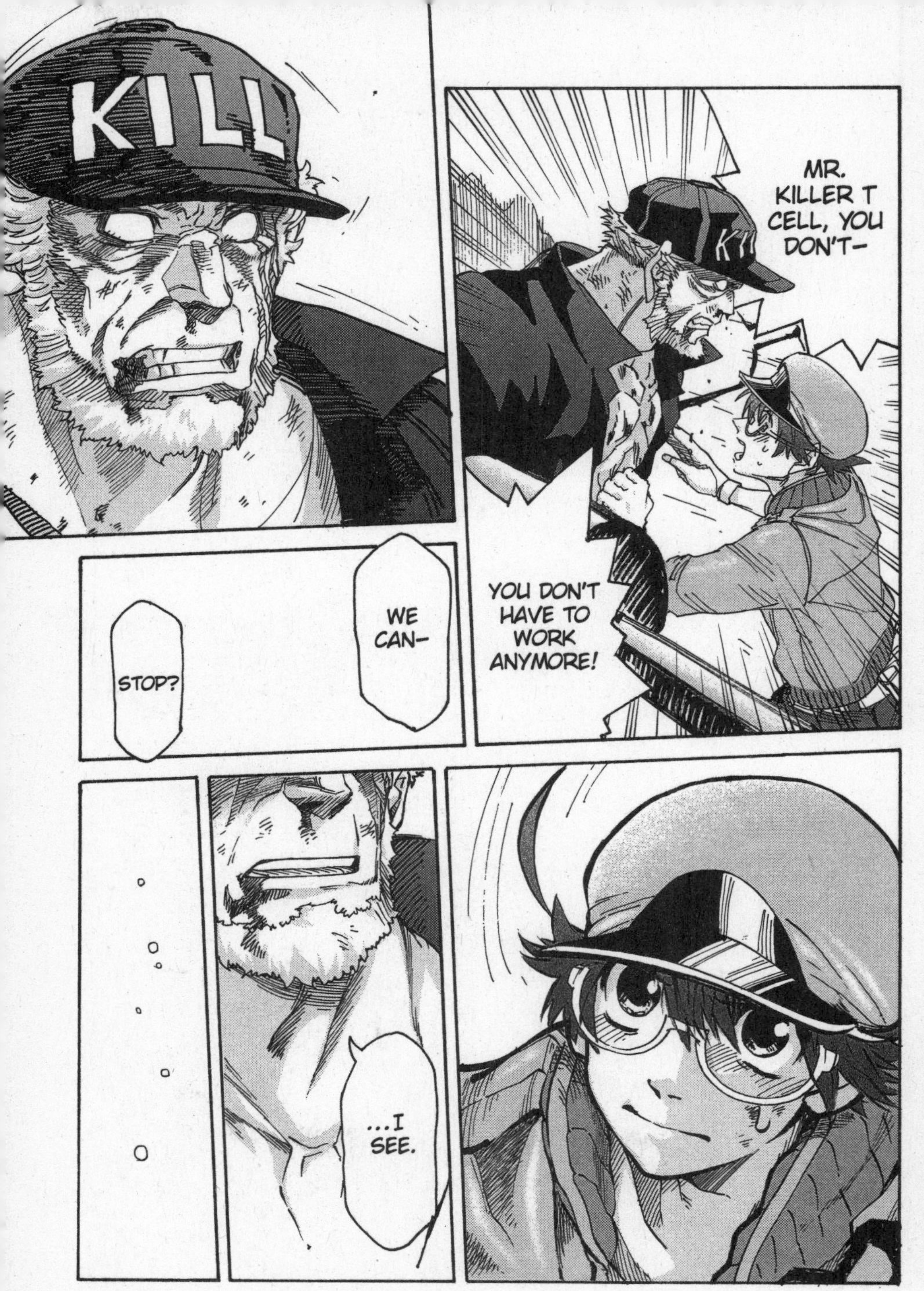
MR. KILLER T CELL, YOU DON'T-
YOU DON'T HAVE TO WORK ANYMORE!
WE CAN-
STOP?
...I SEE.

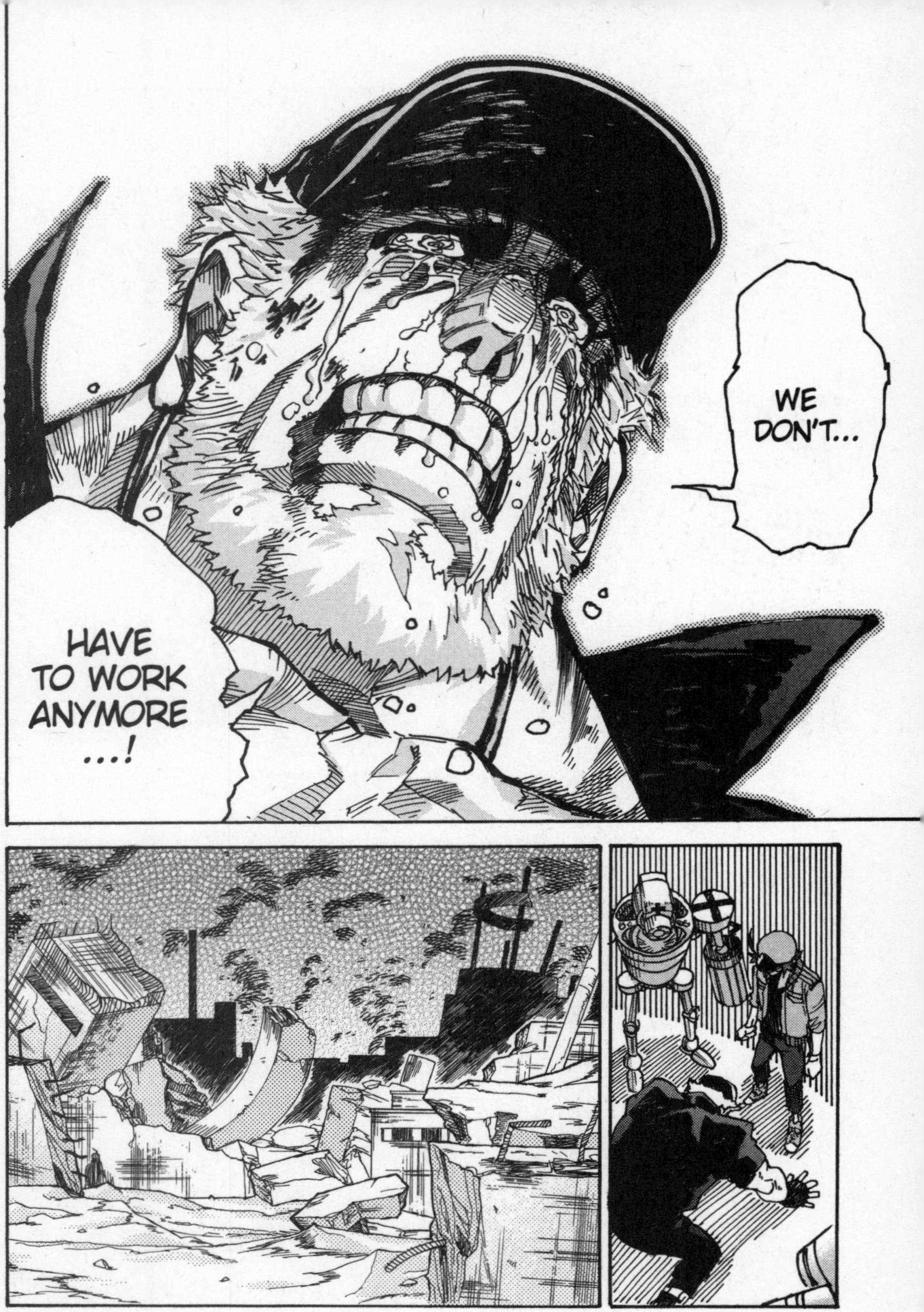
WE DON'T...
HAVE TO WORK ANYMORE ...!

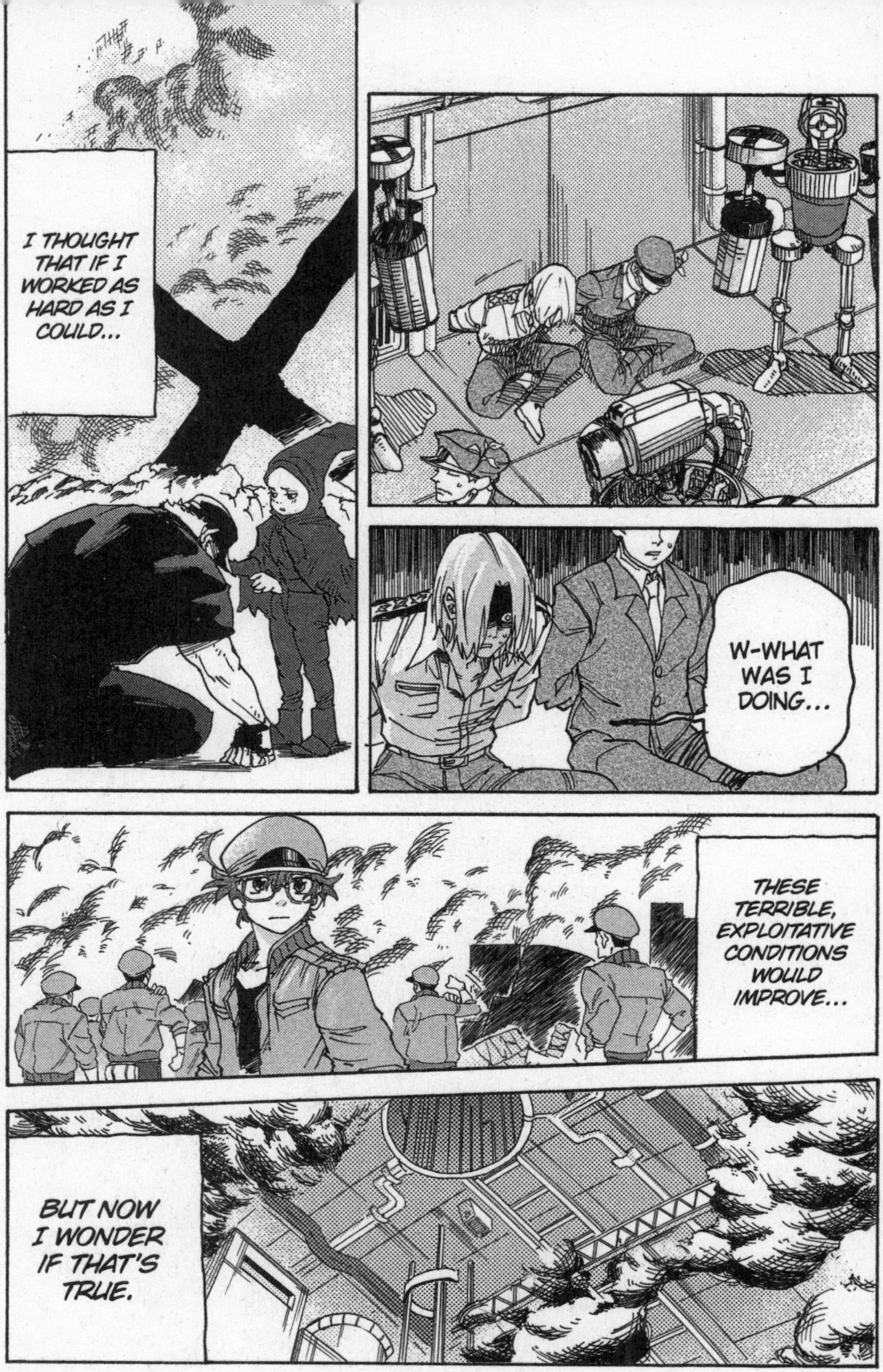
W-WHAT WAS I DOING...
I THOUGHT THAT IF I WORKED AS HARD AS I COULD...
THESE TERRIBLE, EXPLOITATIVE CONDITIONS WOULD IMPROVE...
BUT NOW I WONDER IF THAT'S TRUE.

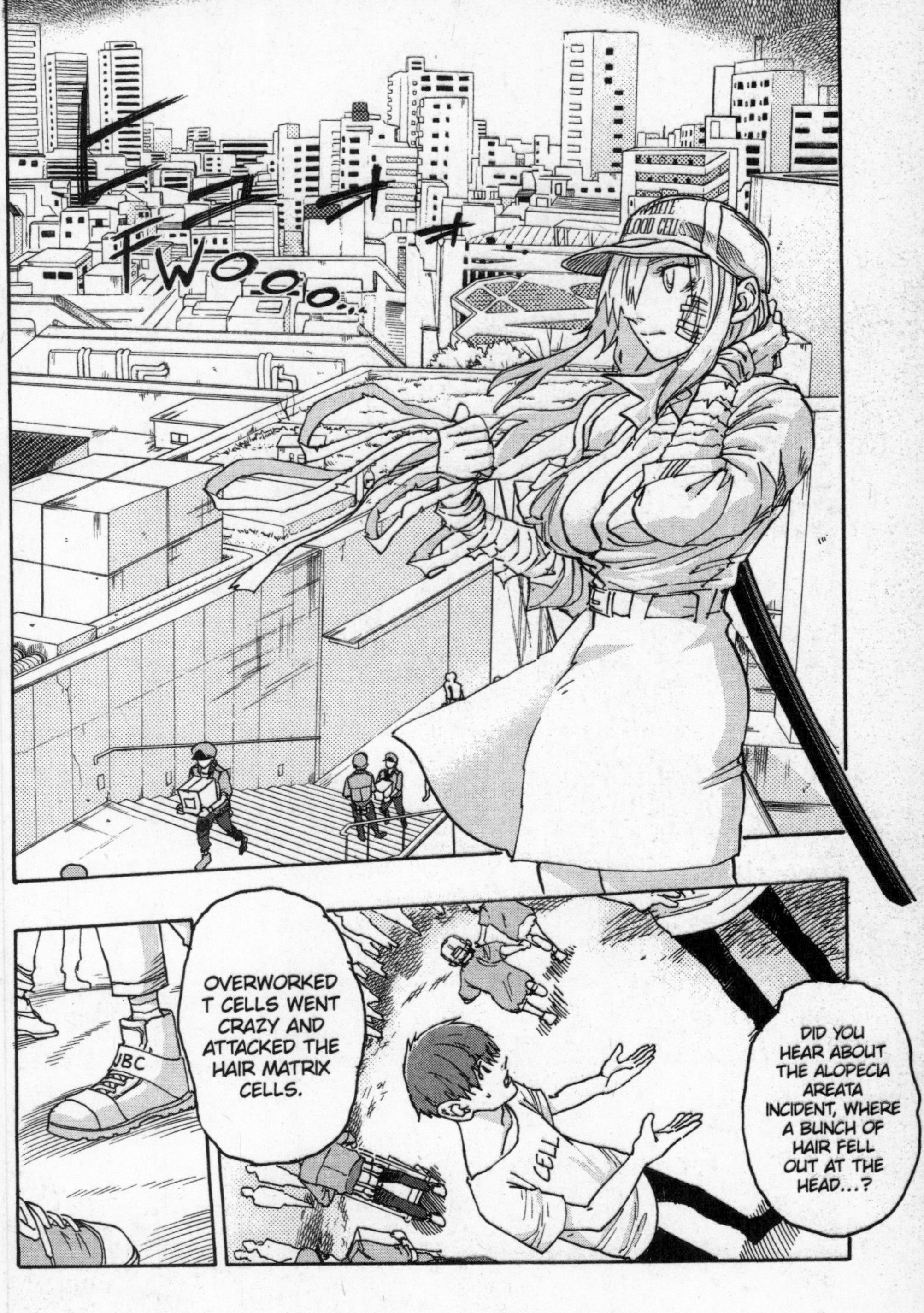
FWOOOO...
DID YOU HEAR ABOUT THE ALOPECIA AREATA INCIDENT, WHERE A BUNCH OF HAIR FELL OUT AT THE HEAD...?
OVERWORKED T CELLS WENT CRAZY AND ATTACKED THE HAIR MATRIX CELLS.
WBC
CELL

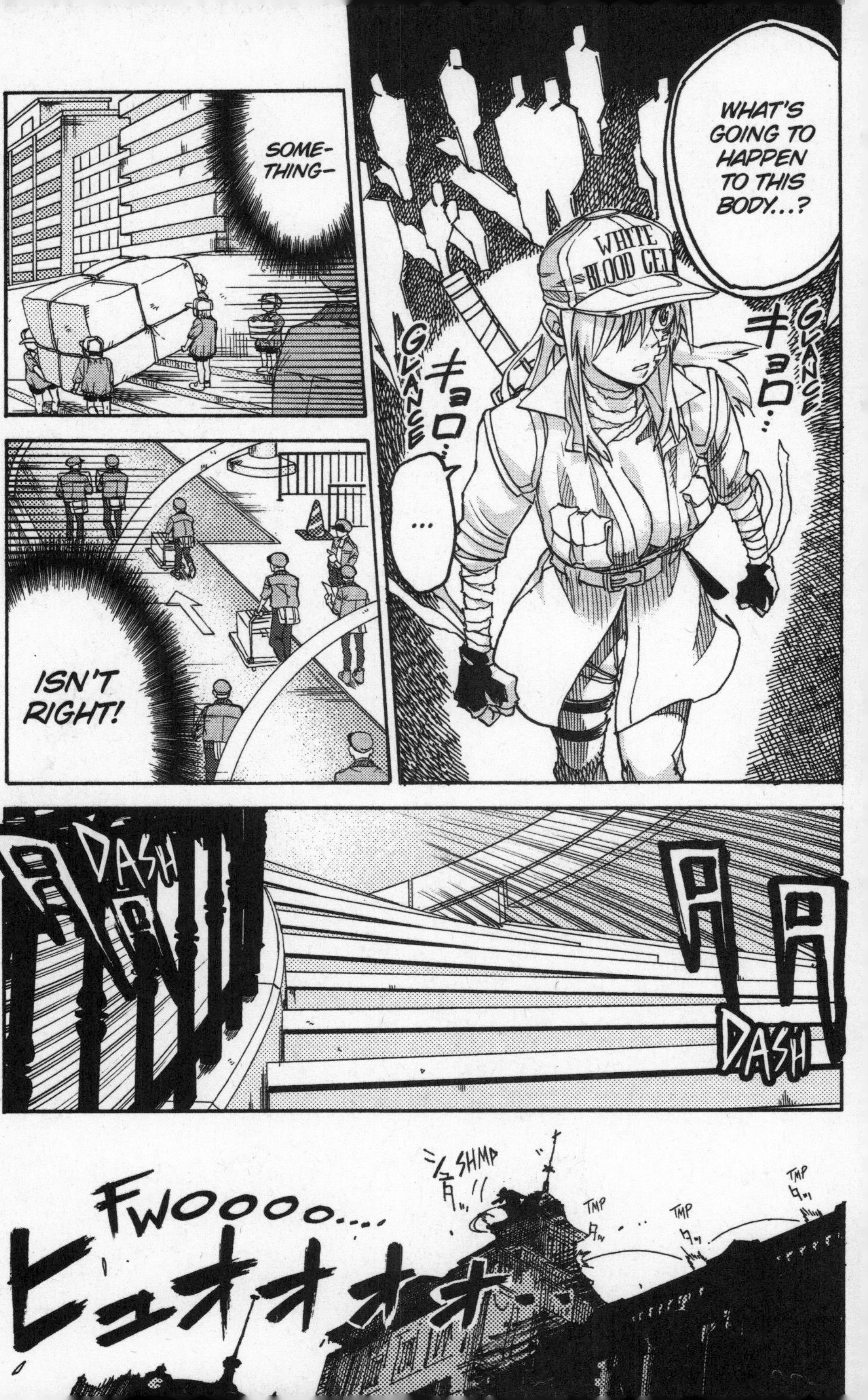
WHAT'S GOING TO HAPPEN TO THIS BODY...?
GLANCE
キョロ...
GLANCE
キョロ...
...
SOME-THING—
ISN'T RIGHT!
DASH
DASH
TMP
TMP
TMP
SHMP
FWOOOO....
ヒュオオオオ...

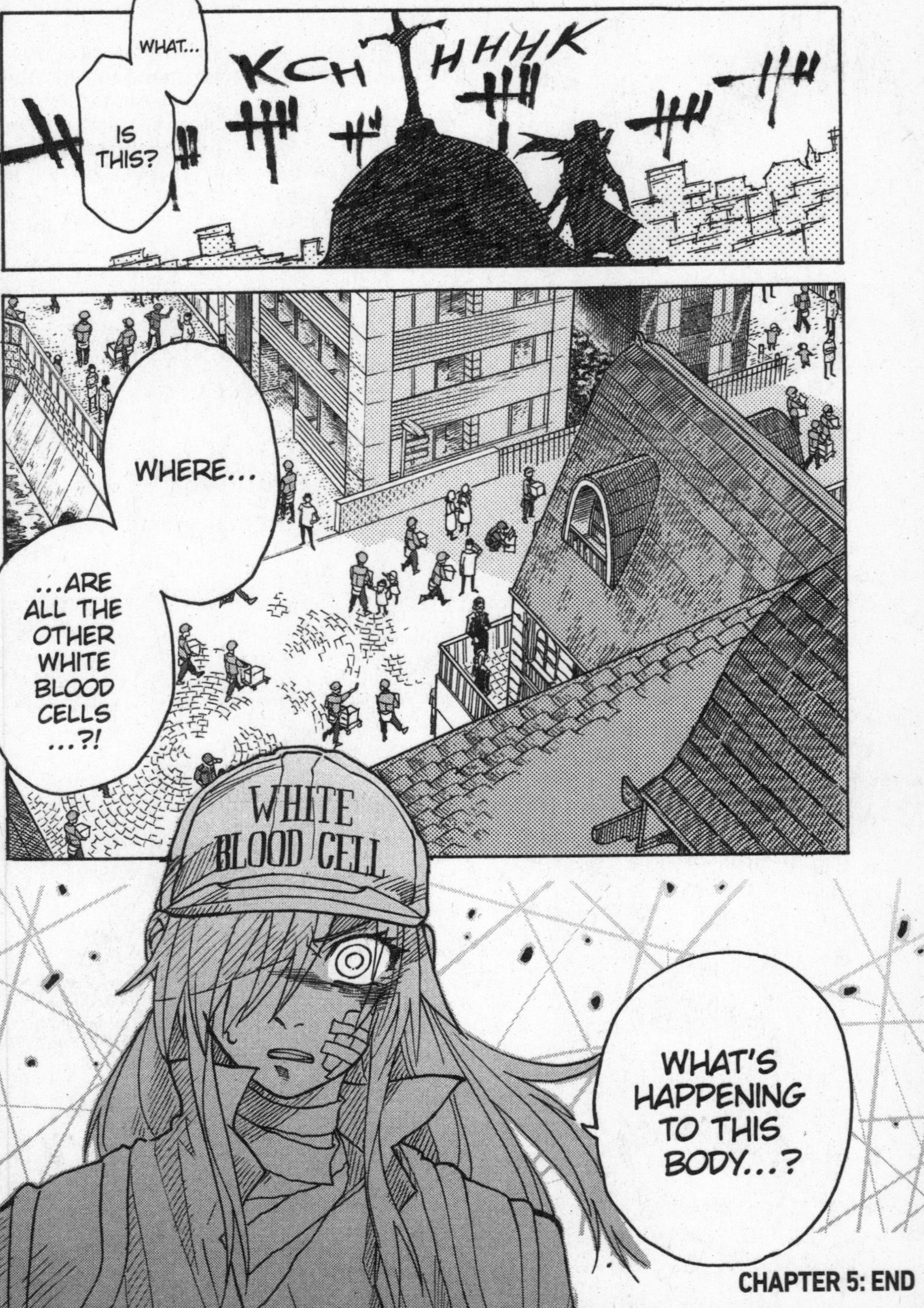
WHAT... IS THIS?
KCHHHHK
WHERE...
...ARE ALL THE OTHER WHITE BLOOD CELLS...?!
WHITE BLOOD CELL
WHAT'S HAPPENING TO THIS BODY...?

CHAPTER 5: END

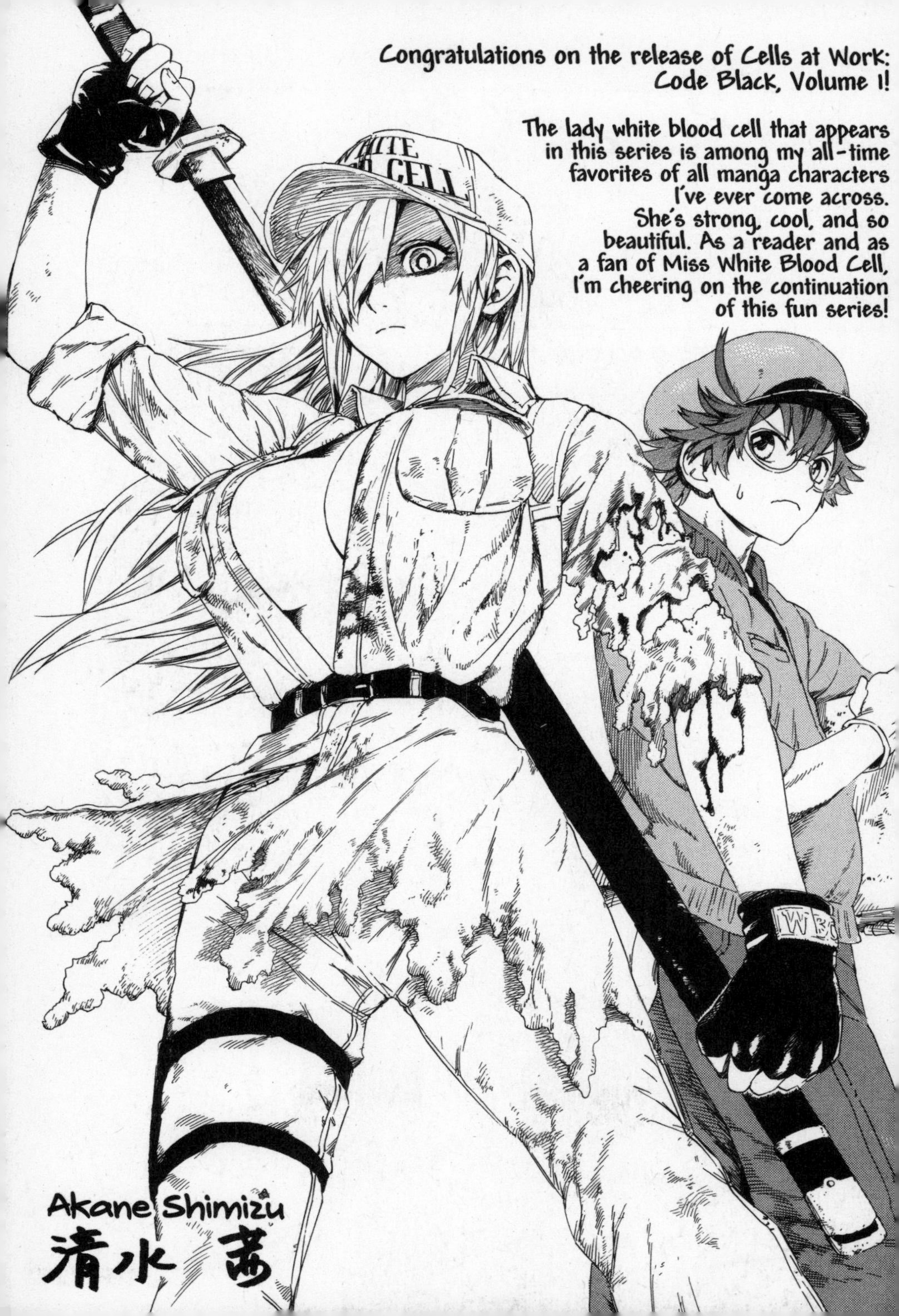

Congratulations on the release of Cells at Work: Code Black, Volume 1!

The lady white blood cell that appears in this series is among my all-time favorites of all manga characters I've ever come across. She's strong, cool, and so beautiful. As a reader and as a fan of Miss White Blood Cell, I'm cheering on the continuation of this fun series!

Akane Shimizu
清水茜

Cells at Work! CODE BLACK vol. 1 is a work of fiction. Names, characters, places, and incidents are the products of the author's imagination or are used fictitiously. Any resemblance to actual events, locales, or persons, living or dead, is entirely coincidental.

A Kodansha Comics Trade Paperback Original.

Published in the United States by Kodansha Comics, an imprint of Kodansha USA Publishing, LLC, New York.

Publication rights for this English edition arranged through Kodansha Ltd., Tokyo.

First published in Japan in 2018 by Kodansha Ltd., Tokyo, as *Hataraku Saibou BLACK* volume 1.

ISBN 978-1-63236-894-2

Printed in the United States of America.

www.kodanshacomics.com

9 8 7 6 5 4 3 2 1

Translator: Yamato Tanaka
Lettering: E. K. Weaver
Editing: Paul Starr
Kodansha Comics edition cover design by Phil Balsman